THE BUSINESS LITIGATION LIBRARY FROM WILEY LAW PUBLICATIONS

CIVIL RICO PRACTICE: CAUSES OF ACTION
Harold Brown, Editor

CIVIL RICO PRACTICE MANUAL
Paul A. Batista

CONFIDENTIALITY ORDERS
Francis H. Hare, Jr., James L. Gilbert, and William H. ReMine

DONOVAN LEISURE NEWTON & IRVINE ADR PRACTICE BOOK
John H. Wilkinson, Editor

LENDER LIABILITY: THEORY AND PRACTICE
Thomas N. Bucknell, Jr., Stephen A. Goodwin, and Marshall C. Stoddard, Jr.

PROVING BUSINESS DAMAGES (SECOND EDITION)
William A. Cerillo

WARRANTY LAW IN TORT AND CONTRACT ACTIONS (TWO VOLUMES)
Ora Fred Harris, Jr. and Alphonse M. Squillante

SUBSCRIPTION NOTICE

This Wiley product is updated on a periodic basis with supplements to reflect important changes in the subject matter. If you purchased this product directly from John Wiley & Sons, Inc., we have already recorded your subscription for this update service.

If, however, you purchased this product from a bookstore and wish to receive (1) the current update at no additional charge, and (2) future updates and revised or related volumes billed separately with a 30-day examination review, please send your name, company name (if applicable), address, and the title of the product to:

Supplement Department
John Wiley & Sons, Inc.
One Wiley Drive
Somerset, NJ 08875
1-800-225-5945

CIVIL RICO PRACTICE: CAUSES OF ACTION

HAROLD BROWN

Editor

Wiley Law Publications

JOHN WILEY & SONS, INC.

New York • Chichester • Brisbane • Toronto • Singapore

I dedicate this book to my wife, Shirley Brown, whose
bright and constant support has always guided me.

In recognition of the importance of preserving what has been
written, it is a policy of John Wiley & Sons, Inc., to have
books of enduring value published in the United States
printed on acid-free paper, and we exert our best efforts
to that end.

Library of Congress Cataloging-in-Publication Data

Civil RICO practice : causes of action / Harold Brown, editor.
     p.   cm. — (Business litigation library)
    Includes bibliographical references.
    ISBN 0-471-53275-4
    1. Organized crime—United States. 2. Corporation law—United
States—Criminal provisions. 3. Racketeering—United States.
4. Civil procedure—United States. I. Brown, Harold, 1915-   .
II. Series.
KF9375.C583   1991
345.73′02—dc20
[347.3052]   91-20261
                                             CIP

Printed in the United States of America

10 9 8 7 6 5 4 3 2 1

PREFACE

This *Civil RICO Practice: Causes of Action* is greatly indebted to a superb group of contributing lawyer-authors. Their craftsmanship provides lasting instruction through a wide variety of models for the use of RICO in civil litigation. By the authors' unraveling of RICO's complex nature for general practitioners, many readers will become indoctrinated in the skills needed to serve the public interest while earning ample rewards as private attorneys general aiding in the enforcement of significant legislation. This exemplification of RICO will also go far to help practitioners participate in curbing repetitious quasi-criminal conduct occurring in an endless variety of categories that would otherwise slip through the net of societal protection. Finally, this book should help to convince both judicial and congressional interests that they should not restrict RICO relief through unfriendly rulings, hobbling amendments, or outright repeal. The book demonstrates that with careful judicial guidance, civil RICO is able to duplicate the nationwide success of the statute's use in outright criminal process, including the government's seizure of vast wealth involved in the prohibited conduct.

In simplest terms, RICO provides a private civil remedy against persons who are guilty either of a pattern of misconduct based on at least two quasi-felonious acts, or of comparable fraud. It is then required to show that there was a relationship between those forms of egregious misconduct and their continuity or threat of future continuity. Finally, civil damages will be due when such racketeering conduct produces damages after its use in investing in an enterprise, acquiring or maintaining an interest in it, conducting its affairs, or conspiring to do any of such acts.

Congress has decreed that such misconduct warrants strong criminal penalties, including seizure of the assets used in their perpetration. It is therefore hardly surprising that in order to aid in promoting compliance, the legislature enacted private recourse, including mandatory treble damages and an allowance for attorneys' fees and costs. After some early setbacks, the courts have provided strong and liberal judicial support for both the criminal and civil remedies, as legislatively decreed. It is, therefore, quite surprising that the statute has been broadly criticized, with many congressional bills offered annually to restrict its private civil remedies. If such efforts succeed in whole or in part, one can resort to the many state RICO statutes allowing private recourse.

This practice manual is primarily directed to aid in teaching practicing lawyers how to understand and employ RICO in their everyday civil practice. In addition to this teaching tool, each chapter provides a very important illustration of the wide varieties of misconduct to which RICO can readily be applied. Actually, each chapter offers a prime example from the broad spectrum of misconduct. These implications deserve amplification.

The use of RICO in franchising covers a huge segment of commercial activity. At the retail level, franchising accounts for over one-third of the gross national product and it is growing apace. By the appropriate inclusion of franchising at the manufacturing and wholesale levels, the percentage of the GNP involved more than doubles. Further, franchising is only one method for distributing products and services; nonfranchised distribution is also subject to the prophylactic control of RICO.

The chapter on gray marketing is a penetrating study of RICO's application to protect all trademarked products or services from violators who fraudulently manipulate the discount prices they obtain for promised resale only in a particular market. Instead of selling in those defined markets, they secretly redirect the products into factory-assigned territories regularly serviced by the appointed distributors. Some consumers may benefit from such illegal duping, but the entire economy can be seriously impacted by the effect of gray marketers on the authorized dealers and the repercussion on the manufacturer's system of distribution.

The chapter on third-party participants illustrates an important avenue to obtain recovery when the direct violators have disappeared or become insolvent. Notoriously, most defrauders fall into that class, at least by the time a final judgment is obtained after years of litigation. Such liability can be found if the solvent party had a sufficient nexus with the illegal process. The chapter could have been called the "deep pocket" gambit.

The chapter on abortion clinics is not meant to be confined to freedom of choice issues. It pertains to an unlimited array of civil rights—First Amendment, labor matters, and similar issues. The key factor is the manner in which the chapter focuses on the abusive means that are involved in the attack on any of these fundamental rights. Although most civil RICO cases have relied upon the use of the mail or wire fraud statutes, RICO defines predicate acts in over 20 federal crimes and eight state felonies. Illustratively, several of these were employed to prove the predicate acts used in the abortion clinic cases. In the state replications of local RICO statutes, the list of criminal activities is much longer and is constantly being expanded.

In the minority stockholders' chapter, the author cogently demonstrates how RICO can be employed to obtain a corporation's restitution for criminal or other egregious misconduct by the company's officers and directors. For example, a major defense contractor may consent to a $200 million fine or repayment to the government for its participation in acquisition conspiracies based on bribery, fraud, extortion, bid-rigging, and deliberate failure to conform to specifications. Acting derivatively on behalf of the culprit corporation, the stockholders' suit provides an almost open-and-shut case for restitution to the corporation by its agents who used and manipulated the enterprise for such malfeasance.

When Congress is peppered with dozens of bills to emasculate the civil remedies of RICO, it should carefully appraise the immense significance of the many categories in which the act has been meritoriously applied to rectify civilly a pattern of criminal-type manipulations. For the first time, the victims of such criminal conduct have been provided with a nationally sponsored plan for obtaining compensation. RICO is therefore the Magna Carta for such forms of civil justice. Although critics may assert that RICO was designed only to challenge the members of organized crime, there can be no injustice in its highly meritorious use to pursue all such malfeasance, no matter what affiliation was involved.

The most important goal of *Civil Rico* is addressed to local practitioners, a group reportedly constituting more than 90 percent of the nation's lawyers. This book should help remove the veil of misunderstanding that has been artfully woven to conceal RICO's purpose and utility. The enforcement of RICO may seem to be an imposing hurdle, but this will disappear when a good-faith learning effort is exerted by counsel. RICO enforcement is intentionally encouraged by the statute's compulsory award of treble damages plus an allowance for attorneys' fees and costs. Congress has thereby sought to induce victims of quasi-criminal conduct to pursue these rights and to encourage their lawyers to prosecute these claims as private attorneys general. Indeed, lawyers who fail to utilize RICO in appropriate cases may be held to an accounting by their former client for professional misconduct and the benefit of quite substantially increased recovery and allowances. Such public policy overcomes all inhibitions and imbues the pursuit of such claims with a governmental blessing.

These noble comments will become all the more evident when one studies each chapter of this book and answers the question of whether the culprits received their just desserts.

ABOUT THE EDITOR

Harold Brown is a graduate of Yale College (magna cum laude) and obtained an LL.B and LL.M from Harvard Law School (magna cum laude). He practices in Boston, Massachusetts, and concentrates in franchise and distribution law. Mr. Brown was the founding member of the ABA Forum Committee on Franchising and served six years on its Governing Council, and he is a member of the NASAA Industry Advisory Board.

He has published numerous articles on franchising, including a monthly publication in the *New York Law Journal* since 1971, and he has lectured on franchising for many associations, law schools, continuing legal education programs, and business groups. He has also testified before many federal and state agencies and legislative committees.

ABOUT THE
CONTRIBUTORS

John C. Fricano is a partner in the firm Skadden, Arps, Slate, Meagher & Flom in the firm's Washington, D.C., office. Before joining the firm, he was chief of the Trial Section of the Antitrust Division, United States Department of Justice, where he served for 20 years. Currently, Mr. Fricano is chairman of the Editorial Advisory Board of the *BNA Civil RICO Report,* and civil law editor of the *RICO Law Reporter.* He has lectured and written extensively on RICO and litigation matters generally. Mr. Fricano wishes to acknowledge the assistance of James J. Gilligan, Esquire, in the preparation of his chapter.

John H. Henn is a partner in the law firm of Foley, Hoag & Eliot in Boston, Massachusetts. He received an A.B., magna cum laude, from Harvard College and his LL.B., cum laude, from Harvard Law School. He is a member of the Boston and Massachusetts Bar Associations. Mr. Henn is an author and lecturer on various subjects, including appellate and deposition practice.

William S. Lerach is a senior partner in the San Diego, California, office of Milberg Weiss Bershad Specthrie & Lerach, a law firm emphasizing securities and antitrust class actions for more than 20 years. Mr. Lerach is a frequent and noted lecturer on class and derivative actions for the American Bar Association and other legal organizations and is considered by many as one of the top securities law practitioners in the United States.

Michael R. McCabe is associated with Milberg Weiss Bershad Specthrie & Lerach in San Diego, California, and has assisted in the prosecution of numerous shareholder civil RICO cases involving defense contractors. Mr. McCabe is a member of the Civil RICO Subcommittee of the Antitrust Section of the American Bar Association.

Jonathan S. Quinn is an associate in the Chicago, Illinois, office of the law firm of Mayer, Brown & Platt, where he concentrates in commercial litigation. Previously, he served as an assistant district attorney in the trial division of the New York County (Manhattan) District Attorney's Office. Mr. Quinn received his B.A. from Haverford College, and he is a 1985 graduate of Northwestern University School of Law, where he was a member of the National Moot Court Team. He is admitted to practice in New York and Illinois.

Richard A. Salomon is a partner in the law firm of Mayer, Brown & Platt, in Chicago, Illinois, with a nationwide litigation practice. He received his B.A. degree from Carleton College and his J.D. from Harvard University. A frequent author and lecturer on ethics and litigation topics, Mr. Salomon has spoken extensively on RICO issues, litigated numerous RICO cases around the country, and testified before the U.S. Congress relating to reform of the civil RICO provisions. He has written several articles on RICO, punitive damages, and related subjects for the *New York Times, Wall Street Journal* and *Chicago Tribune*.

David H. Schwartz received his undergraduate education at Dartmouth College and the University of California, Berkeley. He received his J.D. from the University of California, Hastings College of the Law, San Francisco, California. He is a member of the firm of Hill, Schwartz, Stenson, A Law Corporation in San Francisco, California, specializing in complex commercial litigation and franchise disputes.

SUMMARY CONTENTS

DETAILED CONTENTS

Chapter 3   Civil RICO and Gray Market Diversion

John C. Fricano
Skadden, Arps, Slate, Meagher & Flom
Washington, D.C.

            William S. Lerach
            Michael R. McCabe
            Milberg Weiss Bershad Specthrie & Lerach
            San Diego, California

            David H. Schwartz
            Hill, Schwartz, Stenson
            San Francisco, California

CHAPTER 1

EXPLORING USES OF CIVIL RICO

Harold Brown

USING THIS MANUAL

§ 1.1   Introduction

This RICO practice manual is intended as a working tool, rather than a treatise on federal civil RICO. The statute is quite complex, making it difficult to analyze the Act and to coordinate its many provisions. The manual is designed to demonstrate the application of the Act in a broad variety of factual settings. The specific example in each chapter should be treated as part of a whole category of similar business torts that are ideal for RICO treatment. For example, the case situation set out in **Chapter 5** is the use of civil RICO litigation by abortion clinics against abortion clinic blockaders. The reader should regard it as a model for similar suits for protection of constitutional rights in other factual contexts. The scope of applications illustrated in this book is a realistic demonstration of the broad range of issues that continue to arise in RICO practice.

This practice manual uses actual case situations to illustrate the legal and factual discussion, presented by practicing attorneys recounting their individual experiences. There is obvious duplication in much of this work, which illustrates the finite scope of recurring legal issues. The interesting aspect of this material is its exemplification of the broad range of commercial and noncommercial activity in which RICO can be successfully used.

Throughout the manual, there is exceptionally strong emphasis on the facts of each case. Aside from the Federal Rules of Civil Procedure requirements, there is a fundamental reason for that approach, namely, the skepticism of most courts toward wild accusations designed to obtain treble damages plus an award for attorneys' fees and costs when the provable facts do not warrant such remedies.

Almost all of the predicate acts that constitute a pattern of racketeering under RICO are federal or state crimes, fraud in bankruptcy or securities matters, or trafficking in drugs. The facts underlying such criminal activity are seldom matters of public knowledge. There is, therefore, a real challenge to perform the detective work needed to obtain sufficient facts before filing a complaint. This is necessary, however, to satisfy the requirements of Federal Rule of Civil Procedure 9(b) on particularity of such allegations and to obtain the good faith substantiation demanded by Rule 11. It would take several years as a federal or state prosecutor to become well versed in the trial and appeal of so many felonies, plus years as a securities or commercial law practitioner to achieve skill in suing for bankruptcy or securities fraud. Perhaps for that reason, most civil RICO litigation has been grounded in the predicate acts of mail or wire fraud.[1]

Aside from such legal compulsions, it is simply unwise to depend on general allegations of a conclusory nature without specific allegations of truly egregious conduct. If there are serious deficiencies, it may prove better to omit the RICO claims from a complaint until some meritorious discovery has been obtained on companion counts. That risks exceeding a time bar, but provides a decent opportunity to get enough facts to go beyond the almost useless allegations based on information and belief.

Several publications have tried to explain the riddles in the structure of the RICO statute, but practitioners report that they fall short as a continuing education tool because they do not explain how to apply the Act in a

---

[1] 18 U.S.C. § 1341 (mail fraud) and 18 U.S.C. § 1343 (wire fraud).

daily law practice.[2] In order to bridge the gap from theoretical understanding to the use of RICO as an available remedy in all civil litigation,
the case histories of experienced practitioners should prove quite helpful.
They include a study of their complaints and other material.

§ 1.2 Judicial Construction of RICO

Throughout the text of this manual, there are ample citations to very current appellate rulings on significant issues. The reader is then left to the
self-help research that is always required but especially necessary in this
unique field. Most of the reported cases provide lengthy factual discussions as well as legal theory. They are helpful both as factual precedent
and as the basis for inductive reasoning to resolve the many legal applications. Because the private remedy was adopted at the very end of lengthy
legislative proceedings, there is very little guidance to be gleaned from the
legislative history.

Two crucial legislative omissions have been judicially construed: the
creation of a four-year time bar for civil suits[3] and the availability of
concurrent state jurisdiction.[4] Each of these has eliminated monumental
problems, but they have created new ones of comparable proportions. The
nonstatutory time bar does not contain any legislative prescriptions, leaving room for the sharp judicial differences that have already developed,
especially as to the date of accrual of the claim.[5] Concurrent state jurisdiction raises many federal jurisdictional issues that can only be addressed by citation to persuasive authority because no court will have
precedential control over the decisions of 50 or more state appellate
courts and the entire federal hierarchy.[6]

Criminal enforcement of RICO has been remarkably successful as a
tool to challenge organized crime. The Act has been liberally construed
and its key provisions held constitutional in spite of its severely punishing
terms. That applies with special emphasis to the government's power to

---

[2] See generally P. Batista, Civil RICO Practice Manual (John Wiley & Sons 1987 &
Supp. 1990); RICO-Civil and Criminal, Law and Strategy (Rakoff & Goldstein rev. ed.
1990).

[3] Agency Holding Corp. v. Malley-Duff & Assocs., 483 U.S. 143 (1987). The time bar for
criminal charges in bank fraud cases has been extended to 10 years. See 18 U.S.C.
§ 1344 relating to bank fraud for RICO, and 18 U.S.C. § 3293, extending the 10-year
statute of limitations applicable to bank fraud, including offenses prior to enactment,
unless the prior time bar had already run. These amendments were contained in the
Crime Control Act of 1990, Pub. L. 101-647, 104 Stat. 4862 (approved Nov. 29, 1990).

[4] Tafflin v. Levitt, 493 U.S. 455 (1990).

[5] See Rodriguez v. Banco Central, 917 F.2d 664 (1st Cir. 1990).

[6] Emerich v. Touche, Ross & Co., 846 F.2d 1190 (9th Cir. 1988).

seize assets employed in the crime and to freeze them by means of preliminary decrees,[7] even to the point of depriving defendants of the assets' use for legal defense fees.[8]

Perhaps that success underlies Congressional reluctance to tamper with any substantive part of the statute except for the single section allowing a private cause of action. In spite of the public criticism of the Act's use in civil litigation, Congress has not yet amended that portion of the statute. Furthermore, even if Congress does restrict the private remedy, that will have no direct effect on the RICO statutes that have now been adopted by over three quarters of the states, with wide variances in both civil and criminal application.[9] In the meantime, there is a rapidly expanding list of important applications of the statute in civil practice. Many courts have participated in the effort to address the numerous issues that have arisen, with no end yet in sight.

§ 1.3   The RICO Statute

Although RICO became law in October 1970, until 1980 it was almost exclusively used for criminal prosecutions. The use of civil RICO is relatively new. The legal community has had little opportunity to review RICO's terms, to comprehend RICO's numerous challenges, and to position itself to use RICO in standard civil litigation.

In general, civil RICO provides a private cause of action against persons who engage in a pattern of racketeering activity and commit one or more of four enumerated prohibited acts. The full text of the RICO statute appears in **Appendix A**.

Racketeering activity consists of performance of certain listed predicate acts. The list of predicate acts encompasses any act or threat chargeable or indictable under any of 24 specific federal offenses as well as eight state crimes that are punishable by imprisonment for more than one year. The state crimes include "any act or threat involving murder, kidnapping,

---

[7] Russello v. U.S., 464 U.S. 16 (1983).

[8] *See* United States v. Monsanto, 491 U.S. 600 (1989); Caplan & Drysdale, Chartered v. United States, 491 U.S. 617 (1989) (Blackmun, J., dissenting) (construing Comprehensive Forfeiture Act of 1984, 21 U.S.C. § 853, including its applicability to criminal prosecution under RICO).

[9] *See* RICO Bus. Disputes Guide (CCH) ¶¶ 4000–4520 (1990) for general RICO enactments, and *id.* ¶ 6041 for current adoptions. *See id.* ¶ 2025 for a long list of state specialized RICO laws, such as for drugs and gambling related activities. *See* Arizona v. Pickrel, 136 Ariz. 589, 667 P.2d 1304 (1983); State v. Thompson, 751 P.2d 805 (Utah Ct. App.), *aff'd sub nom.* State v. Fletcher, 751 P.2d 822 (Utah Ct. App. 1988), *rev'd on other grounds sub nom.* State v. Thompson, 1991 Utah LEXIS 17, CCH 1991-1 Trade Cases (CCH) ¶ 69,396 (Utah 1991).

arson, robbery, bribery, extortion, or dealing in narcotics."[10] The federal prohibitions include any act that is indictable under specified sections in title 18 of the United States Code, including such broad categories as mail or wire fraud, plus offenses involving fraud connected with a bankruptcy or fraud in the sale of securities.[11] Given the wide scope of fraud in the use of the mails,[12] in the sale of securities,[13] and in connection with bankruptcy, such offenses can be found in virtually any form of scheme to deceive.

The *pattern of racketeering activity* requires proof of at least two such acts within a 10-year period following enactment of RICO on October 15, 1970.[14] The predicate acts must be related to each other or be or threaten to be continuous.

The congressional thrust in RICO is to "forbid persons from conducting the affairs of an enterprise through a pattern of engaging in the predicate crimes."[15] An *enterprise* is broadly defined to include "any individual, partnership, corporation, association, or other legal entity and any union or group of individuals associated in fact although not a legal entity."[16] The term *person* is defined to include "any individual or entity

---

[10] *Id.* § 1961(1)(A).

[11] *Id.* § 1961(1)(B)(C)(D) & (E). The 24 federal crimes include 18 U.S.C. § 201 (bribery); § 224 (sports bribery); §§ 471–473 (counterfeiting); § 659 (theft from interstate shipment); § 664 (embezzlement from pension and welfare funds); §§ 891–894 (extortionate credit acts); § 1343 (wire fraud); § 1503 (obstruction of justice); § 1510 (obstruction of criminal investigations); § 1511 (obstruction of state or local law enforcement); § 1951 (racketeering); § 1953 (shipping wagering materials); § 1954 (illegal gambling business); §§ 2314–2315 (interstate transport of stolen property); §§ 2341–2346 (trafficking in contraband cigarettes); §§ 2421–2424 (white slave traffic); 29 U.S.C. § 186 (payments and loans to labor organizations, § 501(c) (embezzlement of union funds); plus "any offense involving fraud connected with a (bankruptcy) case" under title 11, "fraud in the sale of securities," or felonious narcotics matters under federal law. Also included are acts indictable under the Currency and Foreign Transactions Reporting Act.

[12] *See* Rakoff, *The Federal Mail Fraud Statute (Part I)*, 18 Duq. L. Rev. 771 (1980). Although mail fraud is extremely broad, good faith has always been a defense. Durland v. United States, 161 U.S. 306, 314 (1896); United States v. Martin-Trigona, 864 F.2d 485, 492–93 (7th Cir. 1982); United States v. Curry, 681 F.2d 406, 417 (5th Cir. 1982).

[13] *See* A. Bromberg, Securities Fraud: SEC Rule 10(b)(5) (1982).

[14] 18 U.S.C. § 1961(5).

[15] *See* Bennett v. Berg, 685 F.2d 1053, 1055 n.10 (8th Cir. 1982), *aff'd in part and rev'd in part,* 710 F.2d 1361 (8th Cir. 1983) (en banc) (including incorporation of the original panel decision). Early leading civil RICO cases are Schacht v. Brown, 711 F.2d 1343 (7th Cir. 1983); Bunker Ramo Corp. v. United Business Forms, Inc., 713 F.2d 1272 (7th Cir. 1983); Cenco, Inc. v. Seidman & Seidman, 686 F.2d 449 (7th Cir. 1982); and USACO Coal Co. v. Carbomin Energy, Inc., 689 F.2d 94 (6th Cir. 1982).

[16] 18 U.S.C. § 1961(4).

capable of holding a legal or beneficial interest in property."[17] The RICO statute focuses on the infiltration of enterprises such as business concerns, labor unions, or government entities.[18]

The statute centers on the four provisions that define prohibited activities.[19] Whenever a pattern of racketeering activity is involved, it is unlawful:

1. To "use or invest income [from such activity] to acquire any interest in, or to establish or operate any enterprise that engages in interstate commerce"[20]

2. "To acquire or maintain any interest or control" in such an enterprise[21]

3. For any person employed or associated with such an enterprise to conduct or participate in such a racketeering pattern of activity[22]

4. For any person to conspire to violate any of the foregoing subsections.[23]

§ 1.4   RICO Penalties

RICO's stiff criminal penalties include a fine of up to $25,000 or 20 years' imprisonment, or both.[24] They also go much further and require the forfeiture to the United States of "any interest . . . acquired or maintained" in violation of one of the "prohibited activities," as well as "any interest in, security of, claim against, or property or contractual right of any kind affording a source of influence over any enterprise he has established, operated, controlled, conducted, or participated in the conduct of."[25] In addition to authorizing the issuance of restraining orders, the statute

---

[17] *Id.* § 1961(3).

[18] *See generally* Blakey & Gettings, *Racketeering Influenced and Corrupt Organizations (RICO); Basic Concepts—Criminal and Civil Remedies,* 53 Temp. L.Q. 1009 (1980). Professor Blakey is widely regarded as a co-author of RICO; the law review article is very extensively annotated, providing a wealth of precedents. An entire issue of Cal. W.L. Rev. Vol. 21, No. 2 (1985) was devoted to a symposium of numerous RICO articles. It was cited generally by the Supreme Court in Sedima, S.P.R.L. v. Imrex Co., 473 U.S. 479 (1985).

[19] 18 U.S.C. § 1962.

[20] *Id.* § 1962(a).

[21] *Id.* § 1962(b).

[22] *Id.* § 1962(c).

[23] *Id.* § 1962(d).

[24] 18 U.S.C. § 1963(a).

[25] *Id.*

empowers the court to authorize the attorney general to seize all forfeited interest or property.[26]

The civil remedies include speedy trial, a private remedy with treble damages and attorneys' fees, and total estoppel effect for a final judgment or decree of the United States.[27] Nationwide venue over individuals and entities is provided for both in criminal and civil matters.[28] Extremely broad powers are granted to the attorney general for civil investigative demands.[29] The Seventh Circuit spoke with more than a modicum of accuracy when it declared that the civil RICO provisions are "constructed on the model of a treasure hunt."[30]

§ 1.5 Unresolved RICO Issues

There are numerous civil RICO issues on which there is substantial disagreement both between and within circuits. For example, there has been dissension as to whether a person may also be the enterprise,[31] as well as whether the enterprise may be both a claimant and a violator.[32] Another unresolved question is whether private claimants are entitled to equitable

---

[26] *Id.* § 1963(d), (e). *See* Russello v. United States, 464 U.S. 16 (1983) (seizure provision of RICO 18 U.S.C. § 1963(b) held constitutional). *See* United States v. Monsanto, 491 U.S. 600 (1989); Caplan & Drysdale, Chartered v. United States, 491 U.S. 617 (1989) (construing the Comprehensive Forfeiture Act of 1984, 21 U.S.C. § 853 (1988), including its applicability to criminal prosecution under RICO. Based on the finding that the United States had putative title to all such spoils, the court declined to allow a reasonable allotment for criminal defense legal fees, in spite of constitutional imperatives for effective legal defense.).

[27] 18 U.S.C. § 1964 (1988).

[28] *Id.* § 1965. Such nationwide venue over corporations and individuals greatly exceeds the comparable provisions covering only corporations under the antitrust laws, 15 U.S.C. § 22 (1988).

[29] 18 U.S.C. § 1968.

[30] Sutliffe, Inc. v. Donovan Cos., 727 F.2d 648, 652 (7th Cir. 1984).

[31] *See* Hirsch v. Enright Ref. Corp., 751 F.2d 628 (3d Cir. 1984), *on remand* 617 F. Supp. 49 (D.N.J. 1985) (holding that "person" and "enterprise" must be separate entities, resulting in reversal of the first civil RICO recovery in federal court after a full trial); *contra,* United States v. Local 560, Int'l Bhd. of Teamsters, 581 F. Supp. 279 (D.N.J. 1984).

[32] *See* Bennett v. Berg, 685 F.2d 1053, *aff'd in part and rev'd in part,* 710 F.2d 1361 (8th Cir. 1983) (en banc). (The panel held that the enterprise could be both a claimant and a violator; the court *en banc* affirmed the panel in all respects except on this issue, in which it held that the enterprise could not be both the claimant and the violator.) Prior to the *en banc* reversal, the panel's opinion was accepted and relied upon in Schacht v. Brown, 711 F.2d 1343 (1983), *cert. denied sub nom.* Arthur Andersen & Co. v. Schacht, 464 U.S. 1002 (1983). The Seventh Circuit view has been adopted by other courts, but there is no general accord.

relief either under the authority of the statute or from a court's general equitable jurisdiction, though the majority is opposed to such a remedy for private entities.[33]

§ 1.6   Mail and Wire Fraud

Without diminishing the significance of the other federal and state crimes enumerated in RICO, it must be pointed out that the federal mail and wire fraud statutes have been used most often to meet the predicate acts requirement.[34] It is erroneous, however, to assume that it is simple to prove the components of these crimes. The mail fraud statute must be read to include "everything designed to defraud by representations as to the past or present, or suggestions or promises as to the future."[35] The act has been employed as a first line of attack against virtually every new deceptive scheme invented by man's ingenuity, at least until such time as specific legislation has been devised to deal with the newest abuses, ranging through securities transactions, loan-sharking, land sales, credit cards, drug distribution, franchising, and pyramid sales schemes.[36]

In a civil proceeding, it is nonetheless necessary to allege and prove specific intent to defraud in order to obtain money or property by fraudulent pretenses or promises, either by devising, participating in, or abetting the scheme, and, for federal jurisdiction, by an anticipated use of the mail or of interstate wire. Although good faith is a defense, this is merely the converse of having to prove fraudulent intent. The fraud must be alleged with particularity,[37] underscored by the special emphasis on counsel's good faith obligation in signing any pleading or court document.[38]

Until *Sedima, S.P.R.L. v. Imrex Co.,*[39] there had been virtually no civil ruling requiring the equivalent of the criminal standard of a showing

---

[33] The trend appears to allow governmental equitable relief, but to deny it to private claimants. *See* Trane v. O'Connor Sec., 718 F.2d 26 (2d Cir. 1983); Dan River v. Icahn, 701 F.2d 278 (4th Cir. 1983); DeMeut v. Abbott Capital Corp., 589 F. Supp. 1378 (N.D. Ill. 1984).

[34] Durland v. United States, 161 U.S. 306 (1896).

[35] *Id.* at 313–14.

[36] *See* United States v. Maze, 414 U.S. 395, 405–07 (1974) (Berger, C.J., dissenting).

[37] *See* Fed. R. Civ. P. 9(b), *relied upon in* Bennett v. Berg, 685 F.2d 1055 (8th Cir. 1982). *See also* Bender v. Southland Corp., 749 F.2d 1205 (6th Cir. 1984) (RICO mail fraud allegations must indicate both intent to defraud and damage causation and be pleaded with particularity under Fed. R. Civ. P. 9(b)), but this must be balanced against the Rule's informational requirement of only a simple statement of the basis of the claim).

[38] *See* Fed. R. Civ. P. 11; Pavelic & LeFlore v. Marvel Entertainment Group, 493 U.S. 120 (1989) (lawyer is individually liable for Rule 11 sanctions).

[39] 473 U.S. 479 (1985).

beyond a reasonable doubt. Almost every court specified proof by a preponderance of the evidence,[40] although some support had been shown for proof by clear and convincing evidence.[41] Factually, a scheme is adequate if it is calculated to deceive persons of ordinary prudence and comprehension, even though no misrepresentations were made. It includes all elements of trickery, whether in the form of half-truths or the concealment of material facts, as well as express misstatements. The damage must be deprivation of tangible, rather than intangible, property or rights.[42] Finally, the anticipated use of the mails or interstate wire may occur either in connection with the accomplishment of the scheme or even as a later act to lull victims.[43]

Perhaps the most interesting aspect of RICO is the fact that written documentation will not act as a barrier to civil recovery. The juridical basis for this important precept is that the criminal act is independent from every attempt to dress it up with cleverly drafted contracts and other documentation, however genuine they may appear. Indeed, in most business torts, such a cosmetic authenticity may play a crucial role in the formulation of the scheme to deceive.[44]

This condensed summary of RICO and the crime of mail fraud seeks to dispel the fear that civil recovery under RICO is an open invitation to converting ordinary business transactions into a bonanza of treble damage recoveries plus attorneys' fees and costs. It also, however, forecasts substantial growth of recourse to RICO, based on mail fraud counts.

---

[40] Armco Indus. Credit Corp. v. SLT Warehouse Co., 782 F.2d 475 (5th Cir. 1986); Eaby v. Richmond, 561 F. Supp. 131, 133–34 (E.D. Pa. 1983); State Farm Fire & Casualty Co. v. Caton, 540 F. Supp. 673, 676 (N.D. Ind. 1982); Parnes v. Heinold Commodities, Inc., 487 F. Supp. 645, 647 (N.D. Ill. 1980) (civil burden of proof); Heinold Commodities, Inc. v. McCarty, 513 F. Supp. 311, 313 (N.D. Ill. 1979); Farmers Bank v. Bell Mortgage Corp., 452 F. Supp. 1278, 1280 (D. Del. 1978).

[41] *See* Swanson v. Babash, Inc., 585 F. Supp. 1094 (N.D. Ill. 1983) (citing Matz, *Determining the Standard of Proof in Lawsuits Brought Under RICO,* Nat'l L.J. 21, col. 1 n.51 (Oct. 1983).

[42] McNally v. United States, 483 U.S. 350 (1987); United States v. Newman, 664 F.2d 12 (2d Cir. 1981); United States v. Hasenstab, 575 F.2d 1035 (2d Cir. 1978); United States v. Mandel, 602 F.2d 653 (4th Cir. 1978) (en banc).

[43] United States v. Maze, 414 U.S. 395 (1974); United States v. Kalem, 416 F.2d 346 (9th Cir. 1969), *cert. denied,* 379 U.S. 952 (1970).

[44] For that reason, the standard merger and integration clause will not bar prosecution of a franchisee's RICO claims. Symes v. Bahama Joe's, Inc., Bus. Franchise Guide (CCH) ¶ 9192 (D. Mass. (1988)), and verdict in Bus. Franchise Guide (CCH) ¶ 9463 (D. Mass. 1989). Similarly, under a little F.T.C. Act, the unfair or deceptive acts or practices were not barred by the fact that in case of the sale of a mobil home, the written license agreement for the space expressly allowed the assessment of a percentage fee of the purchase price for approval of the transfer of a licensed space in a mobil home park. Commonwealth v. DeCotis, 366 Mass. 234, 316 N.E.2d 748 (1974).

§ 1.7   Attorney's Liability for Failing to Bring RICO Claim

Lawyers may themselves be exposed to personal liability when they fail to pursue RICO's expansive remedies including treble damages and allowance for attorneys' fees. If the attorney does not include a RICO count in the pleadings, a franchisee's successful fraud claim will not normally include an award for attorneys' fees or multiple damages. Punitive damages are sometimes available for egregious deceit claims, but not all jurisdictions allow punitive awards and the sizes of the actual awards are quite variable.

If the client's successful fraud claim results only in an award of single damages, his attorney may be liable to him for failure to include a RICO count. Such liability may derive from breach of the lawyer's retainer contract, as well as for tortious conduct arising under a statute such as a little F.T.C. act[45] or for common law negligence. If liability arises under the Massachusetts little F.T.C. act for instance, there can be an award against the attorney for as much as treble, but not less than double damages, plus attorneys' fees and costs. Where a franchisor's attorney actively participates in policy decisions or fails to use due diligence, a defrauded franchisee can sue the franchisor's attorney directly under RICO.[46]

OVERVIEW OF CONTENTS

§ 1.8   Civil RICO's Use Against a Franchisor

Chapter 2 is an exercise in the use of RICO for claims of a diet system franchisee against his franchisor. The presentation is made in three principal parts. The first is a review of applicable sections of the RICO statute and important judicial rulings. The second is a copy of an actually filed complaint, without the real names. The third section is a copy of the fact statement responding to the court's formal interrogatories served on each claimant for civil RICO relief. There follows a copy of court rulings on motions to dismiss.

---

[45] *E.g.* Mass. Gen. L. ch. 93A, §§ 9, 11.

[46] Pinhas v. Summit Health, Ltd., 880 F.2d 1108 (9th Cir. 1989), *cert. denied on attorney-client issue,* 111 S. Ct. 61 (1990), *aff'd on other grounds* 111 S. Ct. 1842 (1991); Courtney v. Waring, 191 Cal. App. 3d 1434, 237 Cal. Rptr. 233 (1987); Pecky Chehalis, Inc. v. C.K. of Western Am., Inc., 304 N.W.2d 91 (N.D. 1981). *See* Rollinson, *Franchisor Attorney Responsibility to Franchise Purchasers,* 2 J. Forum Comm. on Franchises 1 (ABA 1982).

The text covers significant issues that troubled many courts until there was judicial resolution. Chief among these are the standards to prove a pattern for the statutory requirement of pattern of racketeering activity; the elements of proving a scheme to deceive in the use of mail or interstate wire; the conflicting roles of the enterprise; the judicially interpolated time bar; and the question of particularity in pleading.

The franchise complaint is quite explicit in order to satisfy the requirements of Federal Rule of Civil Procedure 9(b) as well as the opposing rule calling for only a plain statement of fact. The complaint also demonstrates two important elements for all RICO pleadings. The first is the need to identify all of the specific details of egregious conduct. The second is to convince the court as early as possible that the special remedies of civil RICO recovery are factually merited.

The third part of the chapter presents a novel judicial way to address the concern that civil RICO is frequently misused. The court balances the conflict in the Federal Rules of Civil Procedure between the need for plain statement of fact and the demand for particularity by posing twenty interrogatories regarding fact and legal claims. That unique process reflects the concern that criminal RICO was primarily designed to challenge organized crime, but that its civil provisions may be applied to garden-variety business torts that do not merit such a strong remedy. Earlier, some courts had a standing rule requiring as much specificity in the complaint as that required for an indictment. As extensively discussed and annotated in **Ch. 2**, that burden has been eased through judicial resolution of the conflicting Federal Rules pleading issues as well as substantive standards, such as those to demonstrate a pattern of racketeering activity or the dichotomy of treating the enterprise as both a victim and a participant in the violation.

The complaint and the RICO statement provide a down-to-earth guide for the practitioner asserting franchisee claims. The particular case encompasses a wide range of substantive problem areas in the franchise relationship,[47] thus giving counsel a series of model counts from which to select for his particular case. The combined import of the three segments of this chapter should assure attorneys for claimants that they will not be prematurely barred by a motion to dismiss; that they will have access to full discovery for an opportunity to reach the jury; and that the court will not impede trial progress by unfriendly treatment.

The chapter concludes with copies of court rulings on motions to dismiss, with extensive analysis that supports the textual discussion in **Chapter 2**. The author has concentrated his practice on franchising, including the reported case.

---

[47] *See generally* H. Brown, "Franchising" Realities and Remedies, (rev. ed. 1991).

§ 1.9 Civil RICO's Use in Gray
Market Diversion Cases

Chapter 3 demonstrates how a plaintiff can invoke RICO with its multiple sanctions and remedies. These are frequently critical to achieving a litigated victory. The focus of this chapter is the gray market, in which unscrupulous wholesalers often fraudulently purchase American-made goods expressly discounted for overseas sale, then resell them in the United States at below-market prices. They reap profits that should accrue to the U.S. manufacturer and its authorized domestic distributors. The author of the chapter has litigated against such gray market diverters on numerous occasions, including representing the claimant in *Shulton, Inc. v. Optel Corp.*[48]

Shulton sought redress for what it determined to be an elaborate and long-running scheme by the defendant wholesalers to commit fraud. Specifically, Shulton alleged that the defendants had conspired to obtain discount-priced BRECK®, OLD SPICE®, and other well-known Shulton products under false and fraudulent pretenses. The alleged scheme depended on the wholesalers' front company to convince Shulton that the merchandise it purchased at Shulton's export (that is, discounted) price was being distributed exclusively overseas. In fact, the defendants were selling the products at wholesale for domestic distribution. By virtue of its complexity, duration, and scope, this duplicitous plan formed the basis of a 23-count complaint.

In *Shulton,* the defendants vigorously resisted the charges in the complaint. During the litigation, Shulton persuaded the court that it was acting as a private attorney general, a role that the crafters of civil RICO had sought to create in the war against organized crime. Prior to filing its complaint, Shulton had conducted an exhaustive, multi-year investigation of the defendants' activity. The fruits of that effort allowed the plaintiff to endow the complaint with substantial detail so that the court could readily accept from the outset that Shulton's case was appropriate for RICO.

Because of its intensive pursuit of the facts, Shulton overcame the defendants' motion to dismiss. It also aligned its cause with the public interest. As discussed in **Chapter 3**, the court's perception of Shulton's lawsuit as promoting the public interest against organized criminal activity twice enabled Shulton to defeat the defendants' strategies to frustrate its recovery. The *Shulton* case and others discussed in the chapter show that once a plaintiff has established its good faith as a legitimate RICO complainant, the full weight of civil RICO can be brought to bear against scheming defendants.

---

[48] No. 85-2925 (NHP) (D.N.J.). See **Ch. 3.**

§ 1.10 The Pattern Requirement in a Manufacturing Context Case

Chapter 4 focuses on 18 U.S.C. § 1961(5) and its requirement of a pattern of racketeering activity. Because the statute does not precisely define pattern of racketeering activity, practitioners must refer to the case law to determine what types of conduct constitute a pattern necessary to sustain a cause of action under RICO. In *H.J., Inc. v. Northwestern Bell Telephone Co.,*[49] the United States Supreme Court addressed the meaning of RICO's pattern requirement in an attempt to further refine (and simplify) the varying interpretations of the requirement. **Chapter 4** explores the ramifications of *H.J., Inc.* with particular focus on RICO issues that have developed in the various federal circuits.

The case involved a pipe manufacturer's claims against a testing laboratory that determined the quality of certain products and affixed its seal of approval on those products that met certain standards. The parties entered into an agreement in 1978 in which the defendant agreed to permit the plaintiff plastic pipe manufacturing company to affix defendant's seal to its products and further agreed to use every legal means available to prevent the unauthorized use of the defendant's seal on items found to be substandard. In 1984, the plaintiff learned that another plastics manufacturer was selling pipe at a price considerably lower than plaintiff's and that this pipe failed to meet the minimum standards of the defendant's testing laboratory but, nonetheless, it carried the defendant's seal of approval. Despite the plaintiff's numerous inquiries to the defendant and the defendant's numerous assurances that the matter was being checked into and that proper action would be taken, no action appeared to have been taken. As it turned out, the seal authorization had been withdrawn by the defendant.

Plaintiff's initial complaint alleged claims of breach of contract, fraud, and conspiracy, but no RICO count. Six months after plaintiff filed its initial complaint, the defendant delisted plaintiff's pipe, purportedly because it failed to meet certain impact tests performed by defendant. Pursuant to Federal Rule of Civil Procedure 15(a), the plaintiff moved to amend its complaint to include new charges under the RICO statute stemming from defendant's wrongful delisting of the plaintiff's goods in retribution for plaintiff's having filed the original suit. The plaintiff's motion for leave to file an amended complaint was granted. As a direct result of the new charges, the plaintiff obtained a favorable settlement. Addition of the RICO claims proved quite useful in focusing the issues.

If this case were filed today, the developing law would probably require the plaintiff's RICO claim to be amended to cover the pattern

---

[49] 492 U.S. 229 (1989).

requirements. The plaintiff's use of RICO was an important element in the settlement discussion.

§ 1.11   Civil RICO's Use in Civil Rights Disputes

Chapter 5 focuses on a nontraditional kind of civil RICO litigation: the relatively new and potentially significant use of RICO suits by abortion clinics against abortion clinic blockaders and trespassers. This application of RICO dramatically illustrates the fact that RICO is no more limited to those commonly thought of as racketeers than is the federal civil rights conspiracy statute[50] limited to its original target, the Ku Klux Klan.

In October 1989, the United States Supreme Court declined to hear a challenge to a successful use of RICO in the lower federal courts against anti-abortion blockaders and trespassers.[51] The case described in **Chapter 5** illustrates a set of facts and a complaint reflecting such a use of RICO. In Massachusetts, starting just before the presidential election of 1988, persons acting in coordination with an incorporated association known as "Operation Rescue" began blockading the entrances to abortion clinics and trespassing inside the premises. The clinics responded with federal and state litigation under applicable federal and state civil rights statutes. Concerned with the applicability of 42 U.S.C. § 1985(3) to claims of interference with women's civil rights, however, the plaintiffs also included a claim under RICO in the federal action. Subsequently, the Supreme Court held that a RICO claim may be included in a state court action.[52]

A RICO claim against abortion clinic blockaders and trespassers can proceed under RICO § 1962(c). The "enterprise" consists of the group of participants who have become, over the course of many blockades and invasions, a "group of individuals associated in fact" under § 1961(4). The pattern of racketeering activity consists of the numerous blockades and trespasses which have occurred within a short period of time, far less than 10 years. These blockades constitute predicate acts for RICO because they violate the Hobbs Act,[53] that is, the blockades and clinic invasions shut down clinics and obviously cause fear in women, and they cause the victims to part with their property interest of contracting with each other for services. The interstate commerce requirement is satisfied both because many clinic patients cross state lines and because clinics

---

[50] 42 U.S.C. § 1985(3).

[51] Northeast Women's Center, Inc. v. McMonagle, _____ U.S. _____, 110 S. Ct. 261 (1989).

[52] Tafflin v. Levitt, 493 U.S. 455 (1990).

[53] 15 U.S.C. § 1951.

purchase out-of-state goods. In sum, the sort of clinic blockades and tres-passes described in **Chapter 5** easily meet the requirements for stating a claim under RICO. Other RICO actions might be sustainable in other, different civil rights contexts.

§ 1.12   Civil RICO's Use in Shareholder Suits

In the late 1980s, a scandal of previously unseen proportions was revealed involving many of the nation's top defense contracting companies doing business with the Department of Defense. The scandal entailed allega-tions of fraud, bribery, and a plethora of other wrongs by these companies against the government in connection with the procurement of and per-formance under defense contracts. In **Chapter 6**, the authors examine the application of civil RICO in a derivative action involving Sundstrand Cor-poration, one of the publicly-owned companies charged in the defense procurement scandal.

This examination involves an overview of the defense procurement scandal and the role of the private bar in the prosecution of large scale corporate misconduct. It then provides a background of the alleged wrongdoing at Sundstrand which formed the basis for civil RICO claims against management, including the alleged illegal billing practices, im-proper tax write-offs, and the bribery of government officials.

The actual civil RICO allegations of the plaintiff shareholders' com-plaint are presented, followed by a review of the district court's disposi-tion of the defendants' motions to dismiss the civil RICO claims, includ-ing relevant portions of the district court's published opinion. The chapter concludes with a review of the subsequent litigation and ultimate settle-ment of this particular civil RICO action.

Wielded wisely, civil RICO is a powerful tool for the private practi-tioner. This chapter provides the practitioner with an informative case his-tory and anatomy of a proper civil RICO case and a useful reference for the application of civil RICO in his or her particular practice.

§ 1.13   Civil RICO's Use Against Suppliers to
Fraudulent Enterprises

Chapter 7 covers the involvement of third-party vendors in relation to the claims of numerous franchisees that they were systematically defrauded by their franchisor. Apparently, the franchisor started with little or no funds, relying upon a major vendor and its financing subsidiary to sell and finance the major equipment required in the operation of the franchised businesses. By the time that the litigation began, or shortly thereafter, the corporate franchisor filed for bankruptcy and the sole owner of the corporation followed suit. Both of them were virtually without assets.

The focal allegations were that the third-party vendor sold to the franchisees the necessary equipment, and its financing subsidiary held a security interest in the equipment. As repossessions mounted, they became fully aware of the franchisor's fraudulent practices, particularly during the lengthy process of reselling equipment that had been repossessed from failing franchisees. The financing subsidiary even pressed the franchisor to take over the payments or to resell the equipment to a new franchisee. In order to pursue the supplier and its subsidiary, the plaintiffs found it essential to establish the supplier's involvement with the franchisor, even in the absence of a principal-agent relationship.

The chapter focuses on the legal premise that the RICO predicate acts of mail and wire fraud do not require the victim to prove all of the elements of common law fraud against the third-party supplier. It is sufficient that the third-party supplier knew of the fraudulent or deceptive practices and furthered the objectives of the fraudulent practices with incidental use of the mails or interstate wires. If such conduct can be shown to have aided or permitted the fraudulent enterprise to carry on its illegal conduct, the third-party supplier may be liable not only to victims who dealt directly with the supplier, but also to those who did not deal directly, because they would not have been victimized but for the support which the third-party supplier gave to the fraudulent enterprise.

It is almost axiomatic that an undercapitalized franchisor will rely on deceptive schemes and that the franchisor will disappear or become judgment-proof by the time the litigation succeeds. Unless the victims are able to find third persons having a sufficient nexus with the insolvent franchise enterprise, neither they nor their lawyers will find it worthwhile to sue. RICO can provide such an opportunity.

CHAPTER 2

CIVIL RICO IN FRANCHISING

Harold Brown

§ 2.1 Introduction

There has been a revived interest in federal civil RICO for redress in franchise matters. Several years ago, a group of print-processing franchisees was able to obtain a very favorable RICO settlement after obtaining a partial summary judgment.[1] They had been induced to buy their franchises through false representations of profits, growth, training, and the like and had then been encouraged to keep operating their unprofitable businesses so that the franchisor and the secured party could realize further revenues through royalties, sale of supplies, and installment payments on the equipment loans. Although the franchisor became insolvent, the court ruled that the financial arm of the equipment manufacturer had a sufficient nexus with the franchisor's enterprise because of its vigorous collection process, pressure on the franchisor to resell the repossessed equipment to new franchisees, and total indifference to the fact that the franchises were being sold even though they were grossly unprofitable.

After a few years of unsuccessful franchise suits, there was a dramatic turnaround. Conceding that its prior cases had been erroneously decided, a federal court ruled that an ice cream franchisor was answerable in RICO for misrepresenting earnings in the sale of separate franchises to operate a retail store and to manufacture the raw products.[2] The district court isolated eight factors from which to deduce whether there was a pattern of racketeering conduct involving at least two predicate acts that were related and demonstrated continuity:

1. The number of independent victims of the alleged activity
2. The number of participants in the alleged crime
3. The purpose of the activity

---

[1] *See* Virden v. Graphics One, Inc., 623 F. Supp. 1417 (C.D. Cal. 1985). Defendants' three motions for summary judgment were defeated.

[2] Symes v. Bahama Joe's, Inc., Bus. Franch. Guide (CCH) ¶ 9192 (D. Mass. 1988), Bus. Fran. Guide (CCH) ¶ 9463 (D. Mass. 1989) (verdict).

4. The result of the activity
5. The method of commission
6. The number of transactions
7. Whether the scheme is ongoing and open-ended
8. The duration of the activity.

The court found the pattern of racketeering because there were allegedly other victims; more than two persons participated; there was alleged continuity over a two-year period; and the activity resulted in the execution of two franchise agreements and an area manufacturing agreement.[3] The court questionably allowed contractual disclaimers to preclude recovery for common law fraud and for deception under the Massachusetts little FTC Act, but it held that the same disclaimers of fraud "cannot shield the franchisor and its executives from accusations of criminal conduct" in the RICO counts.

The following sections examine the important issues the practitioner must consider when framing a RICO complaint on behalf of the defrauded franchisee.

§ 2.2 Pattern of Racketeering Activity

The Supreme Court has stated that RICO is to be read broadly.[4] This is the lesson not only of Congress's self-consciously expansive language and overall approach[5] but also of the Court's express admonition that RICO is to "'be *liberally construed* to effectuate its remedial purposes'."[6] In *Sedima,* the Supreme Court rejected a restrictive interpretation of § 1962(c) that would have allowed a private civil RICO action only when the plaintiff suffered special racketeering damages.

In *Sedima* the Court also suggested the continuity plus relationship test for determining the existence of a pattern of racketeering. Under that test, the Court required interrelated predicate acts that are or threaten to be a

---

[3] The court noted that Nassau-Suffolk Ice Cream v. Integrated Resources, Inc., 662 F. Supp. 1499, 1507 (S.D.N.Y. 1987), had held that the purchase of two ice cream franchises was not dispositive as to the existence of the necessary pattern.

[4] Russello v. United States, 464 U.S. 16 (1983) (while confirming that the seizure provision in RICO's criminal process is constitutional, Court stated Congress intended statute be liberally construed in civil as well as criminal cases).

[5] *See* Act of Oct. 15, 1970, Pub. L. No. 91-452, § 904(a), 84 Stat. 947.

[6] Sedima S.P.R.L. v. Imrex Co., 473 U.S. 479 (1985) (emphasis added) (18 U.S.C. § 1961(5) requires "at least two acts of racketeering activity, one of which occurred after the effective date of this chapter and the last of which occurred within ten years . . . after the commission of a prior act."). *See also* H.J. Inc. v. Northwestern Bell Tel. Co., 492 U.S. 229 (1989).

continuing activity.[7] In *H.J. Inc. v. Northwestern Bell Telephone Co.,*[8] the Supreme Court further delineated the pattern requirement, rejecting a narrow construction of the RICO Act's expansive terms. As for the troublesome concept of continuity, the Court stated: "We adopt a less inflexible approach that seems to us to derive from a common-sense, everyday understanding of RICO's language and Congress' gloss on it. What a plaintiff . . . must prove is a *continuity* of *racketeering activity, or its threat, simpliciter.*"[9] It declared that whether a threat of continued racketeering activity exists must be determined on a case-by-case basis. It, therefore, held that "the continuity requirement is likewise satisfied where it is shown that the predicate acts *are a regular way of conducting defendant's ongoing legitimate business.*"[10]

In many franchise situations, the defendant commits the predicate acts of mail fraud and/or interstate wire fraud as a regular method of doing business with its existing and its potential franchisees. The first reported franchise RICO case that went through trial was *Symes v. Bahama Joe's, Inc.,*[11] in which the jury found RICO violations by both the franchisor and its individual executives, based on a pattern of racketeering activity in mail and wire fraud. In franchising, there is almost a presumption that the activities will be related and will disclose continuity or a threat of continuity.[12]

---

[7] Sedima S.P.R.L. v. Imrex Co., 473 U.S. 479, 496 n.14.

[8] 492 U.S. 229 (1989).

[9] *Id.* at 241 (emphasis added).

[10] *Id.* at 243 (emphasis added).

[11] Bus. Franch. Guide (CCH) ¶ 9192 (1988).

[12] *See, e.g.,* United States v. Pearlstein, 576 F.2d 531, 536–37 (3rd Cir. 1978) (pen distributor franchise scheme used revenue and "typical sales" projections despite insufficient investigation and verification on their validity); United States v. Hildebrand, 506 F.2d 406 (5th Cir. 1975) (misrepresentations about status of products, operations of franchisor, profit potential, and failure to give aid to franchisees in franchise scheme to distribute food cooking device); United States v. Uhrig, 443 F.2d 239 (7th Cir. 1971) (false or exaggerated representations in sales of franchised executive placement businesses); United States v. Cohen, 516 F.2d 1358 (8th Cir. 1975) (affirmed conviction of mail fraud in sale of dealerships for marketing of national brand merchandise in wire rack display stands to be located in stores because there were misrepresentations about the quality of the locations and the profits to be derived); United States v. Seymour, 576 F.2d 1345, 1347 (9th Cir. 1978) (in sustaining conviction for mail fraud in sale of seven franchises, court observed that the "record exhibits a glaring lack of a good faith intent to create a successful leasing business, including a lackadaisical training of dealers and wholly inadequate provisions for dealer field assistance and promotional advertising"); Cacy v. United States, 298 F.2d 227, 228 (9th Cir. 1961) (affirmed conviction for mail fraud based on what government characterized as "the old and familiar franchise racket").

§ 2.3 Mail and Interstate Wire Fraud

Because of complications in proving predicate acts, most franchise claims involve the franchisor's mail and interstate wire fraud. In order to prove mail or wire fraud as a predicate act, it must be shown that the defendant participated in or formed a scheme or activity to defraud and then used the United States mails or interstate telephone wires in furtherance of the scheme or artifice.[13] The mail[14] and wire fraud[15] statutes do not require allegation and proof of common law fraud.[16] *Fraud* has been defined as "wronging one in his property rights by dishonest methods or schemes and usually signifies the deprivation of something of value by trick, deceit, chicane, or overreaching."[17] The intent to defraud or deceive only requires proof of a plan that is "reasonably calculated to deceive persons of ordinary prudence and comprehension."[18] It is, therefore, immaterial whether the intended victims "are gullible or skeptical, dull or bright."[19] The intent may be demonstrated from a "reckless indifference for the truth."[20] The scheme itself may be the source of proving the intent.[21]

The plaintiff need not prove that an affirmative misrepresentation was made, because the violation lies in the formulation of a scheme that is calculated to deceive.[22] Such a scheme may be deduced from misstatements, half-truths, or omissions to state those facts necessary to make the

---

[13] Hofstetter v. Fletcher, 905 F.2d 897 (6th Cir. 1988); Van Dorn Co. v. Howington, 623 F. Supp. 1548 (N.D. Ohio 1985); Bennett v. E.F. Hutton, Inc., 597 F. Supp. 1547 (N.D. Ohio 1984).

[14] 18 U.S.C. § 1341 (1988).

[15] 18 U.S.C. § 1343.

[16] Atlas Pile Driving Co. v. DiCon Fin. Co., 886 F.2d 986 (8th Cir. 1989).

[17] Carpenter v. United States, 484 U.S. 19 (1987) (citing McNally v. United States, 483 U.S. 350, 107 S. Ct. 2875, 2881 (1987)).

[18] Abell v. Potomac Ins. Co., 858 F.2d 1104, 1130 (5th Cir. 1988). *See also* Schreiber Distrib. Co. v. Serv-Well Furniture Co., 806 F.2d 1393 (9th Cir. 1986); Virden v. Graphics One, Inc., 623 F. Supp. 1417 (C.D. Cal. 1985).

[19] United States v. Brien, 617 F.2d 299, 311 (1st Cir. 1980).

[20] United States v. Frick, 588 F.2d 531, 536 (5th Cir.), *cert. denied,* 441 U.S. 913 (1979). *See also* United States v. Boyer, 694 F.2d 58, 59–60 (3rd Cir. 1982); United States v. Perkal, 530 F.2d 604, 605 (4th Cir.), *cert. denied,* 429 U.S. 821 (1976); Kronfeld v. First Jersey Nat'l Bank, 638 F. Supp. 1454 (D.N.J. 1986); Louisiana Power & Light v. United Gas Pipe Line, 642 F. Supp. 781, 803 (E.D. La. 1986) ("knowing intent to defraud may be found when a defendant deliberately proceeds with a reckless indifference for the truth, making representations that are baseless, and shutting his eyes to their probable falsity").

[21] The requisite intent may be shown by examining the scheme itself. Virden v. Graphics One, Inc., 623 F. Supp. 1417; Schreiber Distrib. Co. v. Serv-Well Furniture Co., 806 F.2d 1393.

[22] Atlas Pile Driving Co. v. DiCon Fin. Co., 886 F.2d 986.

statements not misleading in light of the circumstances.[23] The mailed or telephoned communication itself need not be false or inaccurate.[24] To obtain federal jurisdiction for mail or wire fraud, it is enough to show mailings that are completely routine and accurate, provided that such mailings were reasonably anticipated.[25] The contents of the mailings are not an essential part of the scheme to deceive.[26]

The defendants need not be the ones who used the mail or interstate wires.[27] It is enough that the defendants used or caused the use of the United States mails or interstate wires, or had a reasonable basis to foresee that their actions would result in the use of the mails or wires.[28] Such use of the mails or wires does not have to happen concurrently with the fraud.[29] The acts of mail or wire fraud are not limited to those that took place before the execution of the franchise agreements.

---

[23] United States v. Townley, 665 F.2d 579, 585 (9th Cir. 1982).

[24] United States v. Henson, 848 F.2d 1374 (6th Cir. 1988); United States v. Talbot, 590 F.2d 192 (6th Cir. 1978).

[25] United States v. Freitag, 768 F.2d 240 (8th Cir. 1985); Ferleger v. First Am. Mortgage Co., 662 F. Supp. 584 (N.D. Ill. 1987). *See also* United States v. Serino, 835 F.2d 924, 928 (1st Cir. 1987) (mailing need not by itself disclose a scheme to defraud).

[26] United States v. Henson, 848 F.2d 1374 (6th Cir. 1988); United States v. Silvano, 812 F.2d 754, 760 (1st Cir. 1987) (use of mails need not be essential to scheme; mail fraud statute sweeps broadly).

[27] Bennett v. E.F. Hutton Co., 597 F. Supp. 1547, 1560 (N.D. Ohio 1984); United States v. Strong, 702 F.2d 97, 100 (6th Cir. 1983); United States v. Contenti, 735 F.2d 628, 631 (1st Cir. 1984).

[28] United States v. Fermin Castillo, 829 F.2d 1194, 1198 (1st Cir. 1988); United States v. Serino, 835 F.2d 924, 928 (1st Cir. 1987) (sufficient that mailings are incidental to the efforts in furtherance of the scheme; a liberal construction should be given to the "purpose of executing the scheme" language in 18 U.S.C. § 1341); United States v. Silvano, 812 F.2d 754 (1st Cir. 1987) (a mailing need only be closely related to the scheme and reasonably foreseeable as a result of the scheme); Abell v. Potomac Ins., 858 F.2d 1104 (5th Cir. 1988) (use of mails to obtain and transmit application forms); United States v. Henson, 848 F.2d 1374 (6th Cir. 1988); United States v. Robinson, 651 F.2d 1188 (6th Cir. 1981) (causing check to be mailed was in furtherance of the scheme); Virden v. Graphics One, Inc., 623 F. Supp. 1417 (C.D. Cal. 1985) (franchisee used phone to order supplies and mail for payment of rent checks, and the mailings or wire communication were done in aid of the scheme).

[29] Sun Sav. & Loan Ass'n v. Dierdorff, 825 F.2d 187 (9th Cir. 1987) (citing United States v. Sampson, 371 U.S. 75 (1912)); Zola v. Gordon, 685 F. Supp. 354, 372–73 (S.D.N.Y. 1988) (letter mailed after victim has parted with his money sufficient to support mail fraud claim if it is intended to lull plaintiff into false sense of security) (citing United States v. Lane, 474 U.S. 438, 451–52 (1986)); Virden v. Graphics One, Inc., 623 F. Supp. 1417 (C.D. Cal. 1985) (mail and wire communications after execution of franchise scheme formed basis for predicate acts, because fraudulent scheme had not yet reached fruition).

§ 2.4 Misconduct before and after Sale of Franchise

Although fraud in the pre-sale of the franchise is often involved, RICO also covers misconduct after the purchase or execution of the franchise contract. The scheme may involve the sale of products to the franchisees without regard to the actual needs of the franchisee, any other deception, or the concealment of damaging facts. The Seventh Circuit has strongly endorsed the statutory policy of many states confirming that after acquisition of a franchise, the franchisee is virtually deprived of all bargaining power to resist the "opportunistic" conduct of the franchisor.[30] The franchisor and its management are acutely aware of the extreme susceptibility of the existing franchisee to an endless variety of deceptions. Such manipulations must involve the incidental use of the mail or interstate wire, but this can occur if, for example, the franchisee uses the mail to make royalty payments. Such a combination of circumstances gives rise to firm RICO counts after the purchase of the franchise, providing the strongest avenue for legal relief regardless of the terms of the franchise agreement. Indeed, portions of the franchise agreement and other contracts prepared by the franchisor may be an essential tool in proving the conception and perpetration of the scheme to defraud.

§ 2.5 Enterprise As Victim and Violator

RICO centers on the enterprise that is involved in one of the four types of proscribed conduct. Early cases questioned whether an enterprise could be both a victim and a culpable person. Federal appeal courts have reached different conclusions on this issue.[31] The Seventh Circuit determined that the "corporate enterprise should be liable where it is the perpetrator or central figure in the criminal scheme."[32] Another court

---

[30] *See* Wright-Moore Corp. v. RICOH Corp., 908 F.2d 128 (7th Cir. 1990).

[31] *Compare* United States v. Hartley, 678 F.2d 961 (11th Cir. 1982) (a corporation could be simultaneously both a defendant and an enterprise under RICO) *with* United States v. Computer Sciences Corp., 689 F.2d 1181 (4th Cir. 1982) (a corporate division of a computer services firm could not be an enterprise when the corporation was named as the culpable person).

[32] Bernstein v. IDT Corp., 582 F. Supp. 1079 (D. Del. 1984); United States v. Local 560, Int'l Bhd. of Teamsters, 581 F. Supp. 279 (D.N.J. 1984) (a group of union officials could be characterized as a "person" under § 1962(b) and at the same time characterized as an enterprise under § 1962(c)); D'Iorio v. Adonizio, 554 F. Supp. 222 (M.D. Pa. 1982) (corporations and partnerships were properly named to be both RICO enterprises and persons subject to liability in a claim alleging that directors and controlling partners operated the businesses through a pattern of racketeering activity); Griffin v. O'Neal, Jones & Feldman, Inc., 604 F. Supp. 717, 722 (S.D. Ohio 1985); Haroco, Inc. v. American Nat'l Bank & Trust Co., 747 F.2d 384, 402 (7th Cir. 1984) *aff'd on other grounds per curiam*, 473 U.S. 606 (1985).

recognized that a corporation could be named both as an enterprise and
as a culpable person because the corporation could be viewed as the enterprise and also held liable for the conduct of its officers under the general
principles of agency law.[33] The franchisor is clearly liable for the conduct
of its officers and agents, especially those who actively participate in its
policy determinations.[34] The *enterprise* is broadly defined as any entity or
group that is capable of owning property,[35] thus including any business,
government agency, labor union, or any other association, such as a group
of franchisees.

§ 2.6   Time Bar on Commencing Suit

In a monumental decision, the Supreme Court fashioned an imputed time
bar or statute of limitation of four years for RICO misconduct.[36] So long
as the last predicate act falls within that period, the RICO statute specifies that the "second" predicate act "may have occurred as long as ten
years earlier."[37] The Court did not confront the issue of when a RICO
claim accrues. RICO claims have commonly been said to accrue when the
plaintiff knew of or in the exercise of due diligence should have discovered
the wrongs or alleged injuries.[38] The timing of the last predicate act has

---

[33] *See* Schacht v. Brown, 711 F.2d 1343 (7th Cir. 1983) (RICO applies to both insiders
and "outsiders," those merely "associated with" an enterprise who participate directly
or indirectly in the enterprise's affairs through a pattern of racketeering); Miller v.
Affiliated Fin. Corp., 600 F. Supp. 987 (N.D. Ill. 1984) (corporate officers may be held
liable for illegal acts upon proof of direct or indirect participation in the affairs of the
enterprise through a pattern of racketeering activity).

[34] *See* Pinhas v. Summit Health, Ltd., 894 F.2d 1024 (9th Cir.) *cert. denied,* 111 S. Ct. 61
(1990); *see also* Brown, *Caveat Consilium,* 204 N.Y.L.J. 3 (Aug. 30, 1990).

[35] *See* 18 U.S.C. § 1961(4).

[36] Agency Holding Corp. v. Malley-Duff & Assocs., 483 U.S. 143 (1987). The time bar for
criminal charges has been extended to 10 years. *See* 18 U.S.C. § 1344 relating to such
fraud for RICO, and 18 U.S.C. § 3293, extending the 10-year statute of limitations
applicable to such fraud, including offenses prior to enactment, unless the prior time
bar had already run. These amendments were contained in the Crime Control Act of
1990, Pub. L. No. 101–647, 104 Stat. 4789 (1990), reported in RICO Bus. Disputes
(CCH) ¶¶ 4020, 4040 (1991).

[37] *See* 18 U.S.C. § 1961(5).

[38] *See* Rodriguez v. Banco Central, 917 F.2d 664 (1st Cir. 1990) (P.R.) (First Circuit
adopted the rule that RICO statute of limitations begins to run when the plaintiff knew
or should have known of his injury, expressly rejecting Third Circuit rule, which holds
that statute of limitations begins to run after plaintiff knew or should have known of
"the last predicate act"); Cincinnati Gas & Elec. Co. v. General Elec. Co., 656 F. Supp.
49 (S.D. Ohio 1986) (claims by a utility and city against a nuclear reactor maker accrued for RICO statute of limitation purposes when the plaintiffs knew or should have

also been relied upon to determine the accrual of the RICO claim.[39] Under the continuing violations doctrine, an action is timely so long as the last act evidencing the continuing practice falls within the limitation period. When this test is met, relief will be granted with respect to earlier acts that would otherwise be time-barred.[40]

Fraudulent concealment of the cause of action will also toll the statute of limitations. The First Circuit declared that fraudulent concealment would almost always be present when there has been a RICO violation based on fraudulent or criminal activity.[41]

§ 2.7 Substantive Violations

All of the foregoing principles are coordinated in the four RICO provisions that define the "prohibited activities."[42] Whenever a "pattern of racketeering activity" involves at least two "predicate acts," RICO declares it illegal:

1. To "use or invest income" from that racketeering activity to acquire any interest in or to establish or operate any enterprise that engages in interstate commerce

2. "To employ racketeering activity to acquire or maintain any interest or control" in such an enterprise

3. For any person employed by or "associated" with such an enterprise to conduct or participate in such a racketeering pattern of activity

4. For any person to conspire with others to violate any of the three foregoing subsections.

---

known of the alleged fraud, which question was left for jury to decide); *contra,* Granite Falls Bank v. Henrikson, 924 F.2d 150 (8th Cir. 1991) (RICO claim accrues as soon as plaintiff discovered or reasonably should have discovered both existence and source of injury and that injury is part of a pattern).

[39] Moll v. U.S. Life Title Ins. Co., 654 F. Supp. 1012 (S.D.N.Y. 1987); County of Cook v. Berger, 648 F. Supp. 433 (N.D. Ill. 1986) (a county's RICO claim alleging mailings of fraudulently obtained property tax assessment reduction accrued when last overt act was committed).

[40] Bankers Trust Co. v. Feldesman, 648 F. Supp. 17 (S.D.N.Y. 1986).

[41] *See* Rodriguez v. Banco Central, 917 F.2d 664 (1st Cir. 1990); Ingram Corp. v. J. Ray McDermott & Co., 495 F. Supp. 1321 (E.D. La. 1980), *rev'd and remanded on other grounds,* 698 F.2d 1295 (5th Cir. 1983) (a RICO claim predicated on mail and wire fraud in a bid rigging case was not time barred because the applicable statute of limitation was tolled by the fraudulent concealment of the cause of action).

[42] 18 U.S.C. § 1962(a)–(d) (1982). *See* Chief Justice Burger's dissent in United States v. Maze, 414 U.S. 395, 405–407 (1974).

§ 2.8   Other Significant Considerations

Such a simplistic summary does not deal with some of the important concepts that appellate courts continually face, including a steady stream of decisions from the United States Supreme Court. The Court has sustained the constitutionality of the government's power to seize the assets of the enterprise involved in a successful criminal prosecution.[43] There is no need to show damages connected with organized crime.[44] Private injunctions are probably unavailable; the trend appears to be to allow equitable relief to the government but not to private claimants.[45] Arbitration covenants may include RICO claims.[46] Finally, state courts have concurrent jurisdiction over civil litigation.[47]

These brief comments are only intended to lay the foundation for the wide scope of factual and legal issues involved in RICO. There is already a substantial array of appellate decisions, many involving direct opposition between various federal circuits. Concurrent state jurisdiction will create a profundity of state appellate rulings with no assurance of uniformity among the 50 states, the federal circuits, and the United States Supreme Court. It is doubtful that the Court will exercise jurisdiction to resolve conflicts that arise among such an array of state and federal institutions.

§ 2.9   State RICO Statutes

It would be erroneous to overlook the additional governmental players in this drama. First, practitioners must carefully note that over 40 states have enacted their own RICO statutes. In so doing, they have not simply copied the terms of federal RICO in the fashion that numerous states enacted "little" Federal Trade Commission (FTC) Acts. State FTC Acts often employ the exact terms of § 5(a) of the FTC Act, with directions that local courts be "guided" by the interpretations made by federal courts and

---

[43] *See* United States v. Monsanto, 491 U.S. 600 (1989); Caplan & Drysdale, Chartered v. United States, 491 U.S. 617 (1989) (construed the Comprehensive Forfeiture Act of 1984, 21 U.S.C. § 853, including its applicability to criminal prosecution under RICO).

[44] Sedima, S.P.R.L. v. Imrex Co., 473 U.S. 479, 496 n.14 (1985) (emphasis added by Supreme Court).

[45] *See* Trane v. O'Connor Sec., 718 F.2d 26 (2d Cir. 1983); Dan River v. Icahn, 701 F.2d 278 (4th Cir. 1983); DeMeut v. Abbott Capital Corp., 589 F. Supp. 1378 (N.D. Ill. 1984).

[46] Shearson-American Express, Inc. v. McMahon, 482 U.S. 220 (1987).

[47] Tafflin v. Levitt, 493 U.S. 455 (1990).

agencies.[48] Instead, the states have fashioned complete RICO statutes with their own array of predicate acts, to which they are constantly making important additions. Many of these statutes provide for private recourse with substantial variations in their allowable damages, recision rights, and other remedies.

Spurred by judicial as well as business and media comment, Congress has been actively involved in numerous proposals to restrict the provisions for a private RICO remedy. Some of these involve sweeping amendments, such as requiring one or more prior criminal convictions, restricting treble damages, altering the burden of proof, and applying the amendments to pending litigation. In 1990, the House enacted such amendments, but the Senate has been mired in scandals that have prevented committee action. Whatever Congress may enact for federal RICO will have no direct impact on the state RICO statutes. Local jurisprudence has now expanded to the extent that it will readily sustain itself regardless of federal developments both in Congress and in federal courts.

The surge of "new law" cannot be ignored by any civil practitioner, at the risk of professional misconduct under both substantive and ethical standards. Federal RICO cases may now be brought in every state court, aided by whatever the local RICO statute provides. There has yet to be any significant jurisprudence on the complex choice of law issues involved in the application of state RICO laws. The expansive nature of federal RICO is highlighted by the unique nationwide jurisdiction it confers over both corporations and individuals. That extraterritorial statutory tool will be available in state courts for claims filed under the federal RICO statute. Local counsel, confronted with choosing a remedy, must give cardinal attention to the applicability of federal and state RICO claims in both federal and state courts.[49]

§ 2.10   Jurisdictional Questions

There are many fascinating and troublesome issues involving federal and state jurisdiction. At this juncture, it is best to list these questions, some of which may reach monumental status.

Because RICO is a federal statute, it does provide express grounds for federal jurisdiction. The Supreme Court has now affirmed the existence of concurrent state jurisdiction.[50] It is unclear that this would provide a

---

[48] *See, e.g.,* Mass. Gen. L. ch. 93A, § 2(b) (1984).

[49] *See* C&S Nat'l Bank v. Gulf Coast Brokers, Inc., Civ. Action 86-1728 (Dec. 4, 1990) (jury verdict of $7 million, including treble damages and interest, under Florida's RICO statute for swindling bank through "check-kiting" scheme) (*see* 13 (No. 5) Nat'l L. J. 6 (Dec. 19, 1990)).

[50] Tafflin v. Levitt, 493 U.S. 455 (1990).

basis for removal to federal court on the ground that the claim arose under federal law, but the right to transfer has been sustained by the Ninth
Circuit.[51] There is an equally troublesome question regarding the removal
to federal court on the ground of diversity of citizenship, because that
could make a mockery out of the precept of concurrent state jurisdiction
for federal RICO. There would, however, be no room for the so-called art-
ful pleading defense, such as masking a clear violation of the federal antitrust laws to look like an intrastate claim.

It should be noted that concurrent jurisdiction has pitfalls. If a federal
RICO claim could have been joined in a state court proceeding, a judgment in the state law suit will provide a res judicata defense against commencement of a federal RICO claim in federal court. By the same token,
a state RICO claim could normally be joined with a federal RICO claim
in federal court on the ground of pendent jurisdiction if the claims arose
under the same nucleus of operating facts,[52] and a failure to join the state
claim could also constitute res judicata.

Underlying these technical issues is the fact that there have been serious
objections to federal RICO on the ground that it involves "garden variety
fraud" of the kind that is usually consigned to state jurisdiction.[53] Similarly, the Supreme Court has made numerous judicial and legislative
efforts to lessen the burdens on the federal court system. All of these
elements may come into play in judicial and legislative activities.

§ 2.11   Particularity of Allegations

Federal Rules of Civil Procedure Rule 9(b) requires that "[i]n all averments of fraud or mistake, the circumstances constituting fraud or mistake shall be stated with particularity."[54] Rule 9(b) must be read in conjunction with Rule 8(a), which requires only a "short and plain statement
of the claim showing that the pleader is entitled to relief. . . . Thus, it
is inappropriate to focus exclusively on the fact that Rule 9(b) requires
particularity in pleading fraud. This is too narrow an approach and fails
to take account of the general simplicity and flexibility contemplated by
the rules."[55] The purpose of Rule 9(b) is to provide a defendant with fair

---

[51] Emerich v. Touche Ross & Co., 846 F.2d 1190 (9th Cir. 1988).

[52] *See* United Mine Workers v. Gibbs, 383 U.S. 715 (1966).

[53] *See* Arizona v. Pickrel, 136 Ariz. 589, 667 P.2d 1304 (1983); State v. Thompson, 751
P.2d 805, *aff'd sub nom.* State v. Fletcher, 751 P.2d 822 (1988), *rev'd on other grounds
sub nom.* State v. Thompson, 1991-1 Trade Cas. (CCH) ¶ 69,396.

[54] Van Dorn Co. v. Howington, 623 F. Supp. 1548, 1555 (N.D. Ohio 1985).

[55] Michaels Bldg. Co. v. Ameritrust Co. N.A., 848 F.2d 674, 679 (6th Cir. 1988) (quoting
5 C. Wright & A. Miller, Federal Practice and Procedure: Civil § 1298 at 407 (1969)).

notice of the plaintiff's claim so the defendant may prepare a response.[56] RICO claims predicated on mail and wire fraud must satisfy these pleading requirements.[57] In *Cincinnati Gas & Electric Co. v. General Electric Co.*, the court stated:

> plaintiffs must allege that defendant acted with intent to defraud . . . although intent can be averred generally. Moreover, a plaintiff pleading fraud must allege the time, place and contents of the misrepresentations. However, such facts need only be pled in a fashion "sufficient to give defendant notice of the claims against it." The liberal notice pleading procedure of the Federal Rules of Civil Procedure, and of *Conley v. Gibson*, apply in assessing the adequacy of a RICO claim. Therefore, if the pleadings place defendant on notice of the precise misconduct or fraudulent acts claimed, as an alternative to pleading the time, date and places of the wire and fraud violations, Rule 9(b) is satisfied.[58]

At one time, Ohio district courts went to the extreme of requiring that every civil RICO claim contain allegations as specific as those required in an indictment. Such a demand often led to dismissals; it went beyond the needs of "informational" pleading. By insisting on indictable detail in the complaint, such a demand prevented the plaintiff from using discovery to obtain the specific details that were only available in the defendant's records. Such discovery is necessary because it is the only way to obtain exact proof, in much the same way that the government's extensive pre-indictment detective work and use of the grand jury produces proof. Ohio courts now compromise by issuing a special set of 20 interrogatories in a "RICO Fact Statement" (see §§ 2.28 through 2.33), seeking both specific allegations and the legal theories on which the claims are based. These are subject to expansion and amendment as discovery progresses.

§ 2.12 Franchisee Complaint

Sections 2.13 through **2.27** set forth a sample franchisee's complaint using RICO as well as other counts. It is based on a real case and, as with other presentations in this book, the author has employed his direct experience in actual cases whether pending or completed. This should not affect the use of these publicly filed documents for practice commentary. Because

---

[56] *Id.* at 679; Roger v. Lehman Bros. Kuhn Loeb, Inc., 607 F. Supp. 222, 225 (S.D. Ohio 1984).

[57] Van Dorn Co. v. Howington, 623 F. Supp. 1548, 1555 (N.D. Ohio 1985); Bennett v. E.F. Hutton Co., 597 F. Supp. 1547, 1559 (N.D. Ohio 1984).

[58] Cincinnati Gas & Elec. Co. v. General Elec. Co., 656 F. Supp. 49, 75 (S.D. Ohio 1986) (citations omitted).

they are being used for their educational value only, their contents must not be regarded as assertions of fact or legal liability.[59]

The length of the complaint underscores the particularity needed whenever fraud is alleged, especially in the franchise context. It is essential to make extensive investigation before such claims are filed in court because there has been considerable judicial criticism of the misuse of RICO charges for ordinary business complaints. Franchising itself is not well understood,[60] increasing the problems of presentation both to the court and to the jury.

§ 2.13 —Jurisdiction and Parties

UNITED STATES DISTRICT COURT
NORTHERN DISTRICT OF OHIO EASTERN DIVISION

LICENSEE
   Plaintiffs,
 	
V.
 	
DIET FRANCHISOR, PRESIDENT AND
EXECUTIVE VICE PRESIDENT
   Defendants.
	CIVIL ACTION
	NO.:

Verified Complaint and Jury Demand

Nature of the Action

1. This action is brought by plaintiffs. It is brought against defendants Diet Franchisor, President, and Executive Vice President.

2. Diet Franchisor and President developed fraudulent schemes to market franchises for the operation of Diet Franchisor Diet System Centers, which utilize the Diet Franchisor Diet System Program, to overcharge franchisees for mandatory product purchases from the franchisor, to misapply franchisees' advertising contributions, to defraud consumers of Diet Franchisor Diet System Programs, and to prevent franchisees from leaving the system. Executive Vice President actively participated in Diet Franchisor policy determinations.

---

[59] The case presented in this chapter is still pending. As a courtesy to the parties, the actual names have been omitted.

[60] *See generally* H. Brown, Franchising: Realities and Remedies (1991).

3.   As a result of Diet Franchisor's and President's violations of both state and federal law, as hereinafter set forth and alleged, the plaintiffs were induced to purchase and/or operate Diet Franchisor Diet System Centers and to make substantial expenditures of money on the acquisition of such franchises and the establishment and operation of such businesses. The Diet Franchisor Program, which the plaintiffs were induced to sell to the public, was seriously deficient and is alleged to have caused the death of a client of an Alabama franchise.

4.   The conduct of Diet Franchisor and President was in violation of the Racketeer Influenced and Corrupt Organizations Act ("RICO"), 18 U.S.C. § 1961 et. seq., the Wire and Mail Fraud Statutes, 18 U.S.C. §§ 1341 and 1343, and the Federal Trade Commission's Pre-Sale Franchise Disclosure Rule, 16 C.F.R. § 436. Executive Vice President conspired with Diet Franchisor and President to violate 18 U.S.C. § 1962 (a), (b), (c), and (d).

5.   Diet Franchisor's actions constituted breaches of express contract, breaches of the implied covenant of good faith and fair dealing, and breaches of contract based on a promissory equitable estoppel.

6.   The conduct of Diet Franchisor, President, and Executive Vice President was in violation of the local "little" FTC Act, and the regulations promulgated thereunder by the Attorney General under the authority of § 2.

Jurisdiction and Venue

7.   This court has jurisdiction over the claims under 28 U.S.C. § 1332(a). There is diversity of citizenship between the plaintiffs on the one hand and the defendants on the other. All of the claims exceed $50,000, exclusive of interest and costs. This court also has jurisdiction under 18 U.S.C. § 1964.

8.   Venue lies in this District pursuant to the provisions of 28 U.S.C. § 1391 and 18 U.S.C. § 1965.

Plaintiffs

9.   The plaintiffs reside in state A and were the owners of Diet Franchisor franchises located in state A. Licensee-plaintiff devoted her full time and efforts for a period in excess of seven years and to the exclusion of other gainful employment in order to attempt to conduct such business operations successfully. Licensee-plaintiff devoted his part time and efforts for five years and his full-time and effort in excess of two years, to the exclusion of other gainful employment.

10.   In 1982, the plaintiffs telephoned Diet Franchisor in state X from their home in state A regarding a newspaper advertisement by Diet Franchisor for franchises.

11.   Diet Franchisor, President, and Executive Vice President caused to be delivered by interstate mail to the plaintiffs Franchise Offering Circulars dated December 1, 1981, May 1, 1987, and December 2, 1987. The Offering Circular stated that the franchisor generally makes a profit on the sales of its products to franchisees of zero to 25 percent (0%–25%) or zero to 100 percent (0%–100%).

12.   In reliance on representations made by Diet Franchisor's employees at the direction of Diet Franchisor, President, and Executive Vice President, and on those made in the Offering Circulars and in other materials provided by Diet Franchisor, President, and Executive Vice President, and without knowledge of the intentional fraudulent schemes, misrepresentations, and nondisclosures described below, the plaintiffs executed franchise agreements with Diet Franchisor to operate their Diet Franchisor Diet System Centers. The location of the franchise, the date the franchise agreements were executed by the plaintiffs, and the consideration paid were as follows:

Location	Date Executed	Cost
Town A	September 30, 1982	$22,500
Town A Renewal	August 29, 1988	$ -0-
Town B	September 5, 1988	$12,500

13.   The plaintiffs are the owners of two office condominiums at which the Diet Franchisor Diet System Center franchises were operated. The office condominiums were purchased and buildout accomplished for the sole purpose of operating as a Diet Franchisor Diet System Center.

14.   As a direct result of the actions of the defendants, it became impossible for the plaintiffs to operate their businesses in a profitable manner. These actions of defendants included:

  a.   requiring the weekly payment of a 10 percent royalty with a minimum weekly payment of $150 per center whether or not the center is profitable;

  b.   requiring a minimum weekly advertising of $250 per center, a portion of which is allocated to President's company, Ad, Inc.; and demanding an additional advertising expenditure of $575 per week per center, which has since been reduced to $482.50;

  c.   charging exorbitant prices for mandatory products; and

  d.   unreasonably refusing to approve alternate suppliers.

15.   On December 19, 1990 the plaintiffs notified Diet Franchisor that they were terminating the franchise agreements. The plaintiffs

remain liable to the mortgagor for a total of $634,000. Plaintiffs now operate the businesses under the name "Good Bodies."

Defendants

16.   The defendant, Diet Franchisor, is a State X corporation with its principal place of business at Town. Diet Franchisor is in the business of selling franchises for the operation of diet centers that utilize Diet Franchisor Diet System programs. Diet Franchisor requires franchisees to purchase exclusively from it certain dietary products and foods as a part of the Diet Systems Program. Diet Franchisor is wholly owned and controlled by defendant President.

17.   Defendant President is sole shareholder and owner of Diet Franchisor and has been the company's chief executive officer and president since its inception. Upon information and belief, President resides in the state of X. Together with the Executive Vice President, he determines all Diet Franchisor policy matters and controls its conduct in all respects.

18.   The defendant Executive Vice President has been executive vice president of Diet Franchisor since May 1984. He is an independent Certified Public Accountant licensed in the state of X, and through June 1990 also concurrently served as an executive of an independent accounting firm that does exclusive work for Diet Franchisor. Upon information and belief, Executive Vice President resides in the state of X. Executive Vice President actively participated in Diet Franchisor policy determinations. Executive Vice President has stated that his duties include "total charge of franchisee activities."

§ 2.14   —Factual Allegations

UNIFORM ALLEGATIONS

19.   Unless otherwise noted, the allegations in this section are almost identical with complaints filed on or after August 20, 1990 in other lawsuits against the defendants.

The Underlying Transactions and Pattern of Fraudulent Schemes

20.   President established the Diet Franchisor franchise system in 1979. He is Diet Franchisor's president and sole stockholder and is in full charge of its policy and conduct. In 1980, President formed and organized Diet Franchisor. This company owns and operates approximately 36 diet centers in the states of X, Y, and Z. President also owns

Diet Franchisor of Canada, Inc., which has sold 12 franchised centers in Ontario and British Columbia. As of January 1990 there were approximately 396 franchised centers in operation throughout the United States. In 1990, approximately 90 of these centers closed; on December 6, 1990, Executive Vice President declared "the number of open centers changes every morning."

21.   The Diet Franchisor Diet System Centers operate as "outpatient diet clinics" and provide diet services and sell the Diet Franchisor Diet System Program and products to consumers. The consumer pays the Center a fee to enroll in the program. During the program, the consumer purchases products including nutritional supplements (a powdered protein substitute that is added to water), entrees, salad dressing, cookbooks, and other miscellaneous items from the Center. The Center is required to purchase all of these products from Diet Franchisor.

22.   Upon information and belief, President and Diet Franchisor formulated and embarked upon a pattern of intentionally fraudulent schemes, including, without limitation:

a.   a scheme to induce increased purchases of Diet Franchisor franchises and to obtain funds through the payment by franchisees of franchise fees and royalties [the higher weekly royalty of $150 or 10 percent of gross revenues] by fraudulently persuading the franchisees that they would acquire a reasonable opportunity to succeed in their franchised business (the franchise sales scheme);

b.   a scheme to obtain funds from franchisees by requiring that they purchase products solely from Diet Franchisor at prices that resulted in profits to Diet Franchisor which Diet Franchisor, President, and Executive Vice President knew exceeded those stated in the Pre-Sale Offering Circulars and knew were unconscionable (the mandatory products overcharge scheme);

c.   a scheme to obtain funds through franchisees' payments of advertising fees to Diet Franchisor, which in turn directed a portion thereof to Ad, Inc., a company solely owned and controlled by President, resulting in little or no benefit to the franchisees (the advertising fund scheme);

d.   a scheme to get consumers to enroll in Diet Franchisor Diet System Programs, based on knowingly false representations and guarantees concerning the safety and effectiveness of the diet and potential for weight loss (consumer fraud scheme); and

e.   a scheme to prevent the franchisees from leaving the Diet Franchisor system (the policing and sanctions *in terrorem* scheme).

Executive Vice President actively participated in Diet Franchisor policy determinations and assisted President and Diet Franchisor in the execution of these schemes.

23.   In furtherance of these schemes, President, Diet Franchisor, Executive Vice President, and Diet Franchisor employees used the United States mails and interstate telephone wires and other interstate wires: to procure the sale and establishment of diet franchises; to demand and collect franchise fees, royalty payments, advertising fees, and payments for mandatory products; to direct and encourage the franchisees to induce consumers to enroll in the Diet Franchisor Diet System Programs; and to prevent the franchisees from leaving the Diet Franchisor system. President drew money and benefits from this conduct and reinvested them in Diet Franchisor.

24.   In addition to being a participant and vehicle for such schemes, Diet Franchisor failed to fulfill its contractual obligations to the franchisees by failing and refusing to provide a viable system that would allow the franchisees a reasonable likelihood of success, failing to effectively assist the plaintiffs in obtaining suitable site locations, failing to provide effective lease negotiations, failing and refusing to provide adequate support during initial operation of the Center and thereafter, and failing and refusing to provide up-to-date manuals.

25.   Throughout the relationship with the franchisees, Diet Franchisor, President, and Executive Vice President committed deceptive acts and practices that are actionable under the local "little" FTC Act or similar statute and the regulations, if any, promulgated thereunder by the Attorney General.

§ 2.15   —Fraudulent Sales Scheme Allegations

THE FRAUDULENT SALES SCHEME

26.   In order to induce the purchase and establishment of such franchised weight-loss centers at various times, Executive Vice President and Diet Franchisor employees, including Sales Representative, then Diet Franchisor sales representative, at the direction of Diet Franchisor, President, and Executive Vice President, by interstate mail, telephone calls, and in person, repeatedly made intentionally fraudulent oral and written misrepresentations and/or knowingly failed to make full and fair disclosure of certain material facts to prospective franchisees, including the plaintiffs. The representations included, but were not limited to, claims that the franchise system had a proven record that assured that:

  a.   franchisees would receive the benefits of dealing with a full-service franchisor, with a "proven system" of how to operate a successful, profitable company;

b. Diet Franchisor would provide its franchisees with detailed and up-to-date "how-to" manuals regarding all aspects of the business, including what it described as a "unique, specially prepared behavioral guidance manual";

c. Diet Franchisor would provide franchisees with unlimited training and additional assistance after opening;

d. a training college would be established for franchisees;

e. group buying power through Diet Franchisor would lead to additional savings for the franchisees;

f. the franchise development department would provide substantial assistance in site selection, floor plan design, and lease negotiations;

g. constant support and guidance would be provided by Diet Franchisor, including: financial planners and budgeters who would offer expert advice on business planning and budgeting and would periodically monitor sales and expenses and help to establish an effective bookkeeping system; a current portfolio of successful client testimonials that would be provided to the franchisee to use in client solicitation and advertising; and a research project that was being initiated to enable Diet Franchisor to become the authoritative voice in the diet business.

27. Diet Franchisor, Executive Vice President, President, and Diet Franchisor employees knowingly failed to disclose to the plaintiffs that:

a. Diet Franchisor's diet system was no more "proven" than any other diet system; the diet system was constantly changed, creating confusion among the franchisees; many of the described services were unavailable or extremely limited;

b. none of the Diet Franchisor manuals were updated from 1983 until May 1990 nor were they useful; the behavioral guidance manual was superficial, incomplete, and not useful; upon information and belief, the behavioral guidance manual was not unique nor prepared by Diet Franchisor but had been copied from one used by a commercial health club;

c. Diet Franchisor staff members received little training and yet were sent to direct and assist the franchisees; the one-week classroom training was grossly inadequate; certification training classes were shallow and not helpful; little nutritional or dietary information was provided; training seminars emphasized sales and marketing techniques rather than service to the clients; and nutritional counseling skills were not taught;

   d.   Diet Franchisor had no present intention of establishing a training college and one in fact has not been established nor are there any indications that it will be established;

   e.   any savings from group purchases were retained by Diet Franchisor and were not passed along to franchisees; the Diet Franchisor nutritional supplements were not unique and were freely available in the marketplace at substantially lower prices than the prices represented by Diet Franchisor in its Offering Circulars and the even higher prices actually charged by Diet Franchisor;

   f.   site selection assistance consisted merely of the recommendation to locate the Center at a medical center (later changed to strip mall) and a visit from a corporate representative who was not familiar with the town or state, to view the sites selected by franchisee and to give approval or disapproval; and the assistance with lease negotiations resulted in the execution of a three-year lease for a site, the parking lot for which was sold several months later to a developer for construction of a hotel, but the lease did not contain an escape or buy-out provision; Diet Franchisor's unwarranted delay in sending a representative to approve a site cost the plaintiffs $100,000 (their first selected site was sold during the delay period, resulting in plaintiffs' spending $100,000 more on an alternate site);

   g.   support was ineffectual; service representatives were assigned and then quickly replaced, transferred, or resigned; there was no conformity of communications nor completion of programs; grand programs were announced and then never mentioned again; the portfolio of endorsements consisted of out-of-date, unfashionable photographs that were not useful in client solicitations;

   h.   many of the foregoing matters itemized in "a" through "g" have seriously worsened throughout the relationship.

28.   Diet Franchisor, President, and Executive Vice President did not disclose to the plaintiffs that these statements had not been implemented and that Diet Franchisor had failed to take any steps to fulfill the promises; none have in fact occurred. The plaintiffs continued to believe the franchisor would fulfill its promises.

29.   The so-called Federal Trade Commission Pre-Sale Franchise Disclosure Rule, 16 C.F.R. § 436, effective October 21, 1979, promulgated by the Federal Trade Commission pursuant to its rulemaking authority, 15 U.S.C. § 57 (FTC Rule), requires that a franchisor must make accurate specified written disclosures to prospective franchisees at specified times and places. It declares that failure to conform to the

rule constitutes an unfair and deceptive act or practice under § 5(a) of the Federal Trade Commission Act, 15 U.S.C. § 45a.

30. Any failure to disclose to a buyer any fact, the disclosure of which may have influenced the buyer not to enter into the transaction, or any failure to comply with the FTC Rule is actionable as an unfair and/or deceptive act and/or practice under the local "little" FTC Act and the regulations promulgated thereunder by the Attorney General.

31. The Offering Circulars stated that the franchisor would provide initial training consisting of classroom study and hands-on instruction.

32. The Offering Circulars stated that franchisor would assist the franchisee in obtaining a suitable site location for the Center.

33. The recital contained in the Franchise Agreement which was an exhibit to the Offering Circulars stated that the franchisor had developed a business plan and method for providing weight reduction and control and had established an excellent reputation and goodwill with the public.

34. Despite the requirements of the FTC Rule, Diet Franchisor, President, and Executive Vice President did not disclose to the plaintiffs:

   a. that the training was rudimentary and not very useful or helpful, and emphasized sales to clients rather than nutritional and counseling skills; that "hands-on" training consisted of participation as an observer; and that the training manuals used in post-1983 classes were outdated and deficient;

   b. that its site selection assistance was ineffective and slipshod;

   c. that the Diet Franchisor Diet System Program was grossly deficient and that Diet Franchisor intended to change the system by mandating an entirely different diet that eliminated much of the need for the medical monitoring by the physician and nurse, and that it did not produce effective weight loss.

35. As an additional inducement to persuade the plaintiffs to purchase franchises, Sales Representative stated that they would "make a great deal of money in a short time." Sales Representative stated that "the sample income and expense statements in the Offering Circular were overly conservative in order to meet the government disclosure requirements." He assured the plaintiffs that "they would do much better." Later, Diet Franchisor employees, at the direction of Diet Franchisor and President, repeatedly told the plaintiffs that they should make a net profit before taxes of at least 20 percent on gross sales and would make back their initial cash investments through profits within a short time of opening each Center.

36. Under the FTC Rule, the "earnings" representations regarding gross profits triggered a requirement to disclose certain "Earnings

Disclosure" materials; Diet Franchisor, President and Executive Vice President never provided the plaintiffs with such earnings disclosures. The Offering Circulars that Diet Franchisor and President gave the plaintiffs were not the accurate and complete disclosure statements that satisfy the FTC Rule. The FTC Rule declared that these failures constitute a violation of § 5(a) of the FTC Act and are therefore actionable under the local "little" FTC Act and the regulations promulgated thereunder by the Attorney General.

37.   In reliance upon the foregoing representations made by Diet Franchisor's employees at the direction of Diet Franchisor, President, and Executive Vice President, and on those made in the Offering Circulars and in other materials provided by Diet Franchisor, President, and Executive Vice President, and without knowledge of the intentionally fraudulent schemes, misrepresentations, and nondisclosures, the plaintiffs executed Franchise Agreements with Diet Franchisor to operate Diet Franchisor Diet System Centers (Centers).

38.   Despite their investment of money, time, and effort, and contrary to the express representations made to them by Diet Franchisor, the plaintiffs did not receive repayment of their investment within a short time of opening each Center; they have actually had to invest additional monies; and they did not make a net profit of 20 percent on gross sales. Instead, the plaintiffs have suffered substantial losses, with almost no compensation for their own labor.

§ 2.16   —Advertising Fund Scheme Allegations

THE ADVERTISING FUND SCHEME

39.   To induce prospective franchisees to purchase a Diet Franchisor franchise, Diet Franchisor employees, at the direction of Diet Franchisor, President, and Executive Vice President, by interstate mail and telephone calls, made intentionally fraudulent oral and written misrepresentations and/or knowingly failed to make full and fair disclosure of certain material facts regarding Diet Franchisor's advertising programs to prospective franchisees, including the plaintiffs. The franchisees were assured that Diet Franchisor had a system that provided national support in advertising through major publications and periodicals and that full market and media campaigns were available to the franchisees. It was also represented to the franchisees that they would receive the benefit of assistance from an advertising coordinator who would assist with advertising strategy and would provide an advertising handbook for a year-round advertising program with advertisements that were proven traffic builders.

40.   In October 1987, the existing franchisees were informed by Diet Franchisor that it was establishing a National Advertising Fund (NAF). Diet Franchisor stated that the NAF would pay for:

    a.   media advertising and for engaging in test marketing;

    b.   the conduct of surveys for advertising effectiveness; and

    c.   the production of new audio and visual commercials and "ad slicks."

Diet Franchisor represented that all Centers were obligated to make payments to the NAF and would benefit from the national program.

41.   Diet Franchisor, President, and Executive Vice President, in person or by interstate mail, sent to all existing franchisees an Addenda to the Franchise Agreements entitled "National Advertising and Sales Promotions." In reliance upon Diet Franchisor's representations about the NAF, the plaintiffs executed the Addenda. The Addenda required the plaintiffs to pay a $250 weekly contribution for each Center to the NAF. Shortly thereafter, Diet Franchisor waived the plaintiffs' obligation to contribute to the NAF.

42.   By various interstate letters, Diet Franchisor informed existing franchisees of their required contribution to the NAF and made demand for payment.

43.   Upon information and belief, the NAF was not used for its stated purposes. A portion of the fund was paid through the use of interstate mails and/or wires to Ad, Inc., a company wholly owned and controlled by President, resulting in little or no benefit to the franchisees. Upon information and belief, Diet Franchisor did not make weekly contributions to NAF on behalf of the company-owned stores, even though it had promised to do so.

44.   Existing franchisees made written requests to Diet Franchisor by interstate mail for copies of the NAF statement of operation. Diet Franchisor responded by mailing a page of cash receipts and disbursements for the Diet Franchisor Centers in the Plaintiffs ADI (Area of Dominant Influence). Diet Franchisor has never provided the plaintiffs with any audited statement of operation on the use of these Funds.

§ 2.17   —Mandatory Product Overcharge Scheme Allegations

THE MANDATORY PRODUCT OVERCHARGE SCHEME

45.   In order to induce the franchisees to purchase a Diet Franchisor franchise and thereafter make payments to Diet Franchisor for products, Diet Franchisor employees, at the direction of Diet Franchisor,

President, and Executive Vice President, by interstate mail and telephone calls made intentionally fraudulent oral and written misrepresentations and/or knowingly failed to make full and fair disclosure to prospective franchisees, including the plaintiffs, of certain material facts regarding charges for products that franchisees were required to purchase from Diet Franchisor. The representations included, but were not limited to, claims that:

a.   the Diet Franchisor nutritional supplements were unique and specially formulated and were only available from Diet Franchisor; Diet Franchisor had a facility including a laboratory and staff engaged in testing and development of products for Diet Franchisor;

b.   any mark-up over Diet Franchisor's cost was only a "normal mark-up to cover distribution cost"; and

c.   the diet program allowed clients to experience weight loss by eating selected regular grocery foods.

46.   The Offering Circular and Franchise Agreements issued at various times between 1981 and 1989 stated that the franchisee was required to purchase all products including nutritional supplements from Diet Franchisor or from an approved supplier or stated that the franchisee was required to purchase directly from Diet Franchisor all of its requirements of the nutritional supplement.

47.   The Offering Circulars issued at various times between 1981 and 1989 stated that Diet Franchisor was generally making a profit of either zero to 25 percent (0% to 25%), zero to 100 percent (0% to 100%), or zero to 155 percent (0% to 155%) on sale of its products to franchisees. In fact, Diet Franchisor and President have always sold the nutritional supplements at the same prices to all franchisees, and the price has always exceeded the profit ranges stated in the Offering Circulars. The base sales price charged to franchisees for nutritional supplements was $143.64 per case of 36 cartons. The number of packets per carton was reduced from seven to six with no reduction in price. Executive Vice President later declared that Diet Franchisor's cost was approximately $55. This represented a $93.62 gross profit to Diet Franchisor, which as a percentage is 170 percent, which is well in excess of the 0–25%, 0–100%, or 0–155% profit range stated in the various Diet Franchisor disclosure statements. Executive Vice President later declared that the 155 percent figure represented gross profit.

48.   Diet Franchisor, President, and Executive Vice President did not disclose to the plaintiffs that:

a.   the nutritional supplement was not unique and was available in the marketplace at substantially lower prices;

b. Diet Franchisor has always and continues to charge prices substantially in excess of its representations, with profits far in excess of its declarations, for all products bought from it by the franchisees;

c. in addition to the nutritional supplement, there were other Diet Franchisor products that were a mandatory part of the diet program; Diet Franchisor is the sole approved supplier of these products and requests for alternate suppliers have never been processed and were never approved.

49. On several occasions by mail, interstate wire, or in person, franchisees received solicitations from suppliers of the nutritional supplements. The nutritional supplement offered by them to franchisees was substantially identical to that which Diet Franchisor falsely claimed was unique and specially formulated and which Diet Franchisor required the franchisee to purchase at a very substantial mark-up. The suppliers offered to sell the products to the franchisees at prices drastically lower than those charged by Diet Franchisor.

50. Interstate wire and mail requests were made to Diet Franchisor to approve specific alternate suppliers of nutritional supplements. These products were in compliance with Diet Franchisor standards, but the requests were completely and unreasonably ignored, never processed, and none were ever approved.

51. Diet Franchisor has always and continues to charge prices substantially in excess of its express representations, with gross profits far in excess of its written declarations sent to the plaintiffs by interstate mail, and which are unconscionable.

52. The Franchise Agreements outlined a sham procedure for obtaining Diet Franchisor's approval of alternate suppliers of any products or outlined a procedure for obtaining Diet Franchisor's approval of alternate suppliers of products other than the potassium and nutritional supplement. On several occasions franchisees utilized the alleged approval process to seek Diet Franchisor's permission to buy other products such as food items and entrees from alternate suppliers. These requests were completely and unreasonably ignored, never processed, and/or refused. Diet Franchisor has never approved an alternate supplier for any product.

§ 2.18 —Consumer Fraud Scheme Allegations

THE CONSUMER FRAUD SCHEME

53. Prior to the plaintiffs' purchases of their Diet Franchisor Diet System Centers, Diet Franchisor employees, at the direction of Diet

Franchisor, President, and Executive Vice President, by interstate mail and telephone calls, repeatedly made intentionally fraudulent, oral and written misrepresentation and/or knowingly failed to make full and fair disclosure of certain material facts to prospective franchisees, including the plaintiffs, concerning the Diet Franchisor Diet System Program. Diet Franchisor, President, and Executive Vice President knew and intended that the plaintiffs would repeat the misrepresentations to customers in order to induce them to enroll in the program, and this in fact resulted in such customer enrollment. These misrepresentations and sham appearances included but were not limited to:

a. the Diet Franchisor-mandated diet program was a proven, effective, and safe system;

b. the diet program (ketogenic diet) was a two-part plan: the initial plan provided for weight loss of 3 to 4 pounds per week; part two was a maintenance program designed to aid clients in maintaining their ideal weight; and the Diet System was a fast and lasting system which set Diet Franchisor apart from the competition;

c. the name of the franchise, the design of the Center, the use of a local nurse and doctor, and the stressing of medical safety and monitoring were necessary to induce client patronage and clearly distinguished the Diet Franchisor franchise from its competition; and

d. clients of the franchisee would experience fast weight loss by eating selected regular grocery store foods;

e. clients would burn 450 calories with every packet of Brand Name Soup or Juice that they consumed.

54.   In reliance upon these representations, the plaintiffs purchased the Centers and invested time, money, and energy to encourage consumers to enroll in the Diet Franchisor Diet System Program.

55.   Diet Franchisor and President failed to disclose to the plaintiffs that there were serious problems with the diets, including but not limited to:

a. the original ketogenic diet from 1982 was a series of diets containing 500 calories and stated that potassium would be issued if needed; the 1983 mandated ketogenic diet allowed for a daily calorie intake of 500–700 calories, which was and is considered to be physically harmful; the mandated diet had serious side effects, as later corroborated by Diet Franchisor in a Diet Franchisor memo dated January 19, 1989, issued after receiving negative publicity surrounding the death of a client of an Alabama Diet Franchisor franchisee and the wrongful death lawsuit brought by the heirs of the deceased client against Diet Franchisor and the franchisee; the cause of death was stated as hypokalemia, an abnormal depletion of potassium in the circulating blood producing muscle weakness, painful muscle spasms, and postural hypotension; for the first time, franchisees were then instructed to give clients a Dieter's Information Sheet that listed the side effects as: lightheadedness, constipation, cramping, muscle weakness, lower body temperature, hair loss, irregular menstrual cycles, tendency to bruise, bad breath, and dry skin; in April 1990, after a competing franchise system received negative publicity alleging that its diet caused gall bladder problems, Diet Franchisor revised the Dieter's Information Sheet to include gall bladder problems as a possible side effect;

b. the franchisees were obligated to give the clients a written guarantee to the effect that if the client did not lose the guaranteed weight during the program, the client would be allowed to continue at the franchisee's expense until the goal weight was achieved. In fact, however, the Diet Franchisor diet was no more lasting than any diet; most clients regained all, most of, or more than the weight they had lost on the program;

c. upon information and belief, Diet Franchisor's own in-house physician had refused to endorse the ketogenic diet in an advertising campaign;

d. in addition to nutritional supplements, other Diet Franchisor products were a mandatory part of the diet program, and the clients would be induced to purchase Diet Franchisor products rather than buying "grocery store food";

e. clients do not burn 450 calories when consuming Brand Name Soup and Juice.

56. At the 1989 national convention, Diet Franchisor informed franchisees, including the plaintiffs, that a new "high fiber diet" was being implemented and would be mandatory for all Centers by December 31, 1989. President stated that the new high fiber diet would allow for an intake of 800–900 calories and that under this diet there was no concern for potassium loss nor any need for extensive blood analysis. However, Diet Franchisor continued to require the franchisees to conduct the extensive blood analysis every ten weeks at the customer's expense, whether or not it was needed. Upon information and belief, the company-owned centers discontinued the extensive blood analysis for a time (although the fee to the client was not reduced) and later

reinstituted it. Diet Franchisor nonetheless continued to advertise to the public under the service-mark "Diet Franchisor," promoting the image that extensive medical monitoring is essential to the Diet Franchisor Diet System Program. In fact, Diet Franchisor only requires a physician to be present at the Diet Franchisor Diet System Center one evening a week for approximately 4 to 5 hours and the benefits of the physician's attendance to the clients are minimal or nonexistent.

57.   At that same meeting, President assured the franchisees that training, procedural guidelines, and support materials for the new high fiber diet would be available by December 31, 1989. No such materials or substantive training were ever provided to the plaintiffs.

58.   Diet Franchisor and President made representations and guarantees to prospective franchisees, including the plaintiffs, that the high fiber diet would allow for a weight loss of three pounds per week although:

  a.   the high fiber diet did not in fact result in the three pound per week weight loss;

  b.   Diet Franchisor failed and refused to undertake the obligation of providing a diet that would allow for a three pound per week weight loss;

  c.   Diet Franchisor had conducted a survey indicating that weight loss was less than three pounds per week; and

  d.   Diet Franchisor did not provide any data to support the representations and guarantee, despite requests by franchisees.

59.   Existing franchisees requested data to support the claims, but all of these requests were ignored. The average weight loss of clients of the plaintiffs was less than two pounds per week.

60.   During a hearing before a congressional subcommittee on May 7, 1990, President was questioned about the Diet Franchisor advertising claim of up to two to four pounds per week weight loss. President testified that men, obese men, and the morbidly obese tend to lose weight faster than others. President admitted that the advertisements do not contain a disclaimer that weight loss of individuals may vary according to gender or degree of obesity. By interstate letter dated July 5, 1990, Diet Franchisor has now instructed the franchisees that all advertising claims regarding weight loss should be an "average weight loss of over two pounds per week." President testified on December 6, 1990 in a related proceeding that in response to governmental pressure Diet Franchisor has eliminated average weekly weight loss claims entirely from its current advertising. However, the Diet Franchisor franchisees are still required to guarantee two pounds per week weight loss to the clients.

61.   Any misrepresentations of material fact as to a guarantee in connection with the sale or offering for sale of a product is actionable

as an unfair and/or deceptive act and/or practice under the local "little" FTC Act and the regulations promulgated thereunder by the Attorney General.

§ 2.19 —Policing and Sanctions Scheme Allegations

POLICING AND SANCTIONS IN TERROREM SCHEME

62. After fraudulently inducing the franchisees into the Diet Franchisor system, President, Executive Vice President, and Diet Franchisor activated a policing and sanction *in terrorem* scheme whereby they made it impracticable and very difficult for franchisees to leave the system. In furtherance of this scheme, from 1979 to date, President and Diet Franchisor caused certain contract provisions to be incorporated into all contracts between Diet Franchisor and its several hundred franchisees, including the plaintiffs, which were sent and implemented through the use of interstate wires and mails. Executive Vice President actively participated in the implementation of the scheme. These policing and sanction procedures against the franchisees were designed to discourage, intimidate, and prevent the franchisees from leaving the system and to thereby compel them to continue to purchase products from Diet Franchisor, pay royalties, make advertising contributions, and submit to abuses, deceptive schemes, and illegal conduct as detailed in this complaint.

63. The policing procedures included, but were not limited, to:

    a. use of videotaped interviews during which Diet Franchisor employees, at the direction of President and Diet Franchisor, would disclaim making any misrepresentations to the franchisee; but after the videotaping was completed the employees promptly reasserted the misrepresentations;

    b. President's policy of secretly videotaping meetings with franchisees held in the Diet Franchisor conference room, a room which President has specifically fitted with a one-way mirror that allows the proceedings to be secretly videotaped without the knowledge and/or consent of the franchisees. On or about February 1, 1990, President secretly videotaped a meeting with five New England franchisees, including that portion of time in which the franchisees were alone in the room, in violation of State X Rev. Code. Ann. § 2933.52(A)(1);

    c. use of questionnaires in which the franchisees were required to state that no representation regarding earning potential were made by Diet Franchisor employees at the direction of President and Diet Franchisor, when in fact such representations had been made and were restated by Diet Franchisor employees after the franchisee signed the questionnaire;

d. use of threats, reprisals, and intimidation, including the prevention of expansion, of renewal, and termination, plus the loss of location without reimbursement for expensive improvements that Diet Franchisor required them to install and with no monetary compensation for good will; and

e. requiring the franchisee to execute a mutual release upon the sale or closing of a franchise.

64. Diet Franchisor prescribed for the prospective franchisees, including the plaintiffs, contract provisions that were designed to intimidate and prevent the franchisees from seeking redress for the fraudulent misrepresentations and nondisclosures. These contract provisions made by Diet Franchisor and President, and which were intended to shield Diet Franchisor from liability for its misrepresentations and nondisclosures, were non-negotiable clauses in the Franchise Agreements. The provisions also included claims by Diet Franchisor that all prior or contemporaneous promises and representations were merged and superseded by the Franchise Agreement, and Diet Franchisor disclaimed that its employees had made any misrepresentations, warranties, or guarantees as to profits or earnings to induce the franchisee to enter into the Agreement. All of these recitations were false.

65. The Franchise Agreements contain a clause that requires the assignment of telephone number, lease, permits, etc., upon termination. They also contain post-term non-competition covenants. These clauses were incorporated into all Diet Franchisor franchise agreements, including the plaintiffs', and were designed to prevent the franchisees from leaving the system. They included the threatened loss of location, without reimbursement for substantial expenditures for improvements mandated by Diet Franchisor and with no mandatory compensation for plaintiffs' good will. The contracts also included the threat of enforcing repressive non-competition covenants that obligate the franchisee to make illegal and punitive payments to Diet Franchisor after any termination, even if the non-competition covenant is held void and unenforceable. On December 6, 1990, Executive Vice President admitted that the Diet Franchisor franchise system would "end" if the non-competition covenants were not enforced.

66. The non-competition covenant in Section X.C of the Town A and Town B Agreements provides that:

Franchisee agrees that during the term of this Agreement, *it shall not be associated*, directly or indirectly, as employee, proprietor, stockholder, partner, agent, or officer *with the operation of any business competitive with Franchisor.* This shall include the operation of any type of business offering diet, weight control or selling diet and weight control products. This restriction applies to operation (a) within the Area, or (b) within fifty (50) miles from any location from which Franchisor or Franchisees of Franchisor operate. The foregoing restrictions (a) and (b) are distinct and severable.

For a period of one (1) year after the termination or the transfer or other disposition of this Franchise, Franchisee will not so compete as aforesaid in, or within fifty (50) miles of the Approved Location, and if Franchisee does so compete (whether by reason of the unenforceability (sic) of such covenant not to so compete or otherwise), Franchisee shall pay Franchisor royalties in the manner and amount set forth in Section VIII, Paragraph (A) hereof with respect to those revenues, if any, derived by Franchisee from its operation of a weight loss and weight control business within said area or fifty (50) mile limit, such payments to continue for one (1) year or for the balance of the then existing term (whether initial or renewal) of this Agreement, whichever is longer.

(Emphasis supplied)

67.   By its terms the non-competition covenant is binding regardless of the reason for termination, the franchisor's fault, the substantive overbreadth, the excessive time and geographic area, the penal character of the sanctions, and the violation of public policy. It prohibits the franchisee from being associated with "any business competitive with franchisor." Plaintiffs do not and have not ever engaged in Diet Franchisor activities such as the operation of a franchise system; the purchase and sale of many products; the operation of a national advertising fund; and each of the five RICO schemes detailed in this Complaint.

§ 2.20   —Elimination of Services Allegations

EFFECTIVE ELIMINATION OF SERVICE DEPARTMENT AND QUALITY ASSURANCE DEPARTMENT

68.   Between 1987 and 1989, the Diet Franchisor Service Department consisted of approximately 10 service consultants who, Diet Franchisor stated, were responsible for training and for providing constant assistance to franchisees. In addition, Diet Franchisor said that the Quality Control Department was responsible for assessing franchisees who sought expansion and for providing that all Centers met the established quality assurance criteria. Diet Franchisor said this was for the benefit of each franchisee and for all other franchisees and to protect the registered marks.

69.   In fact, the service consultants had received little training from Diet Franchisor, but they were sent to assist the franchisees. Most of the training seminars that they conducted emphasized sales and marketing techniques, rather than how to serve the clients. The Quality Assurance Department conducted random inspections of centers and did not fulfill its promised function. Some centers were never visited.

70.   In December 1989, Diet Franchisor effectively eliminated both the Service Department and the Quality Control Department; thereafter there was only one person responsible for quality assurance. On December 6, 1990, Executive Vice President testified this was done to allow Diet Franchisors to allocate its resources to other areas.

§ 2.21   —Effect of Fraudulent Schemes Allegations

EFFECT OF PRESIDENT'S PATTERN OF FRAUDULENT SCHEMES

71.   At all times relevant hereto, Diet Franchisor has been an enterprise engaged in, and the activities of which affect, interstate and foreign commerce, within the meaning of 18 U.S.C. § 1961(4) and § 1962.

72.   As a result of and in reliance upon the aforesaid acts and false and fraudulent representations and schemes of Diet Franchisor, President, Executive Vice President, and Diet Franchisor employees, made at the direction of Diet Franchisor, President, and Executive Vice President, the plaintiffs:

   a.   purchased franchises and entered into franchise agreements;

   b.   invested substantial time and money in the establishment and conduct of the businesses;

   c.   entered into addenda to the Franchise Agreements whereby they agreed to make payments to the NAF which payments in the form of checks were sent to Diet Franchisor by mail;

   d.   paid and later undertook additional obligations to pay substantial franchise fees and royalty payments and advertising contributions to Diet Franchisor and the NAF pursuant to said agreements, and such payments were in the form of checks and were sent to Diet Franchisor by mail;

   e.   undertook the obligation to pay substantial prices for potassium, nutritional supplements, and other products, payments for which, in the form of checks and/or credit cards, were sent to Diet Franchisor by mail or wire; and

   f.   plaintiffs devoted their full and/or part-time work and efforts to the exclusion of other gainful employment.

73.   By means of the fraudulent schemes described above, Diet Franchisor received substantial funds from the plaintiffs and other franchisees. Also by means of these fraudulent schemes, President, as sole shareholder, received substantial distributions from Diet Franchisor, including $8,637,775 in 1987, $15,893,023 in 1988, and $8,637,775 in 1989. Upon information and belief, the distributions were so excessive that they interfered with the ability of Diet Franchisor to perform its obligations to franchisees, including the plaintiffs, and to maintain a viable franchise system. On December 6, 1990, Executive Vice President testified that Diet Franchisor was aware in 1989 that the diet business was taking a serious downturn. Nevertheless, President received more than $8 million in shareholder distributions in 1989. In 1989–1990 when competing diet franchise systems were reducing royalty and product costs, Diet Franchisor failed and refused to take any affirmative steps.

§ 2.22   —Breach of Contract Count

COUNT I

Breach of Contract

74.   The plaintiffs incorporate and reallege paragraphs 1 through 73 as if fully set forth herein.

75.   Diet Franchisor breached the Franchise Agreements by:

   a.   failing to provide the plaintiffs with adequate initial training;
   b.   failing to provide effective assistance to the plaintiffs with suitable site selection and lease negotiations;
   c.   failing to provide adequate support during initial and later operation of the Diet Franchisor Diet System Center;
   d.   failing to provide up-to-date manuals;
   e.   failing to provide adequate advertising;
   f.   failing to provide competitive pricing for mandatory products purchased from defendants;
   g.   failing to pass on benefits from group purchasing; and
   h.   refusing to furnish a statement of operation of the NAF upon plaintiffs' written request.

76.   The Franchise Agreements between Diet Franchisor and the plaintiffs gave rise to an implied obligation of good faith and fair dealing. In addition, a duty of good faith and fair dealing arose from the substantial imbalance in this long-term relationship in which the parties were engaged in a joint commercial undertaking and in which Diet

Franchisor reserved exclusive and absolute powers over every aspect of their business and thereafter. Diet Franchisor breached these obligations by:

a. failing to provide an adequate system of support;

b. failing to enforce quality control standards over all centers;

c. failing to protect the trademark due to the effective elimination of the quality assurance department and nonenforcement of quality control standards;

d. failing to update manuals in a timely manner;

e. failing to provide a safe, effective diet program with no side effects and a guaranteed weight loss of three pounds per week;

f. mandating a new diet program in September 1989 that was undocumented as to results and failing to provide effective procedural guidelines as to its implementation;

g. failing to develop effective advertising programs;

h. charging an unconscionable mark-up on mandatory products;

i. charging a mark-up on mandatory products that exceeded the stated profit range in its Offering Circulars;

j. failing to consider applications for approval of alternate suppliers and never approving any alternate supplier;

k. failing to make advertising contributions on behalf of company-owned stores;

l. requiring the franchisees, including the plaintiffs, to execute general releases upon numerous events, such as on sale of a franchise;

m. making the plaintiffs' profitable performance of their obligations economically impossible.

77. Diet Franchisor's failure to act in accordance with express promissory representations made to the plaintiffs constituted breaches of contract. The contract was formed in the following manner:

a. Diet Franchisor assured the plaintiffs that:

i. manuals would be updated;

ii. diet programs were safe, effective, and did not have any side effects, and guaranteed weight loss of three pounds per week;

iii. it would make contributions to the NAF on behalf of company-owned stores;

iv. its profit range would not exceed the range stated in its Offering Circulars.

    b. Diet Franchisor intended the plaintiffs to rely on these promissory representations and knew that they so relied;

    c. the plaintiffs reasonably relied upon the representations;

    d. the plaintiffs have been damaged as a result of their reliance on these representations and injustice can only be avoided by enforcing Diet Franchisor's promises.

78. As a direct and proximate cause of Diet Franchisor's breaches of contract set forth in paragraphs 75 through 77 above, the plaintiffs have suffered direct, indirect, and consequential damages, including but not limited to:

    a. the loss of their investment capital;

    b. lost out-of-pocket expenses;

    c. lost business opportunities;

    d. lost profits; and

    e. lost good will.

79. The exact amount of damages sustained by plaintiffs is unascertained at this time, but it well exceeds $50,000.

WHEREFORE, the plaintiffs demand that judgment enter against Diet Franchisor, ordering:

    A. a finding that Diet Franchisor's breaches of contract are willful or in bad faith and therefore are tortious;

    B. an award of monetary damages equal to the plaintiffs' present and future losses, plus interest, costs, and reasonable attorneys' fees as permitted by law;

    C. the rescission of the contractual agreements between the parties;

    D. a nullification of any claims made against the plaintiffs by Diet Franchisor;

    E. such other and further relief the Court deems proper.

§ 2.23   —Deceptive Acts Count

COUNT II

Unfair and Deceptive Acts and Practices

80. The plaintiffs incorporate and reallege paragraphs 1 through 79 as if fully set forth herein.

81. Diet Franchisor, President, and Executive Vice President are persons engaged in trade or commerce as defined by the local "little" FTC Act § X.

82. Diet Franchisor, President, and Executive Vice President have employed unfair or deceptive acts or practices in the conduct of the business, thereby damaging the plaintiffs.

83. These unfair or deceptive acts or practices are actionable under such statutes and the regulations, if any, promulgated by the Attorney General. These unfair or deceptive acts or practices occurred primarily and substantially within plaintiffs' state, in which Diet Franchisor or its agents conduct business.

84. The unfair or deceptive acts or practices employed by Diet Franchisor, President, and Executive Vice President which were made with the intent that franchisees, including the plaintiffs, rely upon them include but are not limited to:

    a. failing to comply with the Federal Trade Commission Pre-Sale Franchise Disclosure Rule, 16 C.F.R. § 436, effective October 21, 1979;

        i. Diet Franchisor's various representations in its prospectus that its profit range on products sold to the plaintiffs would be zero to 25 percent (0%–25%) and zero to 100 percent (0%–100%) were knowingly false when made;

        ii. Diet Franchisor's representations to the plaintiffs that they should realize a net profit of 20 percent of gross sales were knowingly false when made and were not supported by any reasonable basis, and Diet Franchisor failed to offer or to supply the plaintiffs with documentation supporting its assertion as to profit;

        iii. Diet Franchisor's representations to the plaintiffs that they would make back their initial cash investments through profits within a short time of opening the Centers were knowingly false when made and not supported by any reasonable basis, and Diet Franchisor failed to offer to supply the plaintiffs with the earnings data and documentation supporting its assertions as to gross sales, gross profits, and return on investments;

        iv. the failure to comply with the Federal Trade Commission's Pre-Sale Franchise Disclosure Rule is actionable as an unfair and/or deceptive act and/or practice under the local "little" FTC act and the regulations promulgated thereunder by the Attorney General.

    b. failing to disclose to the plaintiffs, in violation of the local "little" FTC act and the regulations promulgated thereunder by the Attorney General, material facts enumerated throughout this complaint which if disclosed to the plaintiffs would have caused the plaintiffs not to purchase the franchises or not to execute the Franchise Agreements and the addenda to Franchise Agreements. These material nondisclosures include but are not limited to the following:

i.   the Diet Franchisor manuals were not updated from 1983 until May 1990 and were not useful;

ii. the original 1982 and the 1983 ketogenic diets and the high fiber diet had serious side effects;

iii. Diet Franchisor was the sole approved supplier of all products, and the requests for approval of alternative suppliers were not considered and were refused;

iv. the nutritional supplements were not unique and were available in the marketplace at substantially lower prices than the prices represented by Diet Franchisor and the even higher prices charged by Diet Franchisor;

v.   Diet Franchisor would not provide effective training or support;

vi. the high fiber diet would not allow for weight loss of three pounds per week; Diet Franchisor had conducted a survey indicating that weight loss of less than three pounds per week would occur; Diet Franchisor would not provide any data to support the representations and guarantees that a weight loss of three pounds per week would occur.

c.   misrepresenting material facts as to guarantees that the high fiber diet would allow for a weight loss of three pounds per week in violation of the local "little" FTC act and the regulations promulgated thereunder by the Attorney General. These misrepresentations as to guarantee included but were not limited to:

i.   making the representations and guarantees to the plaintiffs and requiring the plaintiffs to represent and guarantee to the customers that the high fiber diet would result in a weight loss of three pounds per week although the high fiber diet did not in fact result in the three pound per week weight loss;

ii. making the representations and guarantees to the plaintiffs and requiring the plaintiffs to represent and guarantee to the customers that the high fiber diet would result in a weight loss of 3 pounds per week even though Diet Franchisor failed and refused to undertake the obligation of providing a diet that would allow for a weight loss of three pounds per week;

    iii. making the representations and guarantees to the plaintiffs and requiring the plaintiffs to represent and guarantee to the customers that the high fiber diet would result in a weight loss of three pounds per week although Diet Franchisor had conducted a survey indicating that weight loss of less than three pounds per week would occur;

    iv. making the representations and guarantees to the plaintiffs and requiring the plaintiffs to represent and guarantee to the customers that the high fiber diet would result in a weight loss of three pounds per week although Diet Franchisor did not provide any data to support the representations and guarantees;

    v. President testified before a congressional subcommittee on May 7, 1990 that men and the morbidly obese tend to lose weight faster than the less morbidly obese. President admitted that the advertisements do not contain a disclaimer that individual weight loss may vary according to gender or degree of obesity;

  d. making material misrepresentations of fact enumerated throughout this complaint which were false and/or misleading and had the tendency or capacity to deceive the plaintiffs;

  e. committing unfair acts or practices, including in addition to the conduct set forth above:

    i. not passing along to the franchisees the savings made from their group purchases of products;

    ii. charging an unconscionable mark-up on products;

    iii. unreasonably refusing to consider or to approve alternative suppliers of any product, including the nutritional supplements;

    iv. requiring franchisee to make advertising contributions that resulted in little or no benefit to franchisees;

    v. forcing the plaintiffs to challenge the unlawful penalty provisions of the post-term non-competition clauses.

85. The Diet Franchisor's, President's, and Executive Vice President's commission of unfair or deceptive acts or practices has caused the plaintiffs to suffer direct, indirect, and consequential damages, including but not limited to:

  a. the loss of their investment capital;

  b. lost out-of-pocket expenses;

  c. lost business opportunities;

   d. lost profits; and
   e. lost good will.

86. The unfair or deceptive acts or practices committed by Diet Franchisor, President, and Executive Vice President and complained of above were intentional, willful, and knowing as defined by the local "little" FTC act and the regulations promulgated thereunder by the Attorney General, entitling the plaintiffs to recover punitive damages or damages of not less than double and up to treble their compensatory amount, plus an allowance for their reasonable attorneys' fees and costs.

87. The exact amount of the damages sustained by the plaintiffs is unascertained at this time, but it well exceeds $50,000.

WHEREFORE, the plaintiffs demand that judgment enter against Diet Franchisor and President, ordering:

A. a finding that Diet Franchisor, President, and Executive Vice President used or employed or ordered unfair or deceptive acts and/or practices in violation of the local "little" FTC act and the regulations promulgated by the Attorney General, entitling the plaintiffs to recovery;

B. an award to the plaintiffs of punitive damages or monetary damages in treble but not less than double the amount of their actual damages;

C. an award to the plaintiffs of their reasonable attorneys' fees, interest, and costs;

D. a finding that Diet Franchisor's, President's, and Executive Vice President's violations of the local "little" FTC act and the regulations promulgated thereunder by the Attorney General, estop them from raising any affirmative defenses to this action; and

E. such other and further relief as the Court deems proper.

§ 2.24   —Federal RICO Count

COUNT III

Federal Rico

88. The Plaintiffs incorporate and reallege paragraphs 1 through 87 as if fully set forth herein.

89. On at least two or more separate but related occasions, Diet Franchisor, President, and Executive Vice President have continually

used the aforesaid intentionally fraudulent and deceptive schemes on franchisees, including the plaintiffs, that were designed to:

    a.   induce the plaintiffs to purchase franchises and enter into franchise agreements;

    b.   induce the plaintiffs to invest substantial sums of money in the purchase, establishment, and conduct of the business contemplated by said agreements;

    c.   induce the plaintiffs to enter into addenda to the Franchise Agreements whereby they agreed to make payments to the NAF, which payments in the form of checks were sent to Diet Franchisor by interstate mail;

    d.   undertake obligations to pay and to make payments of substantial franchise fees and royalty payments to Diet Franchisor pursuant to said agreements, which payments in the form of checks were sent to Diet Franchisor by interstate mail;

    e.   undertake the obligation to pay and to make payments for products, including the nutritional supplement, which resulted in profits exceeding Diet Franchisor's declarations; payments for the products through the use of checks were sent to Diet Franchisor by interstate mails or wires;

    f.   require plaintiffs to devote full working time and efforts, to the exclusion of other gainful employment, to the operation of said business.

90.   In furtherance of the aforesaid intentionally fraudulent schemes, Diet Franchisor, President, Executive Vice President, and Diet Franchisor employees made extensive use of the United States mails in repeated violation of 18 U.S.C. § 1341 (mail fraud) to execute, effectuate, facilitate, and further the aforesaid franchise sales, advertising fund, mandatory product overcharge, consumer fraud, and policing and sanction in terrorem schemes on franchisees, including the plaintiffs.

91.   In furtherance of the aforesaid intentionally fraudulent schemes, Diet Franchisor, President, Executive Vice President, and Diet Franchisor employees made numerous interstate telephone calls and made other uses of interstate wire facilities in repeated violation of 18 U.S.C. § 1343 (wire fraud). The use of interstate wire facilities included but were not limited to electronic banking transactions and interstate telephone calls to the plaintiffs to and from state X and state A, the purpose of which was to enter into, execute, effectuate, facilitate, and further the aforesaid schemes in franchise sales, advertising fund, mandatory product overcharge, consumer fraud, and policing and in terrorem sanction.

92.   Each of the aforesaid intentional acts and misconduct of Diet Franchisor, President, Executive Vice President, and Diet Franchisor employees constituted violations of the Mail Fraud Statute, 18 U.S.C. § 1341, and Wire Fraud Statute, 18 U.S.C. § 1343, and constituted instances of "racketeering activity" as defined in 18 U.S.C. § 1961(1).

93.   The multiple acts of racketeering activity by Diet Franchisor, President, and Executive Vice President were interrelated, and were part of a common and continuous pattern of intentionally fraudulent schemes to defraud the franchisees, including the plaintiffs, and perpetrated for the same or similar purpose, thus constituting a "pattern of racketeering activity" as defined in 18 U.S.C. § 1961(5).

94.   Diet Franchisor is an "enterprise" as defined in 18 U.S.C. §§ 1961(4) and 1962.

95.   Through said pattern of racketeering activity:

   a.   Diet Franchisor, President, and Executive Vice President unlawfully, willfully, and knowingly received income derived directly and indirectly and have used and invested, directly and indirectly, such income or the proceeds thereof in Diet Franchisor, the RICO enterprise, in violation of 18 U.S.C. § 1962(a);

   b.   Diet Franchisor, President, and Executive Vice President acquired and maintained, directly and indirectly, an interest in or control of the activities of Diet Franchisor in violation of 18 U.S.C. § 1962(b);

   c.   Diet Franchisor, President, and Executive Vice President conducted and participated, directly and indirectly, in the conduct of said enterprise's affairs in violation of 18 U.S.C. § 1962(c);

   d.   Diet Franchisor, President, and Executive Vice President conspired together to do those things enumerated in subparagraphs a–c above in violation of 18 U.S.C. § 1962(d).

96.   As a result of the foregoing patterns of racketeering activities and violations of law, and the receipt and investment of the monies derived from the schemes, and the acquisition or maintenance of control over the activities of Diet Franchisor, and the conduct of Diet Franchisor's affairs, the franchisees, including the plaintiffs, have been injured in their business and property within the meaning of 18 U.S.C. § 1964(c). The plaintiffs' damages include but are not limited to:

   a.   the loss of their investment capital;
   b.   lost out-of-pocket expenses;
   c.   lost business opportunities;

d. lost profits; and

e. lost good will.

97. The exact amount of damages sustained by the plaintiffs is unascertained at this time, but it well exceeds $50,000.

WHEREFORE, the plaintiffs demand that judgment enter against Diet Franchisor, President, and Executive Vice President, ordering:

A. an award to the plaintiffs of monetary damages in treble the amount of their actual damages;

B. an award to the plaintiffs of their reasonable attorneys' fees, interest, and costs; and

C. such other and further relief as the Court deems proper.

§ 2.25 —Declaratory Relief Request

COUNT IV

Request for Declaratory Relief

98. The plaintiffs incorporate and reallege paragraphs 1 through 97 as if fully set forth herein.

99. Plaintiffs ask this Court for a declaration that the non-competition covenant in the Franchise Agreements (see paragraph 66):

a. is unreasonably broad in duration and distance and is therefore unenforceable and void as a matter of law and of public policy;

b. is unenforceable and void for failure of consideration;

c. which is activated "upon termination" regardless of the reason, including Diet Franchisor's fault as herein alleged, is an attempted illegal penalty and is also contractually void and unenforceable as a matter of public policy;

d. seeks to protect the defendant Diet Franchisor from competition in fields in which the plaintiffs have not engaged and as such is unenforceable, is an illegal penalty, and is void as a matter of public policy;

e. which mandates that a liquidated penalty be paid upon competition, even if the post-term non-competition clauses are unenforceable, is an illegal penalties and void as a matter of public policy;

f. is unenforceable and void due to Diet Franchisor's unclean hands;

g. as a composite, all of such provisions are jointly and sever-
    ally illegal penalties and void as against public policy; and

h. for these and other stated reasons the entire Franchise
    Agreements shall be declared void.

100. The plaintiffs have invested substantial time, effort, and money
in the establishment and development of their business. The plaintiffs
will be irreparably harmed without a declaration that the above provisions are void. Upon such declaration, the plaintiffs pray for such relief
and orders as the Court deems mete and proper.

§ 2.26   —Injunctive Relief Request

COUNT V

Request for Injunctive Relief

101. The plaintiffs incorporate and reallege paragraphs 1 through 100
as if fully set forth herein.

102. Enforcement of the post-term non-competition covenants will
result in the financial collapse of the plaintiffs' business, impair their
ability to generate income with which to fund this litigation, injure their
customers, and possibly subject the plaintiffs to consumer complaints
for failure to deliver the services promised.

103. Any inconvenience on Diet Franchisor is minimal. Diet Franchisor can continue to operate in the same areas by opening company-
owned centers or selling franchises for the territories. Diet Franchisor's
sale of the territories will result in its collection of initial franchise fees
and continuous receipt of royalties, advertising payments, and product
purchase receipts.

104. The Franchise Agreements provide that a violation of the post-
termination non-competition covenant entitles Diet Franchisor to monetary damages. Such a provision is an admission by Diet Franchisor that
it will not be irreparably harmed in the event the plaintiffs are allowed
to deidentify their businesses.

105. Any temporary inconvenience to Diet Franchisor is far outweighed by the irreparable harm that the plaintiffs will suffer if Diet
Franchisor does not accept the assignment of leases and the post-term
non-competition covenants are enforced, or if plaintiffs are not allowed
to deidentify with Diet Franchisor and remain in business at the sites.

106. It is in the public interest to allow the plaintiffs to deidentify
their business. The plaintiffs have built a vested interest in their business

through years of effort and investment. Diet Franchisor has violated both state and federal laws and should not be allowed to enforce unconscionable contract clauses that would result in the frustration of the litigation.

WHEREFORE, plaintiffs respectfully pray that after notice and hearing pursuant to Fed. R. Civ. Pro. 65(a)(1–2) this Court enter a preliminary and a permanent injunction against defendants which:

A.   enjoins the defendants from enforcing the post-term non-competition covenants contained in each of the Franchise Agreements;

B.   enjoins the defendants from claiming that the plaintiffs owe the liquidated penalties set forth in the post-term non-competition covenants.

§ 2.27   —Request for Order Protecting Documents

COUNT VI

Request for Injunctive Relief Including a Temporary Restraining Order and Preliminary Injunction

107. The plaintiffs incorporate paragraphs 1 through 106 as though fully set forth herein.

108. Upon information and belief, the defendants in this action have in their possession, custody, or control documents (as hereafter defined) that relate or refer to the matters set forth in the plaintiffs' complaint.

109. Some or all of said documents are likely to contain statements and information supportive of the plaintiffs' claims or which are likely to lead to such information.

110. Some or all of the documents may be destroyed or disposed of in the usual course of defendants' business, such as under a document retention program, or otherwise be misplaced or lost.

111. Destruction or disposal of any of the documents during the pendency of this litigation would deprive the plaintiffs of material and probative evidence which they are entitled to obtain pursuant to Fed. R. Civ. Pro. 26 (a) and (b)(1) and would substantially prejudice the plaintiffs' ability to investigate and prepare their cases.

112. The plaintiffs have no adequate remedy at law.

113. The defendants cannot be prejudiced by an order to preserve such documents.

WHEREFORE the plaintiffs pray for relief as follows:

A.   that pursuant to Fed. R. Civ. Pro. 65(b) a Temporary Restraining Order issue, enjoining and restraining the defendants from destroying or disposing of any documents which refer or relate to the subject matter of the plaintiffs' complaint or which are likely to lead to such information.

B.   that, after notice and hearing, pursuant to Fed. R. Civ. Pro. 65(a)(1–2) a Preliminary Injunction issue enjoining the defendants as follows, during the pendency of this action:

   i)   to maintain in their present form, retrievability, and at their present location all documents and other materials in their possession, custody, or control which relate to any matter in the complaint or in any pleading which may hereafter be filed by either party, or mention or concern the plaintiffs and/or the plaintiff's Diet Franchisor franchises.

   ii)   the terms "document" and "other materials" are used herein in the broadest sense permissible under the Rules of Civil Procedure. Without limitation, they include any and all tangible things and documents, whether handwritten, typed, printed, or otherwise produced, including but not limited to blueprints, drawings, letters, cables, wires, memoranda, interoffice communications, reports, notes, minutes, recordings, photographs, contracts, agreements, other legal instruments, notebooks, vouchers, ledgers, bills, books, financial records, checks, receipts, files, drafts, worksheets, and any machine-readable records whether punched, carded, taped, or coded electronically, electromagnetically, or otherwise, which can be translated through an appropriate computer, machine, device, or program into usable form, including copies or reproductions of any of the foregoing items upon which written notations that do not appear on the originals have been made;

   iii)   that all documents and other materials covered by such Orders or Injunction as the Court may issue be maintained in their presently labeled folders and file cabinets, data base, or information retrieval system, together with any and all existing indices to the contents of the same, or that otherwise provide access to the same in any manner. The said documents and other materials are to be held in their present or reasonably comparable physical location and availability for inspection, copying, or use and shall be available for inspection by counsel during regular business hours, on reasonable notice, at all times; and

iv)   that such other further relief be granted including a Protective Order, as the Court deems appropriate.

Jury Demand

The plaintiffs demand a trial by jury on all issues so triable.

Respectfully submitted,
Licensee
By their Attorneys,

Dated: _____

_____
A, B, and C (P.C.)

Of Counsel:

_____

Verification

Licensees, being duly sworn, depose and say that they are the plaintiffs in the above-entitled action, that they have read the foregoing Complaint and know the contents thereof, and that the same are true to their personal knowledge, except as to those matters stated to be on information and belief, which they believe to be true.

_____

_____

Dated

Licensee

State of X

Then personally appeared before me the above-named Licensees and acknowledge the foregoing to be their free act and deed.

_____
Notary Public
My Commission Expires: _____

§ 2.28   RICO Fact Statement

The second document included in this chapter is the RICO Fact Statement, which was filed in a related case against the same franchisor. This statement is in response to the written interrogatories propounded to the claimant by the court itself. This unique document is the product of the perceived need for particularity in fraud claims under Federal Rules of Civil Procedure Rule 9(b) balanced against the direction of Rule 8(a) calling for a "short and plain statement of the claim showing that the pleader is entitled to relief."[61]

The court's questions ask for data on both the factual and legal claims, especially on such complex and undecided issues as the multiple facets of the RICO enterprise as a victim and a violator under one or more of the four substantive charges. Even so, such a statement must be amended as discovery proceeds, because, understandably, the facts underlying quasi-criminal conduct are seldom made public or are subjects of general knowledge.

§ 2.29   —Identifying Wrongdoers and Victims

UNITED STATES DISTRICT COURT
NORTHERN DISTRICT OF STATE X
EASTERN DIVISION

DIET FRANCHISOR,
             Plaintiff,
Defendant-in-Counterclaim
 	
V.
 	
LICENSEES,
             Defendants,
Plaintiffs-in-Counterclaim
 	
V.
PRESIDENT AND EXECUTIVE VICE PRESIDENT
   Third-Party Defendants.
	CIVIL ACTION NO. _____

RICO Case Statement

This RICO Case Statement is submitted pursuant to an Order of this Court dated September 11, 1990. The Plaintiffs-in-Counterclaim (plaintiffs) submit the following responses:

1.   State whether the alleged unlawful conduct is in violation of 18 U.S.C. § 1962(a), (b), (c), and/or (d).

---

[61] Van Dorn Co. v. Howington, 623 F. Supp. 1548, 1555 (N.D. Ohio 1988).

Response. It is alleged that the Defendant-in-Counterclaim, Franchisor and the Third-Party Defendants President and Executive Vice President (collectively referred to as the defendants) have violated 18 U.S.C. § 1962(a), (b), (c), and (d).

   2. List each defendant and state the alleged misconduct and basis of liability of each defendant.

Response. Diet Franchisor, President, and Executive Vice President are alleged to have committed multiple acts of mail fraud and wire fraud in the furtherance of fraudulent schemes in order to:

   a. market franchises for the operation and establishment of Diet Franchisor Diet System Centers which utilize the grossly deficient Diet Franchisor Diet System Program and to collect franchise fees, royalties, and advertising payments while providing no benefit to the franchisees;

   b. grossly overcharge franchisees for mandatory product purchases from the franchisor;

   c. misapply franchisees' advertising contributions;

   d. defraud consumers of Diet Franchisor Diet System Programs; and

   e. prevent franchisees from leaving the system, in order to perpetuate the racketeering activity.

Diet Franchisor received income from the pattern of racketeering activity and invested it in the operation of the business. President drew money and benefits from this conduct and invested them in Diet Franchisor. Through the pattern of racketeering activity, Diet Franchisor and President acquired and maintained an interest in and control of Diet Franchisor, the RICO enterprise, which is engaged in, and the activity of which affects, interstate commerce. Diet Franchisor, President, and Executive Vice President actively directed the affairs of Diet Franchisor. Diet Franchisor, President, and Executive Vice President schemed together as independent entities and with Diet Franchisor employees and other independent actors. The latter were:

   a. Ad Inc., an independent advertising agency;

   b. Executive Vice President, an independent Certified Public Accountant licensed in the state of X and an executive of an independent accounting firm;

   c. Attorney X, an independent attorney who is a member of the X Bar; and

   d. Dr. A, M.D., an independent physician licensed in the states of X, Y, and Z.

They conspired to commit acts in violation of 18 U.S.C. § 1962 (a), (b), (c), and (d). Diet Franchisor, President, and the independent actors each actively participated in Diet Franchisor policy determinations. As a result of the predicate acts of Diet Franchisor, President, and Executive Vice President and their illegal schemes to act together and with others, the plaintiffs have been financially injured.

3. List the alleged wrongdoers, other than the defendants listed above, and state the alleged misconduct of each wrongdoer.

Response. Other wrongdoers include the following:

Former Director, the former Diet Franchisor Director of Franchise Sales;

Former Sales Representative, the former Diet Franchisor Sales Representative;

Director of Training, the Diet Franchisor Director of Franchise Training;

Former Director of Franchise Development, the former Diet Franchisor Director of Franchise Development;

Executive Vice President, Diet Franchisor's Executive Vice President and an independent Certified Public Accountant licensed in the state of X and an executive in an independent accounting firm, Diet Franchisor's auditors, acting both as an insider and as an independent person actively participating in these policy determinations;

Attorney X, Diet Franchisor General Counsel and Secretary, acting both as an insider and as an independent attorney who is a member of the state of X bar actively participating in Diet Franchisor policy determinations;

Dr. A, Diet Franchisor's National Medical Director, acting as an insider and as an independent physician licensed in the states of X, Y, and Z, actively participating in Diet Franchisor Policy determinations;

Dr. B, Nutritional Consultant and Director of Nutritional Service; and

Ad Inc., an independent advertising company owned by President, actively participating in the advertising scheme.

The Diet Franchisor employees and independent professionals listed above actively participated in Diet Franchisor's policy determinations. Pursuant to instruction of Diet Franchisor and President, by interstate mail and telephone calls, they knowingly made false statements and failed to make full and fair disclosure to prospective franchisees, including the plaintiffs, of certain material facts concerning the Diet Franchisor system as extensively identified in Response to Question 5(c) below. The misrepresentations and non-disclosures were knowingly made in order to fraudulently induce prospective franchisees, including the plaintiffs, to spend hundreds of thousands of dollars on a deficient system. Diet Franchisor and President received income from the pattern of racketeering activity in the following ways:

a. charging franchisees substantial initial franchise fees, royalties, and advertising fees for services and support that Diet Franchisor had no intention of providing;

b. grossly overcharging franchisees for mandatory product purchases;

c. redirecting a portion of franchisee advertising payments to Ad Inc., a company owned by President and providing no benefit to franchisees; and

d. inducing franchisees to unknowingly repeat to consumers what were misrepresentations about the safety and effectiveness of the Diet Franchisor Diet System Program. This was done in order to induce them to enroll in the program and to make payment for products and services.

The Diet Franchisor employees and independent professionals listed above actively participated in policy determinations in a policing and sanction in terrorem scheme designed to keep the franchisees, including the plaintiffs, in the franchise system in order to allow Diet Franchisor and President to perpetuate their racketeering activity.

Specific examples of the acts committed by the Diet Franchisor employees in furtherance of the schemes are identified in the Response to Question 5(c) below and include but are not limited to:

a. Former Director and Former Sales Representative knowingly made misrepresentations and non-disclosures of certain material facts concerning the services, benefits, and profitability of the Diet Franchisor system to prospective franchisees, including the plaintiffs, in order to induce them to purchase and establish franchised diet centers;

b. Director of Training knowingly made material intentional fraudulent oral misrepresentations to plaintiffs concerning the expected high profitability of the centers;

c. Director of Franchise Development knowingly made material misrepresentations and non-disclosures concerning his real estate expertise and failed to provide effective site selection assistance and provided no assistance with lease negotiations;

d. Executive Vice President knowingly made false oral misrepresentations to the plaintiffs concerning Diet Franchisor's allegedly small mark-up on the plaintiff's mandatory purchases of certain products; Executive Vice President also participated independently in Diet Franchisor policy determinations, including the implementation of the policing and sanction in terrorem scheme.

Further, his accounting firm has performed a severe retaliatory audit on any franchisee who challenged Diet Franchisor's policies;

e. Attorney X actively participated in the determination and implementation of the policies of the several schemes, particularly in the policing and sanction in terrorem scheme to preclude the franchisees from leaving the system;

f. Dr. A actively participated in Diet Franchisor policy determinations, and Dr. A. and Dr. B failed to timely inform the plaintiffs of the serious health risks inherent in the Diet Franchisor Diet System Program, even after there were extensive lawsuits including a claimed death.

Other Diet Franchisor employees and individuals may have participated in the fraudulent schemes. Due to the fact that discovery has not yet been conducted, the plaintiffs are unable to furnish such information.

4. List the alleged victims and state how each victim was allegedly injured.

Response.

a. Plaintiffs were injured by spending hundreds of thousands of dollars through their being fraudulently induced by the defendants to purchase franchises in a grossly deficient system in which: the products involved serious health risks; the plaintiffs had to pay exorbitant prices to purchase mandated products, which prices greatly exceed those declared in the Disclosure Statements given to them before their purchase of the franchises, as well as exorbitant prices for other products; the contract and pre-sale Disclosure Document declared that there were procedures to obtain approval for purchases from other vendors, but such requests for approval were never processed nor were any ever granted; and the advertising funds were not used as represented. They were injured by the fact that they devoted their full working time and efforts, to the exclusion of other gainful employment, in the futile attempt to conduct such business operation successfully. The plaintiffs are further damaged by the fact that they are now forced to defend themselves against Diet Franchisor despite the fact that the relationship between the parties arose as a result of the defendants' numerous violations of federal and state laws.

b. Other Diet Franchisor franchisees, who were injured by the virtually identical Diet Franchisor fraudulent schemes are:

Licensee C, owner of a Diet Franchisor Diet System Center in Connecticut since 1988;

Licensee D, owner of a Diet Franchisor Diet System Center in Indiana until 1990;

Licensees E, owners of a Diet Franchisor Diet System Center in Massachusetts since 1988;

Licensees F, owners of three Diet Franchisor Diet System Centers in New Hampshire since 1982;

Licensees G, owners of four Diet Franchisor Diet System Centers in New Jersey since 1986;

Licensees H, owners of two Diet Franchisor Diet System Centers in Massachusetts since 1983;

Licensee I, owner of a Diet Franchisor Diet System Center in New Hampshire since 1988;

Licensees J, owners of two Diet Franchisor Diet System Centers in Georgia since 1987;

Licensee K, owner of two Diet Franchisor Diet System Centers in South Carolina since 1989;

Licensee L, owner of six Diet Franchisor Diet System Centers in Georgia since 1983;

Licensee M, owner of two Diet Franchisor Diet System Centers in Massachusetts since 1987;

Licensees N, owners of two Diet Franchisor Diet System Centers in Virginia since 1984;

Licensees O, owners of two Diet Franchisor Diet System Centers in Massachusetts since 1986;

Licensee P, owner of a Diet Franchisor Diet System Center in Maryland since 1989;

Licensee Q, owner of a Diet Franchisor Diet System Center in Connecticut since 1989;

Licensee R, owner of a Diet Franchisor Diet System Center in Massachusetts until 1989.

The affidavits of attorney Attorney C and eleven of the franchisees are attached as Exhibit A.

c.   Upon information and belief all of Diet Franchisor franchisees were injured by defendants' fraudulent schemes.

d.   Other victims of defendants' fraudulent schemes include the consumers who were induced to enter the Diet Franchisor Diet System Program and make payments for services and products based on misrepresentations and non-disclosures concerning the safety and effectiveness of the Diet Franchisor diet.

§ 2.30   —Pattern of Racketeering Activity Questions

5.   Describe in detail the pattern of racketeering activity or collection of unlawful debts alleged for each RICO claim. A description of the pattern of racketeering shall include the following information:

(a)   List the alleged predicate acts and the specific statutes that were allegedly violated;

Response. The predicate acts constituted mail fraud in violation of 18 U.S.C. § 1341 and wire fraud in violation of 18 U.S.C. § 1343.

(b) Provide the dates of the predicate acts, the participants in the predicate acts, and a description of the facts surrounding the predicate acts;

Response. Between March 1987 and August 1990, the defendants, their employees, and the independent professionals listed in the Response to Question 3 above, committed predicate acts of mail fraud and wire fraud as part of their regular method of doing business with franchisees including the plaintiffs. The detailed specifications of these predicate acts require completion of discovery because much of the documentation is in the hands of the defendants. Defendants' uses of the interstate wires and mails in furtherance of their fraudulent schemes included the following:

a)   In March 1987, plaintiffs telephoned Diet Franchisor in Ohio from their office in New Hampshire and requested information on Diet Franchisor franchises. Upon information and belief, they spoke to Former Sales Representative. In a follow-up letter dated March 23, 1987, he knowingly made false representations to the plaintiffs about the service and benefits of the Diet Franchisor system. The letter is attached as Exhibit B.

b)   Shortly thereafter, the plaintiffs telephoned Diet Franchisor and requested a Diet Franchisor Franchise Disclosure Document. The defendants caused the Disclosure Document to be sent to plaintiffs by interstate mail. The Disclosure Document contained misrepresentations and omissions of material facts regarding the Diet Franchisor franchise system. Specifically it stated that the franchisor generally makes a profit of zero to 25 percent (0%–25%) on the sale of its products to franchisees. Diet Franchisor has always and continues to charge franchisees, including the plaintiffs, prices that result in profit greatly exceeding the stated range. The Disclosure Document also outlined a procedure for obtaining the franchisor's approval of alternate suppliers of any products.

Requests to Diet Franchisor for such approval were completely and unreasonably ignored, never processed, and/or refused.

c) Between March 1987 and August 1987, Former Sales Representative and Former Director, by interstate telephone and in mailed writing, induced plaintiffs to attend meetings in Manchester, New Hampshire, Boston, Massachusetts, and Akron, Ohio. During those meetings, Former Sales Representative, Former Director, and Director of Training knowingly made false statements about the Diet Franchisor system including statements that plaintiffs could expect to make a 20 percent profit before taxes and would recoup their initial investment within six months.

d) Between November 1987 and January 1988, the Director of Franchise Development, by interstate mail and telephone, knowingly made false statements and non-disclosures about the Diet Franchisor site selection process. Director of Franchise Development failed to disclose that he was not a real estate expert but that his background was in cosmetic sales. He fraudulently induced the plaintiffs to believe that Diet Franchisor's approval of a site was based on expertise and analysis of demographic data.

e) In November 1987, by interstate mail defendants sent plaintiffs Addenda to the Franchise Agreements entitled "National Advertising and Sales Promotions," which required the plaintiffs to make contributions to the NAF, in return for advertising benefits. The plaintiffs executed the Addenda and returned same by interstate mail to Diet Franchisor. By interstate letter dated September 2, 1988, the plaintiffs were informed that their 15 percent contribution to the NAF production fund would be used for new television and print ads. Payments were diverted by Diet Franchisor to Ad Inc., a company owned by President, and resulted in no benefits to the plaintiffs. By interstate letter mailed June 13, 1988, the plaintiffs were informed by Diet Franchisor counsel Attorney X that Diet Franchisor had elected to reactivate the plaintiffs' obligation to contribute to the NAF. Payments in the form of checks were sent to Diet Franchisor by interstate mails. By interstate letters mailed November 2, 1989 and April 12, 1990, the plaintiffs made written requests to Diet Franchisor for a copy of the NAF statement of operation. Diet Franchisor responded by mailing a page of cash receipts and disbursements for the Diet Franchisor Centers in the Boston ADI (Area of Dominant Influence). Diet Franchisor failed to deliver a complete NAF statement of operations.

f) By interstate letter dated July 8, 1988, Former Sales Representative sent the plaintiffs a Franchise Disclosure Document. The

Disclosure Document contained misrepresentations and omissions of material facts regarding the Diet Franchisor system. Specifically, it stated that the franchisor generally makes a profit of zero to 100 percent (0%–100%) on the sale of its products to franchisees. Diet Franchisor has always and continues to charge franchisees prices which result in profit that greatly exceeds the stated range. It further outlined a procedure for obtaining Diet Franchisor's approval of alternate supplies of products other than nutritional supplement. Requests for such approvals were completely and unreasonably ignored, never processed, and/or refused.

g) By interstate letter dated July 22, 1988, the plaintiffs sent Diet Franchisor a check for $12,500 for the purchase of a second franchise center.

h) Between January 1988 and August 1990, Diet Franchisor and President caused Product Price Lists to be sent to the plaintiffs by interstate mail. The payments for the mandatory products were sent to Diet Franchisor by interstate mail and resulted in a profit to Diet Franchisor that exceeded the range stated in the Disclosure Documents.

i) Between March 1987 and January 1989, the defendants and their employees frequently represented to the plaintiffs by interstate wire and mail that the Diet Franchisor diet was a "medically safe, highly reputable weight loss program" and "had no side effects." By interstate letter dated January 19, 1989, after receiving negative publicity after the death of a client of the Alabama franchise, the defendants issued for the first time a Dieter's Information Sheet, which listed risks of extensive and very serious side effects. The defendants required the franchisees to give the Information Sheet to their clients. It was later revised to include gallbladder disease after a lawsuit for such injury was instituted against a competing franchise system. The letter and Dieter Information Sheets are attached as Exhibit C.

j) Between March 1987 and July 1990, the defendants made many representations to the plaintiffs by letter and interstate wire that the Diet Franchisor diet would allow for a weight loss of three pounds per week. Defendants required plaintiffs to make a written guarantee of that weight loss to their clients. By interstate mail and telephone the plaintiffs requested data to support these claims, but all of these were ignored. By interstate letter dated July 5, 1990, Diet Franchisor and President instructed all franchisees that all advertising claims regarding weight loss should be an "average weight loss of over two pounds per week" rather than the previously mandated guarantee of weight loss of three pounds per week. The letter and a copy of a mailed 1989 Diet Franchisor brochure are attached as Exhibit D.

(c)   If the RICO claim is based on the predicate offenses of wire fraud, mail fraud, or fraud in the sale of securities, the "circumstances constituting fraud or mistake shall be stated with particularity." Fed. R. Civ. P. 9(b). Identify the time, place, and contents of the alleged misrepresentations, and the identity of persons to whom and by whom the alleged misrepresentations were made.

Response. At all times as indicated in the Response to Question 5(b) above, the defendants, their employees, and the independent professionals listed in the Response to Question 3 above, knowingly made intentional, fraudulent oral and written misrepresentations and/or knowingly failed to make full and fair disclosure of certain material facts to franchisees, including the plaintiffs. The false representations included but were not limited to claims that the franchise system had a proven record that assured that:

a.   franchisees would receive the benefits of dealing with a full service franchisor, with a "proven system" of how to operate a successful, profitable company;

b.   Diet Franchisor would provide its franchisees with detailed and up-to-date "how-to" manuals regarding all aspects of the business including what it described as a unique, specially prepared behavioral guidance manual;

c.   Diet Franchisor would provide franchisees with unlimited training and additional assistance after opening;

d.   a training college would be established for franchisees;

e.   group buying power would lead to additional savings for the franchisees;

f.   the franchise development department, along with a real estate expert, would provide substantial assistance in site selection, floor plan design, and lease negotiations;

g.   constant support and guidance would be provided, including: financial planners and budgeters who would offer expert advice with business planning and budgeting and would periodically monitor sales and expenses and help to establish an effective bookkeeping system; and a portfolio of successful client testimonials that would be provided to the franchisee to use in client solicitation;

h.   Diet Franchisor had national support in advertising through major publications and periodicals and that full market and media campaigns would be available to the franchisees; franchisees would

also receive the benefit of assistance from an advertising coordinator who would assist with advertising strategy and would
provide an advertising handbook for a year-round advertising program with advertisements that were proven traffic builders;

i.   the Diet Franchisor nutritional supplements were unique and
      specially formulated and were only available from Diet Fran-
      chisor; any mark-up over Diet Franchisor's cost was only a
      "normal mark-up to cover distribution costs"; the diet program
      allowed clients to experience weight loss by eating selected reg-
      ular grocery foods;

j.   the Diet Franchisor-mandated diet program was a "medically
      safe, highly reputable weight loss program" and "had no side
      effects";

k.   the diet program (ketogenic diet) was a two-part plan: the initial
      plan provided for weight loss of three to seven pounds per week;
      part two was a maintenance program designed to aid clients in
      maintaining their ideal weight; and that the diet system was a
      fast and lasting system that set Diet Franchisor apart from the
      competition;

l.   the emphasis on medical safety and monitoring was necessary
      and clearly distinguished the Diet Franchisor franchise from its
      competition; and

m.   clients of the franchisee would experience fast weight loss by eat-
      ing selected regular grocery store foods.

The Defendants failed to disclose to the plaintiffs that:

a.   Diet Franchisor's diet system was no more "proven" than any
      other diet system; the diet system was constantly changed, creat-
      ing confusion among the franchisees; many of the described serv-
      ices were unavailable or extremely limited;

b.   none of the Diet Franchisor manuals have been updated since
      1983, nor were they useful; the behavioral guidance manual was
      superficial, incomplete, and did not relate to the dieting process;
      upon information and belief, the behavioral guidance manual was
      not unique nor prepared by Diet Franchisor, but had been copied
      from one used by a commercial health club;

c.   Diet Franchisor staff members received little training and yet
      were sent to assist the franchisees; the one-week classroom train-
      ing for franchisees was confusing and contradictory; the manuals
      used had sections crossed out; no nutritional or dietary informa-
      tion was provided; training seminars were sporadically held and
      emphasized sales and marketing techniques rather than service
      to the clients; counseling skills were not taught;

d. Diet Franchisor had no present intention of establishing a training college and one in fact has not been established, nor will it be established;

e. any savings from group purchases were retained by Diet Franchisor and not passed along to franchisees; the Diet Franchisor nutritional supplement was not unique and was freely available in the marketplace at substantially lower prices than the prices represented by Diet Franchisor in its Offering Circulars and the even higher prices actually charged by Diet Franchisor;

f. site selection assistance merely consisted of the recommendation to locate the Center at a medical center (later changed to strip mall) and a visit from a corporate representative who was not familiar with the town or state, to view the sites selected by franchisee and to give approval or disapproval; a real estate expert was not used; there was no assistance with lease negotiations;

g. support was ineffectual; service representatives were assigned and then quickly replaced, transferred, or resigned; there was no conformity of communications nor completion of programs; grand programs were announced and then never mentioned again; there were no financial planners or budgeters available to the franchisees; the portfolio of endorsements consisted of five-year old, unfashionable photographs that were not useful in client solicitations;

h. there had never been a national campaign in the media and no such campaigns were to be made available to the franchisees; the advertising handbook was outdated; the franchisees had to devise their own advertisements;

i. in addition to the nutritional supplement, other Diet Franchisor products were a mandatory part of the diet program; Diet Franchisor is the sole approved supplier of these products, and repeated requests for approval of alternate suppliers were never processed or approved;

j. the mandated ketogenic diet allowed for a daily calorie intake of 700 calories, which was and is considered to be medically harmful; the mandated diet had serious side effects as indicated in a Diet Franchisor memo dated January 19, 1989, issued after receiving negative publicity surrounding the death of a client of an Alabama Diet Franchisor franchisee and the wrongful death lawsuit brought by the heirs of the deceased client against Diet Franchisor and the franchisee; the cause of death was stated as hypokalemia, an abnormal depletion of potassium in the circulating blood producing muscle weakness, painful muscle spasms, and postural hypotension; franchisees were then instructed to give clients a Dieter's Information Sheet that listed the side effects as: lightheadedness, constipation, cramping, muscle weakness, lower body temperature, hair loss, irregular menstrual cycles, tendency to bruise, bad breath, and dry skin;

k.   the franchisees were obligated to give their clients a written guarantee to the effect that if the client did not lose the guaranteed weight during the program, the client would be allowed to continue at the franchisee's expense until the goal weight was achieved; the Diet Franchisor diet was no more lasting than any diet; most clients regained all, most of, or more than the weight they had lost on the program;

l.   upon information and belief, Diet Franchisor's own in-house physician refused to endorse the ketogenic diet in an advertising campaign;

m.   in addition to nutritional supplements, other Diet Franchisor products were a mandatory part of the diet program and franchisees were instructed to induce their clients to purchase Diet Franchisor products rather than buying "grocery store food."

The false representations contained in the Offering Circulars stated that the franchisor would provide:

a.   initial training consisting of classroom study and hands-on instruction and that the franchisor would provide the instructors and training materials;

b.   that franchisor would assist the franchisee in obtaining a "suitable site location" for the Center;

c.   that the franchisor had developed a business plan and method for providing weight reduction and control and had established an excellent reputation and good will with the public; and

d.   the franchisor generally makes a profit of zero to 25 percent (0%–25%) or zero to 100 percent (0%–100%) on the sale of its products to franchisees.

The defendants did not disclose to the plaintiffs that:

a.   the training was rudimentary and not useful or helpful, and emphasized sales rather than nutritional and counseling skills; that they would not receive any "hands-on" training, and that the training manuals used in the classes were outdated with the written procedures crossed out and with changes penciled in;

b.   its site selection assistance was ineffective and slipshod, resulting in the plaintiffs' executing a lease and incurring "build out" expenses to establish a Diet Franchisor center, which Diet Franchisor has acknowledged was not an economically viable Diet Franchisor site;

  c.   that the Diet Franchisor Diet System was grossly deficient and that Diet Franchisor intended to change the system by mandating an entirely different diet that eliminated much of the medical monitoring and did not produce effective weight loss; and

  d.   prior franchise agreements did not require the franchisee to purchase the nutritional supplement from Diet Franchisor; Diet Franchisor products in addition to the nutritional supplement were a mandatory part of the diet program; Diet Franchisor is the sole approved supplier of these products, and repeated requests for alternate suppliers are never processed or approved.

(d)   State whether there has been a criminal conviction for violation of the predicate acts;

Response. There has been no criminal conviction for violation of the predicate acts.

(e)   State whether civil litigation has resulted in a judgment in regard to the predicate acts;

Response. There have been no judgments as a result of any litigation with respect to the predicate acts.

(f)   Describe how the predicate acts form a "pattern of racketeering activity"; and

Response. The predicate acts form a continuous and related pattern of racketeering activity in that over the course of several years the defendants, their employees, and the independent professionals listed in the Response to Question 3 above, through numerous predicate acts of mail and wire fraud, have engaged in schemes to:

  a.   market franchises for the operation and establishment of Diet Franchisor Diet System Centers which utilize the grossly deficient Diet Franchisor Diet System Program, and schemes to collect franchise fees, royalties, and advertising payments while providing no benefit to the franchisees;

  b.   grossly overcharge franchisees for mandatory product purchases;

  c.   misapply franchisees' advertising contribution;

  d.   require franchisees to participate in a scheme to defraud consumers of the Diet Franchisor Diet System Programs; and

  e.   prevent the franchisees from leaving the Diet Franchisor system so that the defendants could continue their pattern of racketeering activity.

The schemes were facilitated by numerous misrepresentations and fraudulent concealment of material information over the course of several years. The scheme involved many victims, including the plaintiffs (see Affidavits attached as Exhibit A), and upon information and belief, all other Diet Franchisor franchisees and the consumers who utilized the Diet Franchisor Diet System Programs.

The defendants, their employees and the independent professionals listed in the Response to Question 3 above, have and now are committing the predicate acts of mail fraud and wire fraud as a regular method of doing business with Diet Franchisor's existing franchisees and its potential franchisees.

(g) State whether the alleged predicate acts relate to each other as part of a common plan. If so, describe in detail.

Response. The predicate acts relate to each other as part of a common plan in that through the use of the multiple acts of mail fraud and wire fraud and the material misrepresentations and omissions, the defendants, their employees, and the independent professionals listed in the Response to Question 3 above, were able to defraud the plaintiffs and other victims of very large sums of monies and thereby perpetuate their acquisition and maintenance of control over the activities of Diet Franchisor and the conduct of Diet Franchisor's affairs.

§ 2.31 —Enterprise Questions

6. Describe in detail the alleged enterprise for each RICO claim. A description of the enterprise shall include the following information:

(a) State the names of the individuals, partnerships, corporations, associations, or other legal entities that allegedly constitute the enterprise;

Response. Diet Franchisor is the entity which constitutes the enterprise for all RICO claims.

(b) Describe the structure, purpose, function, and course of conduct of the enterprise;

Response. The enterprise is a corporation whose purpose is to engage in a course of conduct which included committing the predicate racketeering acts to:

a. market franchises for the operation and establishment of Diet Franchisor Diet System Centers which utilize the grossly deficient

Diet Franchisor Diet System Program and to collect franchise fees, royalties, and advertising payments although providing no benefit to the franchisees;

b. grossly overcharge franchisees for mandatory product purchases from the franchisor;

c. misapply franchisees' advertising contributions;

d. compel franchisees to participate in a scheme to defraud consumers of Diet Franchisor Diet System Programs; and

e. compel franchisees to participate in a scheme to prevent franchisees from leaving the system in order to perpetuate the racketeering activity.

(c) State whether any defendants are employees, officers, or directors of the alleged enterprises;

Response. Defendant President is sole shareholder and Chief Executive Officer of the enterprise. Executive Vice President has been and is in full charge of all pre-sale and tenure franchise activities. Other independent actors identified in the Response to Question 3 above have been named but have not yet been joined as defendants.

(d) State whether any defendants are associated with the alleged enterprise;

Response. The defendants are associated with the enterprise.

(e) State whether you are alleging that the defendants are individuals or entities separate from the alleged enterprise, or that the defendants are the enterprise itself, or members of the enterprise; and

Response. President and Executive Vice President are individuals separate from the enterprise.

Diet Franchisor is an entity separate from the enterprise and is the enterprise itself.

Other independent individuals listed in the Response to Question 3 above have been named but not yet joined as defendants, separate from the enterprise.

(f) If any defendants are alleged to be the enterprise itself, or members of the enterprise, explain whether such defendants are perpetrators, passive instruments, or victims of the alleged racketeering activity.

Response. President and Executive Vice President are perpetrators of the alleged racketeering activities.

Diet Franchisor is a perpetrator, passive instrument, and victim of the alleged racketeering activity.

The named but not yet joined independent individuals are co-conspirators and perpetrators of the alleged racketeering activities. They are in the process of being joined as defendants.

7. State and describe in detail whether you are alleging that the pattern of racketeering activity and the enterprise are separate or have merged into one entity.

Response. The enterprise is separate from the pattern of racketeering activity.

8. Describe the alleged relationship between the activities of the enterprise and the pattern of racketeering activity. Discuss how the racketeering activity differs from the usual and daily activities of the enterprise, if at all.

Response. President, Executive Vice President, and the individuals named but not yet joined as defendants, devised, participated, or have abetted the continuation of the pattern of racketeering activity principally through Diet Franchisor, the enterprise. Diet Franchisor was formed to carry on the facially legitimate purposes of operating and selling franchises for the operation of diet centers. In carrying out a modest amount of otherwise legitimate conduct, President, Executive Vice President, and the named independent actors have used Diet Franchisor to engage in a widespread pattern of racketeering activity as described in the Response to Question 5 above.

9. Describe what benefits, if any, the alleged enterprise receives from the alleged pattern of racketeering.

Response. From the pattern of racketeering activities, the enterprise receives franchise fees, royalty fees, advertising payments, and payments for gross overcharges for mandatory products. With the monies collected by the enterprise from its racketeering activity, it has been able to perpetuate such activity and has paid President tens of millions of dollars.

10. Describe the effect of the activities of the enterprise on interstate or foreign commerce.

Response. The enterprise has sold franchises throughout the United States. It has purchased and sold to the plaintiffs and other franchisees tens of millions of dollars of products, in interstate commerce. It has collected tens of millions of dollars from the plaintiff and other franchisees for advertising and royalties through interstate mail. Diet

Franchisor's use of interstate mails and wires broadly affects interstate commerce.

11. If the complaint alleges a violation of 18 U.S.C. § 1962(a), provide the following information:

(a) State who received the income derived from the pattern of racketeering activity or through the collection of an unlawful debt; and

Response. Defendants Diet Franchisor, President, and Executive Vice President received income for the pattern of racketeering activity. President reinvested income into Diet Franchisor and later withdrew tens of millions of dollars, as stated above.

(b) Describe the use or investment of such income.

Response. Defendants Diet Franchisor and President used the income derived from the pattern of racketeering activity to acquire and maintain an interest in the enterprise and to perpetuate the racketeering activity. Upon information and belief, President drew some of the income and used it to establish a similar franchise and/or enterprise in Canada.

12. If the complaint alleges a violation of 18 U.S.C. § 1962(b), describe in detail the acquisition or maintenance of any interest in or control of the alleged enterprise.

Response. Defendants Diet Franchisor and President, through a pattern of racketeering activity, acquired and maintained an interest in the enterprise. President is sole shareholder of the enterprise and both Diet Franchisor and President derived income from the pattern of racketeering activity.

13. If the complaint alleges a violation of 18 U.S.C. § 1962(c), provide the following information:

(a) State who is employed by or associated with the enterprise; and

Response. President and Executive Vice President are employed by and associated with the enterprise. Diet Franchisor is associated with the enterprise. The independent professionals named but not yet joined as defendants have been partially employed by the enterprise. They are in the process of being joined as defendants.

(b) State whether the same entity is both the liable "person" and the "enterprise" under § 1962(c).

Response. President and Executive Vice President are liable persons under § 1962(c). Diet Franchisor is a liable person and is the enterprise under § 1962(c).

14. If the complaint alleges a violation of 18 U.S.C. § 1962(d), describe in detail the alleged conspiracy.

Response. Diet Franchisor, President, and Executive Vice President schemed together as independent entities and with Diet Franchisor employees and with the other independent actors, including:

(a) Ad Inc., an independent advertising agency; and

(b) Executive Vice President, an independent Certified Public Accountant licensed in the state of X, and an executive of an independent accounting firm;

(c) Attorney X, an independent attorney who is a member of the state of X;

(d) Dr. A, M.D., an independent physician licensed in the states of X, Y, and Z.

They conspired to commit acts in violation of 18 U.S.C. § 1962 (a), (b), (c), and (d). Diet Franchisor, President, and Executive Vice President and the independent professionals each actively participated in Diet Franchisor policy determinations.

§ 2.32   —Injury Questions

15. Describe the alleged injury to business or property.

Response. The plaintiffs were injured in that they were fraudulently induced to devote their time, effort, and monies to the exclusion of other employment or investment, to a franchise system that defendants knew would not allow plaintiffs a reasonable opportunity to succeed. The plaintiffs have lost tens of thousands of dollars, and the other franchisees have lost millions of dollars.

16. Describe the direct causal relationship between the alleged injury and the violation of the RICO statute.

Response. But for the defendants' predicate acts of racketeering activity in violation of 18 U.S.C. § 1341 and 18 U.S.C. § 1343 and their material misrepresentation and omissions, the plaintiff would not have been injured. The loss of millions of dollars by the plaintiff and other franchisees was directly caused by the predicate acts.

17. List the damages sustained for which each defendant is allegedly liable.

Response. Each defendant is liable for the plaintiffs' direct, indirect, and consequential damages, including but not limited to their loss of investment capital, lost out-of-pocket expenses, lost business opportunities, lost profits, lost good will, reasonable attorneys' fees, interest, and cost of suit. The plaintiffs' losses are very high, but not yet quantified. They exceed $325,000.

§ 2.33   —Other Causes of Actions Questions

18. List all other federal causes of action, if any, and provide the relevant statute numbers.

Response. There are no other federal causes of action.

19. List all pendent state claims, if any.

Response. Plaintiff pendent state claims are:

a.   breach of contract;

b.   violations of "little" FTC Act;

c.   request for declaratory relief declaring void major parts of the franchise agreement that are an integral part of the policing and in terrorem sanction scheme.

20. Provide any additional information that you feel would be helpful to the court in processing your RICO claim.

Response.

a)   The pattern of racketeering activity has included almost every aspect of egregious fraud that is available in the franchise context. In the past three years, President has personally drawn from the enterprise annual sums in the $8 to 15 million bracket. In one recent year when "sales" were reported by Diet Franchisor in the sum of $34 million, President withdrew about 50 percent of that amount.

b) The money was procured by the enumerated schemes that were not only devised and abetted by President, Executive Vice President, and the other named independent individuals, but have been vigorously and ruthlessly enforced. Because of the alleged illegality of many of these practices, the conduct may well constitute extortion.

c) The response of Diet Franchisor, President, and Executive Vice President to the widespread damage to the plaintiff and many other franchisees has been to demand more money. By letter dated November 2, 1990, from Attorney X, Diet Franchisor announced a new 1990 advertising fund contribution commencing the week ending November 16, 1990. Under this plan, Diet Franchisor has activated the minimum advertising contribution for each center of $250 per week plus an additional $575 per week. In a letter dated November 2, 1990, Executive Vice President stated that the franchisees should "[u]se your skills to create the cash flow, first from the consumer, second from reducing operating costs without compromising the Diet Franchisor operating system, and third from personal resources." The letters are attached as Exhibit E.

Respectfully submitted,
Licensee
By their Attorneys,

Dated: _____

_____
Attorney X

Of Counsel:

_____

Attorneys A, B & C

Certificate of Service

I hereby certify that on the _____ day of _____, 1991, I caused a copy of the RICO Case Statement to be mailed to:

Attorneys D and E

_____
Attorney X

§ 2.34 Memoranda and Orders in Response to Defendants' Motion to Dismiss

In the cases discussed in this chapter, the defendants filed motions to dismiss three of the counts in the complaints for failure to state a claim pursuant to Federal Rule of Procedure 12(b)(6). In the two orders that follow, the court dismisses the § 1962 claim against the franchisor, ruling that the enterprise cannot be both a victim and a participant. However the court declines to dismiss the plaintiff's RICO claims.

UNITED STATES DISTRICT COURT
NORTHERN DISTRICT OF OHIO
EASTERN DIVISION

LICENSEE
    Plaintiffs
 	
V.
 	
DIET FRANCHISOR, PRESIDENT,
AND EXECUTIVE VICE PRESIDENT
    Defendants
	CASE NO.
	
	MEMORANDUM AND ORDER

Presently pending before this court in the above-captioned matter is a motion to dismiss three counts of plaintiffs' complaint filed pursuant to Fed. R. Civ. P. 12(b)(6). Plaintiffs filed their seven-count complaint with this court on October 9, 1990. Defendants' motion to dismiss was filed on November 2, 1990, and plaintiffs filed a memorandum in opposition to this motion on November 14, 1990. Because of the complexity of the issues presented and because the court's ruling on the instant motion may well impact on other causes now pending, this memorandum and order is untypically lengthy. But, it is felt, a fullness of discussion may well be of value to the parties here and to the other similarly situated parties as well.

I. Background

The facts underlying this cause have previously been stated in detail. *See* this court's Findings of Fact and Conclusions of Law, February 12, 1991, regarding cross-motions for preliminary injunction concerning a covenant not to compete contained in franchise agreements between the parties. Thus, a brief summary of the facts is appropriate at this time.

Defendant Diet Franchisor is a national franchisor of Diet Franchisor Centers and is an Ohio corporation with its principal place of business in Ohio. Defendant President is an Ohio resident and is the sole shareholder, director, and president of Diet Franchisor.

Plaintiffs Licensees and _____ are all residents of New Jersey and were Diet Franchisor franchisees from 1986 to 1990. Plaintiffs opened their first franchise in Freehold, New Jersey on June 15, 1987, and subsequently opened three other centers, all in New Jersey. The last center opened on March 3, 1989.

Plaintiffs met with financial difficulties in 1990 and eventually closed all of their centers. On October 9, 1990, plaintiffs commenced this diversity action, alleging the following seven counts:

Count I: Tortious Breach of Contract;

Count II: Deceptive Acts and Unconscionable Commercial Practices in violation of New Jersey Revised Statutes §§ 56:8-2 and 56:8-19;

Count III: Federal RICO Violations, 18 U.S.C. § 1962(a), (b), (c), and (d);

Count IV: Violation of the Franchise Practices Act, New Jersey Revised Statutes §§ 56:10-5 through 56:10-7;

Count V: Declaratory Judgment concerning the covenants not to compete contained in the franchise agreements;

Count VI: Injunctive relief enjoining defendants from enforcing the covenants not to compete, from seeking liquidated damages, and from enforcing certain assignment clauses unless defendants accept assignment of certain leases.

Count VII: Injunctive relief including a temporary restraining order enjoining, *inter alia,* defendants from destroying documents which pertain to the subject matter of plaintiffs' complaint.

Defendants filed no responsive pleading in this action. Rather, on November 2, 1990, they filed the subject motion to dismiss counts II, III, and IV of the complaint. With respect to the cross-motions for preliminary injunction, this court on February 12, 1991, enjoined plaintiffs from violating the covenants not to compete.

II. Analysis

When considering a motion to dismiss for failure to state a claim pursuant to Federal Rule of Civil Procedure 12(b)(6), the court is constrained to accept as true the allegations of the complaint. *Associated General Contractors of California, Inc. v. California State Council of Carpenters,* 459 U.S. 519, 526 (1983), *Scheuer v. Rhodes,* 416 U.S. 232, 236 (1974); *Lee v. Western Reserve Psychiatric Habilitation Center,* 747 F.2d 1062, 1065 (6th Cir. 1984). To dismiss the complaint against defendant, the court would have to find it beyond doubt that the plaintiff can prove no set of facts in support of its claim which would justify the relief sought. *Conley v. Gibson,* 355 U.S. 41, 45–46 (1957).

A. COUNTS II AND IV

With regard to counts II and IV, defendants argue that these counts fail to state a claim for violation of New Jersey law because, pursuant to the choice of law provision in the franchise agreements, Ohio law applies and thus New Jersey law is inapplicable. In support of this argument, defendants primarily rely upon the Sixth Circuit's opinion in *Tele-Save Merchandising Company v. Consumers Distributing Company, Ltd.,* 814 F.2d 1120 (6th Cir. 1987).

In response, plaintiffs contend that the choice of law provisions in the contracts apply only to questions of contract construction, not to non-contract claims such as consumer fraud. Plaintiffs argue that *Tele-Save* is inapposite because the choice of law clause involved there was different than here in that it was broader and applied to non-contract, as well as contract, claims. Plaintiffs also submit that Section 148 of the Restatement (Second) of Conflict of Law should be applied and that § 148 dictates that New Jersey law should apply here. Alternatively, plaintiffs argue that if this court adopts the reasoning of *Tele-Save,* New Jersey law should still apply under Restatement § 187(2), which was recognized by the court in *Tele-Save* and which provides for exceptions to the rule that an effective choice of law by the parties will govern disputes arising out of the contract.

Before this court engages in the task of analyzing the parties[62] respective arguments, it is necessary to first lay a legal foundation which provides guidance on the conflicts of law issue. First, it is a well-accepted principle that a federal court sitting in diversity must apply the conflicts of law rules of the state in which it sits. *See Klaxon v. Stentor,* 313 U.S. 487, 490, 61 S. Ct. 1020, 85 L. Ed. 2d 1477 (1941); *Colonial Refrigerated Transportation, Inc. v. Worsham,* 705 F.2d 821, 825 (6th Cir. 1983); *Detrex Chemical Industries, Inc. v. Employers Insurance of Wassau,* 681 F. Supp. 438, 455 (N.D. Ohio 1987). Therefore, this court must apply Ohio conflict of law principles to determine whether Ohio law or New Jersey law should govern in this case.

In *Tele-Save,* the Sixth Circuit recognized that the Ohio Supreme Court follows the principles of the Restatement (Second) of Conflict of Laws when forced to choose between the laws of two or more forums. Specifically, Ohio gives deference to choice of law contractual provisions under the mandate of Restatement § 187(2).

The Ohio Supreme Court in considering the deference to give contractual choice-of-law provisions has adopted the guidelines of the *Restatement (Second) of Conflict of Laws,* § 187(2) (1971):

---

[62] Three of the agreements (East Brunswick, Princeton, and Wayne) provide that "[t]his agreement shall be construed according to the laws of the State of Ohio." The fourth agreement, that for the Freehold site, provides that "[t]his agreement and the respective rights, duties, and obligations of the parties hereunder shall be construed in accordance with the laws of the State of Ohio without giving effect to principles of conflicts of law." Freehold Agreement § XIX, p. 10.

The law of the state chosen by the parties to govern their contractual rights and duties will be applied, even if the particular issue is one which the parties could not have resolved by an explicit provision in their agreement directed to that issue, unless either

(a) the chosen state has no substantial relationship to the parties or the transaction and there is no other reasonable basis for the parties' choice, or

(b) application of the law of the chosen state would be contrary to a fundamental policy of a state which has a materially greater interest than the chosen state in the determination of the particular issue and which, under the rule of § 188, would be the state of the applicable law in the absence of an effective choice of law by the parties.

Schulke Radio Productions, Ltd. v. Midwestern Broadcasting Company, 6 Ohio St.3d 436, 438–39, 453 N. Ed. 2d 683 (1983).

Tele-Save, 814 F.2d at 1122.

In *Tele-Save,* the plaintiff, an Ohio corporation, sued a Canadian corporation under the Ohio Business Opportunity Plans Act, Ohio Revised Code Chapter 1334, *et seq.* The complaint alleged that the defendant violated these laws by failing, *inter alia,* to provide a disclosure statement in connection with the transaction and by making false and misleading statements. The defendant moved for summary judgment, arguing that the choice of law provision did not allow for use of Ohio law in this lawsuit. The provision stated that "[t]his agreement shall be governed by, and construed in accordance with, the laws of the State of New Jersey." The district granted the motion for summary judgment. In affirming the district court's decision, the Sixth Circuit found that Restatement § 187(2) requires that New Jersey law, rather than Ohio law, governs in this instance. *Id.*

At this juncture, before going any further, it is necessary to address plaintiffs' argument that *Tele-Save* is inapposite and that the choice of law provision here does not preclude a suit pertaining to *non*-contractual matters under another state's laws. In this regard, plaintiffs maintain that the provision here only applies to contract *construction* and that the provision in *Tele-Save* was broader because it covered "governance" of the agreement as well as "construction" of the agreement.

In support of this argument, plaintiffs cite to *Boat Town U.S.A., Inc. v. Mercury Marine Division of Brunswick Corporation,* 364 So. 2d 15 (Fla. App. 4th Dist. 1978). In that case, a Wisconsin manufacturer of marine products, Mercury Marine, brought a breach of contract suit against a Florida dealer, Boat Town U.S.A., who counterclaimed. The trial court found for the Mercury Marine as a matter of law on Boat Town's counterclaim. The counterclaim asserted a violation of the Wisconsin Fair

Dealership Law, but the trial court held that this law was inapplicable to the instant cause.

On appeal, the dealer, Boat Town U.S.A., argued as do defendants herein that Mercury Marine and Boat Town expressly chose Wisconsin law to govern their agreement. Boat Town pointed to a provision much like the one at issue here, which provided that "[t]his agreement and all its provisions are to be interpreted and construed according to the laws of the State of Wisconsin." Boat Town's contention was that this provision reflects the parties' intention that they be bound by Wisconsin law not only as to matters of contract construction, "but also as to the substantive rights and obligations of the parties themselves." *Id.*, 364 So. 2d at 17. Defendants, in effect, urge the same reasoning here.

The Fourth District Court of Appeals disagreed with Boat Town's analysis.[63] The court found that

> a distinction exists between the words "interpretation" and "govern." Interpretation is defined as "(t)he art or process of discovering and expounding the meaning of a . . . written document." Black's Law Dictionary, 4th Ed. 1968. On the other hand, govern means "to direct and control the actions or conduct of, either by established law or by arbitrary will; to direct and control, rule, or regulate, by authority." Black's, *id.* The difference between "interpretation" and "govern" is more than a technical distinction. It goes to the very heart of the purpose underlying a contract.

Id., 364 So. 2d at 17. Plaintiffs would have this court adopt identical reasoning and thus find that *Tele-Save* and Restatement § 187(2) have no application here.

This court finds itself somewhat persuaded by the reasoning of the court in *Boat Town.* However, we must also give close consideration to another Sixth Circuit opinion in the case of *Boatland, Inc. v. Brunswick Corporation,* 558 F.2d 818 (6th Cir. 1977). In that case, the plaintiffs, a Tennessee corporation and its president, filed suit against the defendant alleging, *inter alia,* violation of the Wisconsin Fair Dealership Law. Plaintiffs filed a motion for summary judgment, alleging that the Wisconsin Fair Dealership Law determined the rights of the parties. The contract contained a choice of law provision identical to the one at issue in *Boat Town, viz.,* the contract shall "be interpreted and construed according to the laws of the State of Wisconsin."

The defendant filed a cross-motion for summary judgment, alleging, *inter alia,* that the Wisconsin statute was inapplicable because the choice of law provision only applied to contract construction and not

---

[63] The court, however, ultimately reversed the trial court, holding that Wisconsin law does apply.

contract "governance." The Sixth Circuit disagreed, applying reasoning opposite that of the Florida court and finding that the distinction urged between the terms "governance" and "construction" was a "strained and narrow construction" of the contract language. *Id.*, 558 F.2d at 821–22. *Boat Town*, thus, appears to be of limited precedential value.[64]

This court, however, is not comfortable in strictly following the reasoning of the Sixth Circuit in *Boatland*. Of significance is the fact that the Sixth Circuit specifically found that the parties intended that Wisconsin law apply to *all* of their rights. Here, the court is not faced with any evidence on the issue of the parties' intent. In light of this, it is certainly reasonable to argue that the parties may have intended that another state's laws may apply to the parties' rights other than those involving construction and interpretation of the contract. In other words, the language of the clause in question raises factual issues as to the parties' intent, issues which are clearly inappropriate for resolution under Rule 12(b)(6).

On the issue of the parties intent, the court is especially troubled by the difference in the language between the East Brunswick, Princeton, and Wayne contracts, and that of the Freehold agreement. *See* note 62, *supra*. In the Freehold agreement, the parties specifically provided that all of "the respective rights, duties and obligations" would be construed under Ohio law and that conflicts of law principles would be ignored. This language is akin to the clause involved in *Tele-Save* and is much broader than the language contained in the other three clauses, which merely provide that the contract "shall be construed according to the laws of the State of Ohio." Presumably, if plaintiffs only sought recovery for defendants' conduct as it pertained to the Freehold agreement, *Tele-Save* would apply and the New Jersey counts of the complaint would have to be dismissed. However, all of the contracts are involved in this dispute, and the lack of broad language in the three other clauses evidences an intent that issues involving the parties' rights and duties in noncontractual matters are not to be determined solely by application of Ohio law. Neither party has addressed, much less explained, this difference in the contractual language.

Fortunately, the issue of intent as it pertains to the choice of law question need not be examined in any greater depth. There is a separate and independent reason in support of the proposition that New Jersey law may properly be utilized by plaintiffs in this case. Even if *Tele-Save* is followed, the principles enunciated therein dictate that New Jersey law should be applied to Counts II and IV of plaintiffs' claims. Defendants limit their argument to the claim that § 187(2)

---

[64] *See also* C.A. May Marine Supply Company v. Brunswick Corporation, 557 F.2d 1163 (5th Cir. 1977).

strictly dictates that the court follow the parties' choice of law, but do not address the significant exceptions to this rule. The court in *Tele-Save* expounded upon these exceptions as follows:

> Ohio's receptivity to contractual choice-of-law was further discussed in the recent decision of *Jarvis v. Ashland Oil, Inc.,* 17 Ohio St.3d 189, 478 N.E.2d 786 (1985). In *Jarvis,* the Ohio Supreme Court held that "where the parties to a contract have made an effective choice of the forum law to be applied, the Restatement of the Law 2d, Conflict of Laws (1971) 561, Section 187(2), will not be applied to contravene the choice of the parties as to the applicable law." *Id.* 17 Ohio St.3d at 192, 478 N. Ed. 2d 786. The court then added a narrow limitation to this rule: "[W]here the law of the chosen state sought to be applied is concededly repugnant to and in violation of the public policy of [Ohio], the law of Ohio will only be applied when it can be shown that [Ohio] has a materially greater interest than the chosen state in the determination of the particular issue." *Id.*

Id., 814 F.2d at 1122.

In *Jarvis,* the plaintiff, an Ohio resident, was injured while working for third-party defendant Union Boiler Company (Union), a West Virginia corporation. Union had contracted with defendant Ashland Oil, Inc. (Ashland), a Kentucky corporation, whereby Union would provide labor and services for Ashland at Ashland's facilities. The contract included an indemnification provision whereby Union agreed to indemnify Ashland for injuries arising out of the work performed by Union. The contract also provided that it "shall be construed and the legal relations of the parties hereto shall be determined in accordance with the laws of the State of Kentucky." After plaintiff filed suit against Ashland for his injuries, Ashland filed a third-party complaint for indemnification against Union. Union filed a motion for summary judgment, contending that the indemnification provision was void on public policy grounds. The trial court agreed and granted Union's motion for summary judgment.

On appeal, the court of appeals was faced with the question of whether the trial court properly applied Ohio law in light of the fact that the true parties in interest, Union and Ashland, had agreed that Kentucky law would govern their relationship. In deciding against Union on appeal, the court recognized the two exceptions to the general rule of Restatement § 187(2). The court ultimately found that the exceptions did not apply because Ohio clearly did not have a materially greater interest than Kentucky and that, in any event, the parties had made an "effective choice of law." *Id.,* 17 Ohio St.3d at 192.

Thus, we reason that if either of the two exceptions to § 187(2) apply, the parties have not made an "effective" choice of law. Under

§ 187(2), applied to the facts of this case, the parties' choice of law will govern unless:

1. Ohio has no substantial relationship to the parties or the transaction and there is no other reasonable basis for the parties choice; OR

2. a) application of the law of Ohio would be contrary to a fundamental policy of New Jersey, AND

b) New Jersey has a materially greater interest than Ohio in the determination of plaintiffs' state law claims, AND

c) under Restatement § 188, New Jersey would be the state of the applicable law in the absence of an effective choice of law by the parties.

Plaintiffs argue that the second exception applies in this case. For this exception to apply, three conditions must be fulfilled. First, it must be found that the state laws in question represent a fundamental policy of that state and that application of the chosen state's law would contravene this policy. *Tele-Save*, 814 F.2d at 1123. In this case, plaintiffs seek recovery under the New Jersey Consumer Fraud Act, New Jersey Revised Statutes § 56:8-2, which provides as follows:

The act, use or employment by any person of any unconscionable commercial practice, deception, fraud, false pretense, false promise, misrepresentation, or the knowing, concealment, suppression, or omission of any material fact with intent that others rely upon such concealment, suppression or omission, in connection with the sale or advertisement of any merchandise or real estate, or with the subsequent performance of such person as aforesaid, whether or not any person has in fact been misled, deceived or damaged thereby, is declared to be an unlawful practice; provided, however, that nothing herein contained shall apply to the owner or publisher of newspapers, magazines, publications or printed matter wherein such advertisement appears, or to the owner or operator of a radio or television station which disseminates such advertisement when the owner, publisher, or operator has no knowledge of the intent, design or purpose of the advertiser.

Plaintiffs also seek recovery under the New Jersey Franchise Practices Act, New Jersey Revised Statutes §§ 56:10-5 through 56:10-7, which provides in pertinent part as follows:

56:10-5. Termination of franchise; notice; grounds.

It shall be a violation of this act for any franchisor directly or indirectly through any officer, agent, or employee to terminate, cancel, or fail to renew a franchise without having first given written notice setting forth all the reasons for such termination, cancellation, or intent not to renew to the franchisee at least 60 days in advance of such termination, cancellation, or failure to renew, except (1) where the alleged grounds are voluntary abandonment by the franchisee of the franchise relationship in which event the aforementioned written notice may be given 15 days in advance of such termination, cancellation, or failure to renew; and (2) where the alleged grounds are the conviction of the franchisee in a court of competent jurisdiction of an indictable offense directly related to the business.

56:10-6. Transfer of franchise; notice; approval; agreement of compliance.

It shall be a violation of this act for any franchisee to transfer, assign or sell a franchise or interest therein to another person unless the franchisee shall first notify the franchisor of such intention by written notice setting forth in the notice of intent the prospective transferee's name, address, statement of financial qualification and business experience during the previous 5 years. The franchisor shall within 60 days after receipt of such notice either approve in writing to the franchisee such sale to proposed transferee or by written notice advise the franchisee of the unacceptability of the proposed transferee setting forth material reasons relating to the character, financial ability or business experience of the proposed transferee. If the franchisor does not reply within the specified 60 days, his approval is deemed granted. No such transfer, assignment or sale hereunder shall be valid unless the transferee agrees in writing to comply with all the requirements of the franchise then in effect.

56:10-7. Prohibited practices.

It shall be a violation for any franchisor, directly or indirectly, through any officer, agent or employee, to engage in any of the following practices:

a. To require a franchisee at time of entering into a franchise arrangement to assent to a release, assignment, novation, waiver or estoppel which would relieve any person from liability imposed by this act.

b. To prohibit directly or indirectly the right of free association among franchisees for any lawful purpose.

c. To require or prohibit any change in management of any franchisee unless such requirement or prohibition of change shall be for good cause, which cause shall be stated in writing by the franchisor.

d. To restrict the sale of any equity or debenture issue or the transfer of any securities of a franchise or in any way prevent or attempt to prevent the transfer, sale or issuance of shares of stock or debentures to employees, personnel of the franchisee, or heir to the principal owner, as long as basic financial requirements of the franchisor are complied with, and provided any such sale, transfer or issuance does not have the effect of accomplishing a sale of the franchise.

e. To impose unreasonable standards of performance upon a franchisee.

f. To provide any term or condition in any lease or other agreement ancillary or collateral to a franchise, which term or condition directly or indirectly violates this act.

In *Tele-Save,* the court suggested two ways in which it may be found that a state statute represents a fundamental state policy, gleaned from the official comments to Restatement § 187(2).

> There is no hard and fast rule to determine when a state policy will be considered "fundamental." The Restatement suggests a few guidelines. For example, courts may consider a policy "fundamental" when a large number of significant contacts are grouped in the forum state as opposed to the chosen state. *Restatement (Second) of Conflict of Laws,* § 187 comment g (1971).
>
> . . .
>
> The Restatement also suggests that a statute may embody a "fundamental" state policy if it is "designed to protect a person against the oppressive use of superior bargaining power [as, for example, in a statute] involving the rights of an individual insured as against an insurance company. . . ." *Id.*

Id., 814 F.2d at 1123. With regard to the first consideration, the Restatement provides that "[t]he more closely the state of the chosen law is related to the contract and the parties, the more fundamental must be the policy of the state of the otherwise applicable law to justify denying effect to the choice-of-law provision." Restatement § 187(2), comment g, p. 568.

In this case, there are significant contacts in Ohio, e.g., all four agreements were made and concluded in Akron, Ohio. However, the complaint contains allegations which reflect that New Jersey may also have a number of significant contacts grouped there. For instance, the complaint alleges that many of the claimed fraudulent devices and misrepresentations occurred through the mails and wires, and were received by plaintiffs in New Jersey. Complaint, ¶¶ 15–71. It appears, in other words, that during the course of the franchise relationship, the contacts were fairly evenly divided between Ohio and New Jersey.

In any event, regardless of the distribution of contacts between the states, this court believes that New Jersey's statutes embody a fundamental policy which is significantly strong to allow for the use of the second exception to § 187(2). This policy is that expressed in *Tele-Save* and comment g to the Restatement, *viz.,* the statutes are designed to protect a person against the oppressive use of superior bargaining power. In *Tele-Save,* the court found that the parties therein possessed equal bargaining strength. Here, however, equality of bargaining power is an issue which has yet to be determined to a degree sufficient for purposes of Rule 12(b)(6). The hearing held on December 5 and 6, 1990, pertaining to the cross-motions for preliminary injunction produced no testimony on the issue of whether the franchise agreements are contracts of adhesion, *see,* this court's February 12, 1991 Findings of Fact and Conclusions of Law at 30–31, and the hearing did not otherwise show equality of bargaining strength.

In any event, regardless of what transpired at the hearing, the New Jersey statutes at issue, *inter alia,* seem clearly to be an attempt to cure a recognized lack of bargaining equality between franchisors and franchisees. The legislature stated its purpose in enacting the Franchise Practices Act as follows:

> The Legislature finds and declares that distribution and sales through franchise arrangements in the State of New Jersey vitally affects the general economy of the State, the public interest and the public welfare. It is therefore necessary in the public interest to define the relationship and responsibilities of franchisors and franchisees in connection with franchise arrangements.

N.J.S.A., § 56:10-2. In addition, courts have examined this law's legislative purpose and have concluded that the law was designed, *inter alia,* to protect the franchisee from the superior bargaining positions of the franchisor. *See Westfield Centre Service, Inc. v. Cities Service Oil Company,* 386 A.2d 448, 456, 158 N.J. Super. 455 (N.J. App., Chancery Division 1978); *Marinello v. Shell Oil Company,* 307 A.2d 598, 602, 63 N.J. 402 (1973), *cert. denied* 415 U.S. 920, 94 S. Ct. 1421, 39 L. Ed. 2d 475 (1974).

With regard to the New Jersey Consumer Fraud Act, New Jersey courts have also examined and expressed the underlying purposes of the law, *viz.,* protection of consumers from the unscrupulous practices of commercial sellers. *See DiBernardo v. Mosley,* 502 A.2d 1166, 1167, 206 N.J. Super. 371 (N.J. App., Appellate division 1986), *cert. denied* 511 A.2d 673, 103 N.J. 503; *Barry v. Arrow Pontiac, Inc.,* 494 A.2d 804, 811, 100 N.J. 57 (1985). In light of this, we have no difficulty in finding that the New Jersey Franchise Practices Act and Consumer Fraud Act are based upon a fundamental policy of the state, *viz.,* the protection against the oppressive use of superior bargaining power. Thus, one-half of the first prong to the second exception to § 187(2) if fulfilled.[65]

The other half of this first prong mandates that application of Ohio law be contrary to the fundamental policy underlying the New Jersey

---

[65] Comment g to § 187(2) states that the "forum will apply its own legal principles in determining whether a given policy is a fundamental one within the meaning of the present rule . . ." Applying this directive, the result in our analysis is left unchanged. The Ohio Business Opportunity Purchasers Protection Act, O.R.C. § 1334.01 *et seq.,* was enacted with the same purposes in mind as was the New Jersey Franchise Practices Act. *See* Peltier v. Spaghetti Tree, Inc., 6 Ohio St.3d 194, 197 (1983) (". . . this chapter is designed to regulate the sale of business opportunities and provides significant remedies 'to those who have been misled by dishonest or negligent franchisors.'" (citation omitted)); *Tele-Save,* 814 F.2d at 1125 (Milburn, J., dissenting).

laws. With regard to this portion of the test, the Sixth Circuit has noted, pursuant to comment g to § 187(2), that the chosen law should not be ignored merely because application of the other law (New Jersey) would lead to a different result. *Tele-Save*, 814 F.2d at 1123. The Sixth Circuit, rather, has stated the test in the following manner:

> In order for the chosen state's law to violate the fundamental policy of Ohio, it must be shown that there are significant differences in the application of the law of the two states. *Barnes Group, Inc. v. C & C Products, Inc.*, 716 F.2d 1023, 1031 n. 19 (4th Cir. 1983).

Id. It is clear in this case that there are significant differences in the application of the laws of the states here. The analogous law of Ohio, the Business Opportunity Purchasers Protection Act, Ohio Revised Code § 1334.01 *et seq.*, is not available to plaintiffs because Diet Franchisor is exempt from the Act and plaintiffs are precluded from utilizing the Act. O.R.C. § 1334.12(L), (M). Thus, although common law remedies under Ohio law would be available to plaintiffs, it is clear that significant adverse consequences would result from plaintiffs' attempts to vindicate their rights under Ohio law as opposed to New Jersey law.

Under the second element of the second exception to § 187(2), it must be established that New Jersey has a materially greater interest than does Ohio in the determination of plaintiffs' state law claims. It takes little reflection, and indeed seems axiomatic, that one's state's interest in protecting small and powerless consumers is materially greater than another state's interest in construing and protecting the interstate contracts issued by its domiciliary. For similar, albeit not identical analyses, *see Barnes Group, Inc. v. C & C Products, Inc.*, 716 F.2d 1023, 1030 (4th Cir. 1983) (state's interest in protecting its residents' ability to earn a livelihood and in regulating business relationships within the state is materially greater than other state's interest in protecting the interstate contracts of its domiciliary); *Stickney v. Smith*, 693 F.2d 563, 565 (5th Cir. 1982) (state's interest in protecting injured persons within its borders is materially greater than another state's interest in construing insurance policies issued within its borders); *DeSantis v. Wackenhut Corporation*, 793 S.W.2d 670, 679 (Tex. S. Ct. 1990) (state's interests in its employees, in national employer doing business within its borders, and in its citizens as consumers is materially greater than another state's interest in protecting a national business headquartered in that state).

Several courts have taken a different approach with regard to the analysis under the "materially greater interest" element of the second exception to § 187(2). These courts have indicated that the state with the most significant relationship to the transaction at issue has a materially greater interest in the determination of the subject issue. *See Wright-Moore Corporation v. Ricoh Corporation,* 908 F.2d 128, 132–33 (7th Cir. 1990); *Modern Computer Systems, Inc. v. Modern Banking Systems, Inc.,* 858 F:2d 1339, 1342–43 (8th Cir. 1988); *South Bend Consumers Club, Inc. v. United Consumers Club, Inc.,* 572 F. Supp. 209, 212–13 (N.D. Ind. 1983). These courts, in other words, have deemed the second and third parts to the second exception in § 187(2) to be parallel and have thus analyzed them under the same standards. It is to the third element, then, that this court now turns.

The third element asks whether, if the contract did not provide for a choice of law, New Jersey would be the state of the applicable law under the principles set forth in Restatement § 188. First, it is noted that Ohio follows the general principle that "in cases involving a contract, the law of the state where the contract is made governs the interpretation of the contract." *Nationwide Mutual Insurance Co. v. Ferrin,* 21 Ohio St.3d 43, 44, 487 N.E.2d 568 (1986). The court in *Ferrin* expounded upon this doctrine by emphasizing its view that Section 188 of the Restatement provides the principles to be followed in ascertaining where a contract is made. Section 188 provides as follows:

(1) The rights and duties of the parties with respect to an issue in contract are determined by the local law of the state which, with respect to that issue, has the most significant relationship to the transaction and the parties under the principles stated in Section 6.

(2) In the absence of an effective choice of law by the parties (see Section 187), the contracts to be taken into account in applying the principles of Section 6 to determine the law applicable to an issue include:

   (a) the place of contracting;

   (b) the place of negotiations of the contract;

   (c) the place of performance;

   (d) the location of the subject matter of the contract;

   (e) the domicile, residence, nationality, place of incorporation and place of business of the parties.

These contracts are to be evaluated according to their relative importance with respect to the particular issue.

See Greis Sports Enterprises, Inc. v. Modell, 15 Ohio St.3d 284, 288, 473 N.E.2d 807 (1984) *cert. denied* 473 U.S. 906, 105 S. Ct. 3530, 87 L. Ed. 2d 654 (1985). For purposes of this portion of our analysis, of course, we assume that the parties did not provide for a choice of law.

The five contacts listed in § 188(2), however, cannot be read alone. Rather, § 188(1) requires that these factors be considered in light of the particular contract issue which faces the court and on the question of which state has the most significant relationship to the transaction and parties. This question, in turn, requires an application of the principles stated in § 6 of the Restatement. *Id.*

Section 6 of the Restatement provides as follows:

(1) A court, subject to constitutional restrictions, will follow a statutory directive of its own state on choice of law.

(2) When there is no such directive, the factors relevant to the choice of the applicable rule of law include

(a) the needs of the interstate and international systems;

(b) the relevant policies of the forum;

(c) the relevant policies of other interested states and the relative interests of those states in the determination of the particular issue;

(d) the protection of justified expectations;

(e) the basic policies underlying the particular field of law;

(f) certainty, predictability, and uniformity of result; and

(g) ease in the determination and application of the law to be applied.

Id. The relationship between this section and § 188 can be seen in Comment B to § 188(1) which provides as follows:

The principles stated in Section 6 underlie all rules of choice of law and are used in evaluating the significance of a relationship, with respect to the particular issue, to the potentially interested states, the transaction, and the parties.

Id. Clearly, the Restatement provides that the § 6 principles are to be applied to determine the applicable law, and that the provisions of § 188(2) are only considerations to help guide this analysis.

Thus, pursuant to the mandates of § 188, this court will examine the § 6 principles, while taking the § 188(2) factors into account, to determine whether Ohio or New Jersey law should apply in this situation.

The first precept of § 6(2) provides little guidance. As for the second factor, the relevant policy of Ohio in this matter is far outweighed by the policies of New Jersey which are at issue, *see* discussion above. The third principle, likewise, cuts in favor of New Jersey. Comment f to § 6 helps to disclose this:

In determining a question of choice of law, the forum should give consideration . . . to the relevant policies of all other interested states. The forum should seek to reach a result that will achieve the best possible accommodation of these policies. The forum should also appraise the relative interests of the state involved in the determination of the particular issue. *In general, it is fitting that the state whose interests are most deeply affected should have its local law applied.* (Emphasis added).

In ascertaining the relative interests of New Jersey and Ohio, those of the former state clearly prevail. Ohio's interest stems from its proximity and relation to the actual formation and manifestation of the contract—and it is here where the relevance of the § 188(2) actors becomes significant. An application of these factors to the facts of this case, however, does not conclusively establish that Ohio law should apply. It is true that Ohio was the "place of contracting," inasmuch as the parties signed the agreement there. However, "standing alone, the place of contracting is a relatively insignificant contact." Comment e, § 188. The second factor, the place of negotiation, is also insignificant, as the parties negotiated from different states by the use of the mails and telephones. "This contact is of less importance when there is no one single place of negotiation and agreement, as, for example, when the parties do not meet but rather conduct their negotiations from separate states by mail or telephone." comment c, § 188.

The fourth factor, the location of the contract's subject matter, favors New Jersey; plaintiffs' four franchises were indisputably located in this state. The fifth element clearly dictates an equal interest. Finally, the third factor, place of performance, tends to endorse Ohio as the proper choice, as the applicable franchise fees, etc., were most likely paid there. On the whole, however, in light of the foregoing analysis, the § 188(2) factors do not concretely establish Ohio as the state of interest, and in fact tend to favor New Jersey.

Simply put, New Jersey's interest in this matter is more solid, and thus the third factor of § 6(2) cuts in favor of it. As discussed, plaintiffs are New Jersey citizens and were allegedly wronged there; New Jersey is thus more "deeply affected" than is Ohio, Comment f to § 6.

The fourth, fifth, and sixth elements to § 6(2) collapse upon one another.

> The need for protecting the expectations of the parties gives importance in turn to the value of certainty, predictability and uniformity of result. For unless these values are attained, the expectations of the parties are likely to be disappointed.
>
> Protection of the justified expectations of the parties by choice-of-law rules in the field of contracts is supported both by those factors in Subsection (2) of § 6 which are directed to the furtherance of the needs of the parties and by those factors which are directed to implementation of the basic policy underlying the particular field of law. Protection of the justified expectations of the parties is the basic policy underlying the field of contracts.

Comment b, § 188. The fourth precept of § 6(2) supports the application of New Jersey law, for it is vital to protect the justified expectations of plaintiffs that they would be enabled to utilize the laws of their state in order to redress alleged wrongs. Thus, the fifth and sixth factors also favor New Jersey.

The last element, ease in the determination and application of the law to be applied, is of little significance. The drafters of the Restatement believed this to be a general, ideal goal toward which to strive, but also cautioned that "[t]his policy should not be overemphasized, since it is obviously of greater importance that choice-of-law rules lead to desirable results." Comment j, § 188.

In conclusion, it must be emphasized that a court faced with the task of choosing competing state laws has discretion to consider factors other than those listed in § 6 and can assign more weight to some factors than others depending upon the particular contract issue in question.

> It is not suggested that this list of factors is exclusive. Undoubtedly, a court will on occasion give consideration to other factors in deciding a question of choice of law. Also it is not suggested that the factors mentioned are listed in the order of their relative importance. Varying weight will be given to a particular factor, or to a group of factors, in different areas of choice of law.

Comment (c), § 6. Specifically, this court finds New Jersey's interest in protecting its citizens and consumers to weight heavily in favor of the New Jersey as the applicable choice of law in this case. Furthermore, it is significant to note that Diet Franchisor is a national franchisor dealing with individuals as franchisees across the nation,[66] all of whom should be entitled to benefit from the laws of their respective states. If defendants' argument were accepted, this court would be setting a dangerous precedent wherein any large, national franchisor, by simply inserting a choice of law provision requiring the application of the franchisor's state law, could remove the beneficial effect of the franchisee's state's legislation with the stroke of a pen. This the court simply cannot do. Thus, for these and the foregoing reasons, defendants' motion to dismiss Counts II and IV of the complaint are hereby denied.

B. Count III

The third count of the complaint alleges violations of the Federal Racketeer Influenced and Corrupt Organizations (RICO) Act, 18 U.S.C. § 1962(a), (b), (c) and (d). This statute provides as follows:

---

[66] In fact, Diet Franchisor is a party to several other lawsuits in this court. These suits involve franchisees who are citizens of several other states (e.g., Massachusetts, New Hampshire, Connecticut) and who are seeking to redress alleged injuries wrought by Diet Franchisor in violation of their respective state statutes. Diet Franchisor has pending motions to dismiss in these cases similar to the one at issue here.

(a) It shall be unlawful for any person who has received any income derived, directly or indirectly, from a pattern of racketeering activity or through collection of an unlawful debt in which such person has participated as a principal within the meaning of section 2, title 18, United States Code, to use or invest, directly or indirectly, any part of such income, or the proceeds of such income, in acquisition of any interest in, or the establishment or operation of, any enterprise which is engaged in, or the activities of which affect, interstate or foreign commerce. A purchase of securities on the open market for purposes of investment, and without the intention of controlling or participating in the control of the issuer, or of assisting another to do so, shall not be unlawful under this subsection if the securities of the issuer held by the purchaser, the members of his immediate family, and his or their accomplices in any pattern or racketeering activity or the collection of an unlawful debt after such purchase do not amount in the aggregate to one percent of the outstanding securities of any one class, and do not confer, either in law or in fact, the power to elect one or more directors of the issuer.

(b) It shall be unlawful for any person through a pattern of racketeering activity or through collection of an unlawful debt to acquire or maintain, directly or indirectly, any interest in or control of any enterprise which is engaged in, or the activities of which affect, interstate or foreign commerce.

(c) It shall be unlawful for any person employed by or associated with any enterprise engaged in, or the activities of which affect, interstate or foreign commerce, to conduct or participate, directly or indirectly, in the conduct of such enterprise's affairs through a pattern of racketeering activity or collection of unlawful debt.

(d) It shall be unlawful for any person to conspire to violate any of the provisions of subsections (a), (b), or (c) of this section.

Plaintiffs' RICO claims are predicated upon alleged acts of mail and wire fraud, 18 U.S.C. §§ 1341 and 1343. The complaint charges that defendants utilized these interstate methods of communication to implement fraudulent schemes to market their franchises, to overcharge franchisees for the mandatory purchase of Diet Franchisor products, to misapply advertising contributions from the franchisees, to fraudulently induce franchisees to coerce consumers into the Diet Franchisor program, and to prevent franchisees from leaving the Diet Franchisor system.

In support of their motion to dismiss the RICO claims, defendants argue, first, that plaintiffs' allegations of fraud are insufficient under Fed. R. Civ. P. 9(b), which provides as follows:

In all averments of fraud or mistake, the circumstances constituting fraud or mistake shall be stated with particularity. Malice, intent, knowledge, and other condition of mind of a person may be averred generally.

Specifically, defendants maintain that the element of scienter is not plead with sufficient detail in the complaint. Second, defendants contend that the alleged violation under § 1962(d) fails to properly state a claim because no conspiracy can exist between Diet Franchisor and President and because no other conspirators have been named. Alternatively, defendants claim that even if another entity were properly identified, plaintiffs have not adequately pled the existence of a conspiracy. Third, defendants argue that the § 1962(c) claim necessarily fails as to Diet Franchisor because, under this subsection, the "person" must be separate and distinct from the enterprise alleged. Finally, defendants assert that plaintiffs' fraudulent inducement claims as they relate to the Freehold and East Brunswick agreement are barred by the four year statute of limitations applicable to RICO claims. These arguments will be separately addressed in the order presented.

As mentioned above, defendants' argument with regard to the fraud count primarily asserts that plaintiffs have failed to plead fraudulent intent with the requisite specificity—specifically, that facts have not been pled which support the scienter element. To properly resolve this issue, this court will apply the guidelines contained in the applicable case law on the subject.

Civil RICO pleading requirements in the context of the predicate acts of mail and wire fraud have been previously examined by this court in the case of *Van Dorn Company, Central States Can Co. Division v. Howington,* 623 F. Supp. 1548 (N.D. Ohio 1985). In that case we stated as follows:

> Pursuant to Rule 9(b) of the Federal Rules of Civil Procedure "[i]n all averments of fraud or mistake, the circumstances constituting fraud or mistake shall be stated with particularity." Thus, a RICO claim predicated upon the alleged mail or wire fraud must be set forth with particularity to satisfy Rule 9(b).
>
> . . .
>
> The crime of mail fraud encompasses two well-defined elements. The defendants must first have devised a scheme or artifice to defraud and then used the mails for the purpose of executing the scheme. . . . The elements of the crime of wire fraud also encompasses a scheme to defraud; however, instead of the use of the mails, some use of the interstate telecommunications system must be utilized in the execution of the scheme. . . . The courts have uniformly given the same construction to the language in both the mail and wire fraud statutes with the sole distinction between the crimes being the interstate communication device utilized by the alleged offender.
>
> . . .
>
> When alleging wire and mail fraud as predicate acts of racketeering, a claimant must, pursuant to Rule 9(b), describe with particularity the

circumstances constituting the fraud. The Eighth Circuit described these circumstances in a RICO action to, at a minimum, "include such matters as the time, place and content of false representations, as well as the identity of the person making the misrepresentation and what was obtained or given up thereby."

Id., 623 F. Supp. at 1555 (citations omitted). Applicable Sixth Circuit law, generally, is in accord with these principles. In *Michaels Building Company v. Ameritrust Company, N.A.,* 848 F.2d 674 (6th Cir. 1988), the court warned that the strict pleading requirement of Rule 9(b) should be tempered with the general principles enunciated in Rule 8.

> In ruling upon a motion to dismiss under Rule 9(b) for failure to plead fraud "with particularity," a court must factor in the policy of simplicity in pleading which the drafters of the Federal Rules codified in Rule 8. Rule 8 requires a "short and plain statement of the claim," and calls for "simple, concise, and direct" allegations. Indeed, Rule 9(b)'s particularity requirement does not mute the general principles set out in Rule 8; rather, the two rules must be read in harmony. "Thus, it is inappropriate to focus exclusively on the fact that Rule 9(b) requires particularity in pleading fraud. This is too narrow an approach and fails to take account of the general simplicity and flexibility contemplated by the rules." 5 C. Wright & A. Miller, Federal Practice and Procedure: Civil § 1298, at 407 (1969).

> Given this backdrop admonition of simplicity in pleading, we note that the purpose undergirding the particularity requirement of Rule 9(b) is to provide a defendant fair notice of the substance of a plaintiff's claim in order that the defendant may prepare a responsive pleading.

Id., 848 F.2d at 679 (citations omitted). In addition, the court reiterated what, specifically, is required under Rule 9(b) and Rule 8 for a civil RICO complaint, *viz.,* "the parties and the participants to the alleged fraud, the representations made, the nature in which the statements are alleged to be misleading or false, the time, place, and content of the representations, the fraudulent scheme, the fraudulent intent of the defendants, reliance on the fraud, and the injury resulting from the fraud." *Id.* (footnote omitted).

A review of plaintiffs' sixty-page complaint establishes that this document contains a detailed, fully comprehensive factual background in support of the mail and wire fraud allegations. The factual background comprises the first half of the complaint (71 paragraphs) and details the alleged misrepresentations and material omissions, the time, place, and content of the alleged falsities, the alleged fraudulent scheme, and the alleged reliance and injury. With regard to the scienter requirement, defendants' position is that the plaintiffs are required to allege facts which support the allegation that the alleged misrepresentations were known to be false when made. This court believes that a complaint which in detail alleges both representations (and/or omissions) and that such representations turned out to be false sufficiently alleges the scienter element within the meaning of *Michaels Building*. As stated in that case, the purpose underlying Rule 9(b) "is to provide a defendant fair notice of the substances of a plaintiffs' claim in order that the defendant may prepare a responsive pleading." *Id.*, 848 F.2d at 679. Where the plaintiff alleges that the defendant made certain representations and that the facts represented were false, certainly the defendant is aware of whether the misrepresentations were deceitfully made. Such a defendant, thus, is able to properly prepare a responsive pleading. In any event, to give Rule 9(b) the reading urged by defendants would be to disregard the caveat set forth in *Michaels Building*.[67]

With regard to defendants' second argument in support of dismissal of the RICO claim, plaintiffs do not controvert defendants' assertion that President and Diet Franchisor are incapable of conspiring under § 1962(d). Rather, plaintiffs argue that the identities of the unknown Diet Franchisor employees are within the exclusive control of Diet Franchisor, that no discovery has taken place, and that the unknown actors are in the process of being joined as defendants in this action. Again, we turn to *Michaels Building* for guidance on this issue.

> Courts have held that the rule may be relaxed where information is only within the opposing party's knowledge. *See e.g.,* 5 C. Wright & A. Miller, Federal Practice & Procedure: Civil § 1298, at 416 n. 94 (1969); *Wool v. Tandem Computers, Inc.*, 818 F.2d 1433, 1439 (9th Cir. 1987); *Schlick v. Penn-Dixie Cement Corp.*, 507 F.2d 374, 379 (2d Cir. 1974), *cert. denied*, 421 U.S. 976, 95 S. Ct. 1976, 44 L. Ed. 2d 467 (1975). Especially in a case in which there has been no discovery, courts have been reluctant to dismiss the action where the facts underlying the claims are within the defendant's control. For example, the courts in *Eaby v. Richmond*, 561 F. Supp. 131, 137 (E.D. Pa. 1983), and in *Chambers Development Co. v. Browning-Ferris Industries*, 590 F. Supp. 1528, 1539 (W.D. Pa. 1984), did not grant motions to dismiss under Rule 9(b) because the plaintiffs claimed that they could not plead a RICO complaint with specificity since the facts underlying their claims were particularly within defendants'

---

[67] The primary case relied upon by defendants, Beck v. Manufacturers Hanover Trust Company, 820 F.2d 46 (2d Cir. 1987), does not alter this result. The court there held that plaintiffs must "provide some factual basis for conclusory allegations of intent," and that the "factual allegations must give rise to a 'strong inference' that the defendants possessed the requisite fraudulent intent." *Id.* at 50. This "strong inference" can be established by alleging "facts showing a motive for committing fraud and a clear opportunity for doing so," or, "[w]here motive is not apparent, it is still possible to plead scienter by identifying circumstances indicating conscious behavior by the defendant, . . . though the strength of the circumstantial allegations must be correspondingly greater." *Id.* (citations omitted). Here, plaintiffs have alleged facts which, if true (and the court must consider them true for purposes of Rule 12(b)(6)), constitute strong circumstantial evidence that the alleged scheme was undertaken intentionally.

knowledge. Those courts decided to grant plaintiffs an opportunity to take discovery for sixty days and to file an amended complaint shortly thereafter. *See also Jordan v. Global Natural Resources, Inc.,* 564 F. Supp. 59, 69 (S.D. Ohio 1983); *Imperial Supply Co., Inc. v. Northern Ohio Bank,* 430 F. Supp. 339, 360–61 (N.D. Ohio 1976) (where discovery stayed and information in control of defendants, dismissal of claims improper).

Id., 848 F.2d at 680.

To this date, only limited discovery has taken place and plaintiffs have neither filed an amended complaint nor moved to do so. On March 12, 1991, plaintiffs filed a RICO case statement which does list the actors with whom Diet Franchisor and President are alleged to have conspired. Thus, it is clear that the alleged co-conspirators are not unknown to plaintiffs, who should therefore be given the opportunity to move to amend their complaint pursuant to Rule 15(a) under the reasoning of *Michaels Building.*

Defendants in their third argument seek dismissal of the § 1962(c) claim as it pertains to Diet Franchisor. Defendants contend that Diet Franchisor cannot be sued under this subsection because a "person" under § 1962(c) must be separate and distinct from the "enterprise" alleged. Plaintiffs cite to numerous cases which, according to them, have held that a corporation can simultaneously serve as the "enterprise" and the "person" under § 1962(c).

The cases cited by plaintiffs are of no assistence to them because the Sixth Circuit has decided this issue contrary to their asserted position. In *Puckett v. Tennessee Eastman Company,* 889 F.2d 1481 (6th Cir. 1989), the court affirmed the district court's dismissal of plaintiff's § 1962(c) claim for the reason that a § 1962(c) enterprise cannot be sued as the person under this subsection. The court reasoned as follows:

> It is plain that the language of this subsection precludes the "person" conducting or participating in an enterprise's affairs from simultaneously serving as the "enterprise." *Grider v. Texas Oil & Gas Corp.,* 868 F.2d 1147, 1150 n. 2 (10th Cir. 1989). Because § 1962(c) requires separate legal entities as the "person" and the "enterprise," courts are in substantial agreement that a corporation cannot be named as the liable "person" and simultaneously fulfill the "enterprise" requirement as well. *See, e.g., id.* at 1150; *Schofield v. First Commodity Corp.,* 793 F.2d 28, 29–30 (1st Cir. 1986) (collecting cases); *B.F. Hirsch v. Enright Refining Co.,* 751 F.2d 628, 633–34 (3d Cir. 1984); *Haroco, nc. v. American Nat'l Bank & Trust Co.,* 747 F.2d 384, 399–402 (7th Cir. 1984); *cf. United States v. Hartley,* 678 F.2d 961 (11th Cir. 1982), *cert. denied,* 459 U.S. 1170 & 1183, 103 S. Ct. 815 & 834, 74 L. ed. 2d 1014 & 1027 (1983).

Id., 889 F.2d at 1489. Thus, plaintiffs § 1962(c) claim against Diet Franchisor must be dismissed.

Defendants' final argument asserts that any of plaintiffs' RICO claims associated with the execution of the Freehold and East Brunswick agreements must be dismissed by reason of the RICO four years statute of limitations. Specifically, defendants contend that, because plaintiffs signed these agreements on May 8, 1986 and September 16, 1986, respectively, any claim as it pertains to the alleged pre-contract conduct of defendants must be dismissed as occurring more than four years before the filing of the complaint, which occurred on October 9, 1990.

In response, plaintiffs submit that the RICO statute of limitations period does not begin to run until the claim accrues, which according to them is when either the plaintiff knew or should have known of the injuries alleged, or when the last predicate act upon which the claim is based occurs. Alternatively, plaintiffs contend that fraudulent concealment of the cause of action tolls the statute of limitations.

The issue of when a cause of action under RICO accrues has not been addressed by the Sixth Circuit,[68] and the RICO statute itself is silent on this issue. In *Agency Holding Corporation v. Malley-Duff & Associates,* 483 U.S. 143, 107 S. Ct. 2759, 97 L. Ed. 2d 121 (1987), in which the Supreme Court applied the four year statute of limitations found in the Clayton Act, 15 U.S.C. § 15, to RICO causes of action, the Supreme Court reserved the question.

This court has previously adopted the reasoning of the Third Circuit set forth in *Keystone Insurance Company v. Houghton,* 863 F.2d 1125 (3d Cir. 1988), with some modification. *See The Uniroyal Goodrich Tire Company v. Holland Oil Company,* Case No. C87-297A (N.D. Ohio March 8, 1989). In that case, we held that, construing RICO liberally in order to effectuate its remedial purposes, the statute of limitations enunciated in *Agency Holding* does not begin to run until the last predicate act comprising the alleged scheme has occurred, *id.,* at 5–6.

The court in *Keystone* reviewed several accrual rules and concluded that, in a multiple victim, multiple injury scenario, the best rule is one which focuses both upon plaintiffs' knowledge and upon the pattern element of RICO; the latter element is important because there is no RICO injury without the existence of the pattern elements. *Id.,* 863 F.2d at 1133. The court ultimately established the following accrual rule:

> The rule which we announce provides that the limitations period for a civil RICO claim runs from the date the plaintiff knew or should have known that the elements of the civil RICO cause of action existed unless,

---

[68] The Sixth Circuit has, however, approved of a lower court's jury instructions which charged the jury to determine whether the plaintiff knew or should have known of the alleged fraudulent scheme. *See* Hofstetter v. Fletcher, 905 F.2d 897, 904 (6th Cir. 1988).

as a part of the same pattern of racketeering activity, there is further injury to the plaintiff or further predicate acts occur, in which case the accrual period shall run from the time when the plaintiff knew or should have known of the last injury or the last predicate act which is part of the same pattern of racketeering activity. The last predicate act need not have resulted in injury to the plaintiff but must be part of the same pattern. If the complaint was filed within four years of the last injury or the last predicate act, the plaintiff may recover for injuries caused by other predicate acts which occurred outside an earlier limitations period but which are part of the same "pattern."

Id., 863 F.2d at 1130–31. Thus, the Third Circuit applies the discovery rule to both the pattern element and the injury requirement of a RICO cause of action.

Three other circuit courts have agreed with this reasoning. *See Granite Falls Bank v. Henriksen,* 924 F.2d 150, 154 (8th Cir. 1991); *Bath v. Bushkin, Gaims, Gaines, and Jonas,* 913 F.2d 817, 820 (10th Cir. 1990); *Bivens Gardens Office Building, Inc. v. Barnett Bank of Florida, Inc.,* 906 F.2d 1546, 1553–54 (11th Cir. 1990).[69] These courts have stated the rule in simpler terms, *viz.,* "with respect to each independent injury to the plaintiff, a civil RICO cause of action begins to accrue as soon as the plaintiff discovers, or reasonably should have discovered, both the existence and source of his injury and that the injury is part of a pattern." *Bivens Gardens,* 906 F.2d at 1554–55.

With these standards in mind, it is clear that dismissal of any of plaintiffs' RICO claims on statute of limitations grounds would be inappropriate at this stage. Plaintiffs' position in this regard is not only that they discovered their alleged injuries well past the dates on which the Freehold and East Brunswick agreements were consummated, but also that the pattern did not evolve until after these dates. Thus, under the foregoing analysis, the RICO statute of limitations does not bar plaintiffs' RICO claim.

III. Conclusion

For the foregoing reasons, the defendants' motion to dismiss under Rule 12(b)(6) is hereby granted with regard to plaintiffs' claims against

---

[69] Four other circuits have adopted the rule that the statute begins to run when the plaintiff knows or should have known of his injury. *See* Rodriguez v. Banco Cent., 917 F.2d 664, 666 (1st Cir. 1990); Bankers Trust Co. v. Rhoades, 859 F.2d 1096, 1102 (2d Cir. 1988) *cert. denied* 490 U.S. 1007, 109 S. Ct. 1642, 104 L. Ed. 2d 158 (1989); Pochahontas Supreme Coal Co. v. Bethlehem Steel, 828 F.2d 211, 220 (4th Cir. 1987); State Farm Mutual Automobile Insurance Co. v. Ammann, 828 F.2d 405 (9th Cir. 1987).

Diet Franchisor under 18 U.S.C. § 1962(c). In all other respects, however, the motion is hereby denied.

IT IS SO ORDERED.

_____

U. S. DISTRICT JUDGE

**UNITED STATES DISTRICT COURT
NORTHERN DISTRICT OF OHIO
EASTERN DIVISION**

DIET FRANCHISOR Plaintiffs	CASE NO.
V.	
LICENSEES Defendants	*ORDER*

Currently pending before the court in the above-captioned matters are motions to dismiss filed by Diet Franchisor, President, and Executive Vice President pursuant to Fed. R. Civ. P. 12(b)(6). The pleadings and motions filed in each case to date bear substantial similarities to one another and to two other causes which had been before this court, *Diet Franchisor v. Lignon,* and *Licensee v. Diet Franchisor,* and it is believed that a consolidated resolution of the subject motions to dismiss is appropriate. Further, due to the applicability of the reasoning of this court in the April 23, 1991 order in the *Licensee* case denying Diet Franchisor's motion to dismiss, that opinion (April 23, 1991) will be referred to and relied upon throughout the present analysis. Finally, due to the fact that the counts in each of the relevant complaints and counterclaims make similar allegations, the court will engage in a categorical analysis in order to more efficiently resolve the present dispute.

In each of the motions to dismiss Diet Franchisor contends that the breach of contract counts of each complaint and counterclaim should be dismissed because they characterize the breaches ad tortious, *i.e.,* as "willful" or in "bad faith." According to Diet Franchisor, Ohio law does not recognize a cause of action for "tortious" breach of contract; hence, these counts should be dismissed for failure to state a claim pursuant to Rule 12(b)(6).

A review of the complaints establishes that the claimants and counterclaimants have adequately alleged breach of contract in the complaints and counterclaims. Specifically, the parties claim breach of express contract, breach of implied covenant of good faith and fair dealing, and promissory estoppel. All three theories have been recognized by the Ohio courts as cognizable causes of action. And, while it is true that the complaint also alleges that the breaches were willful and in bad faith, we do not believe that this additional allegation is fatal to the breach of contract count. Where the plaintiff in a breach of contract suit alleges and attempts to show that the breach was willful or in bad faith, the court is constrained to analyze the allegation as one solely for breach of contract and to disregard the extra allegations sounding in tort. *See Battista v. Lebanon Trotting Association,* 583 F.2d 111, 117 (6th Cir. 1976); *Tibbs v. National Homes Construction Corporation,* 52 Ohio App.2d 281, 290–91, 369 N.E.2d 1218 (Warren Cty. 1977). These cases do not stand for the proposition that, where the complaint alleges breach of contract and in addition alleges that the breach was willful, the court should dismiss the complaint *in toto.* Rather, only the allegations regarding the elements of tort should be dismissed.

For the foregoing reasons, the motions to dismiss the breach of contract counts of the complaints and counterclaims are hereby denied. The allegations of willfulness and bad faith, insofar as those allegations relate to the breach of contract claims, must however be dismissed.

Diet Franchisor next argues that the counts in the complaints and counterclaims which attempt to state claims under various state laws must necessarily fail because the choice of law clause in each franchise agreement provide that the agreements shall be construed according to Ohio law. Before this argument is addressed, it is useful to set forth the relevant counts of the complaints and counterclaims and the laws alleged to be violated thereunder, as follows:

1. Case no.   (counterclaim)—unfair and deceptive trade practices under Massachusetts General Laws Chapter 93A (Count II).

2. Case no.   (counterclaim)—unfair and deceptive acts and practices under New Hampshire Revised Statutes Annotated § 358-A:2 (Count II).

3. Case no.   (counterclaim)—unfair and deceptive trade practices under Massachusetts General Laws Chapter 93A (Count II) and violations of the Regulations of the Sale of Business Opportunities Act, Maine Revised Statutes Title 32, Chapter 69-B, and violation of the Unfair Trade Practices Act, Maine Revised Statutes Title 5, Chapter 10 (Count IV).

4. Case no.   (counterclaim)—fraud under Ohio common law (Count II).

5. Case no.   (complaint)—unfair and deceptive acts and practices under Massachusetts General Laws Chapter 93-A (Count II).

5. Case no.   (complaint)—unfair and deceptive trade practices under Connecticut General Statutes § 42-110a *et seq.* (Count II) and violation of Connecticut Fair Conduct in Franchising Act, Connecticut General Statutes § 42-133f (Count IV).

7. Case no.   (complaint)—unfair and deceptive acts and practices
under Connecticut General Statutes § 42-110a *et seq.* and South Carolina Code § 39-5-10 (Count II).
8. Case no.   (complaint)—unfair and deceptive acts and practices
under Indiana Code § 23-2-2.7-1 *et seq.* (Count II).

Diet Franchisor's argument that the choice of law provision bars these
state law claims is unavailing for alternative reasons. First, with regard to
the claims made pursuant to Maine law (counterclaim, Count IV), Connecticut law (complaint, Count IV), and Indiana law (complaint, Count
II), the anti-waiver provisions enacted by the legislatures of these states
nullifies the effect of the choice of law provisions. Maine law provides
that "[a]ny waiver by a consumer of the provisions of this chapter is
contrary to public policy and shall be unenforceable and void." 5 Me.
Rev. Stat. § 214. Connecticut law provides that "[a]ny waiver of the
rights of a franchisee under Section 42-133f or 42-133g which is contained in any franchise agreement entered into or amended on or after
June 12, 1975, shall be void." Conn. Gen. Stat. § 42-133f(f). Finally,

> Indiana has made it unlawful to enter into a franchise agreement "requiring
> the franchisee to prospectively assent to a release . . . [or] waiver . . .
> which purports to relieve any person from liability to be imposed by this
> chapter" or to enter into an agreement "limiting litigation brought for
> breach of the agreement in any manner whatsoever." Ind. Code § 23-2-
> 2.7-1(10).
>
> . . .
>
> The public policy articulated in the nonwaiver provisions of the statute
> is clear: a franchisor, through its superior bargaining power, should not
> be permitted to force the franchisee to waive the legislatively provided
> protections, whether directly through waiver provisions or indirectly
> through choice of law. This public policy is sufficient to render the
> choice to opt out of Indiana's franchise law one that cannot be made by
> agreement.

Wright-Moore Corporation v. Ricoh Corporation, 908 F.2d 128, 132 (7th
Cir. 1990). Thus, pursuant to these code sections, Count IV of the
Coulthard counterclaim, Count II of the Stevens complaint, and Count
II of the Buchanan complaint adequately state claims for which relief
can be granted.
    Second, with regard to the claims invoking Chapter 93A of Massachu-
setts General Laws (counterclaim Count II, counterclaim Count II, complaint Count II), the court is not requested to construe the franchise
agreements, but rather to analyze allegations more properly considered
as based upon a fraud theory sounding in tort. For example, allegations
of unfair trade practices under Mass. Gen. L. ch. 93A does not raise

questions of contract construction. *See Popkin v. National Benefit Life Insurance Company,* 711 F. Supp. 1194, 1200 (S.D.N.Y. 1989), *Computer System Engineering, Inc. v. Qantel Corporation,* 571 F. Supp. 1365, 1371, aff'd 740 F.2d 59 (1st Cir. 1984). The same reasoning would arguably apply, of course, to the substantially similar local "little FTC" acts embodied in New Hampshire, Connecticut, and Indiana law. For these reasons, the court finds that the claims survive scrutiny under Rule 12(b)(6).

Finally, even were the court to find that the choice of law provisions are applicable to the claims herein, we would hold as a matter of law that they are ineffective in the cases at bar. In this regard, we refer substantially to the reasoning set forth by this court in *Licensee v. Diet Franchisor,* case no. (April 23, 1991). In that Memorandum and Order denying a Rule 12(b)(6) motion to dismiss filed by Diet Franchisor, we analyzed Ohio choice of law principles under the guidelines set forth in Restatement (Second) of Conflicts of Laws § 187(2).[70] *See Tele-Save Merchandising Company v. Consumers Distributing Company, Ltd.,* 814 F.2d 1120 (6th Cir. 1987); *Jarvis v. Ashland Oil, Inc.,* 17 Ohio St.3d 189, 478 N.E.2d 786 (1985). At pages 5–26 of our April 23, 1991 opinion, we examined Restatement § 187(2)(b) as applied to the allegations in the *Licensee* complaint and concluded that an application of Ohio law would be contrary to a fundamental policy of New Jersey,[71] that New Jersey has a materially greater interest than Ohio in the determination of plaintiffs' state law claims, and that, under Restatement § 188, New Jersey would be the state of the applicable law absent an effective choice of law by the parties.

The same conclusion is mandated with regard to each of the claims and counterclaims involved in this case. The laws invoked herein are very similar to the laws involved in the *Licensee* case and are based upon the same underlying fundamental policy, viz., protection against consumers/franchisees from the superior bargaining strength of franchisors and/or the unscrupulous practices of commercial sellers. *See, e.g., Wright-Moore Corp., supra; Popkin, supra; Gill v. Petrazzuoli Brothers,*

---

[70] Restatement Section 187(2) provides, in relevant part, as follows:

The law of the state chose by the parties to govern their contractual rights and duties will be applied, even if the particular issue is one which the parties could not have resolved by an explicit provision in their agreement directed to that issue, unless either

(a) the chosen state has no substantial relationship to the parties or the transaction and there is no other reasonable basis for the parties' choice, or

(b) application of the law of the chosen state would be contrary to a fundamental policy of a state which has a materially greater interest than the chosen state in the determination of the particular issue and which, under the rule of § 188, would be the state of the applicable law in the absence of an effective choice of law by the parties.

[71] Plaintiffs in Economou sought recovery under the New Jersey Consumer Fraud Act, N.J. Rev. Stat. §§ 56:8-2 and 56:8-19, and the New Jersey Franchise Practices Act, N.J. Rev. Stat. §§ 56:10-5 through 56:10-7.

Inc., 521 A.2d 212, 217, 10 Conn. App. 22 (Conn. App. 1987); *Bartner v. Carter,* 405 A.2d 194, 201 (Me. 1979); *Rousseau v. Eshelman,* 529 A.2d 862, 864–65, 129 N.H. 306 (N.H. 1987). Further, for the same reasons as those enunciated in the *Licensee* opinion, we believe that application of Ohio law would contravene these public policies, that the states involved herein have a materially greater interest in the outcome of these suits than does Ohio, and that § 188 would mandate the utilization of these states' laws absent the choice of law clause. See *Licensee* at 18–26.

For all of the foregoing reasons, the motions to dismiss Count II of the _____, _____, and _____ counterclaims, and the _____, _____, _____, and _____ complaints, and Count IV of the _____ counterclaim and _____ complaint, must be and are hereby denied.

With regard to case no.   (counterclaim), Count II alleges common law fraud. The basis of Diet Franchisor's motion to dismiss is the contention that the claim fails to plead fraud with particularity as required by Fed. R. Civ. P. 9(b). First, Rule 9(b) is not to be rigidly and mechanistically applied, but must be tempered with the general principles enunciated in Rule 8.

> In ruling upon a motion to dismiss under Rule 9(b) for failure to plead fraud "with particularity," a court must factor in the policy of simplicity in pleading which the drafters of the Federal Rules codified in Rule 8. Rule 8 requires a "short and plain statement of the claim," and calls for "simple, concise, and direct" allegations. Indeed, Rule 9(b)'s particularity requirement does not mute the general principles set out in Rule 8; rather, the two rules must be read in harmony. "Thus, it is inappropriate to focus exclusively on the fact that Rule 9(b) requires particularity in pleading fraud. This is too narrow an approach and fails to take account of the general simplicity and flexibility contemplated by the rules." 5 C. Wright & A. Miller, Federal Practice and Procedure: Civil § 1298, at 407 (1969).

> Given this backdrop admonition of simplicity in pleading, we note that the purpose undergirding the particularity requirement of Rule 9(b) is to provide a defendant fair notice of the substance of a plaintiff's claim in order that the defendant may prepare a responsive pleading.

Michaels Building Company v. Ameritrust Company, N.A., 848 F.2d 674, 679 (6th Cir. 1988) (citations omitted). Second, we believe, in any event, that the extensive complaint adequately states a claim for fraud to satisfy scrutiny under Rule 9(b). *See* Complaint at ¶¶ 24–66.

With regard to the RICO claims asserted by the complainants and counterclaimants in these cases, the motion to dismiss filed by Diet Franchisor sets forth several separate arguments: the RICO claims fail to plead fraud with particularity; the allegations based upon 18 U.S.C.

§§ 1962(c) and (d) fail to state a claim; and many of the claims are barred by the statute of limitations applicable to RICO actions.[72]

The court hereby incorporates in full the reasoning contained in the *Licensee* opinion, *see* Memorandum and Order at 26–37. In that decision, we rejected all of Diet Franchisor's arguments except that pertaining to 28 U.S.C. § 1962(c). The allegations contained in the subject complaints and counterclaims are nearly identical to those of plaintiff in the *Licensee* case, and the respective arguments urged in the motions to dismiss and oppositions thereto are likewise nearly identical. Thus, under the reasoning set forth in our earlier opinion, the motions to dismiss the claims under 18 U.S.C. § 1962(c) are hereby granted. In all other respects, however, the motions to dismiss as they relate to other aspects of the RICO claims are denied.

Conclusion

For the foregoing reasons, the motions to dismiss filed by defendants Diet Franchisor, President, and Executive Vice President in the above-captioned cases are hereby denied in part and granted in part. Plaintiffs' and defendants-counterclaimants' bad faith and willfulness allegations, insofar as they relate to the breach of contract counts (Count I), are hereby dismissed, as is the RICO allegation under 18 U.S.C. § 1962(c). In all other respects, however, the motions to dismiss are hereby denied.

IT IS SO ORDERED.

_____

U. S. DISTRICT JUDGE

---

[72] The motions to dismiss the RICO counts of the _____, _____, and _____ complaints (case nos. _____, _____ and _____) do not include the statute of limitations argument.

CHAPTER 3

CIVIL RICO AND GRAY MARKET DIVERSION

John C. Fricano

§ 3.1   Gray Market Diversion

For years, domestic manufacturers have struggled against the unlawful "diversion" of their merchandise into the so-called gray market. Traditionally, this fight has entailed litigation brought under the federal trademark and customs laws, state law concerning breach of contract, unfair competition, and fraud, and, more recently, the Racketeer Influenced and Corrupt Organizations Act (RICO).[1] Experience teaches that the private right of action under RICO, for reasons that include but by no means are limited to its controversial treble damages remedy, is an essential weapon for domestic consumer products manufacturers to redress and deter gray market activities.

The gray market, or diversion industry, which has been described as "operat[ing] at (or outside) the fringes of legality,"[2] is sustained by legitimate products that are produced domestically and intended for sale in foreign markets, but then improperly resold in this country, or manufactured abroad for consumption outside the United States but exported to this country. In either case, the diversion occurs without the knowledge or consent of the U.S. manufacturer or trademark holder.[3] In both cases the diverter engages in arbitrage by purchasing products in (or intended for) a market where wholesales prices are lower, and reselling them in a market where prices are higher.[4] This price differential is the key factor that makes diversion not just economically feasible but irresistibly profitable. For example, when prices are lower abroad, a distributor can purchase genuine products overseas, pay to ship them into the United States, and still undercut its U.S. competition by offering the diverted merchandise at 20 to 40 percent below prices offered by authorized U.S. distributors. Manufacturers of such goods find themselves in the untenable position of having to compete with, and lose sales to, their own trademarked goods as well as those produced by their foreign subsidiaries or licensees.

The economic impact of the gray market on the profitability of U.S. manufacturers is substantial. The diverter's profits are the legitimate manufacturer's loss. It is estimated that the annual domestic sales of goods sold through the gray market amount to more than $7 billion. The merchandise involved includes diverse products ranging from fragrances and

---

[1] 18 U.S.C. §§ 1961–1968 (1988).

[2] Osawa & Co. v. B&H Photo, 589 F. Supp. 1163, 1170 (S.D.N.Y. 1984).

[3] Miller, *Black Times for Gray Market,* Wash. Post, Dec. 14, 1987, at D5, col. 1; *see* Fricano, *Blackening of the Gray Market,* 2 RICO L. Rep. 533 (RICO L. Rep. Inc.) (Nov. 1985).

[4] *See* W. Goebel Porzellanfabrik v. Action Indus., Inc., 589 F. Supp. 763, 764 n.1 (S.D.N.Y. 1984).

pharmaceuticals to champagne, cameras, textiles and watches.[5] The gray market pervades the entire U.S. economy; virtually all retail buyers, indeed anyone who has purchased goods at a flea market, sidewalk vendor, or so-called discount stores such as 47th Street Photo,[6] have been exposed to gray market goods.

The trade in diverted merchandise not only injures domestic manufacturers but may pose a threat to the health and well-being of the American consumer. Diverters frequently destroy the distributor codes and batch codes on product labels. If a consumer suffers an adverse reaction to a diverted health and beauty aid, fragrance, or pharmaceutical product, the manufacturer cannot trace the batch to remove the potentially harmful merchandise from the market.[7]

In response to the rampant and unsafe practice of diverting pharmaceutical products,[8] Congress passed the Prescription Drug Marketing Act of 1987,[9] which amended the Federal Food, Drug and Cosmetic Act to ban the reimportation of drugs produced in the United States, and to place certain restrictions on the distribution of drug samples. Diversion also is said to threaten American jobs by displacing sales of domestically produced goods with gray market items manufactured abroad.[10]

Nevertheless, diversion is not, in and of itself, illegal.[11] Thus the victimized manufacturer that seeks to be compensated for its losses must articulate a claim under one of a number of recognized legal theories involving the laws of trademarks, breach of contract, or fraud. If the fraud involved is sufficiently persistent and far-reaching, the aggrieved manufacturer can invoke the private cause of action for treble damages and attorneys' fees and costs provided for under RICO.[12]

---

[5] *See* Miller, *Black Times for Gray Market,* Wash. Post, Dec. 14, 1987, at D5, col. 1; Feder, *Gray Market Grew With Rise of Dollar,* N.Y. Times, Dec. 9, 1986, at D4, col. 2; Westerman, *The $7 Billion Gray Market: Where It Stops, Nobody Knows,* Bus. Wk., Apr. 15, 1985, at 86; Wilson, *Hair-Raising Tales: Dirty Tricks, Intrigue Flood Shampoo Wars,* Crain's Detroit Bus., Mar. 26, 1990, § 1 at 1; Fricano, *Blackening of the Gray Market,* 2 RICO L. Rep. 533 (RICO L. Rep. Inc.) (Nov. 1985). *See also* Fieldcrest Mills, Inc. v. Congo Agencies, Inc., slip op. No. 85-305(D) (D.N.J., Apr. 8, 1985).

[6] *See, e.g.,* Vivitar Corp. v. United States, 593 F. Supp. 420 (Ct. Int'l Trade 1984), *aff'd,* 761 F.2d 1552 (Fed. Cir. 1985), *cert. denied,* 474 U.S. 1055 (1986).

[7] *See* Wilson, *Hair-Raising Tales: Dirty Tricks, Intrigue Flood Shampoo Wars,* Crain's Detroit Bus., Mar. 26, 1990, § 1 at 1.

[8] *See, e.g.,* Kilman, *U.S. Charges 3 Concerns and 43 People with Illegal Trading in Discount Drugs,* Wall St. J., Aug. 7, 1985, at 8, col. 1.

[9] Pub. L. No. 100-293, 102 Stat. 95 (1988).

[10] *Bill to Curb Gray Market Imports Debated at Hearing by Senate Judiciary Subcommittee,* Int'l Trade Rep., Apr. 18, 1990, at 551.

[11] *See* United States v. Weinstein, 762 F.2d 1522, 1527 (11th Cir. 1985), *cert. denied,* 475 U.S. 1110 (1986).

[12] 18 U.S.C. § 1964(c) (1988).

§ 3.2   RICO's Importance in Combatting Diversion

Although it is certainly true that a valid RICO claim may intimidate a defendant, and thus precipitate a quick settlement before substantial sums are spent on pre-trial discovery, there are significant substantive reasons for utilizing the statute. The diversion plaintiff who raises a legitimate RICO claim can, wholly apart from stating a claim for treble damages, dispositively alter the dynamics of the case in its favor.

First, and perhaps foremost, in a diversion case RICO often furnishes the injured manufacturer's sole access to federal court. In recent years the courts have limited the utility of the customs and trademark laws against gray market profiteers. For example, § 526 of the Tariff Act of 1930[13] prohibits the importation into the United States of foreign-made goods bearing a trademark owned by a U.S. markholder, without the written consent of that holder. Notwithstanding this straightforward statutory prohibition, the Supreme Court recently ruled, in *K Mart Corp. v. Cartier, Inc.,* that the U.S. Customs Service is not required to intercept such goods as they cross U.S. frontiers.[14] In effect, the Supreme Court shifted to U.S. trademark holders the burden of enforcing § 526's prohibition against the importation of such gray market goods. Compounding the difficulties for domestic manufacturers, the Third Circuit Court of Appeals recently concluded, in *Weil Ceramics & Glass, Inc. v. Dash,* that under the reasoning of *K Mart,* not even private parties can sue under the Tariff Act to bar the importation of these diverted products.[15] If the holding in *Weil* finds favor in other federal circuit courts, the Tariff Act could cease to be an effective shield against the importation of diverted merchandise.

Recent judicial decisions will frustrate as well the efforts of manufacturers who have tried to curb gray market imports by resort to § 32(1)(a) of the Lanham Act,[16] which provides the registered owner of a trademark with a cause of action against anyone who, without consent, uses a "reproduction, counterfeit, copy or colorable imitation" of the mark in such a way as "is likely to cause confusion, or to cause mistake, or to deceive."[17] Domestic manufacturers have sought to invoke the Lanham Act against

---

[13] 19 U.S.C. § 1526 (1988).

[14] 486 U.S. 281, 291 (1988). Justice Kennedy authored a plurality opinion, joined by Justice White, upholding a Customs Service regulation, known as the *common control exception,* 19 C.F.R. § 133.21(c)(1)–(2) (1987), whereunder the Customs Service permits the importation of foreign-manufactured goods bearing trademarks held by domestic companies, if the domestic and foreign manufacturers are part of the same corporate family. *Id.* at 289. Justice Brennan, joined by Justices Marshall and Stevens, filed an opinion concurring in that judgment. *Id.* at 295–96.

[15] 878 F.2d 659, 666 (3d Cir.), *cert. denied,* 110 S. Ct. 156 (1989).

[16] 15 U.S.C. § 1114(1)(a) (1988).

[17] *Id.*

the unauthorized importation of gray market merchandise bearing foreign trademarks that are valid abroad but identical to trademarks controlled in this country by the U.S. manufacturers. Yet two United States courts of appeals recently concluded that domestic markholders have no basis to complain about importation of such products as infringing upon their trademarks unless material differences exist between the foreign-made product and those produced in the United States.[18] The domestic manufacturer also may have to prove that the foreign manufacturer's right to use the trademark is territorially restricted in order to prohibit sale of the foreign-manufactured merchandise in the United States.[19]

Of course, if the domestic manufacturer sells its products to a distributor, intending that they be exported, but the distributor never, in fact, ships the goods out of the country, no cause of action under the trademark or customs laws lies at all. In such cases, the victim must seek another route of access if it wishes to have its claims heard in federal court, where cases and controversies generally can be litigated more swiftly than in many state courts.

Diversion frequently involves breach of contract and common-law fraud, but absent diversity of citizenship between the parties a diversion plaintiff cannot litigate such claims before a federal court. Breach of contract and fraud claims do not provide a statutory basis for injunctive relief, as does the Lanham Act, for example.[20] On the other hand, RICO affords the diversion victim both a federal forum and the possibility of winning the injunctive relief[21] that is often essential to prevent diverters from repeating their transgressions in the future. Therefore, when a U.S. manufacturer discovers that it has been defrauded by one or more gray marketeers, it should consider whether the fraud, by virtue of its scope and duration, gives rise to a valid cause of action under RICO.

Of course, against the advantages of utilizing RICO, the injured manufacturer should weigh the disadvantages of invoking the statute. The burgeoning number of RICO cases in recent years and the perception that most do not promote the explicit purpose of the statute, to stamp out organized crime, have engendered a great deal of judicial hostility toward RICO. For example, many federal district courts and individual judges

---

[18] Lever Bros. Co. v. United States, 877 F.2d 101, 111 (D.C. Cir. 1989); Original Appalachian Artworks Inc. v. Granada Elec. Inc., 816 F.2d 68, 72–73 (2d Cir.), *cert. denied,* 484 U.S. 847 (1987).

[19] *See* Original Appalachian Artworks, Inc. v. Granada Elec. Inc., 816 F.2d 68, 73.

[20] 15 U.S.C. § 1116(a) (1980).

[21] *See, e.g.,* Chambers Dev. Co. v. Browning-Ferris Indus., 590 F. Supp. 1528, 1540 (W.D. Pa. 1984). *But see, e.g., In re* Fredeman Litig., 843 F.2d 821, 828 (5th Cir. 1988). In addition, injunctive relief may be available under state anti-racketeering ("little RICO") statutes. *See, e.g.,* N.J. Rev. Stat. § 2C:41-1 *et seq.* (1987).

have instituted standing orders that require RICO plaintiffs to state with exceeding particularity the facts and circumstances that justify their claims. Failure by a RICO plaintiff to satisfy the requirements of a RICO standing order can result in the dismissal of its claim.

§ 3.3 —Access to Federal Court

Two cases from the author's experience illustrate the utility of RICO to diversion victims seeking to litigate their claims in a federal forum. Shulton, Inc., an international manufacturer of such well known health and beauty aid products as OLD SPICE,® BRECK,® PIERRE CARDIN,® and LADY'S CHOICE® personal care products, was plagued by the illegal diversion of its products by foreign and domestic distributors. Consequently, Shulton began relentlessly to pursue suspected diverters in the federal courts. In *Shulton, Inc. v. René Garcia,*[22] the company sold almost $450,000 worth of OLD SPICE® products at a discounted "export price," significantly lower than its regular domestic wholesale price, because the distributor in question represented that the OLD SPICE® merchandise would be sold exclusively at commissaries operated by the Dominican Republic National Police. Shulton later discovered, however, that the merchandise was never shipped overseas but instead had been resold to a United States distributor. Shulton also uncovered evidence that its customer had been acting on behalf of and in collusion with the U.S. wholesaler to obtain the Shulton merchandise at a fraudulently induced discount price.

In *Shulton, Inc. v. Associated Marketing Systems, Inc.,*[23] the defendants did not approach Shulton seeking "export priced" merchandise purportedly to be shipped overseas, but, in a variation upon the usual theme, represented that they sought discount-priced merchandise to be included in their "Travel Pack" promotional program. Travel Pack purported to offer consumers the opportunity to sample a variety of discounted toiletry products packaged in a canvas tote-bag, called a Travel Pack. The prospect of gaining product exposure through this unusual type of promotional sampling convinced Shulton to sell BRECK® and LADY'S CHOICE® products to the defendants at discounts substantially below the prices charged to regular domestic distributors. Eventually, Shulton uncovered evidence that the defendants did not distribute, and never intended to distribute, Shulton's products through the Travel Pack program, but instead resold the Shulton merchandise at a substantial profit to domestic wholesalers.

---

[22] No. 86-2135-Civ-HASTINGS (S.D. Fla. 1986).

[23] No. 87-3412 (HAA) (D.N.J. 1987) (hereinafter *A.M.S.*).

In both *René Garcia* and *A.M.S.*, because the goods in question were legitimate, purchased domestically, and never exported or reimported, Shulton could count on neither the Lanham Act nor the Tariff Act for relief. But the defendants in both cases made repeated written and oral representations through the U.S. mails and interstate telephone wires that the merchandise would not be sold in the United States wholesale market. Shulton had evidence in both cases that the defendants' representations were fraudulent. Thus, it was in a position to assert that the defendants had violated RICO by engaging in "pattern[s] of racketeering activity"[24] predicated principally upon the mail and wire fraud statutes.[25] These cases were brought in federal court for damages, and injunctions also were sought to prohibit the defendants from trafficking Shulton merchandise in the gray market. Both cases accomplished Shulton's objectives when no federal cause of action other than RICO was available for prosecution.

§ 3.4   Extraterritorial Reach of RICO

RICO should not be cast, however, as a mere stand-in for federal trademark remedies. RICO's inherent advantages in a diversion case are many. For instance, while stating a cognizable claim under the trademark and customs statutes is becoming increasingly difficult, in certain respects RICO's scope actually is expanding. The United States Court of Appeals for the Eleventh Circuit ruled in 1990 that a RICO plaintiff may obtain service of process outside the U.S. against foreign RICO defendants.[26] This development, which was anticipated in 1985,[27] is especially significant for diversion plaintiffs, particularly as world markets continue to expand. Frequently the miscreant in a diversion case is a wholesale distributor based outside the United States who purchased the diverted merchandise

---

[24] 18 U.S.C. § 1961(5) (1988). RICO proscribes, inter alia, the conduct of the affairs of a business enterprise engaged in or affecting interstate commerce through a pattern of racketeering activity. *See* 18 U.S.C. § 1962.

[25] 18 U.S.C. § 1341 (1990) (mail fraud); 18 U.S.C. § 1343 (1990) (wire fraud). In essence, mail fraud consists of the following elements: a scheme or artifice to defraud, or the obtaining of money or property by means of false or fraudulent pretenses, representations, or promises; the use of the mails, for purposes of furthering or executing the scheme or artifice; and the defendant must be associated with the scheme or artifice and must have used or caused the use of the mails. The elements of wire fraud are analogous to mail fraud, except that use of the wires must be interstate or foreign in character. Mail and wire fraud are defined as racketeering acts under RICO. 18 U.S.C. § 1961(1)(B) (1990).

[26] Brink's Mat Ltd. v. Diamond, 906 F.2d 1519, 1522–23 (11th Cir. 1990).

[27] *See* Fricano, *Extraterritorial Reach of RICO to International Transactions: Just A Matter Of Time?*, Int'l Bus. Law., May 1985, at 201.

(under fraudulent circumstances) from the domestic manufacturer's foreign subsidiary or licensee. The Eleventh Circuit's ruling means that a diversion plaintiff need not forego the advantages of a RICO claim in order to make foreign diverters amenable to suit in the United States.[28]

§ 3.5   Criminal Nature of RICO Claims

A further advantage to the prosecution of a RICO claim is that the plaintiff, whose goal is to prove that the diverter was engaged in a pattern of racketeering activity, seeks to uncover evidence implicating the suspected diverter in the commission of federal crimes. In diversion cases the diverter's activities may also constitute violations of the federal food and drug laws. This state of affairs can enure to the RICO plaintiff's benefit, as the author learned when prosecuting a RICO case against a company known as Military Exchange BO, Inc.

The case against Military Exchange demonstrated the lengths to which greedy and unethical persons will go in pursuit of a quick profit. Through the commission of numerous illegal acts, including bribery, counterfeiting, and fraud, Military Exchange, its principals, and co-conspirators unlawfully diverted 58,000 vials of an advanced prescription antibiotic which had been intended by the manufacturer for sale in Central America. After acquiring the pharmaceutical on the basis of false and fraudulent misrepresentations as to the medicine's ultimate destination, Military Exchange stripped off the Spanish-language labels on the vials and replaced them with illegal, forged English labels. These false labels bore fabricated control numbers and expiration dates, which could have led to the consumption of expired product and would have made it impossible to trace the vials in the event of a recall. To make matters worse, the original labels were soaked off by immersing the bottles in warm, soapy water, possibly compromising the sterility of the contents. And although it was never determined whether the defendants stored the antibiotics under the temperature-controlled conditions necessary to prevent tainting of the product, that possibility increased the risk to the public of the defendants' activities. The defendants sold the misbranded drugs for a substantial profit to known United States wholesalers of diverted pharmaceuticals, for ultimate consumption by an unsuspecting American public.

The plaintiff established these facts, in the context of a RICO violation, on a motion for summary judgment brought after the defendant's president

---

[28] The ruling in Brink's Mat Ltd. v. Diamond, 906 F.2d 1519, however, does not expand the power of a federal court to enforce a RICO judgment against a foreign defendant. If the defendant has no assets in the United States from which to satisfy a judgment, problems in collecting a damages award are presented. *See* Fricano, *Extraterritorial Reach of RICO to International Transactions,* Int'l Bus. Law., May 1985, at 206.

asserted his Fifth Amendment rights at his deposition. He feared, and correctly so, that his activities also constituted a criminal violation of the food and drug laws. Consequently, he "took the Fifth" with respect to each and every allegation in the complaint and announced that he would do so again at trial. He further stated that at trial he planned to offer no exhibits or witnesses, nor would he take the stand in his own defense.

This strategy precluded him and his company from contesting the facts, which were supported by substantial circumstantial evidence. In fact, his invocation of the Fifth Amendment itself constituted further evidence of the facts alleged against him.[29] As a result, when the plaintiff moved for summary judgment, its motion essentially was unchallenged, and it was awarded a judgment equivalent to three times its damages plus its attorneys' fees and costs, without having to proceed to trial.

§ 3.6   The Importance of Investigating Before Filing

As the case against Military Exchange demonstrates, the battle against diversion also can be a matter of public, as well as private, interest. Congress created the civil cause of action under RICO so that private litigants might act as "private attorneys general" in the war against organized crime.[30] On the basis of a well-founded RICO complaint, a plaintiff can benefit from the public interest aspects of its case. This point is vividly illustrated by one of the most protracted and hotly contested RICO cases the author has ever litigated, *Shulton, Inc. v. Optel Corp.*[31] This case demonstrates many of the problems that diversion poses for a manufacturer and how they can be dealt with in the context of a RICO suit.

Shulton filed its 23-count complaint in the *Optel* case after discovering a diversion conspiracy so elaborate in its conception and brazen in its execution that Shulton resolved to send a loud and clear message to the entire diversion industry that those who defraud it will be prosecuted to the fullest extent of the law. To accomplish that goal, Shulton turned to RICO.

The *Optel* complaint portrayed a highly organized, sophisticated, and well-financed scheme to commit fraud, beginning some time in 1979 and continuing for almost four years thereafter. Shulton determined that the goal of this fraudulent scheme was to induce it to sell health, beauty aid, and fragrance products (including OLD SPICE,® GEOFFREY BEENE,® NINA RICCI,® PIERRE CARDIN,® BRECK,® and LADY'S CHOICE®)

---

[29] *See* Baxter v. Palmigiano, 425 U.S. 308, 318–19 (1976).

[30] *Hearings on S. 30 Before Subcomm. No. 5 of the House Comm. on the Judiciary,* 91st Cong., 2d Sess. 520 (1970).

[31] No. 85-2925 (NHP) (D.N.J. 1985).

to the defendants at highly reduced prices. At the heart of the scheme was a front company which represented to Shulton that the merchandise sought would be exported to and distributed solely in Central and South America and the Caribbean Basin. Only later, after selling millions of dollars' worth of merchandise to this company and its affiliates at highly reduced "export only" prices, did Shulton discover that most of that merchandise had not been shipped overseas but sold to four of the largest and best known consumer products wholesalers in the secondary, or gray, market, who then resold it in the domestic market at prices lower than the prices charged by Shulton's legitimate wholesale distributors. The complaint alleged that the diversion occurred pursuant to a preconceived plan between the front and the four wholesalers in question, dubbing the latter as the "diverter defendants."

Shulton alleged that as a necessary part of this scheme, to ensure its concealment and success, the front bribed at least two Shulton employees to authorize the sale of the goods at the lower export price, and to arrange for their shipment directly to warehouses maintained by the diverter defendants. The implementation of the scheme as alleged involved numerous violations of six separate federal statutes and state criminal laws: the mail and wire fraud statutes, the National Stolen Property Act,[32] the Travel Act,[33] and state law prohibitions against commercial bribery.[34] The complexity of the scheme gave rise to 23 causes of action, 18 of which were pleaded under the federal and New Jersey RICO statutes.[35] See §§ 3.15 through 3.23.

Before leveling these serious allegations, Shulton first conducted an extensive investigation which enabled it to understand the machinations, scope, and duration of this criminal activity. By the time the case was filed, Shulton had already amassed persuasive evidence of the diverter defendants' complicity in the fraud. This evidence demonstrated, among

---

[32] 18 U.S.C. §§ 2314, 2315 (1990). The National Stolen Property Act prohibits the interstate transportation, sale, or storage of fraudulently obtained or unlawfully converted goods. In diversion cases violations of the statute usually, if not always, can be pleaded as predicate acts. Thus, the diversion plaintiff need not base its RICO claims, as many RICO plaintiffs do, exclusively upon violations of the federal mail and wire fraud statutes.

[33] 18 U.S.C. § 1952 (1990). The Travel Act prohibits travel in interstate commerce for the purpose of committing or promoting unlawful activity.

[34] Under RICO, "racketeering activity" also includes "any act . . . [of] bribery . . . which is chargeable under State law and punishable by imprisonment for more than one year." 18 U.S.C. § 1961(1)(A) (1990).

[35] The New Jersey Anti-Racketeering Act, N.J. Rev. Stat. § 2C:41-1 et seq. (1987), was patterned after RICO (see Curley v. Cumberland Farms Dairy, Inc., 728 F. Supp. 1123, 1138 (D.N.J. 1989)) and is construed in pari materia with the federal act. Shulton, Inc. v. Optel Corp., No. 85-2925 (NHP) (D.N.J. Sept. 29, 1986), slip op. at 46–47, 4 RICO L. Rep. 800 (RICO L. Rep. Inc.) (Nov. 1986).

other things, that the diverter defendants had financed the front's purchases of the merchandise by providing "up front" money and secretly guaranteeing "blind" letters of credit later used by the front to purchase the goods on credit. They also falsified bills of lading to disguise the fact that the products purchased by the front had been transported to the diverter defendants' warehouses, rather than overseas. Through its investigation, Shulton also learned that truckers in the diverter defendants' employ assumed false identities to enter Shulton's premises in Clifton, New Jersey to pick up the merchandise sold to the front.

Other manufacturers who consider bringing RICO claims against diverters might well be advised to follow Shulton's example, in order to avoid the perceived judicial hostility to RICO ascribed to plaintiffs who file bare-bones complaints lacking in those facts necessary to support charges of racketeering. Shulton's decision to develop its case fully, prior to levying such charges, proved crucial to establishing its credentials before the court as the sort of plaintiff that RICO was intended to recruit in the war against organized crime.

§ 3.7   —Alleging Fraud with Particularity

The defendants moved, of course, to dismiss Shulton's complaint, and the diverter defendants unanimously asserted that Shulton had failed to set forth its allegations of their participation in the fraud with the particularity required by Rule 9(b) of the Federal Rules of Civil Procedure.[36] Specifically, they asserted that the complaint did not set forth facts from which it could be inferred that they were knowledgeable participants in the diversion scheme, rather than merely innocent purchasers of the goods diverted by the front. On that basis they argued that the court should not permit such serious accusations of racketeering and fraud to be levied against them. United States District Judge H. Lee Sarokin, to whom the case originally was assigned, appreciated their concern and stated that had such facts been absent from the complaint, he would have dismissed the allegations against the diverter defendants. Shulton had pleaded, however, the specific facts discovered in its investigation concerning the diverter defendants' financing of the front's purchases, the falsified shipping documents, and the entry upon Shulton's premises under false pretenses. Judge Sarokin ruled that these allegations, if proven, would support an inference that the diverter defendants had been accomplices in the fraud.

---

[36] Fed. R. Civ. P. 9(b) provides that "[i]n all averments of fraud or mistake, the circumstances constituting fraud or mistake shall be stated with particularity. Malice, intent, knowledge, and other condition of mind of a person may be averred generally."

He declined, therefore, to dismiss the allegations of fraud against the diverter defendants.

Thus, had Shulton not undertaken its multi-year investigation of the defendants' diversion scheme, it could not have pleaded sufficient facts to address Judge Sarokin's concerns, and the allegations of fraud on which its RICO claims depended (see § **3.14**) may have been dismissed. But because Shulton had thoroughly investigated the circumstances of the fraud, it was able to plead the specific facts indicating that the diverter defendants were culpable participants in the scheme. Shulton not only preserved the right to pursue its RICO claims, but also accomplished the subtle, but no less crucial, objective of demonstrating to the court that this was not a case of "garden variety fraud"[37] but a pervasive, clandestine, highly organized, and criminally conceived and executed conspiracy against which charges of racketeering legitimately had been raised.

Because the diverter defendants failed both to dismiss or discredit Shulton's RICO claims, it seemed they would have to face up to the fact that those allegations, if proven, would expose them as racketeers and saddle them with a judgment for treble damages and fees in the millions of dollars. Instead, however, they seized upon Shulton's investigation of the fraud as a means of "beating the rap."

§ 3.8   Protecting Investigative Files from Discovery

During the initial stages of discovery the defendants learned that Shulton's investigation of the diversion began in 1981, when its senior management became concerned that a substantial amount of Shulton export merchandise was being diverted into the United States wholesale market. The company's internal investigators were directed to find out which customers, if any, were guilty of diverting. The company's law department was directed to oversee and supervise the investigation. When the investigation was first launched, however, the front successfully diverted suspicion from itself by submitting falsified shipping documents purporting to show that the products sold to it actually had been shipped overseas. In addition, Shulton's export manager, who allegedly had been bribed by the front to assist in the concealment of the fraud, exploited his position of trust to vouch for the front's integrity. It was not until September 1982, when the front defaulted on a letter of credit payment for over $350,000, that Shulton learned from the issuing bank that the front had received undisclosed financial backing from the diverter defendants.

---

[37] Parnes v. Heinold Commodities, Inc., 548 F. Supp. 20, 22–23 (N.D. Ill. 1982) ("Litigators, never at a loss for ingenuity, naturally [find] the prospect of treble damages under [RICO] very inviting for garden-variety fraud claims.").

In deposition discovery, the defendants also learned that in 1983 the United States Attorney's Office in Newark, New Jersey had been conducting a grand jury investigation into the front's activities, specifically the payment of bribes and kickbacks to Shulton's employees. Pursuant to the United States attorney's request, Shulton shared with the government the evidence of fraud and bribery that it had uncovered by providing access to the investigative files that it had compiled to date.

Because Shulton had authorized continued sales to its "export" customers, including the front, until its investigators determined that the front was the customer responsible for the diversion, the defendants became convinced that Shulton actually had been aware of and tacitly approved of the diversion. Accordingly, they demanded that the investigators' files be disclosed to them. Shulton refused, of course. The files contained the investigators' contemporaneous notes of confidential interviews with Shulton personnel and numerous third parties regarding the implementation of the defendants' scheme. These notes also reflected the investigators' personal observations, theories, and conclusions about the fraud as the investigation proceeded. Shulton contended that the contents of the files were protected from discovery by the attorney-client privilege[38] and the work product doctrine.[39]

Apart from the fact that Shulton understandably believed it to be unfair to turn over to its adversaries the fruits of its investigation, which had been a time-consuming and expensive undertaking, it argued that it would have been contrary to the public policy underlying RICO's private cause of action. The point of civil RICO is to supplement the prosecutorial resources of the government.[40] Yet if the factual inquiries that potential RICO plaintiffs must conduct to expose "patterns of racketeering activity" (and thus give effect to the statute's purposes) are to be turned against them, then many such private parties may choose to forego the costs of invoking RICO in favor of more modest remedies.

The defendants moved to compel the production of Shulton's investigative files in July, 1987 before federal Magistrate Ronald J. Hedges,

[38] The attorney-client privilege absolutely bars from compelled disclosure the confidential communications between an attorney and his client. *See, e.g.,* Diversified Indus., Inc. v. Meredith, 572 F.2d 596 (8th Cir. 1977).

[39] Documents and other tangible things prepared in anticipation of litigation or for trial by or for a party are commonly referred to as *work product. See, e.g.,* Upjohn Co. v. United States, 449 U.S. 383, 401 (1981). Under Rule 26(b)(3) of the Fed. R. Civ. P., an opposing party may obtain discovery of a party's work product only upon a showing that the party seeking such discovery has substantial need of the materials in the preparation of its own case and is unable without undue hardship to obtain the substantial equivalent of the materials sought by other means.

[40] *See* S. Rep. No. 617, 91st Cong., 1st Sess. 81 (1969); H.R. Rep. No. 1549, 91st Cong., 2d Sess. 56–60, *reprinted in* 1970 U.S. Code Cong. & Admin. News 400007-91. *See also* Sedima, S.P.R.L. v. Imrex Co., 473 U.S. 479, 486–88 (1985).

claiming that Shulton sold merchandise to the front knowing that it would be resold in the domestic market, and accusing the company of asserting the attorney-client privilege and the work product protection to conceal that "fact." Relying on this "cover-up" theory, the defendants argued that they had "substantial need" for Shulton's investigative files that justified compelling their disclosure. What the defendants chose to ignore, however, was that the files had been turned over to the United States attorney, and the facts contained in the file had been disclosed to the defendants in Shulton's answers to their interrogatories and in deposition testimony. Defendants also argued that the disclosure to the government constituted a waiver of the attorney-client privilege and work product protection attaching to the contents of the investigative files, making them discoverable even absent a showing of substantial need.

Magistrate Hedges, recognizing the importance of this matter to both sides, decided to review each of the thousands of pages of documents in the investigative files. After completing his in camera review, he agreed that the files reflected both attorney-client communications and the mental impressions, strategies, and theories of Shulton's law department, matters which normally are shielded from discovery. Having said as much, however, Judge Hedges ruled that the disclosure of the investigative files to the United States attorney effected a waiver not only of Shulton's attorney-client privilege, which Shulton fully anticipated,[41] but also a waiver of Shulton's work product protection. The bottom line was that all of Shulton's investigative files would have to be disclosed to its opponents.

§ 3.9   —Work Product Protection

Magistrate Hedges recognized that the issue of waiver was a complex one, and encouraged Shulton to appeal to Judge Sarokin to review his findings. The defendants severely sharpened their rhetoric on the appeal, attacking the lawsuit itself as part of the "cover-up," which they no longer treated as a matter of speculation but as an established fact. Again they denigrated Shulton's desire to preserve the confidential status of its investigative files as a ploy to conceal its own involvement in the diversion. They continued to assert that Shulton had waived its work product protection when it disclosed the files to the United States attorney.

Once again, Shulton argued that it could not have been engaged in a cover-up when it disclosed the investigative files and the information contained in those files both to federal law enforcement officials and the

---

[41] Because the attorney-client privilege exists to assure the client that any statements he makes when seeking legal advice will be kept strictly confidential between the client and the attorney, any voluntary disclosure by the client of such statements is deemed inconsistent with the confidentiality of the relationship and thus waives the privilege. United States v. AT&T, 642 F.2d 1285, 1299 (D.C. Cir. 1980).

defendants. But the waiver issue would not be brushed aside with ease. There was authority to support the magistrate's ruling that the disclosure to the U.S. attorney waived the work product protection attaching to the investigative files.[42] On the other hand, the seminal decision of the D.C. Circuit in *United States v. AT&T*[43] supported Shulton's position that no waiver had occurred because the disclosure to the United States attorney had not resulted, nor was ever likely to result, in the files' being made available to the defendants.[44] Shulton's task was to persuade Judge Sarokin that the rule of waiver set out in *AT&T* was the correct one.

Shulton did so by directing Judge Sarokin's attention to the public policy implications of the question before him. Shulton noted that the rule of work product waiver adopted by the magistrate could have a chilling effect on future cooperation with federal authorities by private citizens who have civil causes of action against the subjects of criminal investigations. The knowledge that work product materials, otherwise protected from disclosure, will be turned over to a party opponent in civil litigation as a result of rendering such assistance could only serve to inhibit such cooperation. This result, Shulton observed, could not be reconciled with the strong public policy encouraging cooperation between private citizens and government investigators.[45]

In a published opinion dated November 4, 1987,[46] Judge Sarokin reversed Magistrate Hedges' ruling as to waiver of the work product protection, adopting the less stringent rule of waiver set forth in *AT&T*. Applying this standard to the facts before him, he could "imagine no set of circumstances stemming from the disclosure [to the United States attorney] which would have made revelation of the contents of the investigative file to defendants substantially more likely" than if they had not been so

---

[42] *E.g.*, D'Ippolito v. Cities Serv. Co., 39 F.R.D. 610 (S.D.N.Y. 1965).

[43] 642 F.2d 1285 (D.C. Cir. 1980).

[44] *AT&T* held that a party to litigation does not waive the work product protection by disclosing work product materials to a third party, unless the disclosure substantially increases the likelihood that the party's adversary in litigation will gain access to those materials. 642 F.2d at 1299. See § **3.8**.

[45] *See, e.g.*, United States v. Schuster, 717 F.2d 537, 539 (11th Cir. 1983), *cert. denied*, 465 U.S. 1010 (1984) ("there is a strong public policy in favor of encouraging cooperation with law enforcement authorities as a means of detecting, preventing and solving crime"); United States v. LaFatch, 565 F.2d 81, 84 (6th Cir. 1977), *cert. denied*, 435 U.S. 971 (1978) ("In these times of increasing white collar crime, private citizens should be encouraged to cooperate with law enforcement officers in thwarting attempts at bribery and extortion"); Shaw v. United States Dep't of State, 559 F. Supp. 1053, 1064 (D.D.C. 1983) ("Effective criminal law enforcement depends upon the government's ability to encourage the cooperation of private citizens and local law enforcement agencies").

[46] Shulton, Inc. v. Optel Corp., 56 U.S.L.W. 2307, 1987-1 Trade Cas. (CCH) ¶ 67,436 (D.N.J. Nov. 1987).

disclosed. On the whole, then, Judge Sarokin found "the chances that Shulton's sharing of its investigative file with the government would lead to defendants' discovery of the file's contents were exceedingly remote." Accordingly, he ruled that no waiver had occurred.

Furthermore, the court explicitly adopted Shulton's public policy argument as favoring the outcome he reached. He wrote that one should feel free to turn over to the government evidence of crimes, without fearing that doing so will result in confidential information's falling into the hands of one's adversary in a related or contemplated civil proceeding. A finding of waiver on the facts before him, he perceived, would work against the well-recognized public policy goal of encouraging private citizens to assist law enforcement officers in detecting and prosecuting violations of the law. This policy consideration may well have been the deciding factor because the issue was presented in the context of a RICO case. Because the purpose of civil RICO is in part to encourage private parties to enforce RICO against organized criminal activity, it would not be sound policy to discourage such a party from cooperating with the forces of government also investigating the same perpetrators.

Having rejected the defendants' assertion of waiver, Judge Sarokin ruled that they would have to show substantial need for the investigative files before they could be permitted to review them. Before they could make such a showing, he observed, they would have to depose the Shulton employees and other witnesses interviewed during Shulton's investigation, and show them to be unavailable or uncooperative. And so the defendants resigned themselves to the task of deposing the present and former Shulton employees who had been interviewed in the course of Shulton's investigation. They did not undertake this task half-heartedly.

Over the next 18 months the defendants deposed more than 20 Shulton employees, officers, and agents knowledgeable about the facts and circumstances surrounding Shulton's allegations of fraud. Shulton's lead investigator was deposed for seven day-long sessions over the course of several months. Additional Shulton employees and third-party witnesses were deposed, over Shulton's objections, for multiple sessions. Each was subjected to arduous and prolix cross-examination. Without exception, however, these witnesses confirmed, in detail after detail, what was for the defendants the unfortunate truth, that Shulton was not a knowing participant in but rather the unhappy victim of the fraud that had been perpetrated against it.

§ 3.10 Determining Damages

By the summer of 1988, after discovery had proceeded rancorously and exhaustingly for almost two years, the defendants finally appeared ready to come to grips with the substantial record evidence supporting Shulton's

RICO claims, and sought to settle the case. Not surprisingly, the primary impediment to settlement was the matter of calculating Shulton's damages. Defendants maintained that Shulton's damages should be limited to the value of those legitimate profits it could prove it had actually lost as a result of the diversion. On the other hand, Shulton contended that it was entitled to the difference between the fraudulently obtained export price that was paid for the diverted goods and the contemporaneous domestic market price for those same products.

The disparity between the two measures of damages was immense, and the parties saw no room for compromise. The defendants suggested that the court decide this question in the context of a motion *in limine*. It is unclear whether this suggestion arose from the defendants' anxiety that the settlement talks might collapse over this issue or was yet another tactic to defeat Shulton's recovery on grounds not having to do with the merits of the fraud. In any event, United States District Judge Nicholas H. Politan, to whom the case by then had been reassigned, agreed to entertain such a motion, recognizing that the resolution of this issue could facilitate the settlement process. Judge Politan made clear, however, what was at stake. He told the parties that he would not render an advisory opinion. His decision would be binding and would establish the measure of damages that he would instruct the jury to apply at trial.

In their moving papers, the defendants argued that notwithstanding the fraud Shulton had realized a profit, albeit a reduced one, from its dealings with the front. Accordingly, the defendants maintained that Shulton only suffered a compensable loss to the extent that the sale in the U.S. of the diverted merchandise supplanted sales at the higher price Shulton charged for domestic goods. Thus, the defendants reasoned, Shulton could claim no more than the value of proven lost sales, less the profits realized in its transactions with the front. Shulton urged the court to apply in the diversion context the common law principle that when a buyer resorts to fraud to obtain property at less than its full value, the defrauded seller is entitled to recover the difference between the consideration he received and the contemporaneous market value, at the time of sale, of the property he conveyed.[47]

---

[47] 37 Am. Jur. 2D *Fraud and Deceit* § 371, at 503 (1968); *accord, e.g.,* Shapiro v. Midwest Rubber Reclaiming Co., 626 F.2d 63, 68 (8th Cir. 1980), *cert. denied,* 449 U.S. 1079 (1981); Alabama Farm Bureau Mut. Casualty Co. v. American Fidelity Life Ins. Co., 606 F.2d 602, 615 (5th Cir. 1979), *cert. denied,* 449 U.S. 820 (1980); Mitchell v. Texas Gulf Sulphur Co., 446 F.2d 90, 105–06 (10th Cir.), *cert. denied,* 404 U.S. 1004 (1971); Baumel v. Rosen, 412 F.2d 571, 575–76 (4th Cir. 1969), *cert. denied,* 396 U.S. 1037 (1970); Dellefield v. Blockdel Realty Co., 128 F.2d 85, 94 (2d Cir. 1942); Federal-American Nat'l Bank & Trust Co. v. McReynolds, 67 F.2d 251, 254 (D.C. Cir.), *cert. denied,* 290 U.S. 666 (1933); Ortho Pharmaceutical Corp. v. Sona Distribs., Inc., 663 F. Supp. 64 (S.D. Fla. 1987). *See also* Restatement (Second) of Torts § 549(1)(a) & comment c (1977); 37 C.J.S. *Fraud* § 143, at 745 (1943).

Victory for Shulton on the motion *in limine* was not a given. The defendants' theory of damages had substantial appeal from an economic viewpoint. And, as Judge Politan recognized in his opinion, the cases on point in the diversion context were few. Ultimately, as with the work product controversy, Shulton tipped the scales in its favor by directing the court's attention to the public policy implications involved. The difficulties of proof inherent in defendants' proposed rule of damages were manifest. To trace the course into the economy of merchandise diverted nearly 10 years in the past and then identify the actual sales lost to the diverted merchandise would have been phenomenally difficult, if not utterly impossible. The defendants' rule of damages constituted a veritable invitation to commit fraud, because the perpetrator, even if caught, could rely on the difficulties of proof of damages to evade liability for his wrongdoing. This result, Shulton noted, would be directly contrary to the principle that no measure of damages should be an inducement to wrongdoing, or preclude the injured party's recovery, by rendering the measure of damages uncertain.[48]

In his reported opinion,[49] Judge Politan adopted Shulton's measure of damages: the difference between the domestic market price and the fraud-induced export price paid by the front. Lacking substantial precedent to guide him, he steered a course in line with the public policy considerations that Shulton had raised. "If liability is proven at trial," he wrote, "defendant[s] should not be allowed to retain the profits of their fraudulent conduct."[50] The significance of this ruling cannot be overstated. Had Judge Politan ruled in the defendants' favor, he would have established a precedent greatly complicating and encumbering all diversion plaintiffs' proof of their damages; one diversion case after the next likely would scuttle on the question of damages, allowing the perpetrators to reap the benefits of their duplicity. Once again the very context in which the issue was presented helped sharpen the focus upon the public policy considerations, which proved to be the deciding factor in Shulton's favor. Shulton's lawsuit was in keeping with RICO's explicit purpose to encourage private parties to join the war against organized crime. A precedent encumbering the proof of damages in a diversion case would exert precisely the contrary incentive and could not be reconciled with Congress's intent in drafting the RICO statute.

---

[48] *See* Bigelow v. RKO Radio Pictures, Inc., 327 U.S. 251, 264–65 (1946); Story Parchment Co. v. Paterson Parchment Paper Co., 282 U.S. 555, 565 (1931) (citation omitted).

[49] Shulton, Inc. v. Optel Corp., 698 F. Supp. 61 (D.N.J. 1988).

[50] *Id.* at 64.

§ 3.11   RICO's Future in Diversion Cases

Prior to the court's ruling on the motion *in limine*, Shulton already had in its possession evidence establishing beyond serious dispute that the defendants had engaged in a classic pattern of racketeering activity in order to commit fraud. The court's ruling greatly simplified the matter of Shulton's damages, the final element of its prima facie case against the defendants. On the eve of trial, Magistrate Hedges rejected the defendants' renewed motion to compel the production of Shulton's investigative file, finding that in the course of discovery they had learned all there was to learn about the investigation. He ruled that their failure to uncover any evidence to support their theory that Shulton had approved tacitly of the fraud committed against it did not entitle them to discovery of Shulton's work product. And so, as the trial deadline approached, both of the defendants' tactics for evading liability had been defeated. With little other choice, they agreed to a multi-million dollar settlement and consented to broad injunctive relief preventing them from dealing in the products of Shulton or its corporate parent. This outcome resulted largely because Shulton successfully relied on its public interest credentials as a "private attorney general" to persuade the court that Shulton's pursuit of its own interests served the public interest as well.

The discussion of these diversion cases is intended to demonstrate the advantages of RICO, other than its lucrative treble damages remedy, in the diversion context. *Shulton v. Optel,* hard-fought for almost four years, shows that while there are also costs to invoking RICO, the advantages can outweigh them. A diversion plaintiff who uses RICO temperately and carefully prepares his case before initiating litigation will be acknowledged by the court as an actor for the public interest, an asset that can be crucial to the successful prosecution of the plaintiff's claims.

There is some question as to how much longer private plaintiffs will be able to exploit the advantages of RICO. Congress persists in its efforts to develop a statutory remedy for the perceived abuse of the statute. Legislation recently considered by the House of Representatives would have limited the civil RICO remedy to cases that "clearly serve[ ] the public interest and provide[ ] appropriate deterrence against the repetition of egregious criminal conduct."[51] Notwithstanding any such restriction, if enacted, diversion plaintiffs still should find occasion to invoke the statute. The worst diverters rely every day on fraud and duplicity to ply their trade, and they frequently profit at the expense of the public's health and well-being. These diverters, therefore, should remain vulnerable to prosecution under civil RICO. Victims of diversion should take heart, and the perpetrators should take heed.

---

[51] H.R. 5111, 101st Cong., 2d Sess. (1990).

§ 3.12 RICO Complaint Alleging Fraudulent Diversion

Following is a complaint analogous to that filed in *Shulton v. Optel.* Its length indicates the importance of pleading RICO violations with particularity.

UNITED STATES DISTRICT COURT
DISTRICT OF NEW JERSEY

MARTIN, INC.,
a New Jersey corporation,
    Plaintiff,

    vs.

ACME CORPORATION, a Delaware corporation, RICHARD G. ROGERS, individually, WESLEY M. MUNSIN, individually; TOP NOTCH DISTRIBUTORS, INC., a New York corporation, EDWARD BYERS, individually; NATIONWIDE SUPPLY COMPANY, INC., a New York corporation, ADAM QUIN, individually; BAGGINS MERCHANDISING CORP., a New York corporation, HAROLD WINDOM, individually; BAT INDUSTRIES, LTD., a Florida corporation, MICHAEL NERESON, individually; GLOBAL SALES CORPORATION, a New York corporation; UNO INTERNACIONAL DE PANAMA, S.A., a Panama corporation; TEMPLE INTERNATIONAL CORPORATION, a Panama corporation; WORLD COSMETICS, INC., a Florida corporation; TEMPLE INTERNATIONAL CORPORATION, a Florida corporation, MANUEL D. GARCIA, a/k/a "BENITO DURAN," individually, ROBERTO JUAREZ, individually; FOREMOST FORWARDING CO., INC., a New York

CIVIL ACTION
NO. 85-2925

COMPLAINT AND
DEMAND FOR
JURY TRIAL

corporation, DARYL MONTERO,
individually; JUAN ZAPATA, individually;
MIGUEL CERVANTES, individually;
JOHN DOE CORPORATIONS I-X; and
JOHN DOES I-X, individually,
    Defendants.

Plaintiff, Martin, Inc., (Martin) for its complaint against the defendants, alleges, with knowledge respecting its own actions and upon information and belief respecting the actions of the defendants, as follows:

JURISDICTION AND VENUE

1.   This action is brought alleging violations of the Racketeer Influenced and Corrupt Organizations Act (RICO), 18 U.S.C. § 1961 *et seq.,* and the statutory and common law of the state of New Jersey. This Court has jurisdiction over this action by virtue of 18 U.S.C. § 1965(a) (RICO), 28 U.S.C. § 1331 (federal question), 28 U.S.C. § 1332 (diversity of citizenship), and general principles of pendent jurisdiction. The matter in controversy exceeds, exclusive of interest and costs, the sum of $10,000.00.

2.   Venue is predicated on 18 U.S.C. § 1965(a) and (b) and 28 U.S.C. § 1391(a) and (b).

SUMMARY OF THIS ACTION

The Defendants

3.   The corporations listed below are defendants in this action. Each is organized and exists under the laws of the state or country specified and has its principal place of business in the city indicated below:

Corporation	State or Country of Incorporation	Principal Place of Business
Acme Corporation (Acme)	Delaware	New Britain, Connecticut
Top Notch Distributors, Inc. (Top Notch)	New York	Deer Park, New York
Nationwide Supply Co., Inc. (Nationwide Supply)	New York	Westbury, New York
Baggins Merchandising Corp. (Baggins)	New York	Brooklyn, New York

Corporation	State or Country of Incorporation	Principal Place of Business
Bat Industries, Ltd. (Bat)	Florida	Miami, Florida
Global Sales Corporation (Global)	New York	New York, New York
Uno Internacional de Panama, S.A. (Uno)	Panama	Panama City, Panama
Temple International Corporation (Temple of Panama)	Panama	Panama City, Panama
World Cosmetics, Inc. (World)	Florida	Miami, Florida
Temple International Corporation (Temple of Florida)	Florida	Miami, Florida
Foremost Forwarding Co., Inc. (Foremost)	New York	New York, New York
John Doe Corporations I–X	Unknown	Unknown

4. The individuals listed below are defendants in this action. During all or part of the time covered by this action, each was associated with one or more of the defendant corporations in the capacity indicated below:

Individual	Capacity	Corporation
Richard G. Rogers (Rogers)	President and Chief Executive Officer	Acme
Wesley M. Munsin (Munsin)	Chairman of the Board	Acme
Edward Byers (Byers)	President and Chief Executive Officer	Top Notch
Adam Quin (Quin)	President and Chief Executive Officer	Nationwide Supply
Harold Windom (Windom)	Chief Executive Officer and Secretary/Treasurer	Baggins
Michael Nereson (Nereson)	President	Bat

Individual	Capacity	Corporation
Manuel D. Garcia, a/k/a Benito Duran (Garcia)	President and Director	Temple of Florida
	General Manager and part-owner	Temple of Panama
	Director and part-owner	Uno
	Part-owner	World
Roberto Juarez (Juarez)	Treasurer	World
	Treasurer	Temple of Florida
	Accountant	Temple of Panama
	Accountant	Uno
Daryl Montero (Montero)	President	Global
	President and Chairman of the Board	Foremost
Juan Zapata (Zapata)	Part-owner	Temple of Panama
	Part-owner	Global
Miguel Cervantes (Cervantes)	Part-owner	Temple of Panama
John Does I–X	Unknown	Unknown

5.   This is an action for permanent injunctive relief and for damages arising out of defendants' illegal and unlawful conspiracy to defraud Martin. Beginning as early as 1979 and continuing up to and including the date of the filing of this complaint, defendants Global, Uno, Temple of Florida, and Temple of Panama willfully, intentionally, fraudulently, and illegally induced Martin to sell them approximately $9 million worth of Martin merchandise by fraudulently misrepresenting that such merchandise would be exported solely to Central America, South America, and the Caribbean. Because Martin was led to believe that its merchandise would be sold in these markets, Martin agreed to sell its merchandise to Global, Uno, Temple of Florida, and Temple of Panama at the export price, which was significantly below that available to Martin's legitimate domestic distributors and wholesale customers.

6.   Global, Uno, Temple of Florida, and Temple of Panama, however, never intended to, and in fact did not, export the Martin merchandise to Central America, South America, and the Caribbean. Instead, pursuant to a preconceived conspiracy between and among the defendants, the Martin merchandise was transferred to Acme, Top Notch, Nationwide Supply, Baggins, and Bat, under the direction of their principals, Munsin and Rogers, Byers, Quin, Windom, and Nereson respectively, whereby they received the Martin merchandise at prices substantially below those available to Martin's legitimate domestic distributors and

wholesale customers due to the Martin merchandise's having been fraudulently procured by the defendants at the discounted export price.

7. Defendants engaged in a continuous course of commercial bribery by providing illicit payments and/or shares of the profits from defendants' scheme to certain Martin employees and agents in order to initiate, advance, and conceal their fraudulent scheme. In addition, the fraud was initiated, advanced, completed, and concealed through the use of interstate facilities, including the United States mail and wires, by the mailing and/or wiring of, among other things, fraudulent letters of intent, bills of lading, purchase orders, correspondence, and telexes, which falsely indicated or stated that the Martin merchandise would be or had been exported to Central America, South America, and the Caribbean. Finally, defendants transported and sold in interstate commerce the fraudulently obtained and unlawfully converted Martin merchandise knowing the same to have been unlawfully procured from Martin in violation of federal criminal statutes.

8. By reason of the violations set forth below, Martin has sustained and will continue to sustain, among others, the following injuries: (i) Martin has suffered damage by virtue of selling Martin merchandise to defendants at the discounted export price when, in fact, such merchandise was resold in the domestic market; (ii) Martin has suffered damage to its goodwill with respect to its legitimate domestic distributors and wholesale customers by being fraudulently induced to provide Martin merchandise to defendants at prices far below those at which Martin's legitimate domestic distributors and wholesale customers purchase Martin merchandise from Martin; and (iii) Martin has been precluded from developing and maintaining an aggressive and lucrative sales program in certain areas of Central America, South America, and the Caribbean because of the failure of defendants to deliver Martin merchandise to those regions.

§ 3.13 —Parties

In a scheme as complex as that described herein it is as important to describe the parties with particularity as it is the facts constituting the violation. An understanding of who each defendant is and what each is specifically accused of doing is crucial to the court's appreciation of the basis for levying charges of racketeering against each named defendant.

THE PARTIES

9. Plaintiff Martin is a corporation organized under the laws of the state of New Jersey with its principal place of business at 123 First Street,

Wilner, New Jersey 07470. Martin, among other things, manufactures and/or sells personal care and grooming products, including but not limited to the GEOFFREY BEENE GREY FLANNEL and NINA RICCI product lines, PIERRE CARDIN cologne, OLD SPICE, BLUE STRATOS and MANDATE men's toiletries, LADY'S CHOICE solid antiperspirants, BRECK and MISS BRECK hair care products, and CIE fragrances, all of which are trademarked. The products manufactured and/or sold by Martin, including any combination thereof, are hereby defined as "Martin merchandise." Martin sells its merchandise both domestically and internationally, through the Martin U.S.A. Division and the Martin International Division, respectively.

10. Defendant Acme is a corporation organized under the laws of the state of Delaware, with its principal place of business in Braxton, Connecticut. Acme is a foreign corporation licensed to do business in New Jersey and transacts business in New Jersey. Acme, through its Ace Drug Exchange Division, is a national wholesale distributor of name brand and generic pharmaceuticals, medical supplies, and health and beauty aids.

11. Defendant Rogers is the president and chief executive officer of Acme, a position he has held since sometime in 1982. Prior to that time, Rogers was Acme's executive vice president. Rogers is a citizen of the state of Connecticut and transacts business in the state of New Jersey, including but not limited to transactions directly related to this action.

12. Defendant Munsin was the president of Acme's Ace Drug Exchange Division and chairman of the board of Acme until sometime in 1982. Munsin is a citizen of the state of Connecticut and transacts business in the state of New Jersey, including but not limited to transactions directly related to this action.

13. Defendant Top Notch is a corporation organized under the laws of the state of New York, with its principal place of business in Singletree, New York. Top Notch is a national wholesale distributor of health and beauty aids. Top Notch transacts business in the state of New Jersey, including but not limited to transactions directly related to this action.

14. Defendant Byers is the president and chief executive officer of Top Notch. Byers is a citizen of the state of New York and transacts business in New Jersey, including but not limited to transactions directly related to this action.

15. Defendant Nationwide Supply is a corporation organized under the laws of the state of New York, with its principal place of business in Maynard, New York. Nationwide Supply is a national wholesale distributor of drug sundries and health and beauty aids. Nationwide Supply transacts business in New Jersey, including but not limited to transactions directly related to this action.

16.   Defendant Quin is the president and chief executive officer of Nationwide Supply. Quin is a citizen of the state of New York and transacts business in the state of New Jersey, including but not limited to transactions directly related to this action.

17.   Defendant Baggins is a corporation organized under the laws of the state of New York, with its principal place of business in Yonkers, New York. Baggins is in the business, among other things, of selling and distributing, at the wholesale level, drug sundries and health and beauty aids. Baggins transacts business in the state of New Jersey, including but not limited to transactions directly related to this action.

18.   Defendant Windom is the secretary/treasurer and the chief executive officer of Baggins. Windom is a citizen of the state of New York and transacts business in the state of New Jersey, including but not limited to transactions directly related to this action.

19.   Defendant Bat is a corporation organized under the laws of the state of Florida, with its principal place of business in Miami, Florida. Bat is in the business, among other things, of selling and distributing health and beauty aids. Bat transacts business in the state of New Jersey, including but not limited to transactions directly related to this action.

20.   Defendant Nereson is the president of Bat. Nereson is a citizen of the state of Florida and transacts business in New Jersey, including but not limited to transactions directly related to this action.

21.   Defendant Global is a corporation organized under the laws of the state of New York, with its principal place of business in New York, New York. Global is in the business, among other things, of buying and selling health and beauty aid products, purportedly for sale to foreign customers. Global transacts business in the state of New Jersey, including but not limited to transactions directly related to this action.

22.   Defendant Uno is a corporation registered under the laws of Panama, with its principal place of business in Panama City, Panama. Uno, among other things, purportedly sells goods in Central America, South America, and the Caribbean, including fragrances, cosmetics, and health and beauty aids. Uno transacts business in the state of New Jersey, including but not limited to transactions directly related to this action.

23.   Defendant Temple of Panama is a corporation registered under the laws of Panama, with its principal place of business in Panama City, Panama. Temple of Panama, among other things, purportedly sells goods in Central America, South America, and the Caribbean, including fragrances, cosmetics, and health and beauty aids. Temple of Panama transacts business in the state of New Jersey, including but not limited to transactions directly related to this action.

24.   Defendant World is a corporation organized under the laws of the state of Florida, with its principal place of business in Miami, Florida.

World, among other things, purchases and sells health and beauty aid products. World transacts business in the state of New Jersey, including but not limited to transactions directly related to this action.

25.   Defendant Temple of Florida is a corporation organized under the laws of the state of Florida, with its principal place of business in Miami, Florida. Temple of Florida purportedly engages in the business of exporting goods from the United States to Central America, South America, and the Caribbean, including but not limited to the export of fragrances, cosmetics, and health and beauty aid products. Temple of Florida transacts business in the state of New Jersey, including but not limited to transactions directly related to this action.

26.   Defendant Garcia, a/k/a Benito Duran, is the president and a director of Temple of Florida, the general manager and part-owner of Temple of Panama, a director and part-owner of Uno, and the part-owner of World. Garcia is a citizen of the state of Florida and transacts business in the state of New Jersey, including but not limited to transactions directly related to this action. In addition, Garcia has transacted business under the assumed name of Benito Duran.

27.   Defendant Juarez served as the treasurer of World and Temple of Florida and also served as an accountant and financial officer for Garcia's various other business affairs. Juarez is a citizen of the state of Florida and transacts business in the state of New Jersey, including but not limited to transactions directly related to this action.

28.   Defendant Foremost is a corporation organized under the laws of the state of New York with its principal place of business in New York, New York. Foremost engages in the business of international freight forwarding and has acted as the Martin International Division's principal freight forwarder in the United States at all times pertinent to this action. Foremost transacts business in the state of New Jersey, including but not limited to transactions directly related to this action.

29.   Defendant Montero is the president of Global and has held that position since 1978 when Global was formed. Montero is also the chairman of the board and president of Foremost. Montero is a citizen of the state of New York and transacts business in New Jersey, including but not limited to transactions directly related to this action.

30.   Defendant Zapata served as the export manager for the Martin International Division from 1964 to 1983, when he retired. In addition, Zapata is a part-owner of Temple of Panama and Global. Zapata is a citizen of the state of Florida and transacts business in the state of New Jersey, including but not limited to transactions directly related to this action.

31.   Defendant Cervantes served as president and general manager of Martin, S.A., Guatemala, from 1970 to 1983, when he retired. In addition, Cervantes is a part-owner of Temple of Panama. Cervantes is a

citizen of the country of Guatemala and transacts business in the state of New Jersey, including but not limited to transactions directly related to this action.

32.   Defendants John Doe Corporations I–X are various business entities, whose identities are presently unknown to Martin, that engage in the wholesale distribution of health and beauty aid products or engage in the sale of such goods. Such business entities were part and parcel of the scheme to defraud Martin described herein.

33.   Defendants John Does I–X include various officers, directors, or employees of John Doe Corporations I–X, whose identities are presently unknown to Martin, that engage, through their respective corporations, in the wholesale distribution of health and beauty aid products or engage in the sale of such goods. Such individuals were part and parcel of the scheme to defraud Martin described herein.

§ 3.14   —Factual Allegations

The following Statement of Facts demonstrates that in a complex RICO case all the facts, not just the circumstances constituting fraud, should be pleaded with substantial particularity, in order to show the court that the plaintiff has been injured by a true pattern of racketeering activity as contemplated by the RICO statute.

STATEMENT OF FACTS

34.   It is the policy of the Martin International Division in the United States to sell Martin merchandise only for export out of the United States. In addition, the export price, which is considerably lower than Martin's domestic selling price due to lower overhead and other factors, is charged by Martin only to customers who purchase Martin merchandise solely for export. It is against this backdrop that defendants' fraudulent scheme developed.

35.   In 1978 and 1979, the Martin International Division was seeking to develop an aggressive and lucrative sales program in certain areas of Central America, South America, and the Caribbean. Martin wished to penetrate those markets to a much more significant degree than it previously had done. Pursuant to that goal, Martin sought to find a company that could develop such markets for Martin.

36.   In early to mid-1979, Garcia met with Cervantes, the president and general manager of Martin, S.A., Guatemala. Cervantes set the prices for Martin merchandise that was sold for export to Central America, South America, and the Caribbean.

37.   At or about this time, Garcia and Cervantes agreed to a scheme whereby Cervantes would attempt to open an account at Martin for Garcia in order to enable Garcia to purchase Martin merchandise at the export price, which would be set by Cervantes. Thereafter, Garcia would sell the merchandise to domestic wholesale companies for resale in the United States market.

38.   As consideration for his participation in this scheme, Cervantes accepted illicit payments and/or a share of the profits of the scheme from Garcia, which was in direct violation of Martin company policy. All action taken by Cervantes in this scheme was in derogation of his duty of loyalty to Martin and, consequently, beyond the scope of his authority as a Martin employee.

39.   In or about mid-1979, Cervantes and Garcia communicated with Zapata, the export manager for the Martin International Division, and informed him of their fraudulent scheme. Thereafter, Zapata agreed to participate and assist in the scheme to obtain Martin merchandise at the export price and thereafter sell such merchandise to domestic wholesale companies for resale in the United States market.

40.   As consideration for his participation in this scheme, Zapata accepted illicit payments and/or a share of the profits of the scheme from Garcia, which was in direct violation of Martin company policy. All action taken by Zapata in this scheme was in derogation of his duty of loyalty to Martin and, consequently, beyond the scope of his authority as a Martin employee.

41.   Zapata and Cervantes thereafter introduced Garcia to their superiors at the Martin International Division in an attempt to persuade them to sell Martin merchandise to Garcia. Garcia informed Martin that he had contacts in Central America, South America, and the Caribbean which could be important for Martin's export business. Garcia further informed Martin that he owned a company in Panama by the name of Uno through which he would place orders for Martin merchandise.

42.   At or about this time, Martin and Garcia agreed that Martin would sell Martin merchandise to Garcia, provided that Garcia exported such merchandise to certain areas of Central America, South America, and the Caribbean. They further agreed that Martin would sell its merchandise to Garcia at the export price, which represented substantial discounts off the price at which Martin sold its merchandise to its legitimate domestic distributors and wholesale customers. However, because Garcia had not done business with Martin previously, they further agreed that Garcia would enter his orders through a United States company in order to establish a credit history.

43.   To further their fraudulent scheme, Cervantes, Zapata, and Garcia sought a domestic corporate vehicle through which they could

procure Martin merchandise. Accordingly, Zapata, Garcia, and Cervantes communicated with Montero, who was an officer and employee of Foremost, the Martin International Division's principal freight forwarder in the United States. By virtue of these positions, Montero was a trusted agent of Martin.

44.   The above-described defendants sought out Montero because he also owned a company by the name of Global, which was operated out of the same office as Foremost. Montero and Zapata, without Martin's knowledge, had established Global in or about October 1978, purportedly to sell various merchandise to overseas customers. Due to the fact that Zapata's participation in Global was in direct violation of Martin company policy, Montero and Zapata agreed when they established Global that Zapata's name would not be used in connection with that company. Instead, Montero and Zapata agreed that Zapata's share of the profits from Global's operations would be disseminated to Zapata's wife.

45.   After communicating with Zapata, Cervantes, and Garcia, Montero agreed to participate and assist in the fraudulent scheme to obtain Martin merchandise at the export price and thereafter sell such merchandise to domestic wholesale companies for resale in the United States. According to the scheme, Garcia would enter orders for Uno, the company he had established in Panama, through Montero, who would submit such orders under the name of Global to Zapata at Martin for processing. The shipment of such merchandise from Martin would then be handled by Montero by virtue of his position at Foremost.

46.   As consideration for his participation in this scheme, Montero accepted illicit payments and/or a share of the profits of the scheme from Garcia. Such actions were in direct violation of Federal Maritime Commission regulations which governed Montero's activities as a freight forwarder. All action taken by Montero in this scheme was in derogation of his duty of loyalty to Martin by virtue of his status as a Martin agent and, consequently, beyond the scope of his authority as a Martin agent.

47.   Thereafter, the first Uno order for Martin merchandise in the name of Global was received by Martin in or about October 1979. Upon receiving the order, Cervantes and Zapata opened the account at Martin for Global and assigned Martin Customer No. 543 to Global. Furthermore, the substantially discounted export price for the Martin merchandise sold to Global was set by Cervantes.

48.   In furtherance of the fraudulent scheme, Global entered orders on behalf of Garcia and Uno from October 1979 through mid-1980. The Martin merchandise sent pursuant to these orders was delivered, at the direction of Montero, Zapata, and Garcia, to various warehouses in the New York, New Jersey, and Florida areas for purported loading on

ocean vessels bound for Central America, South America, and the Caribbean.

49.   Contrary to the express representations made to Martin by Garcia, however, such merchandise was not exported to Central America, South America, and the Caribbean. Instead, Garcia, on behalf of Global, Uno, Montero, Zapata, and Cervantes, had entered into an arrangement with Defendants Acme, Top Notch, Nationwide Supply, Baggins, and Bat, whereby Garcia provided the above-described companies and their respective principals with the Martin merchandise that Garcia fraudulently procured from Martin.

50.   Defendants Acme, Top Notch, Nationwide Supply, Baggins, and Bat and their respective principals all knowingly participated in the scheme. They also knew that Garcia was falsely and fraudulently representing to Martin that the merchandise he purchased was being exported to Central America, South America, and the Caribbean.

51.   Pursuant to Defendants' fraudulent scheme, Acme, Top Notch, Nationwide Supply, Baggins, and Bat would place their orders for Martin merchandise through their "front"—Garcia—who would then place orders with Martin for Martin merchandise for Uno through Global. Acme, Top Notch, Nationwide Supply, Baggins, and Bat would then prepay Garcia for the fraudulently procured Martin merchandise by wire transferring payments to Garcia's various bank accounts in Panama, the Cayman Islands, and Switzerland, or would guarantee letters of credit, without Martin's knowledge, to pay for the fraudulently procured Martin merchandise.

52.   Cervantes would then set the prices for the ordered merchandise, which were considerably below Martin's normal export price and significantly below the prices available to Martin's legitimate domestic distributors and wholesale customers. After Martin shipped the ordered merchandise to various warehouses at the direction of Zapata, Garcia, and Montero, the warehousing companies were thereafter directed by Garcia and Montero to reconsign the goods to representatives of Acme, Top Notch, Nationwide Supply, Baggins, and Bat.

53.   As part and parcel of this fraudulent scheme, Garcia, with the acquiescence and substantial financial and other assistance provided by Acme, Top Notch, Nationwide Supply, Baggins, and Bat, would thereafter provide illicit payments and/or a share of the profits of the scheme to Zapata, Cervantes, and Montero for their assistance and participation in the fraudulent scheme.

54.   Montero would receive illicit payments and/or a share of the profits from Garcia for Global's participation in the scheme and would then disseminate part of those payments to Zapata through payments to Zapata's wife. In addition, Montero would receive further illicit

payments from Garcia and send part of those sums to Cervantes, who would deposit the illicit proceeds in an account he maintained in Panama under the name of Standard Business Corporation. Finally, Montero would keep a part of the payments as consideration for his illicit participation in defendants' fraudulent scheme.

55. In furtherance of defendants' fraudulent scheme, Garcia, Cervantes and Zapata, without Martin's knowledge, and in direct violation of the duties imposed on Cervantes and Zapata by Martin company policy, established Temple of Panama in or about mid-1980. Temple of Panama was established, with the acquiescence of the other defendants, to enable the defendants to purchase Martin merchandise directly from Martin without the necessity of using Global as an intermediary. Montero agreed to this procedure.

56. In or about mid-1980, Garcia, through the use of the interstate mails, sent Martin a "Temple Fact Sheet" describing the operations of Temple of Panama. The representations contained therein were fraudulent, false, and misleading, and were aimed at leading Martin into believing that Temple of Panama would export the merchandise it purchased from Martin to Central America, South America, and the Caribbean.

57. Garcia sent the Temple Fact Sheet to Zapata at Martin headquarters in Wilner, New Jersey. Zapata, being a silent partner in Temple of Panama with Garcia and Cervantes, passed on the Temple Fact Sheet to his superiors at Martin in order to fraudulently induce Martin to continue to sell Martin merchandise to Garcia.

58. Thereafter, in furtherance of defendants' fraudulent scheme, Temple of Panama sent its first order to Martin for Martin merchandise in or about June 1980. Zapata processed the Temple of Panama order at Martin and assigned Martin Customer No. 543 to Temple of Panama, which was the same number that Zapata and Cervantes had assigned to Global in late 1979. In addition, pursuant to defendants' scheme, Cervantes continued to set the export price for the Martin merchandise purchased by Temple of Panama, even though he knew such merchandise was not being exported.

59. In furtherance of defendants' fraudulent scheme, Garcia also incorporated Temple of Florida in Florida. Temple of Florida was incorporated under the name "Temple International Corporation," the same name that Temple of Panama was registered under in Panama. Thereafter, Garcia's orders were received by Martin in the name of Temple International (hereinafter referred to as Temple of Florida/Temple of Panama).

60. From 1980 to 1982, Temple of Florida/Temple of Panama submitted substantial orders for Martin merchandise. However, contrary to Garcia's representations to Martin, the Martin merchandise so ordered during 1980–1982 was never exported to foreign countries. Instead, in

furtherance of defendants' fraudulent scheme, the Martin merchandise was sold by Temple of Florida/Temple of Panama and World—another Garcia company to which Temple of Florida/Temple of Panama had transferred Martin merchandise—to Acme, Top Notch, Nationwide Supply, Baggins, and Bat for resale in the domestic market.

61.   In accordance with the continuation and furtherance of defendants' fraudulent scheme, the transactions between Temple of Florida/Temple of Panama and World with Acme, Top Notch, Nationwide Supply, Baggins, and Bat were handled in substantially the same manner as the Uno purchases through Global from late-1979 to mid-1980, referred to in paragraphs 47 to 54 above.

62.   Acme, Top Notch, Nationwide Supply, Baggins, and Bat would place their orders for Martin merchandise through Garcia, who would then place orders with Martin for Martin merchandise through Temple of Florida/Temple of Panama. Acme, Top Notch, Nationwide Supply, Baggins, and Bat would then prepay Garcia for the fraudulently procured Martin merchandise by wire-transferring payments to Garcia's bank accounts in Panama, the Cayman Islands, and Switzerland, or would guarantee letters of credit, without Martin's knowledge, to pay for the fraudulently procured Martin merchandise.

63.   Garcia, Zapata and Montero would then arrange for the shipment of the Martin merchandise to Acme, Top Notch, Nationwide Supply, Baggins, and Bat in at least three different ways. First, some Martin merchandise ordered by Temple of Florida/Temple of Panama was shipped to various warehouses in New York and New Jersey at the direction of Garcia, Zapata, and Montero for purported loading on ocean vessels bound for Central America, South America, and the Caribbean. Thereafter, the warehousing companies were directed by Garcia or Montero to reconsign the Martin merchandise to representatives of Acme, Top Notch, Nationwide Supply, and Baggins.

64.   Second, some shipments of Martin merchandise were picked up directly from the Martin plant in Carlton, New Jersey by trucking companies and delivered, per instructions of Garcia, Zapata, and Montero, directly to Acme, Top Notch, and Nationwide Supply, even though the truckers' bills of lading indicated that such goods should be delivered to Temple International, c/o Joseph Santos, Miami, Florida.

65.   Third, other Martin shipments were, in fact, sent to Temple International, c/o Joseph Santos, Miami, Florida, at the direction of Garcia, Montero, and Zapata, where Martin merchandise was unloaded and stored. In various instances, Garcia would direct that such merchandise be transferred to World. Thereafter, Acme, Top Notch, and Nationwide Supply arranged for trucks to transport the Martin merchandise received from Temple of Florida/Temple of Panama and World back to Connecticut and New York for distribution and resale in the domestic

market. In the case of Bat, which was headquartered in Miami, Florida, Garcia would direct Joseph Santos to deliver the fraudulently obtained Martin merchandise to Bat from Joseph Santos' warehouse.

66.   In addition, Garcia transferred some of the Martin merchandise that he and Temple of Florida/Temple of Panama had transferred to World to Beauty International, Inc. (Beauty). The officers of Beauty were Jose Lorenzo (Lorenzo), who is Zapata's brother-in-law, Garcia's wife, and Zapata, who served as the treasurer. Zapata's participation in Beauty was in direct violation of Martin company policy. Zapata, Lorenzo, and Garcia, using his wife as a front, established Beauty, without Martin's knowledge, for the purpose of retailing in the Florida area the fraudulently procured Martin merchandise that Beauty received from World. In this manner, Zapata and Garcia were able to extract more money out of the fraudulent scheme against Martin.

67.   During the time that the Global, Uno, and Temple of Florida/ Temple of Panama orders to Martin were being placed, Zapata, Montero, and Cervantes, pursuant to their fraudulent scheme with Garcia and the other defendants, exclusively handled the Global, Uno, and Temple of Florida/Temple of Panama accounts. Although all other Martin International Division shipping records in the United States contained information concerning the final overseas destination of the Martin merchandise reflected therein, no such information was kept for Global, Uno, and Temple of Florida/Temple of Panama.

68.   By virtue of the fact that Zapata and Cervantes kept control of the Global, Uno, and Temple of Florida/Temple of Panama customer accounts, and the shipping documents for those accounts were handled by Montero, Martin was unaware that Martin merchandise was not being exported by Global, Uno, and Temple of Florida/Temple of Panama, but rather was being transferred to Acme, Top Notch, Nationwide Supply, Baggins, and Bat for resale in the domestic market.

69.   To assure the continuation and concealment of defendants' fraudulent scheme, at various times during 1980, 1981, and 1982, Garcia, on behalf of and with the acquiescence and substantial financial assistance of the other defendants, continued to provide illicit payments and/or a share of the profits of the scheme to Zapata, Cervantes, and Montero for their participation in the scheme to defraud Martin.

70.   Furthermore, as part and parcel of defendants' fraudulent scheme, at various times during 1980, 1981, and 1982, Quin, Munsin, Rogers, Byers, and Windom, through the use of the interstate wires, telephoned Garcia to arrange the purchase and receipt of the fraudulently obtained and unlawfully converted Martin merchandise. Quin, Munsin, and Byers also traveled to Florida during the above-described times to meet with Garcia, in furtherance of their scheme to defraud Martin. Finally, Quin, Munsin, Rogers, Byers, Windom, and Nereson arranged for the interstate transportation, shipment, and sale of the

fraudulently obtained and unlawfully converted Martin merchandise to their respective companies for resale in the United States.

71. In or about mid-1981, salespeople from the Martin U.S.A. Division began noticing that some of their accounts had Martin merchandise in stock that had not been purchased from the Martin U.S.A. Division. They notified Martin headquarters in New Jersey that they believed that such merchandise was being sold to their accounts by customers of the Martin International Division.

72. Zapata was directed by his superiors at Martin to ascertain if Martin International Division customers, including Temple of Florida/ Temple of Panama, were diverting Martin merchandise back into the United States or simply not shipping such merchandise out of the United States. Zapata further was directed to obtain bills of lading, invoices, and other shipping documents from Temple of Florida/Temple of Panama. Zapata thereafter requested such information from Garcia.

73. In or about mid-1981, Garcia, through the use of interstate mails, sent a letter to Zapata at Martin headquarters enclosing numerous ocean and airway bills of lading and other documents purporting to demonstrate that the Martin merchandise purchased by Temple of Florida/Temple of Panama had, in fact, been exported from the United States to various areas in Central America, South America, and the Caribbean.

74. The various ocean and airway bills of lading described in paragraph 73 above, were and are counterfeit, false, and fraudulent. The Martin merchandise reflected therein was not exported or intended for export by Temple of Florida/Temple of Panama. In addition, the letter accompanying the counterfeit, false, and fraudulent bills of lading was itself fraudulent, in that Garcia maintained that all of the Martin merchandise purchased by Temple of Florida/Temple of Panama had in fact been exported.

75. After Zapata received Garcia's letter, which he knew was false and fraudulent, he thereafter sent a memorandum to his superior at Martin. In the memorandum, in furtherance of defendants' fraudulent scheme, Zapata attached Garcia's letter and the enclosed bills of lading that purportedly showed that Temple of Florida/Temple of Panama was exporting Martin merchandise out of the United States. In addition, Zapata falsely and fraudulently stated in his memorandum that he believed Garcia and Temple of Florida/Temple of Panama were in fact exporting Martin merchandise.

76. Thereafter, Zapata's superior, in reliance on Zapata's memorandum, the accompanying Garcia letter and bills of lading, and discussions with Garcia and Zapata, sent a memorandum to his superiors at Martin, in which he concluded that Temple of Florida/Temple of Panama was not involved in diverting merchandise purchased from the Martin International Division back into the United States. Accordingly, Martin

continued to ship its merchandise to Temple of Florida/Temple of Panama, which thereafter, in furtherance of defendants' fraudulent scheme, continued to transfer the Martin merchandise to Acme, Top Notch, Nationwide Supply, Baggins, and Bat.

77.   In furtherance of defendants' fraudulent scheme, Garcia, with the active participation and knowledge of Zapata, Cervantes, and Montero, submitted a proposal to Martin in early 1982 to purchase $1 million of Martin merchandise for export pursuant to letter of credit number T83117 from First American Trust Company of New York (First American).

78.   The letter of credit indicated that Temple of Florida/Temple of Panama was the sole applicant and that Martin was the beneficiary. The letter of credit was issued in favor of Martin by First American on or about July 13, 1982, and was received by Martin on or about July 16, 1982.

79.   Due to delays in shipping, Martin advised Garcia and Temple of Florida/Temple of Panama that the expiration date on the letter of credit would have to be changed from August 11, 1982, to at least August 20, 1982, and that they would have to change the interstate carrier listed in the letter of credit.

80.   In early August 1982, Garcia and Temple of Florida/Temple of Panama falsely and fraudulently represented to Martin, through means of the interstate wires, that the requested changes in the letter of credit had been arranged with First American.

81.   In reliance on the fraudulent representations of Garcia and Temple of Florida/Temple of Panama that the letter of credit had been amended, Martin delivered Martin merchandise to Temple of Florida/Temple of Panama in Florida for a total price of $731,331.06, which price reflected discounts of 40 to 65 percent from the prices Martin charged purchasers of the same products for distribution or resale within the United States.

82.   In late August 1982, First American returned the shipping documents submitted by Martin pursuant to the terms of the letter of credit because the interstate carrier used to deliver the Martin merchandise to Garcia and Temple of Florida/Temple of Panama was not identical to that described in the letter of credit, even though Garcia and Temple of Florida/Temple of Panama had represented to Martin that such change had been made.

83.   On or about September 1, 1982, Garcia and Temple of Florida/Temple of Panama, by means of the interstate wires, falsely and fraudulently represented to Martin that arrangements had been made with First American to accept the shipping documents as submitted by Martin. Martin thereafter resubmitted the shipping documents to First American.

84.   On or about September 15, 1982, First American notified Martin that First American had not received any communication from Garcia and Temple of Florida/Temple of Panama concerning amendments to the letter of credit and that they could no longer hold the shipping documents submitted by Martin.

85.   Martin then called Garcia, who represented to Martin that he would send Martin a copy of a letter to send to First American directing them to honor the letter of credit. On or about September 21, 1982, a copy of the letter was received by Martin from Garcia and a copy was delivered by Martin to First American.

86.   On or about September 23, 1982, First American advised Martin that collateral and financial backing for the letter of credit was not available and that the collateral and financial backing had to be reinstated before the letter of credit could be honored.

87.   On or about September 23, 1982, Garcia falsely and fraudulently represented to Martin that he had reinstated the collateral and financial backing on September 21, 1982, and that he would again contact First American in order to correct the problems with the letter of credit.

88.   On or about September 28, 1982, Martin learned for the first time from First American that (i) the letter of credit was a three-party letter of credit; (ii) the financial backing and collateral was provided by an unidentified third party; (iii) Garcia had waived all rights to change the letter of credit; and (iv) only the unidentified third party could authorize amendments to the letter of credit. First American would not respond to questions concerning the unidentified third party who provided the financial backing and collateral for the letter of credit.

89.   On or about September 29, 1982, First American notified Martin that the letter of credit had expired, and that First American had no obligation under the circumstances to honor the drafts submitted by Martin for payment of the goods ordered and delivered to Garcia and Temple of Florida/Temple of Panama in Florida.

90.   On or about October 4, 1982, Martin representatives met with Garcia in an effort to secure full payment for the outstanding balance of purchases made by Garcia and Temple of Florida/Temple of Panama. Purchases under the letter of credit totaled $731,331.06, of which no money had been paid. Garcia and Temple of Florida/Temple of Panama also owed Martin $368,154.94 for goods purchased from Martin prior to the purchases under the letter of credit.

91.   At the October 4, 1982, meeting, Garcia falsely and fraudulently represented to Martin that if he was paid by his unidentified customer, he would prepare a cashier's check in the full amount of the money owed to Martin. If he did not receive full payment from his unidentified customer, Garcia falsely and fraudulently represented that he would

assign to Martin all of his and Temple of Florida/Temple of Panama's rights to collect the outstanding balance due to them from the unidentified customer. During this meeting, in furtherance of defendants' fraudulent scheme, Garcia at all times falsely and fraudulently represented that his unidentified customer was a "foreign" customer.

92. On or about October 8, 1982, Garcia informed Martin that his unidentified "foreign" customer would pay one-half of the drafts due under the letter of credit, or approximately $365,000.00, with the balance due within 20 days. Thereafter, on or about October 18, 1982, Martin received $365,700.00 from First American pursuant to the letter of credit.

93. Temple of Florida/Temple of Panama's unidentified "foreign" customer and the unidentified third party guarantor on the letter of credit was in fact Acme. Rogers, the president of Acme, signed the letter of credit application on behalf of Acme and Temple of Florida/Temple of Panama in furtherance of defendants' scheme to procure fraudulently Martin merchandise sold for export.

94. In addition, in furtherance of defendants' fraudulent scheme, Acme ultimately received the Martin merchandise transported to Temple of Florida/Temple of Panama in Florida. Acme transported the Martin merchandise—shipped by Martin to Florida pursuant to the letter of credit—back to Connecticut, where such merchandise was thereafter sold in various states, including New Jersey.

95. The balance due under the letter of credit—which amounted to $366,331.00—was never received by Martin even though Acme had received the Martin merchandise shipped to Temple of Florida/Temple of Panama pursuant to the letter of credit. No further payments have been received by Martin pursuant to the First American letter of credit or from any other source.

§ 3.15 —Illegal Conduct of Enterprise Count

Based on the foregoing factual allegations, Martin was able to charge the defendants with no less than nine RICO violations. As the reader will note, this was substantially due to the number of companies involved in the scheme (including Martin, as victim). Focusing on each as the "enterprise" in question gave rise to the numerous RICO violations asserted.

FIRST CAUSE OF ACTION
(For violation of 18 U.S.C. § 1962(c))

96. Martin repeats and realleges paragraphs 1 through 95, inclusive, as if fully set forth herein.

97.   Temple of Florida/Temple of Panama, Uno, and Global constituted enterprises operating in and affecting interstate and foreign commerce. Defendants Acme, Nationwide Supply, Top Notch, Baggins, Bat,
World, Foremost, Munsin, Rogers, Byers, Quin, Windom, Nereson, Zapata, Cervantes, Montero, Juarez and Garcia associated themselves with
the enterprises and conducted and participated in the affairs of the
enterprises through a pattern of racketeering activity in violation of 18
U.S.C. § 1962(c).

98.   Specifically, Acme, Nationwide Supply, Top Notch, Baggins, Bat,
World, Foremost, Munsin, Rogers, Byers, Quin, Windom, Nereson, Zapata, Cervantes, Montero, Juarez, and Garcia, separately and together,
knowingly, willfully, and unlawfully devised and executed a scheme to
defraud Martin through defendants' use of the enterprises in order to
obtain Martin merchandise from Martin at prices substantially below
those available to Martin's legitimate domestic distributors and wholesale customers by means of false and fraudulent statements, representations, or promises and through the commission of numerous criminal
acts.

99.   In furtherance of the above-described scheme to defraud Martin, certain of the false and fraudulent statements made knowingly by
certain defendants, with the approval, acquiescence, and for the benefit of the other defendants, were transmitted through the means of the
United States mails, in direct violation of 18 U.S.C. § 1341. The mailings made to advance the scheme to defraud Martin, each of which
constitutes a distinct and separate offense in violation of 18 U.S.C.
§ 1341, include but are not limited to the following:

(i)   a purchase order sent by Garcia and Montero to Martin in
or about May 1980, on behalf of Global and Uno, falsely and fraudulently indicating that the Martin merchandise reflected therein would
be exported to the Chavez Trading Corporation in Panama, when in fact
such merchandise was not exported to such company;

(ii)   a purchase order sent by Garcia and Montero to Martin in
or about June 1980, on behalf of Global, falsely and fraudulently indicating that the Martin merchandise reflected therein would be exported to Bat, when in fact Bat was a company located in Florida;

(iii)   a purchase order sent by Garcia and Montero to Martin in
or about February 1980, on behalf of Global and Uno, falsely and fraudulently indicating that the Martin merchandise reflected therein would
be exported to Uno in Panama, when in fact such merchandise was not
exported to such company;

(iv)   a purchase order sent by Garcia and Montero to Martin in
or about June 1980, on behalf of Global, falsely and fraudulently indicating that the Martin merchandise reflected therein would be exported to

the Chavez Trading Corporation in Panama, when in fact such merchandise was not exported to such company;

(v)   a purchase order sent by Garcia and Montero to Martin in or about May 1980, on behalf of Global, falsely and fraudulently placing an order for Martin merchandise for purported export to foreign countries and indicating shipping instruction to foreign countries would be forthcoming, when in fact there was no such intent to export such merchandise;

(vi)   a purchase order sent by Garcia to Martin in or about June 1980, on behalf of Temple of Florida/Temple of Panama, falsely and fraudulently indicating that the Martin merchandise reflected therein would be exported, when in fact such merchandise was not exported by such company;

(vii) a purchase order sent by Garcia and Montero to Martin in or about May 1980, on behalf of Global, falsely and fraudulently indicating that the Martin merchandise reflected therein would be exported to Freeport, Ltd. in Jamaica, when in fact such merchandise was not exported to such company;

(viii) a purchase order sent by Garcia to Martin in or about August 1980, on behalf of Temple of Florida/Temple of Panama, falsely and fraudulently indicating that the Martin merchandise reflected therein would be exported, when in fact such merchandise was not exported;

(ix)   a purchase order sent by Garcia to Martin in or about August 1980, on behalf of Temple of Florida/Temple of Panama, falsely and fraudulently indicating that the Martin merchandise reflected therein would be exported, when in fact such merchandise was not exported;

(x)   a "Temple Fact Sheet" sent by Garcia to Martin in or about June 1980, which falsely and fraudulently indicated that Temple of Florida/Temple of Panama had numerous overseas accounts in Central America, South America, and the Caribbean and was the official representative of various lines of products, which in fact Temple of Florida/Temple of Panama did not represent;

(xi)   a letter sent on or about September 18, 1982, from Garcia to Martin with instructions to forward such letter to First American. The letter contained Garcia's fraudulent instructions to First American to amend the Temple of Florida/Temple of Panama letter of credit, even though Garcia knew that only Acme had the power to amend such letter of credit; and

(xii) a letter sent in or about May 1981, from Garcia to Martin enclosing counterfeit, false, and fraudulent bills of lading and stating that all merchandise purchased by Temple of Florida/Temple of Panama had been exported to Central America, South America, and the Caribbean.

100. Additionally, in furtherance of the above-described scheme to defraud Martin, certain of the false and fraudulent statements made knowingly by certain defendants, with the approval, acquiescence and for the benefit of the other defendants, were transmitted by use of the interstate wires in direct violation of 18 U.S.C. § 1343. The false and fraudulent wire transmissions made to advance the scheme to defraud Martin, each of which constitutes a distinct and separate offense in violation of 18 U.S.C. § 1343, include but are not limited to the following:

(i) a telex sent in or about March 1983 from Garcia to Martin, wherein Garcia falsely and fraudulently indicated to Martin that he was attempting to arrange payment for sums owing by Garcia to Martin and that Garcia would be able to sell $6 to 8 million worth of Martin merchandise in the next 12 months;

(ii) a telephone conversation between Juarez and Martin, in or about October 1982, wherein Juarez falsely and fraudulently stated that Temple of Florida/Temple of Panama's unnamed "foreign customer," who in fact was Acme, would commence payment on the sums owing under the letter of credit;

(iii) a telephone conversation between Garcia and Martin, in or about September 1982, wherein Garcia falsely and fraudulently stated he was on his way to First American for a meeting to resolve the letter of credit problems and that all amendments to the letter of credit would be made by the following day;

(iv) a telex sent in or about September 1982 from Garcia's agent to Martin, wherein Garcia's agent falsely and fraudulently stated that Martin representatives would receive payment of outstanding Garcia debts by means of a cashier's check if Martin representatives would fly to Miami on October 4, 1982 to receive such payment;

(v) a telex sent in or about May 1981 from Cervantes to Martin, wherein Cervantes falsely and fraudulently set forth the alleged "export price" at which Martin should sell Martin merchandise to Garcia and Temple of Florida/Temple of Panama, when Cervantes knew that Garcia and Temple of Florida/Temple of Panama were not exporting Martin merchandise, but rather were selling such merchandise directly to Acme, Top Notch, Nationwide Supply, Baggins, and Bat;

(vi) a purchase order telephoned to Zapata at Martin by Montero and Garcia in or about February 1980, on behalf of Global, falsely and fraudulently indicating that the Martin merchandise would be exported to Panama, when in fact such merchandise was not exported;

(vii) a telex sent in or about September 1981 from a Martin, S.A., Guatemala employee to Zapata at Martin, wherein the employee, acting at the direction of Cervantes, set forth new export prices for Martin merchandise that would be sold to Temple of Florida/Temple of Panama, which prices were false and fraudulent given that Cervantes and Zapata knew that Temple of Florida/Temple of Panama would not export such merchandise;

(viii) numerous telephone conversations between Garcia and Martin during the years 1980 to 1982, wherein Garcia and Munsin arranged for the sale, purchase, and transportation to Acme of the fraudulently obtained and unlawfully converted Martin merchandise;

(ix) numerous telephone conversations between Garcia and Rogers in 1982, wherein Garcia and Rogers arranged for the sale, purchase, and transportation to Acme of the fraudulently obtained and unlawfully converted Martin merchandise;

(x) numerous telephone conversations between Garcia and Quin during the years 1980 to 1982, wherein Garcia and Quin arranged for the sale, purchase, and transportation to Nationwide Supply of fraudulently obtained and unlawfully converted Martin merchandise;

(xi) numerous telephone conversations between Garcia and Byers during the years 1980 to 1982, wherein Garcia and Byers arranged for the sale, purchase, and transportation to Top Notch of fraudulently obtained and unlawfully converted Martin merchandise;

(xii) numerous telephone conversations between Garcia and Windom during the years 1979 to 1981, wherein Garcia and Windom arranged for the sale, purchase, and transportation to Baggins of fraudulently obtained and unlawfully converted Martin merchandise;

(xiii) numerous wire transfers of money during the years 1979 to 1982 to Garcia's bank accounts in Panama, the Cayman Islands, and Switzerland by Acme, Top Notch, Nationwide Supply, Baggins, and Bat to aid and finance Garcia's fraudulent purchases of Martin merchandise;

(xiv) numerous telephone conversations during 1981 between Montero and Nationwide Supply, whereby Montero directed Nationwide Supply where and when to pick up the fraudulently procured Martin merchandise from Carlton, New Jersey;

(xv) numerous telephone conversations between Garcia, Zapata, Montero, and Cervantes during the years 1980 to 1982, wherein the above-described defendants would agree to meet for the purpose of Garcia's dispensing illicit payments and/or a share of the profits of the scheme to Zapata, Montero, and Cervantes; and

(xvi) numerous telephone conversations between Garcia, Montero, and representatives of various warehousing companies during the years 1980 to 1982, wherein Garcia or Montero directed such warehousing companies to release Martin merchandise fraudulently procured by Garcia and Montero to representatives of Acme, Top Notch, Nationwide Supply, Baggins, and Bat.

101. Moreover, in furtherance of the above-described scheme to defraud Martin, defendants committed numerous and direct violations of 18 U.S.C. § 2314 by transporting in interstate commerce the unlawfully obtained Martin merchandise knowing the same to have been obtained from Martin by fraud. The Martin merchandise, which has a value far exceeding $5,000, was: (i) shipped at various defendants' direction, with the approval, acquiescence, and for the benefit of the other defendants, from Carlton, New Jersey to warehousing companies in Florida, New York, and New Jersey, and thereafter transported by or for Acme, Nationwide Supply, Top Notch, Baggins, and Bat for sale and distribution in numerous states, including New Jersey; and (ii) delivered at defendants' direction to various trucking companies for purported delivery to Florida, when in fact such merchandise was instead transported to Acme, Nationwide Supply, and Top Notch for sale and distribution in numerous states, including New Jersey, with the approval, acquiescence, and for the benefit of the other defendants.

102. Additionally, in furtherance of the above-described scheme to defraud Martin, defendants have committed numerous and direct violations of 18 U.S.C. § 2315 by receiving, storing, and selling Martin merchandise in interstate commerce, knowing the same to have been unlawfully converted from Martin. The Martin merchandise, which has a value far exceeding $5,000, was transported, stored, distributed and sold in interstate commerce by or for Acme, Nationwide Supply, Top Notch, Baggins, and Bat in numerous states, including New Jersey, with the approval, acquiescence, and for the benefit of the other defendants.

103. In addition, in furtherance of the above-described scheme to defraud Martin, defendants have committed numerous and direct violations of New Jersey Statute 2C:21-10 dealing with commercial bribery (a felony), in that Martin employees Zapata and Cervantes and Martin agent Montero knowingly accepted payments and/or a share of the profits of the scheme offered and conferred from various defendants, with the approval, acquiescence, and for the benefit of the other defendants, as consideration for knowingly violating the duties and fidelities owed to Martin by virtue of their respective employment and agency relationships with Martin.

104. Finally, in furtherance of the above-described scheme to defraud Martin, defendants have committed numerous and direct violations of 18 U.S.C. § 1952 by traveling in interstate and foreign commerce and using the facilities of interstate and foreign commerce, including the wires and mails, to distribute the proceeds of their unlawful activity and

to promote, manage, establish, carry on, and to facilitate the promotion, management, establishment, and carrying on of their unlawful activities. Such unlawful activity referred to above was in fact bribery in violation of New Jersey Statute 2C:21-10, which thereby violated 18 U.S.C. § 1952.

105. The illegal predicate acts described in paragraphs 99 through 104 above constitute a pattern of racketeering activity as defined by 18 U.S.C. § 1961(5).

106. By reason of the aforementioned racketeering enterprise activities, defendants' ability to defraud Martin was immeasurably enhanced because the illegal operation of the enterprises facilitated the fraud and aided its concealment, thereby damaging Martin in its business and property.

§ 3.16   —Conspiracy Count

SECOND CAUSE OF ACTION
(For violation of 18 U.S.C. § 1962(d))

107. Martin repeats and realleges paragraphs 1 through 95 and 99 through 104, inclusive, as if fully set forth herein.

108. Temple of Florida/Temple of Panama, Uno, and Global constituted enterprises operating in and affecting interstate and foreign commerce. Defendants Acme, Nationwide Supply, Top Notch, Baggins, Bat, World, Foremost, Munsin, Rogers, Byers, Quin, Windom, Nereson, Zapata, Cervantes, Montero, Juarez, and Garcia knowingly, willfully, and unlawfully did conspire, agree, and combine together with each other to associate with, conduct, participate in, and further the affairs of the enterprises through a pattern of racketeering activity in violation of 18 U.S.C. § 1962(c). Such conspiracy is unlawful and violates 18 U.S.C. § 1962(d).

109. The object of the conspiracy was to associate with, participate in, and conduct the affairs of the enterprises, in part, by inducing Martin to sell Martin merchandise to the enterprises at substantially reduced prices by fraudulently misrepresenting that such merchandise would be exported to Central America, South America, and the Caribbean. However, in truth and in fact, such merchandise was never intended to be exported by the enterprises but instead was intended to be, and actually was, transferred by the enterprises to Acme, Top Notch, Nationwide Supply, Baggins, and Bat, at prices substantially below those available to Martin's legitimate domestic distributors and wholesale customers.

110. The overt acts committed by defendants to execute and accomplish the above-described unlawful conspiracy include but are not

limited to the illegal predicate acts set forth in paragraphs 99 through 104 above, which constitute a pattern of racketeering activity as defined in 18 U.S.C. § 1961(5).

111. By reason of the above-described unlawful conspiracy, defendants' ability to defraud Martin was immeasurably enhanced because the illegal operation of the enterprises through this conspiracy facilitated the fraud and aided its concealment, thereby damaging Martin in its business and property.

§ 3.17 —Aiding and Abetting Count

THIRD CAUSE OF ACTION
(For violation of 18 U.S.C. § 1962(c))

112. Martin repeats and realleges paragraphs 1 through 95 and 99 through 104, inclusive, as if fully set forth herein.

113. Temple of Florida/Temple of Panama, Uno, and Global constituted enterprises operating in and affecting interstate and foreign commerce. Defendants World, Foremost, Garcia, Juarez, Montero, Zapata, and Cervantes associated themselves with the enterprises and conducted and participated in the affairs of the enterprises through a pattern of racketeering activity in violation of 18 U.S.C. § 1962(c).

114. World, Foremost, Garcia, Juarez, Montero, Zapata, and Cervantes, separately and together, knowingly, willfully and unlawfully devised and executed a scheme to defraud Martin through their use of the enterprises in order to obtain Martin merchandise from Martin at prices substantially below those available to Martin's legitimate domestic distributors and wholesale customers by means of false and fraudulent statements, representations, or promises and through the commission of numerous criminal acts.

115. The illegal predicate acts described in paragraphs 99 through 104 above constitute a pattern of racketeering activity as defined by 18 U.S.C. § 1961(5).

116. Defendants Acme, Nationwide Supply, Top Notch, Baggins, Bat, Munsin, Rogers, Byers, Quin, Windom, and Nereson aided and abetted World, Foremost, Garcia, Juarez, Montero, Zapata, and Cervantes in associating themselves with the enterprises and conducting and participating in the affairs of the enterprises through a pattern of racketeering activity in violation of 18 U.S.C. § 1962(c).

117. Acme, Nationwide Supply, Top Notch, Baggins, Bat, Munsin, Rogers, Byers, Quin, Windom, and Nereson each had knowledge of the illegal operation of the enterprises and lent substantial assistance to World, Foremost, Garcia, Juarez, Montero, Zapata, and Cervantes to

enable them to associate themselves with the enterprises and to conduct and participate in the affairs of the enterprises through a pattern of racketeering activity in violation of 18 U.S.C. § 1962(c).

118. By reason of the aforementioned racketeering enterprise activities and the aiding and abetting of such racketeering enterprise activities, defendants' ability to defraud Martin was immeasurably enhanced because the illegal operation of the enterprises and the aiding and abetting of the illegal operation of the enterprises facilitated the fraud and aided its concealment, thereby damaging Martin in its business and property.

§ 3.18   —Infiltration of Plaintiff Count

FOURTH CAUSE OF ACTION
(For violation of 18 U.S.C. § 1962(c))

119. Martin repeats and realleges paragraphs 1 through 95 and 99 through 104, inclusive, as if fully set forth herein.

120. Martin constituted an enterprise operating in and affecting interstate and foreign commerce. Defendants Acme, Nationwide Supply, Top Notch, Baggins, Bat, World, Foremost, Munsin, Rogers, Byers, Quin, Windom, Nereson, Zapata, Cervantes, Juarez, Montero, Garcia, Temple of Florida/Temple of Panama, Uno, and Global associated themselves with Martin and infiltrated and participated in the conduct of the affairs of Martin through a pattern of racketeering activity in violation of 18 U.S.C. § 1962(c).

121. Specifically, the defendants engaged in a continuous pattern of commercial bribery, whereby Martin employees Zapata and Cervantes and Martin agent Montero were paid by Garcia, with the approval, acquiescence, and substantial assistance of the other defendants, in order to establish and maintain defendants' fraudulent operation and to keep their fraudulent operation from being uncovered by other officials at Martin. By means of the commercial bribery and other related criminal acts by the defendants, defendants were able to associate themselves with Martin and infiltrate and participate in the conduct of the affairs of Martin to Martin's detriment.

122. The consequence of defendants' infiltration and participation in the conduct of the affairs of Martin by, among other things, bribing Martin's agent and employees, was that Martin was induced to sell Martin merchandise at the discounted export price to Temple of Florida/Temple of Panama, Global, and Uno based on fraudulent misrepresentations that such merchandise would be exported to Central America, South America, and the Caribbean. However, in truth and in fact, such merchandise

was never intended to be exported but instead was intended to be, and actually was, transferred to Acme, Top Notch, Nationwide Supply, Baggins, and Bat at prices substantially below those available to Martin's legitimate domestic distributors and wholesale customers.

123. The illegal predicate acts described in paragraphs 99 through 104 above were committed to establish and further defendants' illicit infiltration and participation in the conduct of the affairs of Martin and constitute a pattern of racketeering activity as defined by 18 U.S.C. § 1961(5).

124. By reason of the aforementioned racketeering enterprise activities, defendants' ability to defraud Martin was immeasurably enhanced because the illegal infiltration and participation in the conduct of the affairs of Martin facilitated the fraud and aided its concealment, thereby damaging Martin in its business and property.

§ 3.19 —Conspiracy to Infiltrate Plaintiff Count

FIFTH CAUSE OF ACTION
(For violation of 18 U.S.C. § 1962(d))

125. Martin repeats and realleges paragraphs 1 through 95 and 99 through 104 inclusive, as if fully set forth herein.

126. Martin constituted an enterprise operating in and affecting interstate and foreign commerce. Defendants Acme, Nationwide Supply, Top Notch, Baggins, Bat, Munsin, Rogers, Byers, Quin, Windom, Nereson, Zapata, Cervantes, Juarez, Montero, Garcia, World, Foremost, Temple of Florida/Temple of Panama, Uno, and Global knowingly, willfully, and unlawfully did conspire, agree, and combine together with each other to associate themselves with Martin and infiltrate and participate in the conduct of the affairs of Martin through a pattern of racketeering activity in violation of 18 U.S.C. § 1962(c). Such conspiracy is unlawful and violates 18 U.S.C. § 1962(d).

127. The object of the conspiracy was to associate with, infiltrate, and participate in the conduct of the affairs of Martin for defendants' illicit benefit. Specifically, by means of the conspiracy, the defendants engaged in a continuous pattern of commercial bribery, whereby Martin employees Zapata and Cervantes and Martin agent Montero were paid by Garcia, with the approval, acquiescence, and substantial assistance of the other defendants, in order to establish and maintain defendants' fraudulent operation and to keep their fraudulent operation from being uncovered by other officials at Martin. By means of the commercial bribery and other related criminal acts by the defendants, defendants were able to associate themselves with Martin and

infiltrate and participate in the conduct of the affairs of Martin to Martin's detriment.

128. The consequence of this conspiracy to infiltrate and participate in the conduct of the affairs of Martin by, among other things, bribing Martin's agent and employees, was that Martin was induced to sell Martin merchandise to Temple of Florida/Temple of Panama, Uno, and Global at substantially reduced prices based on fraudulent misrepresentations that such merchandise would be exported to Central America, South America, and the Caribbean. However, in truth and in fact, such merchandise was never intended to be exported, but instead was intended to be, and actually was, transferred to Acme, Top Notch, Nationwide Supply, Baggins, and Bat at prices substantially below those available to Martin's legitimate domestic distributors and wholesale customers.

129. The overt acts committed by defendants to execute and accomplish the above-described unlawful conspiracy include, but are not limited to, the illegal predicate acts set forth in paragraphs 99 through 104 above, which constitute a pattern of racketeering activity as defined by 18 U.S.C. § 1961(5).

130. By reason of the above-described illegal conspiracy, defendants' ability to defraud Martin was immeasurably enhanced because the illegal infiltration and participation in the conduct of the affairs of Martin through this conspiracy facilitated the fraud and aided its concealment, thereby damaging Martin in its business and property.

§ 3.20   —Aiding and Abetting Infiltration Count

SIXTH CAUSE OF ACTION
(For violation of 18 U.S.C. § 1962(c))

131. Martin repeats and realleges paragraphs 1 through 95 and 99 through 104, inclusive, as if fully set forth herein.

132. Martin constituted an enterprise operating in and affecting interstate and foreign commerce. Defendants Zapata, Cervantes, Garcia, Juarez, Montero, Foremost, World, Temple of Florida/Temple of Panama, Uno, and Global associated themselves with Martin and infiltrated and participated in the conduct of the affairs of Martin through a pattern of racketeering activity in violation of 18 U.S.C. § 1962(c).

133. Zapata, Cervantes, Garcia, Juarez, Montero, Foremost, World, Temple of Florida/Temple of Panama, Uno, and Global, separately and together, knowingly, willfully, and unlawfully executed a scheme to defraud Martin through their positions as employees, agents, or customers of Martin, in order to obtain Martin merchandise from Martin at prices substantially below those available to Martin's legitimate domestic

distributors and wholesale customers by means of false and fraudulent statements, representations, promises, and by means of giving and receiving commercial bribes.

134. The illegal predicate acts described in paragraphs 99 through 104 above were committed to establish and further defendants' illicit infiltration and participation in the conduct of the affairs of Martin and constitute a pattern of racketeering activity as defined by 18 U.S.C. § 1961(5).

135. Defendants Acme, Nationwide Supply, Top Notch, Baggins, Bat, Munsin, Rogers, Byers, Quin, Windom, and Nereson aided and abetted Zapata, Cervantes, Garcia, Juarez, Montero, Foremost, World, Temple of Florida/Temple of Panama, Uno, and Global in associating themselves with Martin and infiltrating and participating in the conduct of the affairs of Martin through a pattern of racketeering activity in violation of 18 U.S.C. § 1962(c).

136. Acme, Nationwide Supply, Top Notch, Baggins, Bat, Munsin, Rogers, Byers, Quin, Windom, and Nereson each had knowledge of the illegal infiltration and participation in the conduct of the affairs of Martin and lent substantial assistance to Zapata, Cervantes, Garcia, Juarez, Montero, Foremost, World, Temple of Florida/Temple of Panama, Uno, and Global in order to enable them to associate themselves with Martin and infiltrate and participate in the conduct of the affairs of Martin through a pattern of racketeering activity in violation of 18 U.S.C. § 1962(c).

137. By reason of the aforementioned racketeering enterprise activities and the aiding and abetting of such racketeering enterprise activities, defendants' ability to defraud Martin was immeasurably enhanced because the illegal infiltration and participation in the conduct of the affairs of Martin and the aiding and abetting of the illegal infiltration and participation in the conduct of the affairs of Martin facilitated the fraud and aided its concealment, thereby damaging Martin in its business and property.

§ 3.21   —Counts for Reinvestment of Racketeering Proceeds

SEVENTH CAUSE OF ACTION
(Against Acme, Munsin, and Rogers for
violation of 18 U.S.C. § 1962(a))

138. Martin repeats and realleges paragraphs 1 through 95 and 99 through 104, inclusive, as if fully set forth herein.

139. Acme is an enterprise operating in and affecting interstate commerce. Defendants Acme, Munsin, and Rogers, separately and together,

knowingly, willfully, and unlawfully participated in and executed a scheme with others to defraud Martin for the illicit benefit of Acme and others in order to obtain merchandise from Martin at prices substantially below those available to Martin's legitimate domestic distributors and wholesale customers. Upon information and belief, Acme, Munsin, and Rogers have participated in similar illegal schemes to defraud other manufacturers, and have reinvested the proceeds of these unlawful activities into Acme.

140. Pursuant to the scheme against Martin, Acme, Munsin, and Rogers, acting in concert with Garcia, Juarez, Montero, Zapata, Cervantes, Global, Uno, Temple of Florida/Temple of Panama and World, committed numerous illegal predicate acts, including but not limited to the illegal predicate acts described in paragraphs 99 through 104 above, which constitute a pattern of racketeering activity as defined by 18 U.S.C. § 1961(5).

141. Acme, Munsin, and Rogers received income, directly or indirectly, from the above-described pattern of racketeering activity and used that income, or the proceeds of that income, in the operation of Acme in violation of 18 U.S.C. § 1962(a). Specifically, the income received by Acme, Munsin, and Rogers pursuant to the initial sales by them of the fraudulently obtained Martin merchandise was derived from the pattern of racketeering activity. Thereafter, the proceeds of those initial sales of the fraudulently obtained Martin merchandise were reinvested in Acme by Acme, Munsin, and Rogers, which substantially enhanced Acme's ability to continue and expand its criminal activities against Martin, from which Acme, Munsin, and Rogers received further income and used that income to further Acme's participation in the scheme against Martin.

142. By reason of the aforementioned racketeering enterprise activities, the ability of Acme, Munsin, and Rogers to defraud Martin was immeasurably enhanced because the illegal receipt of the income from the pattern of racketeering activity used in the operation of Acme facilitated the continuation of the fraud, expanded its scope, and aided its concealment, thereby damaging Martin in its business and property.

EIGHTH CAUSE OF ACTION
(Against Top Notch and Byers
for violation of 18 U.S.C. § 1962(a))

143. Martin repeats and realleges paragraphs 1 through 95 and 99 through 104, inclusive, as if fully set forth herein.

144. Top Notch is an enterprise operating in and affecting interstate commerce. Defendants Top Notch and Byers, separately and together, knowingly, willfully, and unlawfully participated in and executed a scheme with others to defraud Martin for the illicit benefit of Top Notch and others in order to obtain merchandise from Martin at prices

substantially below those available to Martin's legitimate domestic distributors and wholesale customers. Upon information and belief, Top Notch and Byers have participated in similar illegal schemes to defraud other manufacturers and have invested the proceeds of those unlawful activities into Top Notch.

145. Pursuant to the scheme against Martin, Top Notch and Byers, acting in concert with Garcia, Juarez, Montero, Zapata, Cervantes, Global, Uno, Temple of Florida/Temple of Panama and World, committed numerous illegal predicate acts, including but not limited to the illegal predicate acts described in paragraphs 99 through 104 above, which constitute a pattern of racketeering activity as defined by 18 U.S.C. § 1961(5).

146. Top Notch and Byers received income, directly or indirectly, from the above-described pattern of racketeering activity and used that income, or the proceeds of that income, in the operation of Top Notch in violation of 18 U.S.C. § 1962(a). Specifically, the income received from Top Notch and Byers pursuant to the initial sales by them of the fraudulently obtained Martin merchandise was derived from the pattern of racketeering activity. Thereafter, the proceeds of those initial sales of the fraudulently obtained Martin merchandise were reinvested in Top Notch by Top Notch and Byers, which substantially enhanced Top Notch's ability to continue and expand its criminal activities against Martin, from which Top Notch and Byers received further income and used that income to further Top Notch's participation in the scheme against Martin.

147. By reason of the aforementioned racketeering enterprise activities, the ability of Top Notch and Byers to defraud Martin was immeasurably enhanced because the illegal receipt of the income from the pattern of racketeering activity used in the operation of Top Notch facilitated the continuation of the fraud, expanded its scope, and aided its concealment, thereby damaging Martin in its business and property.

NINTH CAUSE OF ACTION
(Against Nationwide Supply and Quin
for violation of 18 U.S.C. § 1962(a))

148. Martin repeats and realleges paragraphs 1 through 95 and 99 through 104, inclusive, as if fully set forth herein.

149. Nationwide Supply is an enterprise operating in and affecting interstate commerce. Defendants Nationwide Supply and Quin, separately and together, knowingly, willfully, and unlawfully participated in and executed a scheme with others to defraud Martin for the illicit benefit of Nationwide Supply and others in order to obtain merchandise from Martin at prices substantially below those available to Martin's legitimate domestic distributors and wholesale customers. Upon information and belief, Nationwide Supply and Quin have participated

in similar illegal schemes to defraud other manufacturers and have invested the proceeds of those unlawful activities into Nationwide Supply.

150. Pursuant to the scheme against Martin, Nationwide Supply and Quin, acting in concert with Garcia, Juarez, Montero, Zapata, Cervantes, Global, Uno, Temple of Florida/Temple of Panama, and World, committed numerous illegal predicate acts, including but not limited to the illegal predicate acts described in paragraphs 99 through 104 above, which constitute a pattern of racketeering activity as defined by 18 U.S.C. § 1961(5).

151. Nationwide Supply and Quin received income, directly or indirectly, from the above-described pattern of racketeering activity and used that income, or the proceeds of that income, in the operation of Nationwide Supply in violation of 18 U.S.C. § 1962(a). Specifically, the income received by Nationwide Supply and Quin pursuant to the initial sales by them of the fraudulently obtained Martin merchandise was derived from the pattern of racketeering activity. Thereafter, the proceeds of those initial sales of the fraudulently obtained Martin merchandise were reinvested in Nationwide Supply by Nationwide Supply and Quin, which substantially enhanced Nationwide Supply's ability to continue and expand its criminal activities against Martin, from which Nationwide Supply and Quin received further income and used that income to further Nationwide Supply's participation in the scheme against Martin.

152. By reason of the aforementioned racketeering enterprise activities, the ability of Nationwide Supply and Quin to defraud Martin was immeasurably enhanced because the illegal receipt of the income from the pattern of racketeering activity used in the operation of Nationwide Supply facilitated the continuation of the fraud, expanded its scope, and aided its concealment, thereby damaging Martin in its business and property.

§ 3.22 —Counts for Violation of State Anti-Racketeering Laws

Because the New Jersey Racketeering Act is patterned after the federal RICO statute, Martin's nine federal RICO claims also gave rise to nine counts under the New Jersey act.

TENTH CAUSE OF ACTION
(For violation of the New Jersey Racketeering Act)

153. Martin repeats and realleges paragraphs 1 through 95 and 97 through 106, inclusive, as if fully set forth herein.

154. The activities of the defendants described in Count I above constitute the operation of the affairs of Temple of Florida/Temple of Panama, Uno, and Global (the enterprises) through a pattern of racketeering activity in direct violation of New Jersey Statute 2C:41-2(c).

155. The illegal predicate acts described in paragraphs 99 through 104 above constitute a pattern of racketeering activity as defined by New Jersey Statute 2C:41-1.

156. By reason of the aforementioned racketeering enterprise activities, defendants' ability to defraud Martin was immeasurably enhanced because the illegal operation of the enterprises facilitated the fraud and aided its concealment, thereby damaging Martin in its business and property.

ELEVENTH CAUSE OF ACTION
(For violation of the New Jersey Racketeering Act)

157. Martin repeats and realleges paragraphs 1 through 95, 99 through 104, and 108 through 111, inclusive, as if fully set forth herein.

158. Defendants Acme, Nationwide Supply, Top Notch, Baggins, Bat, Munsin, Rogers, Byers, Quin, Windom, Nereson, Zapata, Cervantes, World, Foremost, Juarez, Montero, and Garcia, knowingly, willfully, and unlawfully did conspire, agree, and combine together with each other to associate themselves with, conduct, participate in, and further the affairs of Temple of Florida/Temple of Panama, Uno, and Global (the enterprises described in Count II above) through a pattern of racketeering activity in violation of New Jersey Statute 2C:41-2(c). Such conspiracy is unlawful and violates New Jersey Statute 2C:41-2(d).

159. The overt acts committed by defendants to execute and accomplish the above-described unlawful conspiracy include but are not limited to the illegal predicate acts set forth in paragraphs 99 through 104 above, which constitute a pattern of racketeering activity as defined by New Jersey Statute 2C:41-1.

160. By reason of the above-described illegal conspiracy, defendants' ability to defraud Martin was immeasurably enhanced because the illegal operation of the enterprises pursuant to the conspiracy facilitated the fraud and aided its concealment, thereby damaging Martin in its business and property.

TWELFTH CAUSE OF ACTION
(For violation of the New Jersey Racketeering Act)

161. Martin repeats and realleges paragraphs 1 through 95, 99 through 104, and 113 through 118, inclusive, as if fully set forth herein.

162. The activities of defendants World, Foremost, Juarez, Montero, Garcia, Zapata, and Cervantes described in Count III above constitute

the operation of the affairs of Temple of Florida/Temple of Panama, Uno, and Global (the enterprises) through a pattern of racketeering activity in direct violation of New Jersey Statute 2C:41-2(c).

163. The illegal predicate acts described in paragraphs 99 through 104 above constitute a pattern of racketeering activity as defined by New Jersey Statute 2C:41-1.

164. Defendants Acme, Nationwide Supply, Top Notch, Baggins, Bat, Munsin, Rogers, Byers, Quin, Windom, and Nereson aided and abetted World, Foremost, Garcia, Juarez, Montero, Zapata, and Cervantes in associating themselves with the enterprises and conducting and participating in the affairs of the enterprises through a pattern of racketeering activity in violation of New Jersey Statute 2C:41-2(c).

165. Acme, Nationwide Supply, Top Notch, Baggins, Bat, Munsin, Rogers, Byers, Quin, Windom, and Nereson each had knowledge of the illegal operation of the enterprises and lent substantial assistance to World, Foremost, Juarez, Montero, Zapata, Cervantes, and Garcia in order to enable them to associate themselves with the enterprises and to conduct and participate in the affairs of the enterprises through a pattern of racketeering activity in violation of New Jersey Statute 2C:41-2(c).

166. By reason of the aforementioned racketeering enterprise activities and the aiding and abetting of such racketeering enterprise activities, defendants' ability to defraud Martin was immeasurably enhanced because the illegal operation of the enterprises and the aiding and abetting of the illegal operation of the enterprises facilitated the fraud and aided its concealment, thereby damaging Martin in its business and property.

THIRTEENTH CAUSE OF ACTION
(For violation of the New Jersey Racketeering Act)

167. Martin repeats and realleges paragraphs 1 through 95, 99 through 104, and 120 through 124, inclusive, as if fully set forth herein.

168. The activities of the defendants described in Count IV above constitute the association with Martin (the enterprise) and the infiltration and participation in the conduct of the affairs of Martin through a pattern of racketeering activity in direct violation of New Jersey Statute 2C:41-2(c).

169. The illegal predicate acts described in paragraphs 99 through 104 above constitute a pattern of racketeering activity as defined by New Jersey Statute 2C:41-1.

170. By reason of the aforementioned racketeering enterprise activities, defendants' ability to defraud Martin was immeasurably enhanced because the illegal infiltration and participation in the conduct of the

affairs of Martin facilitated the fraud and aided its concealment, thereby damaging Martin in its business and property.

FOURTEENTH CAUSE OF ACTION
(For violation of the New Jersey Racketeering Act)

171. Martin repeats and realleges paragraphs 1 through 95, 99 through 104, and 126 through 130, inclusive, as if fully set forth herein.

172. Defendants Acme, Nationwide Supply, Top Notch, Baggins, Bat, Munsin, Rogers, Byers, Quin, Windom, Nereson, Zapata, Cervantes, Juarez, Montero, Garcia, Foremost, World, Temple of Florida/Temple of Panama, Uno, and Global knowingly, willfully, and unlawfully did conspire, agree, and combine together with each other to associate themselves with Martin (the enterprise described in Count V above) and infiltrate and participate in the conduct of the affairs of Martin through a pattern of racketeering activity in violation of New Jersey Statute 2C:41-2(c). Such conspiracy is unlawful and violates New Jersey Statute 2C:41-2(d).

173. The overt acts committed by defendants to execute and accomplish the above-described unlawful conspiracy include but are not limited to the illegal predicate acts set forth in paragraphs 99 through 104 above, which constitute a pattern of racketeering activity as defined by New Jersey Statute 2C:41-1.

174. By reason of the above-described illegal conspiracy, defendants' ability to defraud Martin was immeasurably enhanced because the illegal infiltration and participation in the conduct of the affairs of Martin pursuant to the conspiracy facilitated the fraud and aided its concealment, thereby damaging Martin in its business and property.

FIFTEENTH CAUSE OF ACTION
(For violation of the New Jersey Racketeering Act)

175. Martin repeats and realleges paragraphs 1 through 95, 99 through 104, and 132 through 137, inclusive, as if fully set forth herein.

176. The activities of defendants Zapata, Cervantes, Garcia, Juarez, Montero, Foremost, World, Temple of Florida/Temple of Panama, Uno, and Global described in Count VI above constitute the association with Martin (the enterprise) and the infiltration and participation in the conduct of the affairs of Martin through a pattern of racketeering activity in direct violation of New Jersey Statute 2C:41-2(c).

177. The illegal predicate acts described in paragraphs 99 through 104 above constitute a pattern of racketeering activity as defined by New Jersey Statute 2C:41-1.

178. Defendants Acme, Nationwide Supply, Top Notch, Baggins, Bat, Munsin, Rogers, Byers, Quin, Windom, and Nereson aided and abetted Zapata, Cervantes, Garcia, Juarez, Montero, Foremost, World, Temple of Florida/Temple of Panama, Uno, and Global in associating themselves with Martin and infiltrating and participating in the conduct of the affairs of Martin through a pattern of racketeering activity in violation of New Jersey Statute 2C:41-2(c).

179. Acme, Nationwide Supply, Top Notch, Baggins, Bat, Munsin, Rogers, Byers, Quin, Windom, and Nereson each had knowledge of the illegal infiltration and participation in the conduct of the affairs of Martin and lent substantial assistance to Zapata, Cervantes, Garcia, Juarez, Montero, Foremost, World, Temple of Florida/Temple of Panama, Uno, and Global in order to enable them to associate themselves with Martin and infiltrate and participate in the conduct of the affairs of Martin through a pattern of racketeering activity in violation of New Jersey Statute 2C:41-2(c).

180. By reason of the aforementioned racketeering enterprise activities and the aiding and abetting of such racketeering enterprise activities, defendants' ability to defraud Martin was immeasurably enhanced because the illegal infiltration and participation in the conduct of the affairs of Martin and the aiding and abetting of the illegal infiltration and participation in the conduct of the affairs of Martin facilitated the fraud and aided its concealment, thereby damaging Martin in its business and property.

SIXTEENTH CAUSE OF ACTION
(Against Acme, Munsin and Rogers for violation of the New Jersey Racketeering Act)

181. Martin repeats and realleges paragraphs 1 through 95, 99 through 104, and 139 through 142, inclusive, as if fully set forth herein.

182. The activities of defendants Acme, Munsin, and Rogers described in Count VII above constitute a violation of New Jersey Statute 2C:41-2(a) in that Acme, Munsin, and Rogers received income, directly or indirectly, from a pattern of racketeering activity as defined by New Jersey Statute 2C:41-1, and as described in paragraphs 99 through 104 above, and used that income, or the proceeds of that income, in the operation of Acme (the enterprise).

183. By reason of the aforementioned racketeering enterprise activities, the ability of Acme, Munsin, and Rogers to defraud Martin was immeasurably enhanced because the illegal receipt of the income from the pattern of racketeering activity used in the operation of Acme facilitated

the continuation of the fraud, expanded its scope, and aided its concealment, thereby damaging Martin in its business and property.

SEVENTEENTH CAUSE OF ACTION
(Against Top Notch and Byers
for violation of the New Jersey Racketeering Act)

184. Martin repeats and realleges paragraphs 1 through 95, 99 through 104, and 144 through 147, inclusive, as if fully set forth herein.

185. The activities of defendants Top Notch and Byers described in Count VIII above constitute a violation of New Jersey Statute 2C:41-2(a) in that Top Notch and Byers received income, directly or indirectly, from a pattern of racketeering activity as defined by New Jersey Statute 2C:41-1, and as described in paragraphs 99 through 104 above, and used that income, or the proceeds of that income, in the operation of Top Notch (the enterprise).

186. By reason of the aforementioned racketeering enterprise activities, the ability of Top Notch and Byers to defraud Martin was immeasurably enhanced because the illegal receipt of the income from the pattern of racketeering activity used in the operation of Top Notch facilitated the continuation of the fraud, expanded its scope, and aided its concealment, thereby damaging Martin in its business and property.

EIGHTEENTH CAUSE OF ACTION
(Against Nationwide Supply and Quin
for violation of the New Jersey Racketeering Act)

187. Martin repeats and realleges paragraphs 1 through 95, 99 through 104, and 149 through 152, inclusive, as if fully set forth herein.

188. The activities of defendants Nationwide Supply and Quin described in Count IX above constitute a violation of New Jersey Statute 2C:41-2(a) in that Nationwide Supply and Quin received income, directly or indirectly, from a pattern of racketeering activity as defined by New Jersey Statute 2C:41-1, and as described in paragraphs 99 through 104 above, and used that income, or the proceeds of that income, in the operation of Nationwide Supply (the enterprise).

189. By reason of the aforementioned racketeering enterprise activities, the ability of Nationwide Supply and Quin to defraud Martin was immeasurably enhanced because the illegal receipt of the income from the pattern of racketeering activity used in the operation of Nationwide Supply facilitated the continuation of the fraud, expanded its scope, and aided its concealment, thereby damaging Martin in its business and property.

§ 3.23   —Common Law Fraud Count

NINETEENTH CAUSE OF ACTION
(Common law fraud)

190. Martin repeats and realleges paragraphs 1 through 95 and 99 through 104, inclusive, as if fully set forth herein.

191. Defendants entered into a scheme whereby they agreed to defraud Martin in order to obtain Martin merchandise at the discounted export price for sale through Acme, Nationwide Supply, Top Notch, Baggins, and Bat in the domestic market.

192. Pursuant to that scheme, Garcia, Montero, Global, Uno, and Temple of Florida/Temple of Panama knowingly and with fraudulent intent, with the knowledge, approval, assistance, and acquiescence of the other defendants, fraudulently misrepresented to Martin that they planned to export Martin merchandise to Central America, South America, and the Caribbean. Defendants intended that Martin would rely upon that fraudulent misrepresentation.

193. In reliance upon the fraudulent misrepresentation, Martin sold Martin merchandise to Garcia, Montero, Global, Uno, and Temple of Florida/Temple of Panama at the export price, which was considerably below that available to Martin's legitimate domestic distributors and wholesale customers. In furtherance of defendants' scheme, Garcia, Montero, Global, Uno, and Temple of Florida/Temple of Panama thereafter transferred the Martin merchandise to Acme, Nationwide Supply, Top Notch, Baggins, and Bat for resale in the domestic market.

194. By reason of defendants' fraudulent misrepresentations, Martin has been damaged.

§ 3.24   —Breach of Contract Count

TWENTIETH CAUSE OF ACTION
(Against Acme, Garcia and Temple of Florida/
Temple of Panama for breach of contract)

195. Martin repeats and realleges paragraphs 1 and 2, 9 and 10, 23, 25 and 26, and 77 through 95, inclusive, as if fully set forth herein.

196. Defendants Garcia and Temple of Florida/Temple of Panama acted as agents for their undisclosed principal, defendant Acme.

197. In or about mid-1982, Garcia and Temple of Florida/Temple of Panama entered into a contract with Martin, on their own behalf and on behalf of Acme.

198. Under that contract, Martin agreed to sell to Temple of Florida/ Temple of Panama approximately $1 million worth of Martin merchandise for export to Central America, South America, and the Caribbean.

199. Pursuant to the contract, Garcia, Temple of Florida/Temple of Panama, and Acme procured a letter of credit from First American to pay for their purchase of the Martin merchandise. Martin was unaware that Acme was a co-applicant on the letter of credit.

200. Pursuant to the contract, Martin shipped $733,331.06 of Martin merchandise to Temple of Florida/Temple of Panama in Florida. Acme thereafter transported such merchandise back to its headquarters in Connecticut.

201. At Acme's direction, First American refused to honor the letter of credit and release the funds due Martin for the merchandise it shipped. Ultimately, Acme only authorized First American to release $365,700 under the letter of credit, even though Garcia and Temple of Florida/Temple of Panama represented to Martin on behalf of their undisclosed principal, Acme, that the remainder of the money due under the letter of credit would shortly be paid to Martin.

202. Garcia, Temple of Florida/Temple of Panama, and Acme breached their contract with Martin when Garcia, Temple of Florida/ Temple of Panama and Acme refused to pay Martin the remainder of the money due for delivery of the Martin merchandise.

203. By reason of the breach of contract with Martin by Garcia, Temple of Florida/Temple of Panama, and Acme, Martin has been damaged.

§ 3.25   —Fraud in Inducement of Contract Count

TWENTY-FIRST CAUSE OF ACTION
(Fraud in the inducement of the contract)

204. Martin repeats and realleges paragraphs 1 through 95 and 99 through 104, inclusive, as if fully set forth herein.

205. Defendants entered into a scheme whereby they agreed to defraud Martin in order to obtain Martin merchandise at the discounted export price for sale by Acme, Top Notch, Nationwide Supply, Baggins, and Bat in the domestic market.

206. Pursuant to defendants' scheme, by falsely and fraudulently representing that Global and Uno intended to export Martin merchandise to Central America, South America, and the Caribbean, defendants knowingly and with fraudulent intent induced Martin to enter into a contract with Global and Uno, whereby Martin sold Martin merchandise to Global and Uno at the export price, which was considerably

below that which Martin's legitimate domestic distributors and whole-sale customers would have had to pay. Defendants intended that Martin would rely on that misrepresentation.

207. In furtherance of defendants' scheme, Global and Uno there-after transferred the Martin merchandise to Acme, Nationwide Supply, Top Notch, Baggins, and Bat for resale in the domestic market.

208. By reason of the defendants' fraudulent inducement of the con-tract with Martin, which Martin relied upon in entering the contract with Global and Uno, Martin has been damaged.

TWENTY-SECOND CAUSE OF ACTION
(Fraud in the inducement of the contract)

209. Martin repeats and realleges paragraphs 1 through 95 and 99 through 104, inclusive, as if fully set forth herein.

210. Defendants entered into a scheme whereby they agreed to de-fraud Martin in order to obtain Martin merchandise at the discounted export price for sale by Acme, Top Notch, Nationwide Supply, Baggins, and Bat in the domestic market.

211. Pursuant to defendants' scheme, by falsely and fraudulently rep-resenting to Martin that Temple of Florida/Temple of Panama intended to export Martin merchandise to Central America, South America, and the Caribbean, defendants knowingly and with fraudulent intent in-duced Martin to enter into a contract with Temple of Florida/Temple of Panama, whereby Martin sold Martin merchandise to Temple of Flor-ida/Temple of Panama at the export price, which was considerably be-low that which Martin's legitimate domestic distributors and wholesale customers would have had to pay. Defendants intended that Martin would rely on that misrepresentation.

212. In furtherance of defendants' scheme, Temple of Florida/Temple of Panama thereafter transferred the Martin merchandise to Acme, Top Notch, Nationwide Supply, Baggins, and Bat for resale in the domestic market.

213. By reason of the defendants' fraudulent inducement of the con-tract with Martin, which Martin relied upon in entering the contract with Temple of Florida/Temple of Panama, Martin has been damaged.

TWENTY-THIRD CAUSE OF ACTION
(Against Acme, Garcia, and
Temple of Florida/Temple of Panama for
fraud in the inducement of the contract)

214. Martin repeats and realleges paragraphs 1 and 2, 9 and 10, 23, 25 and 26, and 77 through 95, inclusive, as if fully set forth herein.

215. Defendants Garcia, Temple of Florida/Temple of Panama, and Acme entered into a scheme in or about mid-1982, whereby they agreed to defraud Martin in order to obtain Martin merchandise at the export price for sale by Acme in the domestic market.

216. Pursuant to the scheme, by falsely and fraudulently representing to Martin that Temple of Florida/Temple of Panama intended to export Martin merchandise purchased pursuant to a letter of credit to Central America, South America, and the Caribbean, Garcia, Temple of Florida/ Temple of Panama, and Acme knowingly and with fraudulent intent induced Martin to enter into a contract with Temple of Florida/Temple of Panama, whereby Martin sold Martin merchandise to Temple of Florida/ Temple of Panama at the export price, which was considerably below that available to Martin's legitimate domestic distributors and wholesale customers. Garcia, Temple of Florida/Temple of Panama, and Acme intended that Martin would rely on that misrepresentation.

217. In furtherance of the scheme, Temple of Florida/Temple of Panama thereafter transferred the Martin merchandise purchased under the letter of credit to Acme for resale in the domestic market.

218. In addition, in furtherance of the scheme, Acme, which was an undisclosed co-applicant in the letter of credit with Temple of Florida/ Temple of Panama, directed First American not to pay Martin for merchandise delivered pursuant to the letter of credit and ultimately authorized First American to release only one-half of the amount due to Martin.

219. By reason of Garcia's, Temple of Florida/Temple of Panama's and Acme's fraudulent inducement of the contract with Martin, which Martin relied upon in entering the contract with Temple of Florida/Temple of Panama, Martin has been damaged.

§ 3.26 —Prayer for Relief

WHEREFORE, Martin prays for judgment as follows:

(a) an injunction (i) permanently prohibiting all of the defendants, their subsidiaries, affiliates, agents, servants, employees, and all persons acting in concert or participation with them, from obtaining or selling, or attempting to obtain or sell, Martin merchandise except with the full knowledge, consent, and approval of Martin, and (ii) requiring the return to Martin of all the Martin merchandise that has not been resold by defendants in the domestic market;

(b) an award to Martin of such damages as it shall prove at trial, trebled;

(c) an award to Martin of punitive damages;

(d) an award to Martin for the costs of this action, together with reasonable attorneys' fees; and

(e) an award to Martin of any such further relief as this Court may deem just and proper.

MARTIN HEREBY DEMANDS THAT THIS ACTION BE TRIED BEFORE A JURY.

CHAPTER 4

CIVIL RICO IN MANUFACTURING

Richard A. Salomon
Jonathan S. Quinn

§ 4.1   Fact Situation in Manufacturing Context

The defendant is a testing laboratory which contracts with manufacturers of plastic piping to certify, along the lines of the Underwriters Laboratory, the quality of certain products in the plumbing industry and affixes its seal of approval on those products that meet certain standards. Defendant and the plaintiff entered into a contract in 1978 in which defendant agreed to permit the plaintiff plastics manufacturing company to affix defendant's seal of approval to its products and further agreed to use every legal means available to prevent the unauthorized use of defendant's seal on items found to be substandard.

In mid-1984, the plaintiff learned that another plastics manufacturer was selling piping at a price considerably lower than the plaintiff's and that this pipe failed to meet the minimum standards of defendant's testing laboratory but, nonetheless, it carried defendant's seal of approval. The

177

plaintiff took its concerns to officials of defendant and, despite numerous assurances that the matter was being checked into and that proper action would be taken, the defendant took no action, even though, as it turned out, the competitor's seal authorization had actually been withdrawn (delisted) in May 1984 by defendant.

According to the plaintiff, officials of defendant knew that the manufacturer of the substandard piping had been delisted throughout the period of May to August 1984 but specifically deceived the plaintiff and intentionally concealed this information. Although the competing manufacturer had been delisted in May 1984, it continued to sell its product bearing defendant's seal to customers and suppliers until approximately October 1984. Because of its lower prices, the plaintiff lost substantial revenues which it claimed it would otherwise have received from suppliers.

Finally, in August 1984, the plaintiff sent a series of telexes to officials of the defendant to further demand information on the status of the substandard piping. Two telexes ultimately sent by high-ranking officials of the defendant disclosed that the defendant, in fact, had delisted the other manufacturer in May 1984. Still, no public announcement of this delisting occurred at any time either before or immediately after these telexes. Moreover, the defendant took no enforcement action of any kind against the manufacturer after the May delisting to force either recall of the uncertified products or to ensure the disclosure of this information to customers and suppliers.

The plaintiff filed suit in May 1985 in the Circuit Court of Geneva County, Alabama, alleging claims of (a) breach of contract (referring to the language in the agreement to "use every legal means available to prevent unauthorized use of the [seal] on unlisted items or on listed items found to be substandard"); (b) fraud and concealment; and (c) conspiracy. The action was removed by defendant from state court to federal court in Alabama, which subsequently transferred the case, because of the doctrine of forum non conveniens, to the Northern District of Georgia.

Six months after the plaintiff filed its initial complaint, defendant delisted the plaintiff's piping, purportedly because it failed to meet certain impact tests performed by defendant. Pursuant to Federal Rule of Civil Procedure 15(a), the plaintiff moved to amend its complaint (see § 4.5) to include new charges under the RICO statute stemming from defendant's wrongful delisting of the plaintiff as harassment for its having filed the suit. The plaintiff's motion for leave to file an amended complaint was granted, and the Second Amended Complaint in this action was filed in February 1986. The plaintiffs alleged, inter alia, that the wrongful delisting constituted additional evidence of fraud by defendant and that such facts offered indisputable evidence that a pattern of racketeering existed, as required by the RICO statute. It is this complaint, set out in §§ **4.6** through **4.11** with the names of the parties altered, that forms the basis for the discussion in this chapter.

In February 1987, the parties arrived at a settlement agreement that terminated the action. Although the merits of the lawsuit were never adjudicated, the plaintiff received a favorable settlement, largely because of the addition of the RICO claim, which proved quite useful in focusing the issues.

§ 4.2   Pattern of Racketeering Activity

Due to the developing law in the area, the plaintiff's RICO claim (see § **4.6** through **4.11**) might have to be amended if this case were filed today, in light of evolving decisions related to the pattern requirement. In fact, the most controversial issue in RICO jurisprudence today is the meaning of *pattern.*

Section 1962 of the RICO statute specifies that there can be no violation of the statute unless there exists a pattern of criminal activity. The statute, however, does not define a pattern beyond stating that there must be "at least two acts of racketeering activity" within a 10-year period.[1]

Although there has never been agreement by the courts on what constitutes a pattern of racketeering activity, the pattern element posed little, if any, difficulty for plaintiffs prior to the issuance of the Supreme Court's decision in *Sedima, S.P.R.L. v. Imrex Co.,*[2] in which it stated that "[w]hile two such acts [of racketeering activity] are necessary, they may not be sufficient." Before *Sedima,* many courts imposed no limitations at all on the pattern element beyond the minimal requirements set forth in the RICO statute,[3] but the Supreme Court rejected that minimalist view in *H.J. Inc. v. Northwestern Bell Telephone Co.,*[4] finding that any two "predicate" acts of racketeering within 10 years of each other may constitute a pattern if they merely relate in some way to the affairs of the enterprise.

The Supreme Court's decision in *Sedima* required the lower courts to reconsider the question of what constitutes a pattern. In the now-famous footnote 14 of its opinion, the Court opined that the definition of pattern in § 1961(5) was merely a starting point for judicial interpretation. The Court determined that, based upon RICO's legislative history, in order to satisfy the pattern element of the offense a plaintiff must prove continued criminal activity or a threat of continued activity (the *continuity element*)

---

[1] 18 U.S.C. § 1961(5) (1988).

[2] 473 U.S. 479, 496 n.14 (1985).

[3] 18 U.S.C. § 1961(5).

[4] 492 U.S. 229 (1989).

and a relationship between the predicate acts (the *relationship element*).[5]
Unfortunately, the Court did not specifically discuss what was meant by
either continuity or relationship.

In the aftermath of the *Sedima* decision, the lower courts struggled to
develop a test for the pattern of racketeering requirement. In particular,
the courts differed over whether it is necessary to show merely multiple
acts or more than one fraudulent "scheme" in order to demonstrate a pattern of racketeering activity. At one end of the spectrum, the Eighth and
Tenth Circuits adopted the highly restrictive position that plaintiffs must
prove two distinct criminal schemes—as opposed to episodes or transactions—in order to prove a pattern, which is a position much more favorable to the defendant.[6] At the other end of the spectrum, a few circuits,
such as the Second and Eleventh, effectively disregarded footnote 14 of
Sedima and adhered to their pre-*Sedima* interpretation of the pattern element, that multiple predicate acts constituting a single fraudulent scheme
can create civil RICO liability.[7] Other circuits, however, adopted a more
middle-of-the-road approach, making a case-by-case, flexible, multiple-
factor factual inquiry.[8]

In *H.J. Inc. v. Northwestern Bell Telephone Co.,*[9] the Supreme Court
confirmed the *continuity plus relationship test* of *Sedima* and rejected the
Eighth Circuit's multiple schemes requirement. The Court held that continuity or a threat of continuing criminal activity could be proven in a variety of ways, "thus making it difficult to formulate in the abstract any
general test for continuity."[10] The Court stated that continuity "is both a
closed- and open-ended concept, referring either to a closed period of repeated conduct, or to past conduct that by its nature projects into the future with a threat of repetition."[11] "A party alleging a RICO violation may
demonstrate continuity over a closed period by proving a series of related
predicates extending over a substantial period of time. Predicate acts extending over a few weeks or months and threatening no future criminal
conduct do not satisfy this requirement."[12] Alternatively, a party may

---

[5] Sedima, S.P.R.L. v. Imrex Co., 473 U.S. 479, 496 n.14.

[6] *See, e.g.,* Superior Oil v. Fulmer, 785 F.2d 252 (8th Cir. 1986); Torwest DBC, Inc. v. Dick, 810 F.2d 925 (10th Cir. 1987).

[7] *See, e.g.,* United States v. Ianniello, 808 F.2d 184 (2d Cir. 1986), *cert. denied,* 483 U.S. 1006 (1987); Bank of Am. Nat'l Trust & Sav. Ass'n v. Touche Ross & Co., 782 F.2d 966, 971 (11th Cir. 1986).

[8] *See, e.g.,* Barticheck v. Fidelity Union Bank, 832 F.2d 36 (3d Cir. 1987); Morgan v. Bank of Waukegan, 804 F.2d 970 (7th Cir. 1986).

[9] 492 U.S. 229 (1989).

[10] *Id.* at 241.

[11] *Id.*

[12] *Id.* at 242.

prove a pattern of racketeering activity by proving a "specific threat of repetition extending indefinitely into the future" or that the "predicate acts or offenses are part of an ongoing entity's regular way of doing business."[13] No one factor is determinative; rather, courts must examine the facts of each case to determine when the threat of long-term criminal activity is present.

§ 4.3   Pattern Requirement since *H.J. Inc.*

What, if any, guidance does the *H.J. Inc.* decision give in adding definition to the fuzzy picture of the continuity requirement? In the first place, the Supreme Court rejected the two most extreme approaches: the pro-defendant, multiple schemes approach of the Eighth Circuit, and the pro-plaintiff approach of the courts that held the pre-*Sedima* position that a pattern is established simply by proving any two predicate acts that are not "sporadic" or "isolated."

At the time the lawsuit, whose pleadings are presented in §§ **4.5** through **4.11**, was filed, the 11th Circuit subscribed to the more lenient, pro-plaintiff position. In 1986, the 11th Circuit had rejected the multiple schemes test and held that two or more separate uses of the mails or wires perpetrated in the course of a single fraudulent scheme are separate racketeering acts constituting a pattern.[14] In effect, the *H.J. Inc.* decision rejected both that approach and the more restrictive approach and implicitly approved an intermediate approach, the fact-based, multi-factor test followed by most circuits.

Under a strict *H.J. Inc.* analysis, the plaintiff in the sample lawsuit presented here may have to amend its complaint to ensure that no court would grant a dismissal or summary judgment in favor of the defendant merely because its alleged activities were close-ended over a short period of time with no threat of ongoing activity. In pleading the pattern element, a plaintiff should describe the relationship between the enumerated predicate acts in great detail in order to demonstrate the existence of a pattern of racketeering. In addition, a plaintiff should allege that the acts are sufficiently continuous so as to constitute a pattern.

Nonetheless, *H.J. Inc.* did not define a pattern in any meaningful detail, and courts still have considerable discretion in applying the elements. A recent 11th Circuit decision, for example, casts some doubt on the extent to which *H.J. Inc.* has truly tightened the pattern requirement. In *United*

---

[13] *Id.*

[14] *See* Bank of Am. Nat'l Trust & Sav. Ass'n v. Touche Ross & Co., 782 F.2d 966, 971 (11th Cir. 1986) (nine separate acts of fraud over three years constitutes a pattern).

States v. Hobson,[15] the 11th Circuit Court of Appeals affirmed, on remand, the RICO conviction of a criminal defendant who had been con-
victed based solely on a single episode of importation of marijuana from
Colombia. The court held that, notwithstanding *H.J. Inc.,* the pattern of
racketeering was sufficient, given the defendant's series of acts relating to
the shipment. The court concluded that the series of acts "by its nature
project[ed] into the future with a *threat of repetition.*"[16]

On the other hand, a recent decision by a federal district court in Georgia indicates that, in light of *H.J. Inc.,* a single scheme that lasts only a
short period of time and affects only one victim is insufficient. In *Homes
by Michelle, Inc. v. The Federal Savings Bank,*[17] the court dismissed a
RICO claim filed by the officers of a home-building company against
their lender alleging that the bank had caused the builder's subsequent default on acquisition loans by failing to provide agreed-upon construction
financing. The court concluded that under the definition of continuity,
plaintiffs had not satisfied the requirements of *H.J. Inc.*

Rather than adopting a uniform definition of the elusive pattern requirement, post-*H.J. Inc.* courts have enunciated the factors to be considered on a case-by-case basis:

1. The number of predicate acts committed
2. The seriousness of the offenses
3. The number of victims
4. The time period involved
5. The number of separate schemes
6. The likelihood that the acts would be continued.[18]

§ 4.4 Application of Pattern Requirement to Manufacturing Case

In light of recent case law, plaintiffs must be careful to plead with particularity the continuity required to sustain a RICO claim. In the sample
pleadings, such a determination would likely turn on the question of what
the purpose of defendant's allegedly fraudulent scheme was. In order to
satisfy the continuity element of the pattern requirement under *H.J. Inc.,*

[15] 893 F.2d 1267 (11th Cir. 1990).

[16] *Id.* at 1269 (emphasis added).

[17] 733 F. Supp. 1495 (N.D. Ga. 1990).

[18] *See, e.g.,* Swistock v. Jones, 884 F.2d 755 (3d Cir. 1989); Management Computer
Servs., Inc. v. Hawkins, Ash, Baptie & Co., 883 F.2d 48 (7th Cir. 1989).

the plaintiff here would have to demonstrate either a "specific threat of repetition," or show that the predicate acts are part of the defendant's "regular way of doing business."[19]

The schemes alleged in this action—to allow and encourage the manufacturer of the substandard piping to sell that piping bearing the defendant's seal; to fraudulently conceal from plaintiff and others the fact that the manufacturer of the substandard piping had been delisted; and to fraudulently conceal the fact that it allowed certain manufacturers to use reprocessed materials—arguably show, by their nature, a threat of future criminal conduct. Nonetheless, it is possible that, under *H.J. Inc.,* even accepting the plaintiff's allegations as true, the purpose of the schemes might be deemed to have been achieved and the scheme completed. Under that hypothetical scenario, a court might find that the plaintiff had not alleged any additional facts to suggest a threat of continuity. In order to sustain a colorable action considering *H.J. Inc.,* the plaintiff today might be wise to allege additional facts about the manner in which defendant might inflict future injury on the plaintiff or other parties. A civil RICO plaintiff would be well advised to anticipate and prepare for the defendant's inevitable motion to dismiss. Toward this end, the plaintiff should conduct, prior to filing suit, research of law in the circuit in which the action was commenced regarding pattern, as well as other issues, such as person/enterprise.

The facts in the sample case are distinguishable from *H.J. Inc.* In *H.J. Inc.,* the respondent telephone company had, over the course of a six-year period, paid bribes to five utilities commissioners in an effort to obtain unfair and unreasonable rate hikes. The Supreme Court held that the lower courts had erred in dismissing the petitioner telephone customers' RICO claim. The alleged criminal activity in *H.J. Inc.*—bribing public officials—was capable of repetition and thus created a genuine threat of future racketeering activity against the same victims. Additionally, the predicate acts occurred over a substantial period of time. In short, the scheme was both open-ended and extended over a substantial period of time. As already noted and in light of developing case law, plaintiff herein would be well advised to amend the complaint to fortify the acts constituting the pattern.

Although the merits of the sample lawsuit were never adjudicated, plaintiff received a favorable settlement, largely because of the RICO claims, which proved quite useful in focusing the issues. Once a determination has been made that a valid basis for a RICO claim exists, including satisfaction of the pattern elements, counsel should consider in appropriate cases meeting with opposing counsel to discuss the imminent filing of

---

[19] 492 U.S. at 242.

a RICO suit. If the pattern elements have been convincingly established, one of the principal bases for the dismissal of a RICO claim at an early stage will have been overcome.

§ 4.5   Motion to File Amended Complaint

IN THE UNITED STATES DISTRICT COURT
FOR THE NORTHERN DISTRICT OF GEORGIA
ATLANTA DIVISION

PLATTEN PLASTIC CONDUIT & PIPE CORPORATION, a Corporation, Plaintiff, v. FLUID DYNAMICS FOUNDATION, a Corporation, Defendant.	CIVIL ACTION NO. C85-9999-A

PLAINTIFF'S MOTION FOR LEAVE
TO FILE SECOND AMENDED COMPLAINT

Plaintiff, Platten Plastic Conduit & Pipe Corporation ("Platten Plastic"), by its attorneys, moves this Court to grant it leave to file its Second Amended Complaint, pursuant to Rule 15(a) of the Federal Rules of Civil Procedure. In support of this motion, Platten Plastic states as follows:

Introduction

1.   Since the filing of its First Amended Complaint on October 31, 1985, Platten Plastic has discovered additional evidence of wrongdoing by defendant, Fluid Dynamics Foundation ("FDF") and has incurred additional damages that must be included in a Second Amended Complaint. In part, as a result of this additional evidence of misconduct and other information uncovered, Platten Plastic seeks to amend its First Amended Complaint to bring a related claim under the Racketeer Influenced and Corrupt Organizations Act ("RICO"), 18 U.S.C. §§ 1961–1964. These amendments will not prejudice FDF or the additional defendants because these parties have in their own possession all of the relevant documents that support these fraud-based claims and the resulting concealment. Indeed, the individual defendants named in the

amended complaint have either already been deposed in this case or were otherwise put on notice.

2.   The instant case was only recently transferred to this Court after considerable delay and after defendant FDF's efforts to remand and transfer this case based on the doctrine of *forum non conveniens* were resolved. FDF's attempts to prevent the filing of the First Amended Complaint and to dismiss or have summary judgment granted on the original complaint were previously rejected by the Court. At a motions calendar hearing on January 23, 1986, Platten Plastic informed this Court and opposing counsel that it was considering filing a newly amended complaint. Consistent with the Court's request, Platten Plastic has promptly filed the attached Second Amended Complaint.

3.   The grounds supporting the filing of this amended complaint, including the fact that defendants will not be prejudiced, are outlined in greater detail below.

New Evidence

4.   On or about October 1, 1985, FDF delisted Platten Plastic's two-inch ABS foam core pipe, purportedly because this pipe failed certain impact tests performed by FDF. After filing its First Amended Complaint on October 31, 1985, Platten Plastic discovered that FDF had improperly tested and violated standard testing procedures in evaluating Platten Plastic's two-inch foam core pipe. It is submitted that FDF, intending to harass Platten Plastic for filing this suit, intentionally departed from proper testing procedures to insure that Platten Plastic's pipe would fail these tests. A second amendment of Platten Plastic's complaint is necessary, therefore, to include these new facts, allegations, and this claim, along with the damages arising thereunder.

5.   Discovery occurring both before and after the filing of Platten Plastic's First Amended Complaint has shed light on the chronology of events leading up to this litigation. In particular, depositions taken of FDF's officers and employees have clarified the roles of these individuals in the overall scheme to defraud Platten Plastic. In addition, the depositions have disclosed further evidence of fraud by defendants affecting parties other than Platten Plastic. In order to incorporate this evidence and to amplify the allegations of the original and amended complaints and to state them with more particularity, in accordance with Rule 9 of the Federal Rules of Civil Procedure, amendments to the First Amended Complaint are necessary.

RICO Claim

6.   On July 1, 1985, the United States Supreme Court issued two opinions, *Sedima, S.P.R.L. v. Imrex Co.,* 105 S. Ct. 3275 (1985) and

American National Bank v. Haroco, Inc., 105 S. Ct. 3291 (1985), which held that a private litigant does not have to establish a prior criminal conviction by defendants or put forward allegations of a distinct "racketeering" injury before being able to state a claim for relief under RICO. These stated requirements had been engrafted on the statute by numerous lower courts. Because of the serious nature of the RICO allegations, Platten Plastic did not file its RICO claim until after the *Sedima* and *Haroco* opinions had issued, subsequent lower court decisions were released further clarifying the scope of RICO, and Platten Plastic had made a careful examination of all relevant RICO allegations. In particular, the newly discovered facts regarding the wrongful delisting of Platten Plastic (¶ 4 *supra*) constitute additional evidence of fraud by FDF and offer Platten Plastic additional and indisputable evidence that a "pattern of racketeering" existed, as required by the RICO statute. Accordingly, Platten Plastic requests leave of this Court to amend its complaint to add the RICO claim.

Additional Damages

7.   Platten Plastic suffered additional damages as a result of FDF's wrongful delisting in October 1985. In addition, Platten Plastic has calculated more precisely the damages resulting from lost sales, as previously alleged in the original and first amended complaints. As a result, it must amend its complaint to reflect these new damage figures.

No Prejudice to Defendants

8.   The defendants will not be prejudiced by an order granting Platten Plastic leave to file its Second Amended Complaint. All relevant documents and information are already in their hands and little additional discovery arising out of any new claims will be necessary. FDF was on notice that Platten Plastic contemplated filing a second amended complaint, since it mentioned this fact at the January 23, 1986 motion call. Moreover, FDF, having removed and transferred this case to this Court, is principally responsible for the delays which have resulted.

9.   Each of the FDF officers and employees named in the Second Amended Complaint has made, contributed to, or knowingly acquiesced in the making of false statements that furthered FDF's scheme to defraud Platten Plastic. Further, the officers and employees of FDF named in the complaint will not be prejudiced by this filing because four of the proposed defendants have already been deposed in this case. All of the defendants have been aware of the existence of the case and many, if not all, have been involved in its defense since its inception. Pursuant to Rule 15(a) of the Federal Rules of Civil Procedure, Platten Plastic must

amend its complaint to add these individuals as defendants so that they may be held legally responsible for their fraudulent activities.

10. In addition, FDF recently hired new counsel who is actively involved in the defense of the case and who, upon information and belief, had little or no familiarity with this case before January, 1986. Therefore, it cannot be claimed that counsel would be prejudiced by any amendments to FDF's complaint to add a new cause of action or additional allegations related to previously filed claims.

WHEREFORE, plaintiff Platten Plastic requests that this Court grant it leave to file the attached Second Amendment Complaint.

§ 4.6 Manufacturer's Complaint

IN THE UNITED STATES DISTRICT COURT
FOR THE NORTHERN DISTRICT OF GEORGIA
ATLANTA DIVISION

PLATTEN PLASTIC CONDUIT & PIPE CORPORATION, a Corporation, Plaintiff, vs. FLUID DYNAMICS FOUNDATION, a Corporation, REBECCA THATCHER, EMIL TRENT, ROBERT BERNSON, WARD BUTLER, REED TATE, and SAM KUSAK, Defendants.	CIVIL ACTION NO. C85-9999-A

SECOND AMENDED COMPLAINT

Plaintiff Platten Plastic Conduit & Pipe Corporation, by its attorneys, hereby complains of defendants as follows:

JURISDICTION AND VENUE

1. Jurisdiction of this Court is founded upon the provisions of Title 28, United States Code, § 1332 (diversity of citizenship) and upon the provisions of Chapter 96, United States Code, Racketeer Influenced and Corrupt Organizations (RICO), Title 18 U.S.C. §§ 1961–1964. Specifically, this civil action is brought under 18 U.S.C. § 1964(c),

which provides that any person injured in his business or property by reason of a violation of 18 U.S.C. § 1962 may sue in the United States District Court for threefold damages.

2.   Venue in this Court is founded upon 18 U.S.C. § 1965(a), in that defendants reside in the Northern District of Georgia, or may be found in that district, or are transacting business, directly or through agents, in that District.

Parties

3.   Plaintiff Platten Plastic Conduit & Pipe Corporation ("Platten Plastic") is a corporation incorporated under the laws of the State of Delaware with its principal place of business in Platten, Alabama. Platten Plastic is a manufacturer of foam core plastic pipe and is one of only a few manufacturers in the United States that produces this product. Its principal customers are located in the Southeastern United States, the Mid-West, and the State of Texas. Much of the plastic pipe produced by Platten Plastic is used in manufactured homes, such as mobile homes.

4.   Defendant, Fluid Dynamics Foundation ("FDF") is a corporation incorporated under the laws of the State of Michigan with its principal place of business in Ann Arbor, Michigan and with its Southeastern Regional Office in Atlanta, Georgia. FDF is licensed as a non-profit corporation which purports to evaluate and test various products, including plastic piping, against standards promulgated by itself and other organizations, in particular the American Society for Testing Materials ("ASTM").

5.   Defendant Rebecca Thatcher ("Thatcher"), upon information and belief, is a resident of the State of Michigan and at all relevant times herein alleged was President and Chief Operating Officer of FDF.

6.   Defendant Emil Trent ("Trent") is a resident of the State of Michigan and at all relevant times herein alleged was employed by FDF as Manager of its Plastics Listing Program.

7.   Defendant Robert Bernson ("Bernson") is a resident of the State of Michigan and at all relevant times herein alleged was employed by FDF as Director of Listing Programs.

8.   Defendant Ward Butler ("Butler") is a resident of the State of Michigan and at all relevant times herein alleged was an Executive Vice President of FDF.

9.   Defendant Reed Tate ("Tate") is a resident of the State of Georgia and at all relevant times herein alleged was Regional Manager for FDF, Southeast Region.

10.   Defendant Sam Kusak ("Kusak"), upon information and belief, is a resident of the State of Michigan and at all relevant times herein alleged was employed by FDF as Director of Regional Services.

§ 4.7 —Substantive Allegations

SUBSTANTIVE ALLEGATIONS

11.   After testing a manufacturer's product, FDF may authorize the manufacturer to place an FDF seal on the product. This seal purports to represent that the product has been tested by FDF and meets the requisite standards in the industry, as determined primarily by the ASTM. Pipe manufacturers pay a substantial annual listing fee to FDF for the right to use this seal. In addition, FDF purports to maintain a listing of all products that have been tested and approved to bear the FDF seal. If FDF determines, during regular plant inspections or product testing, that a pipe product which has been previously tested and approved no longer meets the requisite standards, FDF must take appropriate and effective action to ensure that the noncompliance is corrected. If subsequent evaluations of the product indicate that corrective measures have not been taken, FDF must "delist" the product and prevent its further sale until the product is brought into compliance with the requisite standards.

12.   When a product is said to be "listed" by FDF, it is a representation that the product meets the requisite standards and is approved to bear the FDF seal. This seal is a widely recognized sign of quality in the plastic pipe and other industries and a widely recognized sign that the product to which it is affixed complies with public health and safety requirements. For example, the United States Department of Housing and Urban Development ("HUD") recognizes the FDF standard and criteria for plastic pipe as complying with Federal Manufactured Home Construction Safety Standards. Plastic pipe, such as that produced by Platten Plastic, which is installed in manufactured homes must meet these federal standards before HUD will approve federally-funded mortgages for these homes. FDF is one of only a few organizations whose seal HUD recognizes as being in compliance with these federal standards.

13.   On or about December 5, 1978, and yearly thereafter, Platten Plastic entered into a contract (the "Contract") with FDF, whereby FDF agreed to test Platten Plastic's pipe products and list those products meeting the applicable standards, in exchange for the payment of listing fees by Platten Plastic. A true and correct copy of this Contract is attached hereto as Exhibit A. In exchange for the right to use FDF's seal in 1984, for example, Platten Plastic paid FDF $3,702.00 in listing fees. In 1985, Platten Plastic paid FDF $5,017.00 in listing fees.

14.   As part of its Contract with FDF, Platten Plastic is required to file, and has filed, yearly affidavits certifying, *inter alia,* that it will place

the FDF seal only on products complying with FDF standards or criteria. Throughout the period from December 5, 1978 until the present, Platten Plastic has in all respects complied with the aforementioned Contract with FDF, has regularly produced only pipe meeting all applicable FDF standards, and has placed the FDF seal only on pipe meeting those standards.

15.   Pursuant to Policy No. 18, attached to and incorporated in the aforementioned Contract with Platten Plastic, FDF promised and agreed to "use every legal means available to prevent unauthorized use of the [FDF] seal on unlisted items or on listed items found to be substandard." In addition, from 1978 to the present, FDF, through its written policies, advertisements and related literature, has repeatedly represented to Platten Plastic specifically and to the plastic pipe industry in general that FDF would protect the integrity of its seal against unauthorized use or infringement by other manufacturers. True and correct copies of policy statements, advertisements, and other related literature distributed, directly or indirectly, to the industry and the public by FDF are attached hereto as Group Exhibit B.

(i) Concealment of Bramble Delisting

16.   Bramble Plastics Corporation ("Bramble") is a manufacturer of plastic pipe and, at all relevant times alleged herein, was a competitor of Platten Plastic in the South and Southeastern United States.

17.   Throughout the relevant time period, and in particular during 1984, Bramble manufactured and sold ABS foam core (F-628) and solid wall (D-2661) plastic pipe in Platten Plastic's trade area. This pipe bore the FDF seal, or was shipped in pallets of pipe bearing the FDF seal purportedly to demonstrate that the shipment as a whole met the standards and qualifications associated with the FDF seal. However, notwithstanding the presence of the FDF seal on ABS foam core and solid wall plastic pipe produced by Bramble during 1984, this pipe was of highly inferior quality and did not meet the minimum standards necessary for FDF approval.

18.   In early 1984, FDF found Bramble in violation of FDF standards and, on or about May 9, 1984, it delisted Bramble's ABS F-628 foam core and D-2661 solid wall plastic pipe and prohibited Bramble from using the FDF seal on this pipe. FDF did not inform any governmental body, plastic pipe manufacturer (including Platten Plastic) or buyer, consumer, the public, or any other person or entity (other than Bramble) of the delisting of Bramble's ABS foam core and solid wall plastic pipe.

19.   Notwithstanding this delisting, Bramble continued throughout the summer and fall of 1984 to manufacture and sell these delisted pipe products and to place the FDF seal on this pipe. Moreover, Bramble was able to sell this pipe at a greatly discounted price because it was using

inferior materials and cost-cutting production methods which did not meet FDF standards.

20.   As a result of these discounts, in or about June 1984 certain regular customers of Platten Plastic, including Waters, Incorporated ("Waters") and Triple J, Inc. ("Triple J"), unaware of the delisting, began purchasing significant volumes of plastic pipe from Bramble, which they would otherwise have purchased from Platten Plastic. This caused Platten Plastic, at this same time, to experience a sudden and severe decrease in its sales of ABS foam core pipe from the previous year's levels.

21.   Throughout the months of May, June, July, August and September 1984, Platten Plastic's sales severely eroded, as compared to prior years, as its customers turned to the cheaper Bramble pipe. During this same time period, Platten Plastic employees continually came across Bramble pipe in the marketplace which was clearly of substandard quality. Nonetheless, while this pipe had been delisted, it bore the FDF seal.

22.   During this period, for example, Harvey Dallas ("H. Dallas"), Vice President of Platten Plastic, made regular sales visits to plastic pipe buyers and observed plastic pipe purchased from Bramble which was of inferior quality and which, by its very appearance, did not meet FDF standards. This pipe either bore the FDF seal or was shipped with pipe bearing the FDF seal so as to lead the purchaser to believe that it had FDF approval. The customers who had purchased the pipe all believed that the pipe was FDF-approved.

23.   Platten Plastic was greatly disturbed by this influx of clearly substandard Bramble pipe into the marketplace, and by the accompanying decrease in its own sales of foam core plastic pipe, particularly since it had taken great care and expended substantial sums of money to ensure that *its own* pipe met all applicable FDF and other standards. As a result, during the months of June, July, August and September 1984, Platten Plastic and others made repeated telephone inquiries to FDF regarding Bramble's authorization to use the FDF mark on its plastic pipe. Notwithstanding the delisting of Bramble in May 1984, FDF repeatedly told Platten Plastic and other inquiring parties that Bramble did have authorization to use the seal on D-2661 solid wall and F-628 foam core pipe. These representations by FDF and its personnel were false and fraudulent and known to be so when made. Defendants made these representations intentionally, knowingly, and recklessly with the intent to deceive Platten Plastic and the market in general.

24.   The fraudulent misrepresentations described in paragraph 23 include the following:

(a)   On or about May 14, 1984 and again on May 18, 1984, Jason Dallas ("J. Dallas"), President of Platten Plastic, telephoned from his office in Alabama to defendant Tate at FDF's regional office in Atlanta, Georgia. J. Dallas discussed the inferior quality of Bramble's plastic pipe products and, during both conversations, asked whether Bramble was listed by FDF for the marketing of ABS D-2661 and F-628 pipe. Despite the fact that FDF had delisted Bramble as to these two products only a few days prior to these two phone conversations, Tate both times falsely stated that Bramble was listed.

(b)   J. Dallas saw Platten Plastic's sales plummet and observed that Bramble was still selling substandard pipe during June 1984. On or about July 6, 1984, he called Tate at FDF's Atlanta office to find out why FDF had not taken corrective action against Bramble for selling substandard pipe. Tate was initially evasive on this point, but, when asked whether Bramble was listed for D-2661 and F-628 pipe, he once again falsely assured Mr. Dallas that Bramble was still FDF-listed.

(c)   During the summer of 1984, H. Dallas had, on various sales visits, observed Bramble pipe in the yards of pipe purchasers and had found Bramble pipe shipments containing numerous trade names, with some pipe bearing the FDF seal and others not. This pipe was of very poor quality. Much of the pipe was very brittle, with thin walls and substandard lengths. Puzzled by the mixture of FDF and non-FDF pipe and its overall poor quality, H. Dallas called Tate, on or about July 9, 1984 and again on July 13, 1984, to inquire about the status of Bramble's pipe. When he asked Tate whether Bramble was listed at that time for ABS solid wall pipe under D-2661 and ABS foam core pipe under F-628, Tate stated that Bramble pipe was indeed listed, under the tradename Excel, in FDF's most recent listing directory, which had been published in March 1984. This statement was false and misleading since FDF had delisted this same line of pipe in May 1984, a fact which was known by Tate at all relevant times. Tate also represented in both of these phone conversations that he knew of no problem with Bramble's pipe, a patently false statement since FDF had held administrative hearings (attended by Tate himself) regarding the poor quality of Bramble's pipe prior to the May delisting and had in fact delisted this pipe.

(d)   On or about July 12, 1984, J. Dallas called Tate to renew his complaints about the poor quality of Bramble's pipe. He asked Tate whether Bramble was still listed for D-2661 and F-628 pipe and, if so, why. Tate again falsely stated that Bramble was listed and that its pipe products were of satisfactory quality.

(e)   On or about July 16, 1984, J. Dallas called FDF's national office in Ann Arbor, Michigan and spoke by telephone sequentially to defendants Trent, Bernson, Butler and Thatcher. He asked each one whether Bramble was listed by FDF for ABS solid wall pipe under D-2661 and foam core pipe under F-628. Defendants Trent, Bernson and Butler, individually, each falsely stated that Bramble was listed by FDF. Defendant

Thatcher responded in a highly misleading manner by stating (1) that the entity Bramble was listed, (2) that its contract with FDF was still in force, and (3) that it had the right to use the FDF seal. On this same day, J. Dallas called Tate in Atlanta, asked the same question, and again was told, falsely, that Bramble was listed.

(f)   After having received further indications that Bramble was marketing substandard pipe under the FDF seal, J. Dallas called Tate on or about July 27, 1984 to determine the status of Bramble's listing with FDF. Notwithstanding his prior representations regarding the adequacy of Bramble's pipe, Tate admitted that FDF had in the past required Bramble to destroy a substantial amount of substandard pipe. Nonetheless, he falsely stated and assured J. Dallas that Bramble still had an FDF listing.

(g)   On or about the last week of July 1984, Harvey Bovina ("Bovina"), Vice President and General Manager of Waters and a regular customer of Platten Plastic, telephoned defendant Trent, Manager of FDF's Plastics Listing Program, in Ann Arbor, Michigan. The call originated from Waters's offices in Texas. Bovina asked Trent whether Bramble's plastic pipe was approved by FDF. Notwithstanding that Bramble had been delisted in May 1984, defendant Trent fraudulently and knowingly concealed this fact and misrepresented to Bovina that Bramble was listed and that its plastic pipe was FDF-approved.

(h)   On or about August 23, 1984, H. Dallas called Tate at FDF's Atlanta office to report to him on the poor quality of Bramble's pipe which he had observed in various pipe purchasers' yards. He then asked Tate to meet him at a pipe purchaser's yard so that Tate could see first-hand the poor quality of Bramble's pipe. Notwithstanding his July 27 statement to J. Dallas that FDF had recently required Bramble to destroy substantial amounts of pipe, Tate refused the offer, stating that he was unaware of any problem with Bramble's pipe. This statement was patently false, since Tate knew that FDF had (1) held administrative hearings (attended by Tate himself) regarding the poor quality of Bramble pipe, (2) delisted Bramble's foam core and solid wall pipe in May, (3) made numerous special inspections of Bramble's plant during the relevant period (including inspections by Tate), and (4) required Bramble to destroy substantial amounts of substandard plastic pipe.

(i)   By late August 1984, J. Dallas could no longer accept FDF's repeated oral assurances that Bramble was listed when it was clear that Bramble was selling substandard pipe. Accordingly, on or about August 24, 1984, he sent a telex to defendant Bernson, FDF's Director of Listing Programs, wherein he specifically demanded confirmation that Bramble was listed for D-2661 and F-628 pipe. That same day, he then called Bernson at FDF's Ann Arbor, Michigan office and explained that he had sent the telex so as to force Bernson to respond in writing. He told Bernson that he needed a written record of the FDF's findings regarding Bramble before pursuing further inquiry through other means, including legal action. In spite of this, Bernson falsely maintained during this phone conversation that Bramble was FDF-listed.

25.   During this same period, Platten Plastic also complained to the Federal Trade Commission ("FTC") and the Alabama Attorney General's Office regarding Bramble's deceptive trade practices. Only after Platten Plastic had lodged these complaints and FDF had received J. Dallas's August 24, 1984 telex forcing it to respond in writing did it admit that Bramble had been delisted in May. By two telexes, dated August 27, 1984, defendant Trent, Manager of FDF's Plastics Listing Program, finally informed Platten Plastic and J. Dallas that FDF had withdrawn Bramble's authorization to apply the FDF mark on these products on May 9, 1984. True and correct copies of these telexes are attached hereto as Exhibits C and D.

26.   On August 28, 1984, one day after FDF had sent the two telexes referred to in paragraph 25, Sal Holmes ("Holmes"), purchasing agent for Triple J, met with defendant Tate at Triple J's offices in Cordele, Georgia. Holmes repeatedly asked defendant Tate whether Bramble's plastic pipe had FDF approval. Despite the fact that defendant Trent had admitted only one day earlier that Bramble had been delisted in May 1984, defendant Tate knowingly concealed Bramble's delisting and refused to reveal to Holmes, and H. Dallas, who was also in attendance, that the Bramble pipe in question did not have FDF approval. Instead he merely referred them to FDF's March 1984 listing directory and showed Holmes and H. Dallas that Bramble was listed in that directory.

27.   On or about August 30, 1984, J. Dallas had occasion to talk by telephone to Tate at his home in Atlanta, Georgia. Tate indicated that he had visited Bramble's plant after his meeting with Holmes at Triple J and had found substandard pipe, which Bramble was ordered to destroy. Notwithstanding this, he still falsely maintained that Bramble was listed for its foam core and solid wall pipe.

28.   Upon information and belief, prior to and during this period, certain employees at FDF's Atlanta office were offered illegal payments or other remuneration by Bramble in exchange for intentionally ignoring and concealing from others Bramble's manufacture and sale of substandard pipe. In addition, in early September 1984, an employee of FDF's Atlanta office, who during 1984 had been charged with the duty of inspecting Bramble's plant, suddenly left the employ of FDF and became employed by Bramble.

29.   After repeated complaints from Platten Plastic, the Office of the Attorney General for the State of Alabama commenced an investigation

of Bramble's deceptive trade practices in September 1984. Only after this investigation had begun and Platten Plastic had been in contact with the FTC did FDF issue an "Official Notice," dated September 25, 1984, stating that Bramble was not authorized to affix the FDF seal on any of its ABS solid wall or foam core pipe products. This notice, which on its face indicates that it was sent to public health officials throughout the United States, was issued nearly five months after FDF had delisted these products.

30.   Notwithstanding Bramble's long history of abusing the FDF seal and selling substandard pipe, FDF, on or about November 2, 1984, reinstated Bramble's listing for ABS foam core pipe, the same type of pipe produced by Platten Plastic. At the time of its relisting, Bramble was still producing substandard pipe, and much of the substandard pipe that it had produced after its May 1984 delisting was still in the marketplace and had not been recalled by FDF.

31.   On information and belief, none of Bramble's customers during the period from May to September 1984 would have purchased ABS foam core or solid wall plastic pipe from Bramble had they known that these products did not meet FDF standards. Because Bramble was able to produce its substandard pipe at a lower cost, many of Platten Plastic's regular customers, believing the pipe to be FDF-approved, shifted their purchases from Platten Plastic to Bramble during this period. For example, during 1984, Holmes of Triple J purchased $125,000 in pipe from Bramble at a very low price that he would otherwise have purchased from Platten Plastic. In addition, Waters purchased substantial amounts of pipe from Bramble which it otherwise would have bought from its regular foam core pipe supplier, Platten Plastic. As a result of these lost sales to Triple J, Waters, and other customers, Platten Plastic suffered losses of approximately $700,000.

(ii) FDF Approval of Use of Substandard Materials

32.   FDF Standard No. 14 applies to plastic piping and requires, among other things, that plastic piping system components be produced from virgin, rather than reprocessed, materials. Virgin materials are materials that have not been subjected to use or reprocessing other than that required for their initial manufacture. Virgin materials are usually stronger than reprocessed materials.

33.   Notwithstanding the requirements of Standard 14, FDF, for nearly all of 1985 and for at least the two years prior thereto, knowingly violated its own standards and allowed and approved the use of reprocessed materials. Only after Platten Plastic had learned of the use of reprocessed materials by its competitors and complained to FDF in September 1985 did FDF notify foam core and solid wall pipe producers,

by letter of October 1, 1985, that reprocessed plastic materials were not authorized for use in FDF-listed material formulations. A true and correct copy of this letter is attached hereto as Exhibit E.

34.   FDF authorized many of Platten Plastic's competitors, including Cleary Plastic Pipe & Products of Cleary, Alabama ("Cleary") and Crocket Inc. ("Crocket"), to use reprocessed rather than virgin materials. (Crocket is essentially a successor corporation to Bramble, with some former Bramble principals having ownership and/or management interest in the company.) Because reprocessed materials are substantially less costly than virgin materials, these producers were able to sell plastic pipe at a lower price than they would have been able to had they been required to use materials meeting FDF and underlying ASTM standards. Cleary's authorization to use reprocessed materials was not withdrawn by FDF until on or about November 11, 1985. The date for withdrawal of authorization from Crocket is not known.

35.   At all relevant times herein alleged, Platten Plastic was placed at a significant competitive disadvantage with respect to its competitors whom FDF had authorized to use substandard reprocessed materials. As a result, Platten Plastic suffered significant monetary losses.

(iii) FDF Harassment of Platten Plastic

36.   Because FDF had refused to take effective action against Bramble for selling substandard pipe, Platten Plastic, on or about March 6, 1985, filed its original complaint against FDF in the Circuit Court of Geneva County, Alabama for breach of contract, fraud and conspiracy.

37.   On or about June 11, 1985, two FDF employees conducted FDF's first annual inspection of Platten Plastic for 1985. They inspected both Platten Plastic's plant and its pipe and indicated in their Field Inspection Report that they found no violations of FDF standards. A true and correct copy of the Field Inspection Report is attached hereto as Exhibit F.

38.   During this inspection of Platten Plastic's plant, samples of plastic pipe were collected and were then sent to FDF's laboratories in Ann Arbor, Michigan for testing. By letter dated July 17, 1985, defendant Kusak, Director of Regional Services for FDF, represented to Platten Plastic that Platten Plastic's two-inch ABS foam core pipe had failed FDF's impact testing at its laboratories in Ann Arbor, Michigan. In this letter, FDF insisted that Platten Plastic investigate the matter and arrange for a resampling within thirty days. FDF further threatened that "FAILURE TO [INVESTIGATE] WILL RESULT IN DELISTING OF THE PRODUCTS . . . ." A true and correct copy of this letter is attached hereto as Exhibit G. Kusak sent a second letter, dated July 31, 1985, correcting an error in the July 17, 1985 letter and representing to Platten Plastic that the pipe in question had failed FDF impact testing at

both 73°F and 32°F. A true and correct copy of this letter and the attached test results are attached hereto as Exhibit H.

39. Platten Plastic was both surprised and perplexed by Kusak's July 17 and July 31 letters, since its record of compliance with FDF standards was well-known. FDF made at least three inspections of its plant each year during the period from 1979 to 1985, and additional tests were conducted at its laboratories in Ann Arbor, Michigan. Platten Plastic's plant and its product regularly passed all inspections and testing.

40. On or about August 13, 1985, Kusak made a special visit to Platten Plastic's plant to collect additional samples of Platten Plastic's two-inch ABS foam core pipe for retesting. Notwithstanding the representations in his July 17 and July 31 letters, Kusak on this visit noted no violations of FDF standards. Moreover, during the visit he observed impact testing on Platten Plastic's two-inch ABS foam core pipe and admitted in his Field Inspection Report that all pipe samples passed the impact tests. A true and correct copy of this Field Inspection Report is attached hereto as Exhibit I.

41. Nonetheless, by letter dated October 1, 1985, defendant Trent represented to J. Dallas that performance retesting had been completed on the pipe collected during the August 13 special visit. He represented that this pipe, like the samples collected at the June 11 visit, had failed the impact tests at 73°F and 32°F, and was therefore not in compliance with applicable FDF standards. Defendant Trent then informed J. Dallas as follows:

> "Effective immediately, as a result of the retest failure, 2" ABS foam core pipe is removed from your official Listing and authorization is withdrawn to apply the FDF Mark to all 2" ABS foam core pipe produced by Platten Plastic Conduit & Pipe Corporation.
>
> To qualify for reinstatement, you are required to determine the cause of the unsatisfactory retest results, and report the findings and corrective actions in writing to FDF within 30 days of receipt of this notification. We will conduct an inspection (special visit) to verify that corrective action has been taken, and to collect retest samples. During this period, no new 2" ABS foam core pipe can be produced and bear the FDF Mark. Further, all existing inventory of 2" ABS foam core pipe with the FDF Mark is hereby placed on hold and must remain in inventory until the time of the special visit."

A true and correct copy of this letter is attached hereto as Exhibit J.

42. Certain that its pipe met all applicable standards, Platten Plastic, by telex dated October 7, 1985, demanded that FDF retest additional samples of two-inch foam core pipe to be supplied by Platten Plastic. By letter dated November 4, 1985, Trent informed Platten Plastic that the additional pipe samples submitted by Platten Plastic had been retested

and were in compliance with all applicable standards. No explanation was offered as to why the earlier samples had failed. A true and correct copy of this letter is hereto attached as Exhibit K.

43.   Platten Plastic subsequently obtained the pipe samples collected during the August 13 special visit which purportedly had failed the impact retests. Platten Plastic then had these samples examined by Manitou Plastic Products Co. of Chicopee, Massachusetts and Carlin Pressure, Inc., of Tacoma, Washington. These companies concluded in early November 1985 that FDF had tested the pipe by impacting it with a tup (a heavy metal weight) which was either damaged or shaped improperly. Moreover, the faulty configuration of the tup would have been clearly apparent and visible to the naked eye of the tester. FDF's use of an improper impacting tup caused Platten Plastic's pipe specimens to fail the impact test even though the specimens met all applicable FDF standards. FDF's testing of Platten Plastic's pipe was a serious departure from standard testing procedures. Prior to this time, Platten Plastic never had its pipe tested in such a wholly improper manner.

44.   FDF and its officers and employees intentionally, knowingly and recklessly used improper impact testing so as to ensure that Platten Plastic's two-inch ABS foam core pipe would fail these tests even though the pipe met all applicable FDF standards. FDF falsely represented in its July 17, July 31, and October 1, 1985 letters (Exhibits G, H, and J respectively) that Platten Plastic's two-inch ABS pipe was not in compliance with applicable FDF standards. FDF made these false representations intentionally, knowingly and recklessly, and with the intent to harass and punish Platten Plastic for commencing and pursuing this litigation. FDF's delisting of Platten Plastic's two-inch foam core pipe prevented Platten Plastic from selling this pipe from October 1, 1985 until November 6, 1985, when Platten Plastic received Trent's November 4 letter relisting this product. As a result of the five week delisting of Platten Plastic's two-inch ABS foam core pipe, Platten Plastic suffered substantial monetary losses due to lost sales and other consequential losses.

§ 4.8   —Breach of Contract Count

COUNT I

Breach of Contract

45.   Platten Plastic repeats and realleges paragraphs 1–44.

46.   FDF, by the terms of its own policies and pursuant to the Contract with Platten Plastic, agreed to "use every legal means available to

prevent unauthorized use of the [FDF] seal on unlisted items or on listed items found to be substandard" (Exhibit A, Policy No. 18). FDF breached this agreement by:

(a)   knowingly allowing and encouraging Bramble, a competitor of Platten Plastic, to sell in Platten Plastic's trade area ABS foam core and solid wall plastic pipe products bearing the FDF seal when such products were inferior in quality and did not meet with FDF's minimum standards and when Bramble was not authorized to use the FDF seal on such products; and

(b)   knowingly allowing and encouraging Platten Plastic's competitors, including Cleary and Crocket, to use reprocessed materials, as defined by ASTMD-883, in the production of their plastic pipe, when applicable requirements of Standard 14, in accordance with the material section of D-2661 and F-628 of Standard 14, mandate that only virgin materials may be used.

47.   In entering into the aforementioned Contract with Platten Plastic, FDF further agreed to authorize Platten Plastic to use the FDF seal on all products meeting applicable FDF standards. Platten Plastic, in turn, paid valuable consideration for the right to use the FDF seal. FDF, by delisting Platten Plastic's two-inch foam core pipe in October 1985 when it knew that such pipe met all applicable FDF standards, violated this agreement with Platten Plastic.

WHEREFORE, Platten Plastic demands judgment on Count I against FDF in an amount in excess of $700,000 for FDF's breaches of the Contract and the resulting loss to Platten Plastic. Because these breaches were willful and in wanton disregard for the contractual rights of Platten Plastic, Platten Plastic also demands judgment against FDF for $3,000,000 in punitive damages.

§ 4.9   —Common Law Fraud Count

COUNT II

Common Law Fraud

48.   Platten Plastic repeats and realleges paragraphs 1–47.

49.   As more specifically set forth in paragraphs 16–31, Platten Plastic and others made repeated inquiries to FDF and the individual defendants regarding Bramble's authorization to use the FDF seal on its ABS foam core and solid wall pipe. In responding to these inquiries, defendants fraudulently concealed the fact that Bramble had been

delisted as to these products in May 1984. Defendants further intentionally, knowingly and recklessly misrepresented that Bramble was listed as to these products. In addition, defendants intentionally and falsely represented that FDF would inquire into the matter and take appropriate action if Bramble was selling substandard product.

50.   As more fully set forth in paragraphs 32–35, defendants knowingly authorized certain of Platten Plastic's competitors, including Cleary and Crocket, to use reprocessed materials in violation of FDF standards. Defendants fraudulently concealed this material fact from Platten Plastic.

51.   As more fully set forth in paragraphs 36–44, during the period from July to November 1985, FDF employees fraudulently misrepresented that Platten Plastic's two-inch ABS foam core pipe failed proper FDF impact tests and therefore did not meet all applicable FDF standards. Defendants further intentionally, knowingly and recklessly performed improper testing on this pipe and concealed (1) that its impact tests were contrived to ensure their failure and (2) that in fact Platten Plastic's two-inch foam core pipe met all applicable FDF standards throughout this time period.

52.   Each of the misrepresentations or omissions referred to in the preceding paragraphs 49–51 was made by FDF intentionally, knowingly and recklessly with the intent to deceive Platten Plastic and the market in general. Defendants' actions were fraudulent and constituted material, willful misrepresentations which Platten Plastic was forced to follow or justifiably relied upon to its detriment.

WHEREFORE, Platten Plastic demands judgment on Count II against all defendants for an amount in excess of $700,000 in compensatory damages and $3,000,000 in punitive damages for defendants' willful and reckless fraudulent conduct.

§ 4.10   —Civil Conspiracy Count

COUNT III

Civil Conspiracy

53.   Platten Plastic repeats and realleges paragraphs 1–52.

54.   Upon information and belief, FDF and the individual defendants entered into a conspiracy with Bramble and its agents to defraud Platten Plastic and others by concealing the delisting of Bramble products in May 1984 and by allowing Bramble to use the FDF seal without meeting the minimum requirements as set forth by FDF itself. The purpose and

effect of this conspiracy was to provide Bramble with an unfair trade advantage in exchange for the payment of substantial continued listing fees and, upon information and belief, other possibly illicit payments by Bramble to FDF.

55.   Upon information and belief, FDF and the individual defendants further conspired with Crocket (successor corporation of Bramble), Cleary, and possibly other manufacturers to provide these manufacturers with an unfair trade advantage by allowing them to manufacture plastic pipe using reprocessed, rather than virgin, materials, all in violation of FDF's own standards.

56.   In furtherance of these conspiracies, defendants fraudulently concealed the misuse of its seal by Platten Plastic's competitors and/or falsely assured Platten Plastic that it would remedy any reported abuses. These misrepresentations and omissions, which are more fully set forth above, were to the detriment of Platten Plastic because they prevented and forestalled Platten Plastic from protecting itself by legal action or otherwise.

WHEREFORE, Platten Plastic demands judgment on Count III against all defendants for an amount in excess of $700,000 in compensatory damages and $3,000,000 in punitive damages for defendants' conspiracies to defraud Platten Plastic.

§ 4.11   —RICO Count

COUNT IV
RICO

57.   Platten Plastic repeats and realleges paragraphs 1–56.

58.   Platten Plastic brings this suit under 18 U.S.C. § 1964(c), because it has been injured in its business or property by reason of a violation of 18 U.S.C. § 1962.

59.   Defendants Thatcher, Trent, Bernson, Butler, Tate and Kusak were at all relevant times "persons," as defined in 18 U.S.C. § 1961(3).

60.   FDF is and was at all relevant times an "enterprise," as defined in 18 U.S.C. § 1964(4), which engaged in or the activities of which affected interstate commerce. FDF inspects and lists plumbing-related products produced in various states. These products are sold through and have a direct effect on interstate commerce. The individual defendants were at all relevant times associated with the aforementioned enterprise and its business operations and affairs. Alternatively, FDF and the individual defendants together comprised an "enterprise," as defined in 18 U.S.C. § 1964(4), which at all relevant times was engaged in or the activities of which affected interstate commerce.

61.   In order to continue to collect listing fees and, upon information and belief, other possibly illicit payments from plastic pipe manufacturers, defendants devised schemes or artifices to defraud Platten Plastic and others by (a) allowing and encouraging Bramble to sell plastic pipe products bearing the FDF seal which did not meet FDF standards; (b) fraudulently concealing from Platten Plastic, other manufacturers, customers and the public that Bramble's authorization to sell ABS foam core and solid wall plastic pipe had been withdrawn in May 1984; and (c) fraudulently concealing the fact that, in violation of its own standards, it had authorized certain manufacturers, including Cleary and Crocket, to use reprocessed materials, all as more fully set forth in paragraphs 16–35.

62.   After Platten Plastic discovered defendants' fraudulent schemes and commenced the instant litigation, defendants sought, in furtherance of these schemes, to harass Platten Plastic into abandoning its suit by delisting Platten Plastic's two-inch foam core pipe in October 1985, all as more fully set forth in paragraphs 36–44.

63.   Defendants, through the actions as described in paragraphs 11–56, engaged in a "pattern of racketeering," as defined in 18 U.S.C. § 1961(5), including the commission of acts violating 18 U.S.C. § 1341 (mail fraud) and 18 U.S.C. § 1343 (wire fraud). This pattern of racketeering activity included repeated criminal conduct and schemes which were separate in time both prior to and after the filing of the instant lawsuit.

64.   As described heretofore, defendants conducted or participated, directly or indirectly, in the conduct of the affairs of FDF or, alternatively, an enterprise consisting of FDF and the individual defendants, through a "pattern of racketeering activity," in violation of 18 U.S.C. § 1962(c), as a part of a fraudulent scheme to permit and facilitate Platten Plastic's competitors to misuse the FDF mark in exchange for substantial listing fees. On information and belief, defendants also engaged in these fraudulent schemes to obtain other possibly illicit remuneration.

65.   Specifically, having devised these schemes to defraud Platten Plastic and in order to execute or attempt to execute these schemes or artifices, FDF committed the following acts (more specifically described above) which were violations of 18 U.S.C. § 1341 (mail fraud) and 18 U.S.C. § 1343 (wire fraud), and which were part of a pattern of racketeering activity through which defendants conducted FDF's affairs in violation of 18 U.S.C. § 1962(c):

(a)   On or about the dates listed below, defendants transmitted in interstate commerce certain signs, signals, and sounds in violation of 18 U.S.C. § 1343 (wire fraud):

Approximate Date of Phone Call	Inquiring Party (Caller) and Location	Defendant Making Misrepresentation Over Phone and Location
5/14/84	J. Dallas Platten, Alabama	Tate Atlanta, Georgia
5/18/84	J. Dallas Platten, Alabama	Tate Atlanta, Georgia
7/6/84	J. Dallas Platten, Alabama	Tate Atlanta, Georgia
7/9/84	H. Dallas Platten, Alabama	Tate Atlanta, Georgia
7/12/84	J. Dallas Platten, Alabama	Tate Atlanta, Georgia
7/13/84	H. Dallas Platten, Alabama	Tate Atlanta, Georgia
7/16/84	J. Dallas Platten, Alabama	Trent Ann Arbor, Michigan
7/16/84	J. Dallas Platten, Alabama	Bernson Ann Arbor, Michigan
7/16/84	J. Dallas Platten, Alabama	Butler Ann Arbor, Michigan
7/16/84	J. Dallas Platten, Alabama	Thatcher Ann Arbor, Michigan
7/16/84	J. Dallas Platten, Alabama	Tate Atlanta, Georgia
7/27/84	J. Dallas Platten, Alabama	Tate Atlanta, Georgia
7/30/84	H. Bovina (Waters) Hurst, Texas	Trent Ann Arbor, Michigan
8/23/84	H. Dallas Platten, Alabama	Tate Atlanta, Georgia
8/24/84	J. Dallas Platten, Alabama	Bernson Ann Arbor, Michigan
8/30/84	J. Dallas Platten, Alabama	Tate Atlanta, Georgia

The contents of these phone calls and the intentionally fraudulent misrepresentations and omissions made by defendants or their agents during these calls are specifically set forth in paragraphs 24 and 27.

(b)   On or about the dates listed below, defendants caused to be placed in a post office or other authorized depository for mail the following described letters to be delivered by the United States Postal Service, all in violation of 18 U.S.C. § 1341 (mail fraud):

Date	Addressee	Author	Exhibit
07/17/85	J. Dallas	Kusak	G
07/31/85	J. Dallas	Kusak	H
10/01/85	J. Dallas	Trent	J

The contents of these letters and the fraudulent misrepresentations and omissions made by defendants therein are specifically set forth in paragraphs 38–41.

66.   Each and every defendant conspired to defraud Platten Plastic, and each act of mail and wire fraud alleged in paragraph 65 was in furtherance of defendants' fraudulent schemes and conspiracy. Each of these mail fraud and wire fraud violations was a part of a pattern of racketeering activity (as defined in 18 U.S.C. § 1961(5)) carried out by defendants in the conduct of the affairs of FDF, or of the enterprise consisting of FDF and the individual defendants, and in violation of 18 U.S.C. § 1962(c).

67.   As a result of the foregoing, Platten Plastic was injured in its business or property by reason of a violation of 18 U.S.C. § 1962(c) and has been damaged in an amount in excess of $700,000.

WHEREFORE, Platten Plastic respectfully requests:

(1)   that judgment be entered on Count IV against all defendants for an amount in excess of $700,000;

(2)   pursuant to 18 U.S.C. § 1964(c), that said award be trebled;

(3)   that it recover the costs of this action and reasonable attorneys' fees; and

(4)   that it be awarded such other relief as this Court may deem just and proper.

CHAPTER 5

CIVIL RICO IN CIVIL RIGHTS DISPUTES

John H. Henn

§ 5.1   Suits Against Abortion Clinic Blockaders

In 1970, Congress enacted the Racketeer Influenced Corrupt Organizations Act[1] (RICO) in an attempt "to seek eradication of organized crime in the United States by strengthening the legal tools in the evidence-gathering process, by establishing new penal prohibitions, and by providing enhanced sanctions and new remedies to deal with the unlawful activities of those engaged in organized crime."[2] Twenty years after its enactment, however, RICO has been used successfully in contexts far removed from what would traditionally be referred to as organized crime. For example, a construction worker harassed by her union because she was a

---

[1] 18 U.S.C. §§ 1961–1968 (1988 & Supp. 1989).

[2] Organized Crime Control Act of 1970, Pub. L. No. 91-452, 84 Stat. 922 (1970) (codified in scattered sections of 18 U.S.C.) (Statement of Findings and Purpose).

woman[3] and an executive who was terminated because he raised questions about company practices[4] both successfully sued for treble damages and attorneys' fees[5] under the RICO statute.[6]

This chapter focuses upon a significant new arena for civil RICO litigation: the court battle between abortion clinics and abortion clinic blockaders. The blockaders, commonly referred to collectively as "Operation Rescue," have united with the common goal of "closing down" abortion providers.[7] Although the United States Supreme Court granted to women nearly 20 years ago the constitutional right to choose abortion,[8] women seeking to exercise that right are often obstructed by Operation Rescue's systematic and widespread blockades of abortion and family planning facilities. "Just as Southern politicians once stood in the doorways of schoolhouses to prevent African-American school children from passing through to exercise their constitutionally-protected right to desegregated education, today anti-abortion blockaders stand in the doorways of abortion clinics to prevent women from passing through to exercise their constitutional right to choose abortion."[9]

This chapter discusses how RICO may be successfully employed by abortion clinics and their potential clients in the arsenal of weapons against anti-abortion blockaders. In October 1989, the propriety of using RICO in this context was confirmed when the United States Supreme Court declined to hear a challenge to its use against anti-abortion blockaders and trespassers,[10] thereby letting stand a Third Circuit Court of Appeals decision upholding a RICO jury verdict against the blockaders.[11] **Section 5.2** details Operation Rescue blockades in Massachusetts and their effect on women in that state. **Section 5.3** outlines Planned Parenthood League of Massachusetts' legal attack against these

---

[3] Hunt v. Weatherbee, 626 F. Supp. 1097 (D. Mass. 1986).

[4] Williams v. Hall, 683 F. Supp. 639 (E.D. Ky. 1988).

[5] *See* 18 U.S.C. § 1964(c).

[6] Indeed, RICO is no more limited in its application to conventional notions of "racketeers" than is the federal civil rights conspiracy statute, 42 U.S.C. § 1985(3), limited in application to its original target, the Ku Klux Klan.

[7] *See* Operation Rescue, *Join Us In Operation Rescue* (pamphlet announcing blockades in New York City during the week of Apr. 30 to May 7, 1988) [hereinafter Join Us In Operation Rescue].

[8] *See* Roe v. Wade, 410 U.S. 113 (1973).

[9] Henn & Del Monaco, *Civil Rights and RICO: Stopping Operation Rescue,* 13 Harv. Women's L. J. 251 (1990).

[10] Northeast Women's Center, Inc. v. McMonagle, 110 S. Ct. 261 (1989).

[11] Northeast Women's Center, Inc. v. McMonagle, 868 F.2d 1342 (3d Cir. 1989), *cert. denied,* 110 S. Ct. 261 (1989).

activities, including lawsuits initiated in both federal[12] and state[13] courts in Massachusetts. **Sections 5.4** through **5.6** discuss the legal framework of a RICO claim, demonstrating its applicability to abortion clinic blockades, and also address various arguments that might be raised in opposition to the use of RICO in the abortion clinic context. A sample complaint based on the issues in this case filed in federal court is excerpted in §§ **5.7** through **5.12.**

§ 5.2 Factual Background

Although abortion clinics have endured picketing and "sidewalk counseling" for years, systematic and widespread blockading of clinics began during the 1988 presidential campaign, usually by an organization calling itself Operation Rescue. Operation Rescue and various affiliated organizations sought to "close down abortion mills and prevent abortion mill employees or pregnant mothers from entering the clinics."[14] During that presidential campaign, blockaders sealed off abortion clinics for days at a time, preventing clinics from functioning and substantially disrupting the community.[15] On one day in October 1988, police arrested over 2,000 blockaders in blockades that occurred in 27 different cities.[16]

Abortion clinic blockaders have pursued their goals through a variety of criminal tactics, including trespass, traffic offenses, giving false names to police officers, disorderly conduct, and creating a public disturbance.[17]

---

[12] Planned Parenthood League of Mass., Inc. v. Operation Rescue, No. 88-2329-MA (D. Mass. filed Oct. 18, 1988) [hereinafter *PPLM I*]. A sample complaint based on this case is excerpted in §§ **5.7–5.12.**

[13] Planned Parenthood League of Mass., Inc. v. Operation Rescue, No. 89-2487 (Mass. Super. Ct. filed Apr. 19, 1989) [hereinafter *PPLM II*], preliminary injunction aff'd, 406 Mass. 701 (1990). In September 1990, contempt judgments pursuant to the injunctions were entered against abortion clinic blockaders. *See id.* (Mass. Super. Ct. Order Sept. 25, 1990) (ruling that "the defendants' conduct in blocking the doors to the plaintiffs' clinics . . . constitutes 'clear and undoubted disobedience' of the injunction, and the Court finds and concludes that each of those defendants . . . is in civil contempt of that order.") This case was tried to the court on the question of a permanent injunction on Mar. 25–Apr. 10, 1991.

[14] Operation Rescue Newsletter, Apr. 30–May 7, 1988.

[15] *Operation Rescue Demonstrations Spark 2,000 Arrests in 27 U.S. Cities,* Boston Globe, Oct. 30, 1988, at 41, col. 1.

[16] *Id.*

[17] *See* Mark Sherman, *Prolifers Vow To Pack Jails In City,* Atlantic Constitution, Aug. 5, 1988, at 1A, col. 4; *107 Protesters are arrested in Blockade of Conn. Clinic,* Boston Globe, Oct. 23, 1988, at 34, col. 1.

Courts have issued numerous injunctions against anti-abortion block-ades,[18] as well as civil contempt orders when these injunctions were vio-lated.[19] Nearly all of the injunctions have been upheld on appeal.[20]

Operation Rescue's activities in Massachusetts illustrate the broad range of abortion blockade tactics utilized by the blockaders, and the ef-fect that the blockades have both on women seeking abortions and on the surrounding communities. For example, the organization known as "Operation Rescue: Boston" has blocked access to Massachusetts abor-tion providers on more than 30 occasions between October 1988 and

---

[18] *See* National Org. for Women v. Operation Rescue, 726 F. Supp. 1483 (E.D. Va. 1989) (permanent injunction); National Org. for Women v. Operation Rescue, 726 F. Supp. 300 (D.D.C. 1989) (preliminary injunction); Cousins v. Terry, 721 F. Supp. 426 (N.D.N.Y. 1989) (preliminary injunction); West Hartford v. Operation Rescue, 726 F. Supp. 371 (D. Conn. 1989) (preliminary injunction); Aradia Women's Health Center v. Operation Rescue, No. 8801539 (W.D. Wash. Jan. 10, 1989) (preliminary injunction); Roe v. Operation Rescue, 710 F. Supp. 577 (E.D. Pa. 1989) (permanent injunction); New York State Nat'l Org. for Women v. Terry, 704 F. Supp. 1247 (S.D.N.Y. 1989), *aff'd*, 886 F.2d 1339 (2d Cir. 1989) (permanent injunction); Roe v. Operation Rescue, No. 88-5157 (E.D. Pa. June 30, 1988) (temporary restraining order); New York State Nat'l Org. for Women v. Terry, No. 88-3071 (S.D.N.Y. May 5, 1988) (temporary re-straining order); Planned Parenthood League of Mass., Inc. v. Operation Rescue, No. 89-2487 (Mass. Super. Ct. Order July 24, 1989) (preliminary injunction) *aff'd*, 406 Mass. 701 (1990); New York State Nat'l Org. for Women v. Terry, No. 8318/88 (N.Y. Super. Ct. Orders Apr. 28, 1988 and May 2, 1988) (temporary restraining orders); Planned Parenthood of Monmouth County, Inc. v. Cannizzaro, 204 N.J. Super. 531, 499 A.2d 535 (Ch. Div. May 2, 1985) (permanent injunction).

[19] Roe v. Operation Rescue, No. 88-5157 (E.D. Pa. Dec. 7, 1988); New York State Nat'l Org. for Women v. Terry, 697 F. Supp. 1324 (S.D.N.Y. 1988), *aff'd*, 886 F.2d 1339 (2d Cir. 1989). *See also* Craig Wolff, *Judge Fines 10 for Protests Over Abortion*, N.Y. Times, Feb. 28, 1990, at B1, col. 6 (Judge Robert J. Ward, a federal judge in Manhattan, ex-plained that "coercive action [in the form of large fines against individual blockaders] was necessary because his previous orders had been ignored by Operation Rescue.").

[20] New York State Nat'l Org. for Women v. Terry, 886 F.2d 1339 (2d Cir. 1989) (affirming entry of permanent injunction and entry of summary judgment in plaintiffs' favor); Northeast Women's Center, Inc. v. McMonagle, 868 F.2d 1342 (3d Cir.) (relying on RICO; remanding and indicating that lower court could issue a broader injunction), *cert. denied*, 110 S. Ct. 261 (1989); Portland Feminist Women's Medical Center v. Advocates For Life, Inc., 859 F.2d 681 (9th Cir. 1988) (affirming preliminary injunc-tion as modified); Northern Va. Women's Health Center v. Balch, 617 F.2d 1045 (4th Cir. 1980) (affirming permanent injunction and contempt citations); Planned Parent-hood League of Mass., Inc. v. Operation Rescue, 406 Mass. 701, 550 N.E.2d 1361 (1990); Bering v. SHARE, 106 Wash. 2d 212, 721 P.2d 918 (1986), *cert. dismissed*, 479 U.S. 1050 (1987) (upholding permanent injunction restricting places where protesters could demonstrate); Parkmed v. Pro-Life Counselling, Inc., 91 A.D.2d 551, 457 N.Y.S.2d 27 (1982) (affirming preliminary injunction as modified).

September 1990.[21] Municipalities, as a result, have expended significant financial resources for police assistance.[22]

As reflected in the papers filed in the *PPLM I* and *PPLM II* litigations, a typical blockade has involved as many as 300 to 400 people surrounding a clinic in an attempt to block entry. Some blockaders sit or stand in any entrance area where access can be blocked by a sufficient mass of bodies, while others attempt to create chain-like barriers by interlocking arms or even chaining themselves to others. Ordinarily, blockaders also "go limp" once they are in position and disregard police orders to move.

Blockaders also usually try to gain entrance to the interior of clinics' offices and, once inside, occupy the waiting area and chain or lock themselves to each other and to fixtures of the building. Even when the blockaders fail to gain entrance into a building, their tactics cause many clinic directors to stop all procedures because usual clinic medical protocol requires ready access to hospitals for emergency situations.

Preventing women and staff from passing through clinic doorways is not the blockaders' only goal. Blockades also permit "sidewalk counselors" to confront clinic patients on the sidewalks and try to convince them to abandon their efforts to have an abortion. These counselors typically shove pictures of fetuses at women, scream at them about baby "killing," and pursue them as they retreat.[23] While some sidewalk counselors are doing this, others are falsely advising that the clinics are closed. Indeed, merely because of the noise and confusion, women often have trouble speaking to clinic employees to determine whether the targeted clinic is in fact open.

Patients and staff who manage to penetrate the blockades still cannot feel safe or secure. When protective "corridors" have been formed by police officers, designed to let the clinics' patients pass, the corridors are often narrow and easily collapsed or at least squeezed by the pushing and jostling of the blockaders and their supporters. Moreover, many women

---

[21] Walker & Epperson, *67 Abortion Protesters Arrested Outside 2 Clinics,* Boston Globe, July 23, 1989, at 17, col. 2; Longcope, *59 Antiabortion Protesters Arrested on Cape,* Boston Globe, Sept. 1, 1989, at 23, col. 3; Freeman & Shea, *28 Abortion Protesters Arrested,* Springfield Union News, Sept. 9, 1989, at 1, col. 3; Howe, *48 Arrested in Blockade at Hub Abortion Clinic,* Boston Globe, Sept. 24, 1989, at 34, col. 2; *Police Arrest 69 Abortion Foes at Clinic,* Boston Globe, Oct. 15, 1989, at 43, col. 1.

[22] *See* Graham, *Demonstrations a "Financial Strain" on Town,* Boston Globe, Mar. 5, 1989, at 40, col. 1. (the chairman of the Brookline Board of Selectmen predicted that one single day's arrest of anti-abortion demonstrators would cost the town $10,000 to $20,000.).

[23] English, *Anti-Abortion Picketers In Brookline Show Passion But No Compassion,* Boston Globe, Oct. 17, 1988, at 19, col. 1.

will elect not to be escorted into the clinic from fear of being photographed by the media.

Operation Rescue: Boston blockades in Massachusetts have generated over 1500 arrests as of January 1990.[24] Neither arrests nor the criminal process have been much of a deterrent. In part, this is a result of the blockade tactics themselves. Not only do blockaders go limp when arrested but, to the extent they are not actually held in custody, they simply return to their positions by the clinic entrances. In addition, some have chained themselves to axles of police buses[25] or chained their necks to clinic doors. These tactics make arrests difficult and hinder police efforts to dismantle blockades.

Once arrested, Operation Rescue's members seek to paralyze the criminal justice system by filling jails and courthouses. They refuse to state their names or to pay the nominal administration fees that ensure release, and they normally demand jury trials.[26] As a result, towns like Brookline and Worcester, Massachusetts, have faced financial crises from the costs of arresting and housing anti-abortion protesters.[27] Brookline, for example, has on occasion deployed every available police officer and borrowed buses and wagons for transport.[28] The town has also been forced to detain the blockaders in a recreation center when holding cells at the jail were full.[29] Overall, the activities of Operation Rescue and its affiliated organizations have seriously disrupted the various communities in Massachusetts. Moreover, the disruption promises to persist, as Operation Rescue:

---

[24] *See* Bickelhaupt & Kennedy, *Boston Abortion Protest Blunted by Police, Rain,* Boston Globe, Oct. 23, 1988, at 33, col. 3; Bickelhaupt, *In Brookline, Abortion Protest Triggers 8 Arrests,* Boston Globe, Nov. 27, 1988, at 1, col. 3; Martins, *Scores Arrested During Brookline Abortion Protests,* Boston Globe, Jan. 1, 1989, at 29, col. 5; Callahan, *Antiabortion Protests Held in Brookline: 200 Arrested,* Boston Globe, Mar. 5, 1989, at 1, col. 5.

[25] Walker & Epperson, *67 Abortion Protesters Arrested Outside 2 Clinics,* Boston Globe, July 23, 1989, at 21.

[26] *See* Operation Rescue Update (Sept. 1988) (newsletter) (encouraging blockaders to use the name "Baby Doe" when arrested and noting that they will be held until they reveal their correct names); McQuillan, *Eight Arrested in Hub's "Largest Abortion Demo,"* Boston Herald, Nov. 27, 1988, at 1 (protesters refused to pay $15 arrest processing fee).

[27] Graham, *Demonstrations a "Financial Strain" on Town,* Boston Globe, Mar. 5, 1989, at 40 (discussing Brookline's "very difficult situation").

[28] Bickelhaupt & Kennedy, *Boston Abortion Protest Blunted by Police, Rain,* Boston Globe, Nov. 27, 1988, at 1 (noting that virtually the entire Brookline police force and 45 state troopers were called upon to deal with anti-abortion activists); Callahan, *Antiabortion Protests Held in Brookline: 200 Arrested,* Boston Globe, Mar. 5, 1989, at 1, col. 5. (Brookline police force borrowed Massachusetts Bay Transportation Authority buses and wagons from Boston police department.)

[29] Armstrong, *Jailed Abortion Foes Get Gift of Support,* Boston Herald, Mar. 6, 1989, at 7, col. 1.

Boston leaders have vowed to continue and perhaps increase the number of blockades in the area.[30]

In addition to disrupting the community, Operation Rescue blockades substantially interfere with a woman's constitutional right to choose abortion. Many women will not even try to approach a blockaded clinic, reasonably fearing for bodily harm or privacy. In addition, women who do try to gain access often fail to do so.

Delay in obtaining a desired abortion poses significant health and safety risks, which increase as the procedure is postponed or delayed. Abortion is obviously time-sensitive; as the pregnancy progresses, the procedure becomes more risky and complicated.[31] If delay forces a woman to undergo a second rather than first trimester abortion, she will likely be subjected to a two day "laminaria" procedure that is normally quite safe and medically appropriate but may result in serious risks (endometritis, infertility, or even death) should the woman be unable to enter the clinic on the second day of the procedure.

In addition to health problems, blockades that delay abortions may impose significant psychological burdens on women, especially if a pregnancy resulted from rape or incest. Moreover, even if a woman succeeds in entering the clinic to receive her scheduled abortion, the hostile yelling outside the clinic, the display of gruesome signs in the windows of a waiting room, and the rattling of the clinic entrance doors can obviously be quite disturbing.

§ 5.3 Legal Proceedings

In order to ensure the health and safety of women seeking abortions or other family planning services at health care facilities in eastern Massachusetts, as well as to prevent those engaged in Operation Rescue from harassing and intimidating clinic patients and staff, Planned Parenthood sought legal redress in the federal and state courts of Massachusetts.

In October 1988, Planned Parenthood and others brought suit in federal court in Massachusetts against Operation Rescue: Boston, and dozens of alleged clinic blockaders. Significant for the purposes of this chapter, the suit included a RICO claim. Excerpts from the actual complaint filed in that suit, including the RICO count, are included in §§ 5.7 through 5.12.

---

[30] Remarks of Operation Rescue Director Constance Smith, *quoted in* Bickelhaupt & Kennedy, *Boston Abortion Protest Blunted by Police, Rain,* Boston Globe, Nov. 27, 1988, at 35.

[31] *See* Mishell, *Control of Human Reproduction, Contraception, Sterilization and Pregnancy Termination,* in Obstetrics and Gynecology 357 (D. Danforth 5th ed. 1986) ("complication rates are three to four times higher for second trimester abortions than for first trimester abortions.").

As may be observed from a review of the complaint, it contains very specific and particular facts to support the allegations. This detail and specificity are necessary to comply with Federal Rule of Civil Procedure 9(b), which requires predicate acts underlying a RICO claim to be stated with particularity if they involve fraud.[32] Moreover, pleading with this particularity is consistent with Federal Rule of Civil Procedure 11, which requires all pleadings to be "well grounded in fact."

Planned Parenthood also filed a separate state court action in April 1989[33] pursuant to the Massachusetts civil rights statute.[34] The state claim did not include a RICO count because at the time of filing it was unclear whether a state court exercised jurisdiction over RICO claims.[35] Moreover, unlike many state civil rights acts, the Massachusetts statute, like RICO, expressly provides for an award of compensatory damages, costs, and attorneys' fees against those who by "threats, intimidation or coercion" seek to interfere with other persons' constitutional rights.[36] That statute also expressly provides for injunctive relief.[37]

§ 5.4   Application of RICO to Anti-Abortion Blockaders

RICO makes it unlawful for any person to (a) use income derived from a pattern of racketeering activity to acquire, establish, or operate an enterprise engaged in interstate commerce;[38] (b) acquire or maintain an interest in or control of an enterprise engaged in interstate commerce through a pattern of racketeering activity;[39] (c) conduct or participate in the affairs of an enterprise through a pattern of racketeering activity;[40]

---

[32] *See, e.g.,* Bennett v. Berg, 685 F.2d 1053 (8th Cir. 1982), *cert. denied,* 464 U.S. 1008 (1983) (involving predicate acts of mail fraud); Gregoris Motors v. Nissan Motors Corp., 630 F. Supp. 902 (E.D.N.Y. 1986) (involving predicate acts of fraud, bribery, and extortion).

[33] Planned Parenthood League of Mass., Inc. v. Operation Rescue, No. 89-2487 (Mass. Super. Ct. Apr. 19, 1989). This action has subsequently become the principal case pursued by the plaintiffs.

[34] Massachusetts has a strong state civil rights act that does not require state action. *See* Mass. Gen. L. ch. 12, §§ 11H–I (1986); Redgrave v. Boston Symphony Orchestra, 855 F.2d 888, 900–01 (1st Cir. 1988), *cert. denied,* 488 U.S. 1043 (1989).

[35] It is now clear that state courts have concurrent jurisdiction over civil RICO claims. *See* Tafflin v. Levitt, 493 U.S. 455 (1990).

[36] Mass. Gen. L. ch. 12, §§ 11H–I (1986).

[37] There is a question as to whether injunctive relief is available under RICO. See § 5.6.

[38] 18 U.S.C. § 1962(a) (1988).

[39] *Id.* § 1962(b).

[40] *Id.* § 1962(c).

and (d) conspire to do any of the above.[41] Since anti-abortion blockaders are not seeking by their activities to acquire or maintain an interest in an enterprise engaged in commerce, the subsections of the statute applicable to abortion clinic blockades are § 1962(c) and (d).

A claim based on § 1962(c) must separately demonstrate both the existence of an "enterprise" and a "pattern of racketeering activity." The statute defines an *enterprise* to include any "group of individuals associated in fact although not a legal entity."[42] An *association-in-fact enterprise* may be "a group of persons associated together for a common purpose of engaging in a course of conduct," which is proven by "evidence of an ongoing organization, formal or informal, and by evidence that the various associates function as a continuing unit."[43]

In order to demonstrate a *pattern of racketeering activity,* a plaintiff must show, at a minimum, the commission of two statutorily defined predicate acts within a 10-year period.[44] These predicate acts may constitute any one of a long list of federal statutory offenses and state law felonies.[45] Two or more predicate acts constitute a pattern when there is a relationship between the predicate acts and either continuous predicate acts or a threat that the activity comprising the predicate acts will continue.[46]

Notwithstanding the use of the word "racketeer" in the title of the statute, RICO's prohibitions generally apply to everyone.[47] And, of course, at least one court of appeals has specifically upheld the use of RICO against anti-abortion blockades, subject to certain limitations.[48]

---

[41] 18 U.S.C. § 1962(d) (1988 & Supp. 1989).

[42] 18 U.S.C. § 1961(4) (1988).

[43] United States v. Novia Turkette, 452 U.S. 576, 583 (1981).

[44] 18 U.S.C. § 1961(5).

[45] *Id.* at § 1961(1).

[46] H.J., Inc. v. Northwestern Bell Tel. Co., 492 U.S. 229, 109 S. Ct. 2893 (1989). Predicate acts are related when they "have the same or similar purposes, results, participants, victims, or methods of commission, or otherwise are related by distinguishing characteristics and are not isolated events." 109 S. Ct. at 2901 (quoting 18 U.S.C. § 3575(e)). Continuity can be demonstrated by a series of related predicate acts committed over a substantial period of time. *Id.* at 2902. Alternatively, a plaintiff can prove a threat of continuous activity by, inter alia, showing that the defendant regularly commits the predicate acts in the course of its business or that the predicate acts themselves include a specific threat of repetition. *Id.*

[47] *See* Sedima, S.P.R.L. v. Imrex Co., 473 U.S. 479, 493–500 (1985) (rejecting notion that one must prove "racketeering injury" to bring RICO suit).

[48] *See* Northeast Women's Center, Inc. v. McMonagle, 868 F.2d 1342, 1348–50 (3d Cir. 1989) (court of appeals noted with approval the following limitations imposed by the district court: "[n]o portion of this Judgment shall be construed by any law enforcement officer so as to restrain the peaceful protesting, picketing, demonstrating, chanting, or leafletting by the defendants on the sidewalks abutting [the adjacent] road") (citing Northeast Women's Center, Inc. v. McMonagle, 665 F. Supp. 1147, 1164 (E.D. Penn. 1987)). *Cf.* West Hartford v. Operation Rescue, 915 F.2d 92 (2d Cir. 1990) (municipality failed to state a Hobbs Act claim which could serve as a predicate act for an

The actions of Operation Rescue and its affiliated organizations fit squarely within RICO's requirements. Anti-abortion blockaders have engaged in numerous distinct yet related predicate acts in violation of federal law. Moreover, the blockaders threaten, and even expressly promise, to continue these acts, which are carried out as part of the activity of an organized group or enterprise.

A group of people associated together for the common purpose of physically blocking women from obtaining abortions qualify as an enterprise within the RICO statute. Such a group usually is an ongoing organization, functioning as a continuing unit that engages in activities other than blockading. For example, Operation Rescue's actions and literature demonstrate that its members have engaged for over two years in a "conspiracy" to close down abortion clinics. Operation Rescue has blockaded abortion clinics across the country, and Operation Rescue: Boston and its leaders blocked access to Massachusetts abortion providers 19 times in just over one year (1989). In addition, these organizations and their members engage in a variety of planning and promotional activities designed to make their blockades as effective as possible. As a result, Operation Rescue and its local chapters fit the RICO definition of association-in-fact enterprises existing independently of their predicate acts.[49]

§ 5.5   —Hobbs Act Application

The predicate act requirement is satisfied when anti-abortion blockaders violate the Hobbs Act,[50] which RICO explicitly lists among the crimes that can constitute predicate acts.[51] The elements of a Hobbs Act violation are that defendants (1) induce their victims to part with property, (2) through the use of fear, and (3) with an adverse effect on interstate commerce.[52]

---

actionable RICO claim against Operation Rescue blockaders; although the court of appeals noted that the abortion clinic may have an actionable RICO claim based on extortion, the town could not support such a claim.).

[49] *See* United States v. Novia Turkette, 452 U.S. 576, 583 (1981).

[50] 18 U.S.C. § 1951(a) (1988) provides:

Whoever in any way or degree obstructs, delays or affects commerce or the movement of any article or commodity in commerce, by robbery or extortion or attempts or conspires so to do, or commits or threatens physical violence to any person or property in furtherance of a plan or purpose to do anything in violation of this section shall be fined not more than $10,000 or imprisoned not more than twenty years, or both.

[51] 18 U.S.C. § 1961(1) (1988 & Supp. 1989).

[52] United States v. Local 560, Int'l Bhd. of Teamsters, 780 F.2d 267, 281 (3d Cir. 1985), *cert. denied,* 476 U.S. 1140 (1986). *Accord,* United States v. De Parias, 805 F.2d 1447, 1450 (11th Cir. 1986), *cert. denied,* 482 U.S. 916 (1987).

The property element of a Hobbs Act violation has been liberally construed to include violation of intangible property rights, such as business and contractual relationships.[53] Because women cannot at present safely perform abortions on themselves,[54] they must enter into contractual relationships with medical providers who can perform abortion procedures. Since a blockade poses an obvious obstacle to women's ability to enter into these contracts, both the women and the abortion providers are deprived of property as defined by the Hobbs Act.

The fear element of a Hobbs Act violation encompasses fear of economic loss, including the loss of contractual relationships, or the loss of the opportunity to enter into such relationships.[55] Finally, the interstate commerce element of a Hobbs Act violation is easily met, because interstate commerce for the purposes of the Hobbs Act appears to apply with commerce clause breadth. Hence, even a de minimis effect on interstate commerce, which occurs whenever the victim purchases goods manufactured out-of-state, is enough to satisfy the interstate commerce requirement.[56]

---

[53] United States v. Hathaway, 534 F.2d 386, 395–96 (1st Cir.), *cert. denied,* 429 U.S. 819 (1976). *See also* United States v. Lewis, 797 F.2d 358, 364 (7th Cir. 1986), *cert. denied,* 479 U.S. 1093 (1987); Feminist Women's Health Center v. Roberts, No. C86-161Z (W.D. Wash. May 5, 1989) (clinic's "right to continue to operate its business" is property right protected under the Hobbs Act); Texas Air Corp. v. Air Line Pilots Ass'n Int'l, No. 88-0804 (S.D. Fla. July 14, 1984) (use of extortionate fear in effort to compel sale of business interfered with property right protected under Hobbs Act); United States v. Nadaline, 471 F.2d 340 (5th Cir. 1973), *cert. denied,* 411 U.S. 951 (1973) (right to solicit business is property right protected under Hobbs Act). Although the court in United States v. Aquon, 851 F.2d 1158, 1175 (9th Cir. 1988), suggested that the Hobbs Act should be interpreted more narrowly in light of the Supreme Court's decision in McNally v. United States, 483 U.S. 350 (1987) (narrowing definition of property in mail fraud context), other courts have rejected this suggestion. *See, e.g.,* United States v. Local 560, 694 F. Supp. 1158, 1188 (D.N.J. 1988) (indicating that definition of property under Hobbs Act "may well be more inclusive of 'intangible' rights" than in mail fraud context); Northeast Women's Center, Inc. v. McMonagle, 868 F.2d 1342, 1350 (3d Cir. 1989) ("rights involving conduct of business are property rights"); United States v. International Bhd. of Teamsters, 708 F. Supp. 1388, 1398 n.5 (S.D.N.Y. 1989) (disagreeing with United States v. Aquon). *See also* West Hartford v. Operation Rescue, 915 F.2d 92 (2d Cir. 1990) ("property" does not encompass "altered official conduct" which was allegedly sought by blockaders); *accord* Brookline v. Operation Rescue, No. 89-0805-MA (D. Mass. Apr. 29, 1991).

[54] Technology that would permit self-administered abortion through medication, such as France's "RU 486," is not yet available in the United States.

[55] *See* United States v. Bucci, 839 F.2d 825, 827–28 (1st Cir. 1988) (citing United States v. Hathaway, 534 F.2d 386, 394, 396 (1st Cir. 1976)).

[56] *See* United States v. Frasch, 818 F.2d 631, 634–35 (7th Cir. 1987); United States v. Anderson, 716 F.2d 446, 447, 450 (7th Cir. 1983) (holding that extortion of abortion clinic physician affected interstate commerce because clinic's business was threatened and, inter alia, it purchased goods from out of state). Thus, every clinic in the country, even those with no out-of-state patients, should be able to meet the Hobbs Act's interstate commerce requirement.

In sum, clinic blockades should constitute Hobbs Act predicate acts under RICO. Blockaders extort intangible property interests from the women seeking abortions, and from the clinics that seek to serve them. These women have a constitutional right to enter into contractual relations to obtain an abortion; the abortion providers have a property interest in continuing to provide abortion services. Because the blockades deprive the women and the clinics of these interests through threats of physical harm, intimidation, and harassment, the predicate act requirement of RICO is satisfied.[57]

In the context of abortion clinic blockades, there is usually no question about the existence of a pattern of activity that violates the Hobbs Act. For example, Operation Rescue and/or its local chapters have blockaded and trespassed inside clinics throughout the country vastly more often than two times in the last 10 years, typically staging blockades almost monthly. These repeated acts of Hobbs Act extortion are separate yet related violations and should easily constitute a pattern of racketeering activity.[58]

§ 5.6 Objections to RICO Applicability

RICO claims based on Hobbs Act violations may be used against anti-abortion blockaders notwithstanding the claim that the blockaders have no economic motive for their activities.[59] Indeed, anti-abortion blockaders do have a negative economic motive: they seek to shut down abortion clinics and prevent them from operating. Blockaders literally use force to prevent women from obtaining and clinics from providing abortion services. Although the blockaders may not receive an economic benefit from interfering with contracts, they intend to and do inflict great economic harm and can potentially drive a health facility out of business.[60] Moreover, the blockaders do not need to have an economic motive. Lack of economic

---

[57] *See* Hunt v. Weatherbee, 626 F. Supp. 1097, 1103 (D. Mass. 1986) (coercing female employee into buying raffle ticket benefiting union constituted Hobbs Act violation satisfying predicate act requirement of RICO).

[58] *Id.* at 1103–04.

[59] *Cf.* Northeast Women's Center, Inc. v. McMonagle, 110 S. Ct. 261 (1989) (White, J., dissenting). Justice White argued that the Supreme Court should grant certiorari to determine whether RICO liability could be imposed when neither the enterprise nor the pattern of racketeering activity had any profit-making element. *Accord* National Org. for Women v. Scheidler, No. 86C-78888 (N.D. Ill. May 28, 1991).

[60] Any economic motive requirement can be satisfied by a motive to cause economic harm, even if there is no corresponding economic benefit. *See* Northeast Women's Center, Inc. v. McMonagle, 868 F.2d 1342, 1350 (3d Cir. 1989); United States v. Anderson, 716 F.2d 446, 450 (7th Cir. 1983); Feminist Women's Health Center v. Roberts, No. C86-161Z, slip op. at 7 (W.D. Wash. May 5, 1989).

motive is not a defense to a Hobbs Act conviction, and it should not serve as a defense to liability under a RICO claim that is based on Hobbs Act predicate acts.[61] Consistent with this interpretation, two federal appellate courts have recently held anti-abortionists criminally liable for violations of the Hobbs Act.[62]

A second basis for criticizing the use of RICO against anti-abortion blockaders is that it may potentially chill first amendment activity. But even assuming that a blockade is meaningfully characterized as "expressive," blockades are not protected by the first amendment. The landmark first amendment case of *Cox v. Louisiana*,[63] which expanded first amendment protection, explicitly stated that "a group of protesters could not insist on the right to cordon off a street, or entrance to a public or private building, and allow no one to pass who did not agree to listen to their exhortations."[64] Operation Rescue blockaders seek to do even more than this: they seek to block access to all individuals, regardless of whether they stop to listen.

First amendment defenses are particularly questionable when used by anti-abortion blockaders because, in contrast to the civil rights activists of the 1960s with whom they compare themselves,[65] Operation Rescue and its affiliates seek to deprive others of constitutional rights. The claim of Operation Rescue blockaders to be like civil rights activists of the 1960s is "at best, disingenuous: . . . the civil rights movement sought to extend constitutional rights to all Americans. Operation Rescue wants to deny those rights to one class of citizens: women."[66]

Finally, RICO has not in reality posed any threat to first amendment rights, quite apart from the fact that blockades do not have first amendment protection in the first place. Operation Rescue leaders have been subjected to stiff monetary penalties on non-RICO claims (usually for

---

[61] *See, e.g.,* Northeast Women's Center, Inc. v. McMonagle, 868 F.2d 1342, 1350.

[62] *Id.;* United States v. Anderson, 716 F.2d 446.

[63] 379 U.S. 536 (1965).

[64] *Id.* at 555. Similarly, anti-abortion blockaders cannot use the Supreme Court's decisions in NAACP v. Claiborne Hardware, 458 U.S. 886 (1982), and Organization For a Better Austin v. Keefe, 402 U.S. 415 (1971), to their advantage. In *Claiborne Hardware,* the Supreme Court made clear that the first amendment does not protect against violence or threats of violence. 458 U.S. at 893, 916. Moreover, unlike women seeking abortions, the persons seeking an injunction in *Claiborne Hardware* were not asserting (because they could not) any fundamental constitutional right to sell hardware or other goods. In *Organization For a Better Austin,* in contrast to cases involving anti-abortion blockades, there was no evidence of "any disruption of pedestrian or vehicular traffic." 402 U.S. at 417.

[65] *See* Julian Bond, *Dr. King's Unwelcome Heirs,* N.Y. Times, Nov. 2, 1988, at A27, col. 1.

[66] *Id.*

contempt of court)[67] and have made clear that they neither fear nor have any intention of paying them. Thus, in the minds of the blockaders themselves, exposure to financial liability poses no obstacle to the expression of their views.

Nevertheless, RICO claims against anti-abortion blockaders should be sensitive to first amendment concerns and be focused on physical actions such as blockading and trespassing, and not on verbal conduct. Abortion clinics have not used RICO against leafleting or posters or non-disruptive picketing, of the sort that has been occurring on the streets outside their doors for over 15 years. Only when anti-abortionists began to block those doors and invade and trespass upon clinic property have RICO claims been pursued.[68]

Using RICO against abortion clinic blockaders employs a federal statute to protect "civil rights." That is, RICO is used against an association of persons who seek through multiple criminal acts to prevent women from exercising their constitutional rights to obtain abortions. This use comports with the civil rights tradition of protecting the exercise of constitutional rights from physical interference. Whether a blockade's target is a desegregated school, a voting booth, or an abortion clinic, federal civil rights kinds of remedies are needed, of which RICO serves as one. Indeed, in light of the recent decision by the United States Supreme Court to grant certiorari[69] in a case presenting the question of whether the civil rights conspiracy act[70] can be applied to abortion clinic blockades in order to protect women,[71] RICO may be the only federal civil rights remedy available.

Despite the obvious benefits to using RICO against anti-abortion blockaders, one possible limitation is that women and clinics may not be able to obtain an injunction against further violations of the statute.[72] This is not

---

[67] *See* Roe v. Operation Rescue, No. 88-5157 (E.D. Pa. Dec. 7, 1988); New York State Nat'l Org. for Women v. Terry, 697 F. Supp. 1324 (S.D.N.Y. 1988), *aff'd*, 886 F.2d 1339 (2d Cir. 1989). See also § **5.2.**

[68] Indeed, the Third Circuit in Northeast Women's Center, Inc. v. McMonagle acknowledged constitutional limits on RICO's use in this context. The court noted that "the jury found that Defendants' actions went beyond mere dissent and publication of their political views. Hence, it concluded, the blockaders could rightfully be found guilty of violating RICO, which has been broadly applied "in contexts far beyond those originally intended." 868 F.2d 1342, 1348.

[69] Bray v. Alexandria Women's Health Clinic, 111 S. Ct. 1070 (1991), *granting cert. from* National Org. for Women v. Operation Rescue, 914 F.2d 582 (4th Cir. 1990).

[70] 42 U.S.C. § 1985(3) (1989).

[71] Bray v. Alexandria Women's Health Clinic, 111 S. Ct. 1070. The questions presented are quoted at 59 U.S.L.W. 3576 (Feb. 26, 1991).

[72] *Compare* Religious Technology Center v. Wollersheim, 796 F.2d 1076, 1081–88 (9th Cir. 1986) (no private injunctive relief), *cert. denied,* 479 U.S. 1003 (1987) *with* Bennett v. Berg, 685 F.2d 1053, 1064 (8th Cir. 1982) (suggesting injunctive relief may be available), *cert. denied,* 464 U.S. 1008 (1983).

a major drawback, however, because women and clinics suing blockaders can almost invariably allege pendent state law causes of action and obtain injunctions under them.[73]

§ 5.7   Complaint Against Anti-Abortion Blockaders

IN THE UNITED STATES DISTRICT COURT
FOR THE DISTRICT OF AMES

PLANNED PARENTHOOD FEDERATION OF AMES, INC.; ABC CLINIC, INC.; XYZ CLINIC, INC., JOHN DOE, M.D., REBECCA ROE,
      Plaintiffs,
 	
   v.
 	
OPERATION SAVE: AMES; [here list each individual defendant]; JOHN SMITH(S) AND JANE SMITH(S), the last two being fictitious names, the real names of said defendants being presently unknown to plaintiffs, said fictitious names being intended to designate organizations or persons who are members of defendant organizations, and others acting in concert with any of the defendants who are engaging in, or intend to engage in, the conduct complained of herein,
      Defendants.
	CIVIL ACTION
	No.
	CLASS ACTION
	
	SAMPLE
	VERIFIED COMPLAINT
	FOR INJUNCTIVE
	RELIEF AND DAMAGES

Plaintiffs, by their undersigned attorneys, allege as follows:

Preliminary Statement

1.   Plaintiffs seek injunctive and related relief to ensure the health and safety of women seeking abortions or other family planning services

---

[73] *See, e.g.,* Northeast Women's Center, Inc. v. McMonagle, 868 F.2d 1342, 1347, 1355–56 (injunctive relief granted under state law claims of trespass and interference with contractual relations); West Hartford v. Operation Rescue, 726 F. Supp. 371, 381 (D. Conn. 1989) (injunction granted on probability of success of pendent state public nuisance claim).

in Ames health care facilities. Plaintiffs require immediate injunctive relief to prevent defendants and those acting in concert with them from carrying out "Operation Save," their plan being to blockade family planning clinics in Ames and harass and intimidate the clinics' patients and staff.

2. Plaintiffs and the classes they seek to represent are organizations and clinics representing and serving women who seek abortion and other family planning services, physicians, and affected women. Plaintiffs seek to protect their constitutional, statutory, and common law rights to obtain and provide abortions and other family planning services, and to prevent illegal interference with their exercise of these rights.

3. Based on their prior illegal Operation Save blockades and related actions in other cities, and their announced intentions to conduct an "Operation Save: Ames" blockade and related actions on [dates], defendants will try to illegally blockade access to abortion providers, obstruct the provision of abortion and other family planning services, intimidate, harass and restrain women attempting to use the services of the clinics, and "clog up" the administration of the police and the courts. Defendants have stated that they will conduct these actions somewhere in Ames on [dates], but purposely have not indicated which providers they will specifically target. Defendants' actions will greatly increase the health risks faced by women seeking counseling, abortions, and other services in the targeted facilities, and therefore plaintiffs require immediate injunctive relief.

§ 5.8 —Jurisdiction and Parties

JURISDICTION AND VENUE

4. This Court has subject matter jurisdiction under 28 U.S.C. § 1331, 28 U.S.C. § 1343, 18 U.S.C. § 1964 and principles of pendent jurisdiction.

5. Venue in this District is proper under 28 U.S.C. § 1391(b) because the claims arise here.

PARTIES

Plaintiffs

6. Plaintiff Planned Parenthood Federation of Ames, Inc. (Planned Parenthood) is a non-profit Ames corporation whose principal office is at _____. It maintains clinics in Bestford (at [address], a

residential area) and Carlson ([address]), Ames, that provide abortion and other family planning services. Planned Parenthood's patients regularly include women who travel to its clinics from other states. Planned Parenthood has been determined to be exempt from federal income tax under § 501(c)(3) of the Internal Revenue Code of 1954, as amended. It brings this action on its own behalf and as a representative of the classes of counseling organizations, clinics and women described below.

7.   Plaintiff ABC Clinic, Inc. (ABC) is a non-profit Ames corporation whose principal place of business is in a residential area at [address], Bestford, Ames. ABC has been determined to be exempt from federal income tax under § 501(c)(3) of the Internal Revenue Code of 1954, as amended. It brings this action on its own behalf and as a representative of the classes of clinics and women described below.

8.   Plaintiff XYZ Clinic, Inc. (XYZ) is an Ames corporation whose principal place of business is at [address], Bestford, Ames. It brings this action on its own behalf and as a representative of the classes of clinics and women described below.

9.   Plaintiff John Doe, M.D., is a resident and citizen of Ames, a physician licensed to practice medicine in Ames, and the medical director of Planned Parenthood's clinics. He brings this action on his behalf and as a representative of the classes of women and physicians described below.

10.   Plaintiff "Rebecca Roe" is a fictitious person, who is representative of all the women seeking to obtain an abortion at the plaintiff clinics on [dates]. None of the real women so scheduled for those dates has so far been willing to risk the potential breach of confidentiality attendant upon being a party herein.

Defendants

11.   Defendant Operation Save also known as Operation Save: Ames for purposes of planned actions in Ames on [dates], is an unincorporated association of organizations and individuals with offices in _____. Its purpose is to organize and coordinate disruptions of abortion and family planning facilities, including the blockades scheduled for Ames on [dates]. Operation Save's literature lists its address as _____, and its telephone number as _____.

12.   According to Operation Save's literature, defendant Roger Rescue, acting in concert with other defendants and others unknown, is the founder and National Director of Operation Save. Upon information and belief, he resides in _____, and has been arrested in numerous cities for staging Operation Save blockades.

13–39.   [Here list and describe all other organizational and individual defendants, including all information specific to each as to why each is or can be expected to be involved in blockades.]

40. Defendants "John Smith(s)" and "Jane Smith(s)" are fictitious names, the real names of said defendants being presently unknown to plaintiffs. These fictitious names are intended to designate organizations or persons who are members of defendant organizations, and others acting in concert with any of the defendants who are engaging in, or intend to engage in, the conduct complained of herein.

§ 5.9   —Class Action Allegations

CLASS ACTION ALLEGATIONS

Plaintiff Classes

41. Pursuant to Fed. R. Civ. P. 23, plaintiffs bring this action on their own behalf and as representative parties on behalf of the following similarly situated classes, each of which classes will be adversely affected by defendants' intended conduct as described below:

(a)   all women who seek abortions or other services of any sort at any clinics or medical offices in Ames;

(b)   all physicians who perform or who may perform abortions within Ames;

(c)   all counseling organizations within Ames that provide counseling to women with respect to reproduction matters;

(d)   all clinics within Ames that provide services, including abortion and abortion counseling services, to women.

42. The members of each of the plaintiff classes of all women, physicians, counseling organizations, and clinics are so numerous that joinder of all members is impracticable. The questions of law and fact presented herein are common to the claims of all members of each of the respective plaintiff classes. The claims of the named plaintiffs are typical of the claims of the members of each of the respective plaintiff classes. The named plaintiffs will fairly and adequately protect the interests of the members of the respective plaintiff classes.

43. Because defendants' actions raise issues generally applicable to plaintiffs and all others similarly situated, final injunctive relief with respect to plaintiffs and the classes they represent and with respect to defendants is the only appropriate method for the fair and efficient adjudication of the controversy. Questions of law and fact common to the members of the classes predominate over any questions affecting only individual members. Maintenance of this action as a class action is superior to other available methods for the fair and effective adjudication of the controversy.

§ 5.10 —Factual Allegations

FACTS APPLICABLE TO ALL CLAIMS

Operation Save: Ames

44. Defendants, pursuant to a conspiracy that they have entitled Operation Save, plan to close down abortion facilities in Ames on [dates], by trespassing on, sitting in, or blocking access to such facilities, intimidating and harassing patients and visitors, staging disruptive protests, and otherwise disrupting and interfering with the operations of such facilities.

45. Defendants do not accept the United States Supreme Court decisions protecting a woman's right to choose abortion, and they intend to interfere with the rights of women attending the targeted clinics and providers, including women who travel from out-of-state. *Id.*, Exhibit D.

46. Upon information and belief, defendants in carrying out Operation Save will be joined by approximately 500 people from various states.

47. Defendants' own literature calling for volunteers to come to Ames states: [quote].

It further states with respect to whether it will be deterred by actions of law enforcement personnel: [quote].

48. Defendants' own literature also states that they intend to "clos[e] down abortion mills" to "prevent abortion mill employees or pregnant mothers from entering" the clinics. Defendants' instructions to their co-conspirators acknowledge that they are likely to be arrested, and state that even if the police make arrests and seek to "disperse the crowd, the goal you must have is to keep the doorway occupied."

49. Defendants have arranged pre-blockade meetings in _____, Ames on [dates] but have not publicly identified which clinics, hospitals, or physician's offices they will target. Upon information and belief, defendants intend to keep this aspect of Operation Save secret in order to frustrate attempts to protect and guarantee women's access to the clinics and providers.

Past "Rescues"

50. Upon information and belief, defendant Roger Rescue first conceived of Operation Save in 1983. Since that time defendant Rescue and one or more of the other defendants have published anti-abortion literature and organized the following "rescues" by distributing fliers and staging rallies and training sessions.

51–91. [Here describe, incident by incident, each blockade and/or trespass that has occurred in your own jurisdiction over the last 12 to 24 months, or those in other jurisdictions that lead you to believe that your jurisdiction will experience comparable incidents.]

§ 5.11   —Allegations of Injury

INJURY TO PLAINTIFFS

92.   Defendants' actions have the effect of denying or disrupting access to the targeted clinics so that many women postpone their scheduled services. Such delays in childbirth and abortion services significantly increase the health risks faced by the women affected, particularly women undergoing the two-day laminaria procedure performed by some of the plaintiff clinics.

93.   Unless defendants' planned activities are enjoined, substantial and irreparable damage will be inflicted upon women patients, to their health, their safety, and their rights to choose an abortion, including women who travel from out-of-state. In addition, substantial and irreparable harm will be done to the clinics' and physicians' rights to conduct their businesses.

94.   Because of the actions of defendants and those acting in concert with them, plaintiffs have been required to take additional steps to secure the safety of their patients and staff. Plaintiff clinics have had to spend additional time counseling patients scheduled to obtain abortions or family planning services on [dates] in order to warn them of the possible disruptions and help them decide whether or not to postpone their appointments. Plaintiff clinics also have had to arrange for additional staff, make special arrangements with local police, and hire additional police details for the days of the expected blockades.

95.   Plaintiffs have no adequate remedy at law.

* * *

§ 5.12   —RICO Counts

CLAIMS FOR RELIEF

COUNT V: 18 U.S.C. § 1962(c) (RICO)

108. This cause of action is brought against all defendants except Operation Save, pursuant to the provisions of 18 U.S.C. § 1962(c). Alternatively, it is brought against all defendants including Operation Save.

109. All defendants are "persons" within the meaning of 18 U.S.C. §§ 1961(3) and 1962(c).

110. Operation Save is an "enterprise" within the meaning of 18 U.S.C. §§ 1961(4) and 1962(c). Alternatively, all defendants, and others known and unknown to plaintiffs, are associated in fact for the purpose of depriving plaintiffs of their constitutional, statutory, and common law rights. This association in fact constitutes an "enterprise" within the meaning of 18 U.S.C. §§ 1961(4) and 1962(c).

111. Plaintiffs are "persons" within the meaning of 18 U.S.C. § 1961(3) and for purposes of the civil remedies provision, 18 U.S.C. § 1964(c).

112. Operation Save is an enterprise engaged in and the activities of which affect interstate commerce within the meaning of 18 U.S.C. § 1962(c).

113. At all times relevant hereto, all of the defendants were associated with Operation Save within the meaning of 18 U.S.C. § 1962(c).

114. Beginning in approximately [date], defendants have engaged in a conspiracy to infringe and tortiously interfere with plaintiffs' constitutional, statutory, and common law rights and licenses to obtain and provide abortions, family planning, and other medical services, described in detail above. Defendants have called this conspiracy Operation Save and/or Operation Save: Ames.

115. On numerous occasions from [date] through the present, for the purpose of executing the aforesaid scheme, the defendants engaged in acts of extortion in violation of 18 U.S.C. § 1951(b)(2) and § 1952(a)(2) and (3), and Ames Gen. Laws ch. 265, § 25, in that, through the use of fear instilled by various protest activities, they attempted and conspired to induce facilities that provide abortions, their employees, and patients to part with intangible property rights against their will, including but not limited to the right of the facilities to provide abortion services and the right of patients to obtain abortion services or to enter into a contractual relationship with the facilities.

116. Defendants have announced publicly that they intend to carry out this conspiracy at facilities in Ames on [dates].

117. The unlawful conduct described above constitutes a "pattern of racketeering activity" within the meaning of 18 U.S.C. §§ 1961(1) and (5).

118. Defendants conducted and participated, directly and indirectly, in the conduct of the affairs of Operation Save through a pattern of racketeering activity within the meaning of 18 U.S.C. §§ 1961(1) and 1961(5) in violation of 18 U.S.C. § 1962(c).

119. All defendants committed or aided and abetted the commission of at least two acts of extortion, described above, and intend to commit

or aid and abet the commission of additional acts of extortion in Ames on [dates].

120. Some plaintiffs already have been injured in their business and/or property as a result of defendants' activities. If defendants are allowed to fulfill their stated intentions, plaintiffs will be injured in their business and/or property, as a result of defendants' activities, in an amount still to be determined.

COUNT VI: 18 U.S.C. § 1962(d) (RICO)

121. Defendants have conspired and agreed among themselves and with others whose identities are unknown to plaintiffs to commit the violations of 18 U.S.C. § 1962(c) described above, thereby injuring plaintiffs.

CHAPTER 6

CIVIL RICO IN SHAREHOLDER SUITS INVOLVING DEFENSE CONTRACTORS

William S. Lerach
Michael R. McCabe

§ 6.1   Introduction

As a result of the Supreme Court's counsel in *Sedima, S.P.R.L. v. Imrex Co.*[1] that the provisions of the Racketeer Influenced Corrupt Organizations Act (RICO)[2] were to be "read broadly," the private practitioner

---

[1] 473 U.S. 479, 497 (1985).

[2] 18 U.S.C. §§ 1961–68 (1988).

received a license to invoke the statute when faced with an appropriate set
of facts. Armed with this mandate, a prime opportunity to utilize civil
RICO arose in the late 1980s with the revelation of massive fraud within
the defense contracting industry in connection with the procurement and
performance of government contracts. For attorneys representing the
shareholder-owners of public companies implicated in the scandal, civil
RICO was an appropriate tool in the effort to remedy the harm caused
these corporations.

This chapter examines such a shareholder civil RICO case involving defense contractor Sundstrand Corporation from the pleading stage to its
conclusion. The background of the defense procurement scandal which
gave rise to the Sundstrand class and derivative litigation[3] and the place
and the role of the private bar in the prosecution of widespread corporate
misconduct are discussed in § 6.2. To illustrate a successfully pled civil
RICO action, §§ 6.3 through 6.6 provide a summation of the allegations
of the *Shields* complaint, including specific excerpts of the complaint's
civil RICO allegations. **Sections 6.7** through **6.12** provide relevant portions of defendants' motions to dismiss, and plaintiffs' response, which
normally follow the filing of a civil RICO complaint. Thereafter, § 6.13
presents the district court's analysis of the defendants' motions to dismiss
the *Shields* complaint's civil RICO claims, including excerpts of the relevant portions of the district court's published opinion. Finally, § 6.14
briefly reviews the subsequent litigation and ultimate settlement of the
Shields action. Upon conclusion, it is hoped that the reader will have been
provided an informative civil RICO case history and pleading model for
future reference in his or her particular practice.[4]

§ 6.2   The Defense Procurement Scandal

There was revealed during the late 1980s in the United States a scandal of
previously unseen proportions implicating many of the nation's largest defense contractors in widespread allegations of fraud, bribery, and corrup-

---

[3] The Sundstrand litigation was styled Shields v. Erikson, No. 88 C 8207 (N.D. Ill. 1988),
and will hereinafter be referred to as *Shields*.

[4] It should be noted that civil RICO actions have also been filed against management on
behalf of other defense contractors who have found themselves called to task by the
government for unlawful procurement activities, including Northrop Corp. (Goldberg
v. Jones, Case No. CV 88-7332 KN(Kx) (C.D. Cal. 1988)); Cubic Corp. (Miller v.
Zable, Civ. No. 88-1195 B(M) (S.D. Cal. 1988)); Computer Communications Technology Corp. (Abbey v. Bahre, Civ. No. 89-0589 E(Cm) (S.D. Cal. 1988)); Teledyne, Inc.
(Shields v. Singleton, Case No. C715-183 (L.A. Sup. Ct. 1988)); Litton Industries (The
Wildflower Partnership v. Hoch, Civ. No. 89-1967 RG(Sx) (C.D. Cal. 1988)); and
TRW, Inc. (Cummings v. Mettler, Case No. 1:89CV0176 (N.D. Ohio 1988)).

tion in connection with the acquisition of and performance under military defense contracts with the government. A partial list of the companies implicated in the scandal reads like a veritable *Who's Who* of the defense contracting industry, including such familiar faces as Northrop Corporation, Litton Industries, Teledyne, TRW, Hughes Aircraft, McDonnell-Douglas Corporation, Rockwell International, Boeing Industries, General Dynamics, Lockheed Corporation, and Sundstrand Corporation.

Following one of the largest and most far-reaching federal criminal investigations in United States history, many of these companies have found themselves criminally and/or civilly charged with sundry illegalities in connection with contracts with the Department of Defense. These investigations and charges entail allegations of bribery of government officials by industry "consultants," the unlawful acquisition and use of confidential bidding information, false claims for payment, parts substitution and falsification, false test certifications, and improper billing and accounting practices.[5]

As the government proceeded with its criminal and civil investigations and prosecutions, those companies charged with wrongdoing have successively fallen in line with criminal guilty pleas, consent decrees, and civil settlements. In addition to substantial penalties and fines, prosecuted corporations face additional damages in the form of temporary suspension or permanent debarment from government contracts, forced completion of existing defense contracts at no profit, required retesting and recertification of suspect products at no cost, the implementation of institutional safeguards against further abuse,[6] the expense and disruption of lost employee and management time, weakened borrowing power from private and institutional lenders, loss of contracts in the commercial sector, substantial civil damage awards and settlements from "whistle-blower" lawsuits,[7] and loss of good will and standing in the business community.

---

[5] The defense contracting industry is no stranger to fraud and unlawful business practices. Indeed, as the defense contracting industry prospered in the 20th century, the industry found itself subject to repeated and increasing scandals involving fraud and bribery, so much so that industry insiders have observed that "dirty tricks" have become an "entrenched part of the industry's culture." *See, The Defense Scandal—The Fall Out May Devastate Arms Merchants,* Business Week, July 4, 1988, at 28.

[6] These corporate safeguards are primarily designed to protect the government from future fraud in connection with the procurement and performance of defense contracts. Such intracorporate therapeutics may include continuing ethics programs for company employees, independent corporate ombudsmen to act as liaisons between employees and management, and the requirement of costly internal audits and investigations.

[7] The so-called whistle-blower or *qui tam* actions are usually brought by industry employees who uncover fraud by their employers against the government. These individuals are responsible for revealing much of the wrongdoing that was occurring at many of the nation's defense contractors. Brought pursuant to the federal False Claims Act, 31 U.S.C. §§ 3729–3732, these actions are filed under seal, and the Department of Justice

The defense procurement scandal is but one of a number of recent instances of widespread misconduct in America's corporate and investment communities and is unfortunately coupled with a suspect ability of the Securities and Exchange Commission and the Department of Justice to actively and effectively prosecute the cases that arise.[8] Moreover, although the government's criminal and civil prosecutions may serve to protect the government and taxpayers in the future and also provide some monetary recovery for the United States Treasury, these prosecutions do nothing directly on behalf of the shareholder-owners of these companies, either to compensate for damages suffered or to challenge the conduct of upper management responsible for permitting the illegalities to occur.

As a consequence, vigorous private enforcement of the statutory remedies in the securities laws and civil RICO through representative class and shareholder derivative actions is required.[9] Indeed, the Supreme Court has repeatedly observed that "[p]rivate enforcement . . . provides a necessary supplement to Commission action," by both affording relief to those injured by violations of the securities laws and serving as a deterrent to future wrongdoing.[10] These considerations are just as important, if not

---

is allowed a prescribed period of time in which to decide whether or not to assume prosecution of the case on behalf of the government. The plaintiff, or *relator,* shares in any recovery obtained on behalf of the government.

[8] *See, e.g.,* Defense Procurement Fraud, Report of the Government Accounting Office, June 1988 (discussing staff turnover, management, and case monitoring problems which have hindered effective prosecution of defense procurement fraud). These difficulties are enhanced further by the incredible scope of the defense procurement scandal and a perception that the Securities and Exchange Commission has been lax in its duties. Indeed, Representative Dingle observed at a May, 1987 Congressional Committee hearing regarding defense procurement fraud that "the Securities and Exchange Commission seems to have abandoned its policies of demanding such disclosures" and "the Pentagon Inspector General told this Subcommittee that he has 45 of the top 100 defense contractors under criminal investigation." Hearings, Subcommittee on Oversight and Investigations, Committee on Energy and Commerce, Mar. 4–5, 1987 at 1–3.

[9] The important role of representative actions is a product of the reality of diverse shareholder ownership of public corporations. As one court observed:

In our complex modern economic system where a single harmful act may result in damages to a great many people there is a particular need for the representative action as a device for vindicating claims which, taken individually, are too small to justify legal action but which are of significant size if taken as a group. In a situation where we depend on individual initiative, particularly the initiative of lawyers, for the assertion of rights, there must be a practical method for combining these small claims, and the representative action provides that method.

Escott v. Barchris Constr. Corp., 340 F.2d 731, 733 (2d Cir.), *cert. denied,* 382 U.S. 816 (1965) (footnote omitted).

[10] J.I. Case Co. v. Borak, 377 U.S. 426, 432 (1964). *See also,* Mills v. Electric Auto-Lite Co., 396 U.S. 375, 396–97 (1970).

more so, today.[11] Moreover, RICO contains an express private right of action which Congress hoped would "enhance the effectiveness of [the Act's] prohibitions" and provide "a major new tool" as part of what Congress intended as "an aggressive initiative to supplement old remedies and develop new methods for fighting crime"[12]—which is exactly what cheating the Defense Department is.

Thus, for the practitioner representing minority shareholders, revelation of the procurement scandal involving huge publicly owned corporations presented a new challenge to hold management accountable for the substantial harm to the companies under their stewardship. Moreover, the duration and pervasiveness of the wrongdoing occurring within these companies opened the door for the shareholders' lawyer to apply civil RICO to the errant officers and directors through the vehicle of a class and derivative action on behalf of the shareholders and the corporation.[13]

The substantive requirements of civil RICO can readily be met in a class and derivative corporate fraud case provided the practitioner is careful in the framing of his or her allegations and organizes the complaint in a manner allowing the reviewing court to be clear on the propriety of the civil RICO theories for relief. To illustrate this, the following sections present a close look at the *Shields* litigation.

§ 6.3 Shareholders' RICO Suit

Sundstrand Corporation is one of the publicly-owned defense contractors embroiled in the defense contract procurement scandal of the 1980s. In the case of *Shields v. Erikson*,[14] counsel for the shareholders found prime circumstances in which to plead a civil RICO case against management.

---

[11] Indeed, combined with the fall of the corrupted junk bond market, revelation of a poisoned commodities market, and the more recent collapse of many of the nation's savings and loan associations, to name a few of such scandals, the defense procurement debacle has truly made the 1980s the "Decade of Deceit" for corporate America.

[12] *Sedima*, S.P.R.L. v. Imrex Co., 473 U.S. 479, 498 (1985).

[13] Dean Rostow has called the derivative suit "the most important procedure the law has yet developed to police the internal affairs of corporations." Rostow, *To Whom and For What Ends Is Corporate Management Responsible?: The Corporation in Modern Society*, 48 (E. Mason ed. 1959). Similarly, United States Supreme Court Justice Jackson long ago observed,

> This remedy born of stockholder helplessness was long the chief regulator of corporate management and has afforded no small incentive to avoid at least grosser forms of betrayal of stockholders' interests. It is argued, and not without reason, that without it there would be little practical check on such abuses.

Cohen v. Beneficial Indus. Loan Corp., 337 U.S. 541, 548 (1949).

[14] No. 88 C 8207 (N.D. Ill. 1988).

By way of background, Chicago-based Sundstrand Corporation was a leading producer of equipment for the United States Department of Defense with over 40 percent of its revenues and profits coming from defense contract work. Upon discovery of an alleged pattern of illegal conduct in which Sundstrand allegedly overcharged the government more than $100 million on several government contracts, Sundstrand found itself subject to extensive federal law enforcement investigations and two separate grand jury investigations. On October 21, 1988, Sundstrand pled guilty to a four-count criminal information which charged Sundstrand with defrauding the United States through three separate criminal conspiracies and through the submission of fraudulent claims for payment to the government. As part of the guilty plea and plea agreement, Sundstrand was required to pay the United States government a criminal fine of $115 million.[15]

In accepting the plea agreement and guilty plea to four felony counts, Judge Stanley J. Roszkowski of the United States District Court for the Northern District of Illinois made the following observations, among others:

> I would be remiss in my duty in accepting this agreement if I did not comment on some of the particulars of this sordid affair. It is difficult—no, it's impossible—for the court to understand the atmosphere which was created to cause large numbers of people to engage in these various illegal conspiracies. If it were only one or two remote acts, perhaps it might be more understandable as a misunderstanding of the facts or the legal responsibility, but that is not the case here.
>
> What we have here is an ongoing course of criminal conduct spanning many months and even years. Many people had to be deeply involved for the various illegal schemes to succeed. It seems to this court that these schemes succeeded because of an attitude, a mindset, created by the company that it was all right to cheat and lie and steal from the government, although it is apparent from the factual basis submitted in this case that the defendant did not treat its other commercial customers the same way. . . .
>
> One would think that someone in authority would have said not only do we have a duty to our best customer to deal with it fairly, honestly, and ethically, that duty rises above ordinary standards of business conduct. Our

---

[15] This was the largest criminal fine ever imposed upon a defense contractor in the history of the United States. Sundstrand also settled administrative claims with the government by agreeing to pay $71.3 million to the Defense Department and to implement substantial and material changes in its accounting systems. In addition, as a result of a separate grand jury investigation, an implicated subsidiary of Sundstrand also pled guilty to a felony in the United States District Court for the Western District of Washington. As a part of that plea agreement and in settlement of civil claims, the subsidiary paid the government a total of $12,320,000.

duty is the same as that of a trustee, a fiduciary, for we are dealing with the taxpayers, in effect, with ourselves and our employees.

Instead, not only did Sundstrand not take this position, in addition to deceitful conduct it engaged in to overcharge the government, it also created a scheme to cheat the government out of the taxes which it clearly owed. It compounded the crimes several times over when it did this.

And even after it was aware of the investigation into its illegal conduct, it continued to engage in conduct to cover up its illegal acts.[16]

When details of the illegalities were publicly revealed, the shareholders' counsel filed the *Shields* civil RICO action against the officers and directors of Sundstrand in the United States District Court for the Northern District of Illinois. The plaintiffs asserted substantive civil RICO claims under § 1962(c) and (d), which, respectively, prohibit activities relating to the conduct or control of an enterprise through a pattern of racketeering activity and prohibit conspiring to violate any of the provisions of the statute.[17]

RICO § 1962(c) requires pleading the following elements:

1. The existence of a RICO "enterprise"
2. The existence of a "pattern of racketeering activity"
3. A nexus between defendants and either the pattern of racketeering activity or the enterprise
4. Resulting injury to plaintiffs in their "business or property."[18]

These elements were readily met under the facts presented in the *Shields* action. The alleged enterprise[19] was the corporation, Sundstrand

---

[16] Transcript of Guilty Plea at 68–70, United States v. Sundstrand, CR 20021 (N.D. Ill. 1988).

[17] 18 U.S.C. 1962(c) provides:

It shall be unlawful for any person employed by or associated with any enterprise engaged in, or the activities of which affect, interstate or foreign commerce, to conduct or participate, directly or indirectly, in the conduct of such enterprise's affairs through a pattern of racketeering activity or collection of unlawful debt.

18 U.S.C. 1962(d) provides:

It shall be unlawful for any person to conspire to violate any of the provisions of subsections (a), (b), or (c) of this section.

[18] Sedima, S.P.R.L. v. Imrex Co., 473 U.S. 479, 496 (1985). The reader should be mindful that the *Shields* complaint pre-dated the more recent United States Supreme Court decision of H.J. Inc. v. Northwestern Bell Tel. Co., 109 S. Ct. 2893, 2900 (1990), which further refined the concept of pattern of racketeering activity to require, among other things, a plaintiff or prosecutor to show "that the racketeering predicates are related, and that they amount to or pose a threat of continued criminal activity."

[19] 18 U.S.C. § 1961(c)(4).

Corporation. Similarly, the required nexus between the defendants and the enterprise was quite clear, because the defendants were alleged to be either past or present controlling officers and/or directors of Sundstrand or one of Sundstrand's subsidiaries implicated in the government's allegations of wrongdoing. That the defendants' alleged wrongdoing resulted in injury to plaintiffs in their business or property was also readily met by general allegations of damage.

The *Shields* complaint also met the "pattern of racketeering activity" requirement of RICO[20] by detailing no less than five separate schemes to defraud the government in connection with the procurement of or performance under defense contracts with the government. The first scheme alleged that a Sundstrand subsidiary engaged in improper and illegal billing practices on fixed price contracts with the government for the design, development, and production of aerospace components and systems used on commercial and military aircraft and spacecraft. Despite contractual terms to the contrary, the officer and director defendants were alleged to have caused Sundstrand to improperly include cost overruns in overhead billing rates charged to the Defense Department under the contracts. In essence, it was alleged under this scheme that the defendants caused Sundstrand to knowingly "low ball" bids on the fixed price contracts, knowing that there would be overruns which would later be recouped by billing the costs as overhead.

The second scheme alleged that officers and directors of Sundstrand billed personal expenses to government contracts through another Sundstrand subsidiary. These alleged improper billings included charges for liquor, gifts, travel by spouses, country club memberships, jewelry, and other personal matters, and it was further alleged that these charges were misallocated and billed as administrative overhead and then were improperly submitted to and paid for by the Defense Department.

The third scheme alleged a plan to defraud the government through improper tax write-offs by setting up a series of sham sales transactions between Sundstrand and another company. In this scheme, the sales transactions were allegedly structured in a manner in which Sundstrand purported to, but did not, lose money on sales of inventory to the other company, and then later took tax write-offs on the supposed losses. In addition, the defendants were alleged to have caused Sundstrand to take steps to conceal the truth from the IRS by making false statements about the purported sales and rewriting the subject contracts to conceal material facts concerning the true nature of the transactions.

The fourth scheme alleged the bribery of government officials to further the award of government contracts to Sundstrand. In this scheme, the defendants were alleged to have caused or allowed Sundstrand to bribe

---

[20] *Id.* at 1961(c)(5).

Defense Department and other public officials for the purpose of influencing them to favor Sundstrand in the award of government contracts. The defendants were also alleged to have caused Sundstrand to hide unlawful bribes and gratuities to government employees in the corporation's books by recording them as normal business transactions and even billing them to the government as part of Sundstrand's overhead.

The fifth scheme alleged that the defendants caused a wholly owned subsidiary of Sundstrand to file false and fraudulent claims for payment with the government. In this scheme, the defendants were alleged to have included costs unallowable under the contracts, such as patent litigation costs, to be improperly billed under an existing rate agreement with the Department of Defense.

The plaintiffs predicated their RICO theory on the defendants' alleged numerous violations of the mail fraud statute,[21] the wire fraud statute,[22] and the bribery statute.[23]

§ 6.4 Shareholders' Complaint

Before turning to the actual civil RICO allegations of the *Shields* complaint, a brief synopsis of the substance and structure of the entire complaint is in order, to give the reader one suggested approach in organizing and drafting a civil RICO complaint involving widespread corporate wrongdoing.[24]

First, the *Shields* complaint included a section entitled "Introduction and Overview of Action." This section provided a seven-page summary of the basic facts and nature of the action and the claims for relief being asserted. This section was designed to serve as a summary of the entire complaint and is recommended for inclusion in any complex complaint. In litigations involving large-scale corporate fraud, the complaint can often be quite lengthy (indeed, in the Northrop shareholders' derivative action, the complaint was over 110 pages long and included a table of contents). As a consequence, this prefatory section provides the reader with a useful "road map" of the entire action.

The *Shields* complaint then properly pled, under separate heading, the jurisdiction and venue of the district court in which the action was filed.

---

[21] 18 U.S.C. §§ 1341, 1342.

[22] 18 U.S.C. §§ 1343, 1342.

[23] 18 U.S.C. §§ 201, 202.

[24] The authors wish to acknowledge the drafting expertise of Patricia M. Hynes and Robert P. Sugarman, both partners in the New York City office of Milberg Weiss Bershad Specthrie & Lerach, who were primarily responsible for drafting the *Shields* complaint.

For an action filed in federal court, Federal Rule of Civil Procedure 8(a) requires allegations of jurisdiction. In *Shields,* federal jurisdiction was founded on 18 U.S.C. §§ 1964(c) and 1965(a) (RICO), 15 U.S.C. § 78(aa) (§ 27 of the 1934 Securities and Exchange Act for alleged proxy violations), and 28 U.S.C. § 1331 (diversity jurisdiction). In factual support of venue, the complaint alleged that the challenged wrongful conduct occurred in the Northern District of Illinois, where the complaint was filed, that Sundstrand's principal place of business was located in that district, that most of the defendants were residents of or had conducted business affairs in that district, and that many of the percipient witnesses resided in that district.

The third section of the *Shields* complaint, denominated "Parties," identified the named parties and also alleged the basis for the liability of the individual defendants, that is, whether primary or secondary. With respect to the officer and director defendants, their exact roles and responsibilities at Sundstrand or one of Sundstrand's subsidiaries were pled with as much particularity as possible. With little, if any, access to intracorporate information, perhaps the greatest difficulty for the shareholder's attorney in a large corporate fraud case is to tie upper-level management to the underlying wrongdoing. In the Parties section, the plaintiffs alleged that those defendants with executive or operating officer and/or directorial status at Sundstrand had positions of authority which allowed them to control the conduct of Sundstrand. Likewise, the complaint alleged that, by virtue of their positions as officers or directors, each of these defendants owed a duty to Sundstrand and its shareholders to ensure that its business was carried on lawfully. Moreover, the complaint detailed, as much as practicable, the exact duties of the officer and/or director defendants by reason of their particular positions within Sundstrand and/or membership on corporate board committees, like the audit and finance committee.

The fourth section of the *Shields* complaint was entitled "Derivative Allegations." Here, the plaintiffs attempted to comply with the pleading requirements of Rule 23.1 of the Federal Rules of Civil Procedure, which requires particularized factual allegations that the board of directors of the company either refused a shareholder demand to bring the action or that it would have been futile for the shareholder to demand the board of directors to do so.[25]

---

[25] Though beyond the scope of this chapter, a large obstacle facing the derivative practitioner is complying with Fed. R. Civ. P. 23.1, which sets forth strict pleading requirements in order to maintain a derivative action, providing, in pertinent part:

[T]he complaint shall also allege with particularity the efforts, if any, made by the plaintiff to obtain the action the plaintiff desires from the directors or comparable

§ 6.5   —RICO Allegations

After the allegations summarized in § 6.4, civil RICO allegations analogous to the following were made:[26]

PATTERN OF RACKETEERING ACTIVITY

I. Scheme to Defraud the United States and the Department of Defense (Billing Cost Overruns)

A.   Mail Fraud

1.   The ABC Group (ABC) was an operating unit of the Corporation, with headquarters in Anywhere, State, engaged in the design, development, and production of aerospace components and systems (hereinafter hardware) used on military and commercial aircraft and spacecraft. The majority of ABC's sales were made to the United States Department of Defense.

2.   The majority of the Corporation's defense contracts were firm, fixed price contracts requiring the Corporation to perform each contract for a set price regardless of the total costs incurred by the Corporation in the performance of the contract.

3.   The Corporation was required to submit to the Defense Department monthly reports regarding the Corporation's actual overhead, as well as a Final Overhead Rate Submittal setting forth the Corporation's actual overhead rates for the preceding calendar year. Government regulations prohibited the Corporation from including any cost overruns in the Corporation's overhead billing rates.

4.   The Corporation was required, pursuant to government regulations, to submit to the Defense Department a disclosure statement accurately describing the Corporation's cost accounting practices and to amend that disclosure statement when necessary to accurately describe the Corporation's cost accounting practices.

---

authority and, if necessary, from the shareholders or members, and the reasons for the plaintiff's failure to obtain the action or for not making the effort.

In *Shields,* although the court upheld plaintiffs' RICO allegations, the complaint was dismissed for failing to plead futility of demand with sufficient particularity. This pleading defect was cured in the second amended *Shields* complaint and, on Aug. 23, 1989, Judge Plunkett held that plaintiffs had adequately pled futility of demand under Rule 23.1.

[26] The paragraph numbers of the actual *Shields* complaint have been changed here, but the references to exhibits are in the original allegations. In addition, the names of the individual defendants have been omitted.

5.   From at least August 1981 to and including at least June 3, 1985, the defendants individually and collectively devised and intended to devise a scheme and artifice to defraud the United States government and the Defense Department of money and design rights, and to obtain money and property from the United States government and the Department of Defense by means of false and fraudulent pretenses, representations, and promises.

6.   It was the object of the scheme to make illegal profits for the Corporation by concealing cost overruns on design and development contracts, as well as other mischarged development costs, totalling more than $50 million in the Corporation's overhead billing rates paid by the Defense Department.

7.   It was part of the scheme that defendants caused or permitted the Corporation to bid intentionally for design and development contracts at less than the Corporation's estimated costs to perform those contracts in order to ensure that the Corporation would receive the contracts and would retain the design rights to the hardware developed pursuant to those contracts.

8.   It was further part of the scheme that the defendants would and did cause or permit the Corporation to instruct its engineers working on design and development contracts to charge costs to the contract only until either actual costs reached a budgeted ceiling or cost overruns were anticipated.

9.   It was further part of the scheme that when actual costs reached the budgeted ceiling or cost overruns were anticipated, the defendants caused or permitted the Corporation to instruct its engineers to charge the cost overruns on design and development contracts to the Corporation's overhead accounts and to conceal the existence of the cost overruns by issuing a memo closing the direct contract charge account and falsely reporting that all work had been completed.

10.   It was further part of the scheme that defendants caused or permitted the Corporation to receive from the Defense Department progress payments that included monies for the cost overruns on design development contracts as well as other mischarged development costs, which had been concealed in the Corporation's overhead billing rates.

11.   It was further part of the scheme that defendants caused or permitted the Corporation to misrepresent in various submissions to the Defense Department the fact that cost overruns on design and development contracts, as well as other mischarged development costs, were concealed in overhead billing rates submitted to and paid by the United States Defense Department.

12.   In furtherance of the scheme, defendants caused or permitted a directive to be issued by the Corporation to destroy an internal report which questioned the practice of charging cost overruns to overhead, and defendants caused or permitted the Corporation and its employees to repeatedly deny that such a practice was in place.

13.   As a result of the scheme, defendants wrongfully caused or permitted the Department of Defense to pick up approximately 55 to 65 percent of the cost overruns, which amounted to in excess of $50 million.

14.   On October 21, 1988, the Corporation pled guilty to Count I of a Criminal Information (88 Cr. 0001) in the Northern District of State, which included the allegations substantially similar to those set forth in paragraphs 1 to 13 above, charging it with conspiring with others to defraud the United States and the Defense Department of money and that the object of the conspiracy was to make illegal profits by concealing millions of dollars in cost overruns on design and development contracts, as well as other mischarged costs in the Corporation's overhead billing rates (Exhibit B, at 1 to 13).

15.   In pleading guilty to Count I, the defendants caused or permitted the Corporation to admit in open court "that those participating in this conspiracy took numerous actions to further its objective, including the Corporation's submission to the Defense Department of fraudulent overhead billing rates containing the overruns, and of false statements denying the overruns were included in these rates. As a result of the conspiracy, the Corporation obtained millions of dollars in Defense Department payments to which it was not entitled." (Transcript of Guilty Plea at 21, Exhibit E attached hereto).

16.   For the purpose of executing such scheme and artifice and attempting so to do, defendants placed and caused to be placed in post offices and authorized depositories for mail matter to be sent and delivered by the U.S. Postal Service and did take and receive therefrom matter, and knowingly caused to be delivered by mail according to the direction thereon such matter, all in violation of 18 U.S.C. §§ 1341 and 1342.

B.   Wire Fraud

17.   The allegations in paragraphs 1 to 16 are repeated and realleged as though fully set forth herein.

18.   For the purpose of executing such scheme and artifice and attempting so to do, the defendants transmitted and caused to be transmitted by means of wire communication in interstate commerce writings, signs, signals, pictures, and sounds, all in violation of 18 U.S.C. §§ 1343 and 1342.

II. Scheme to Defraud the United States and the Department of Defense (Billing Personal Expenses and Misallocating Costs)

A.   Mail Fraud

19.   Service Corporation (Service) was a wholly owned subsidiary of the Corporation, incorporated in State and headquartered in Anywhere, State. Service was engaged primarily in marketing and servicing the products of ABC and XYZ, another subsidiary of the Corporation located in _____.

20.   The Corporation accounted for Service costs as an indirect cost allocated between ABC and XYZ. Defendants caused or permitted the Corporation to not allocate Service costs between ABC and XYZ in proportion to the benefits derived from those costs. Defendants caused or permitted the Corporation to include in ABC's General and Administrative (G&A) overhead billing rate paid by the Defense Department millions of dollars in misallocated Service costs.

21.   From at least January 1, 1980 to at least January 1, 1987, in the Northern District of State and elsewhere, the defendants individually and collectively devised and intended to devise a scheme and artifice to defraud and for obtaining money and property by means of false and fraudulent pretenses and promises, in that defendants caused or permitted the Corporation to include in ABC's G&A overhead billing rate paid by the Defense Department millions of dollars in unallowable indirect costs, including but not limited to charges for liquor, babysitting, gifts, travel by executives' spouses, cigarettes, candy, saunas, golf, tennis, country club dues, movies, jewelry, clothes, airline club memberships, dog kennels, snowplowing at executives' homes, radar detectors, air shows, advertising, entertainment, lobbying costs, acquisition costs, non-business travel, excess compensation, and servants for executives and their spouses.

22.   On October 21, 1988, the Corporation pled guilty to Count IV of a Criminal Information (88 Cr. 0001) in the United States District Court for the Northern District of State, which included allegations substantially similar to those set forth in paragraphs 19 to 21 above, charging the Corporation with submitting false claims in the form of progress payment billings which the Corporation knew to contain millions of dollars in unallowable and misallocated indirect general and administrative costs. (See Exhibit B pp. 34 to 37). In pleading guilty, defendants caused or permitted the Corporation to admit that "the unallowable G&A cost contained in the fraudulent progress payments billings included charges for personal items for employees. Also included in the fraudulent progress payments billings were misallocated G&A Service Corporation costs, which should properly have been allocated to Data Control,

another subsidiary of the Corporation. By the inclusion of these unallowable and misallocated G&A costs in its progress payment billings, the Corporation obtained millions of dollars of Defense Department payments to which it was not entitled." (Transcript of Guilty Plea, Exhibit E, at 47).

23.   For the purpose of executing such scheme and artifice and attempting so to do, the defendants placed and caused to be placed in post offices and authorized depositories for mail matter to be sent and delivered by the U.S. Postal Service and did take and receive therefrom matter, and knowingly caused to be delivered by mail according to the direction thereon such matter, all in violation of 18 U.S.C. §§ 1341 and 1342.

B.   Wire Fraud

24.   The allegations in paragraphs 19 to 23 are repeated and realleged as though fully set forth herein.

25.   For the purpose of executing such scheme and artifice and attempting so to do, the defendants transmitted and caused to be transmitted by means of wire communication in interstate commerce writings, signs, signals, pictures, and sounds, all in violation of 18 U.S.C. §§ 1343 and 1342.

III. Scheme to Defraud the Internal Revenue Service

A.   Mail Fraud (Phony Tax Writeoffs)

26.   The SJ Company, Inc. (SJ) was a corporation with its corporate offices in _____. SJ was engaged in the long-term warehousing of manufacturers' inventory for the manufacturers' possible future use. SJ operated warehouses at various locations, including one in Somewhere, State, approximately 30 miles from Anywhere, State.

27.   Under the tax laws of the United States, a business could write off a loss from the sale of the inventory only if the sale was bona fide. A sale of inventory was bona fide under the tax laws of the United States only if the seller totally relinquished control of the inventory.

28.   Aviation Mechanical (Aviation) was a division of ABC, having its principal office at 4747 Harrison Avenue, Anywhere, State.

29.   From October 19, 1979, the defendants, individually and collectively, caused or permitted the Corporation to enter a contract with SJ for SJ to acquire certain Aviation parts previously stored in the Corporation's own warehouses. Prior to shipping the selected Aviation parts to SJ's Somewhere warehouse, the defendants caused or permitted the Corporation to generally prepare the parts for long-term storage. Upon receipt of the Aviation parts, SJ determined the quantity of each part

received, prepared a computerized inventory of the parts, and placed the parts in storage. On a monthly basis, SJ supplied the Corporation with a computer tape reporting the current inventory of parts acquired from the Corporation then in SJ's warehouse. Defendants caused or permitted the Corporation to add SJ's monthly computerized inventory control system to that of the Corporation so that it could track the availability of parts at SJ. When the Corporation wanted to reacquire any of the Aviation parts shipped to SJ, the Corporation informed SJ and SJ shipped the requested parts to the Corporation.

30.   Defendants caused or permitted the Corporation to record on its books and records a purported loss equal to the Corporation's book value for the Aviation parts at the time they were shipped to SJ less the amount paid for those parts by SJ.

31.   Defendants caused or permitted the Corporation to take tax write-offs amounting to millions of dollars on the Corporation's federal income tax returns reflecting the purported loss that the Corporation recorded on its books and records for parts shipped to SJ.

32.   On or about April 6, 1983, the Internal Revenue Service (IRS) issued Revenue Ruling 83-59, disallowing a tax write-off for transactions similar to those arranged by defendants between the Corporation and SJ by holding that under the tax laws of the United States the seller of the inventory had not relinquished sufficient control to constitute a bona fide sale.

33.   From at least April 7, 1983 to and including at least December 4, 1984, in the Northern District of State and elsewhere, the defendants devised and intended to devise a scheme and artifice to defraud the United States and the Internal Revenue Service of money by means of false and fraudulent pretenses, representations and promises.

34.   It was the object of the scheme for the defendants to insure the Corporation's ability to take millions of dollars in federal income tax write-offs for purported losses on the shipment of Aviation parts to SJ by concealing the true nature and extent of control exercised by the Corporation over the parts after shipment.

35.   It was part of the scheme that the defendants caused or permitted the Corporation to make false statements to and conceal material facts from the Internal Revenue Service in response to questions asked by the IRS regarding the control exercised by the Corporation over parts shipped to SJ.

36.   It was further part of the scheme that the defendants caused or permitted the Corporation to rewrite its contract with SJ to conceal material facts from the IRS regarding the control exercised by the Corporation over parts shipped to SJ.

37. On October 21, 1988, defendants caused the Corporation to plead guilty to Count III of a Criminal Information (88 Cr. 0001) in the Northern District of State, which included allegations substantially similar to those allegations contained in paragraphs 26 to 36 above, charging the Corporation with conspiring with others to defraud the United States and the IRS by obstructing the IRS in its ascertainment of the correct amount of federal income taxes owed by the Corporation and that the object of the conspiracy was to ensure the Corporation's ability to take millions of dollars in federal income tax write-offs for purported losses on the Corporation's parts shipped to SJ.

38. In pleading guilty, the defendants caused or permitted the Corporation to admit that "to accomplish the object of this conspiracy, the Corporation concealed the true nature and extent of control exercised by the Corporation over the parts shipped to SJ to prevent the IRS from disallowing the write-off because no bona fide sale had taken place. Those participating in the conspiracy took numerous actions to further its objective, including causing the Corporation to execute a contract with SJ which was intended by the Corporation to conceal the control exercised by the Corporation over parts shipped to SJ." (Transcript of Guilty Plea, Exhibit E, at 40–41).

39. For the purpose of executing such scheme and artifice and attempting so to do, the defendants placed and caused to be placed in post offices and authorized depositories for mail matter to be sent and delivered by the U.S. Postal Service and did take and receive therefrom matter, and knowingly caused to be delivered by mail according to the direction thereon such matter, all in violation of 18 U.S.C. §§ 1341 and 1342.

B. Wire Fraud

40. The allegations in paragraphs 26 to 39 are repeated and realleged as though fully set forth herein.

41. For the purpose of executing such scheme and artifice and attempting so to do, the defendants transmitted and caused to be transmitted by means of wire communication in interstate commerce writings, signs, signals, pictures, and sounds, all in violation of 18 U.S.C. §§ 1343 and 1342.

IV. Bribery

42. From at least February 1980 to at least November 9, 1986, in the Northern District of State and elsewhere, the defendants caused or permitted the Corporation to corruptly give and to aid in the giving of things of value to public officials of the Defense Department and to other persons, including spouses of public officials, totalling more than

$100,000, for the purpose of influencing official acts of public officials of the Defense Department in violation of 18 U.S.C. § 201(b).

43. On October 21, 1988, the defendants caused the Corporation to plead guilty to Count II of a Criminal Information (88 Cr. 0001) in the Northern District of State, charging the Corporation with a conspiracy to give more than $100,000 in illegal gratuities to government personnel and their spouses. (Exhibit B, at 14–24). In connection with that guilty plea, the defendants caused or permitted the Corporation to admit that it "conspired to give Defense Department personnel and their spouses gifts and entertainment totalling thousands of dollars because of the personnel's official acts." The defendants have also caused or permitted the Corporation to admit that "in carrying out this conspiracy, the conspirators took numerous actions, including the Corporation's concealment of the identities of the Defense Department personnel accepting the gratuities through the use of the term "customer" in lieu of the recipients' names and positions on the Corporation's expense reports." (Transcript of Guilty Plea, Exhibit E, at 29.)

V. Scheme to Defraud the United States Department of Defense (False Claims by XYZ)

A.   Mail Fraud

44.   From at least January 1980 through at least March 1985, the defendants individually and collectively devised and intended to devise a scheme and artifice to defraud the United States and the Defense Department of money and to obtain money from the United States and the Department of Defense by means of false and fraudulent pretenses, representations, and promises.

45.   It was part of the scheme that the defendants would and did cause or permit XYZ, a wholly-owned subsidiary of the Corporation, located in _____, to present and cause to be presented to the United States Department of Defense claims for payment, knowing that such claims were false, fictitious, and fraudulent in that they were based upon a Forward Pricing Rate Agreement (FPRA) between XYZ and the Department of Defense which fraudulently included unallowable costs, including $234,169 of patent litigation costs.

46.   The FPRA was negotiated on January 30, 1980, and was based, in part, on XYZ's knowing and unlawful inclusion of the unallowable patent litigation costs in its supporting data.

47.   XYZ's inclusion of the unallowable patent litigation costs had the effect of fraudulently increasing the General and Administrative (G&A) rate by approximately 0.4 percent in the FPRA negotiated on January 30, 1980. This FPRA was in effect from January 30, 1980 to June 8, 1981. XYZ

used the fraudulently inflated FPRA between January 30, 1980 and June 8, 1981 to price approximately $20 million of government contracts.

48.   In March 1985, the defendants caused XYZ to present its invoice A5-1380 to a prime contractor knowing that the prime contractor would then make a claim for payment against the United States Department of Defense. The invoice was false and fraudulent in that it was based, in part, on the January 30, 1980 FPRA which fraudulently included the $234,169 of patent litigation costs.

49.   XYZ's use of the fraudulently inflated January 30, 1980 FPRA to price government contracts resulted in a loss to the United States of approximately $80,000.

50.   On October 19, 1988, the defendants caused or permitted XYZ to plead guilty to one felony count in the Western District of State (Cr. 88-0002), which included allegations substantially similar to those contained in paragraphs 44 to 49, charging XYZ with submitting false, fictitious, and fraudulent claims to the United States Department of Defense.

51.   For the purpose of executing such scheme and artifice and attempting so to do, the defendants placed and caused to be placed in post offices and authorized depositories for mail matter to be sent and delivered by the U.S. Postal Service and did take and receive therefrom matter, and knowingly caused to be delivered by mail according to the direction thereon such matter, all in violation of 18 U.S.C. §§ 1341 and 1342.

B.   Wire Fraud

52.   The allegations in paragraphs 44 to 51 are repeated and realleged as though fully set forth herein.

53.   For the purpose of executing such scheme and artifice and attempting so to do, the defendants transmitted and caused to be transmitted by means of wire communication in interstate commerce writings, signs, signals, pictures, and sounds, all in violation of 18 U.S.C. §§ 1343 and 1342.

COUNT I
VIOLATION OF THE RACKETEER INFLUENCED AND CORRUPT ORGANIZATIONS ACT OF 1970 (RICO)

54.   Plaintiffs repeat and reallege as though fully set forth herein the allegations contained in paragraphs 1 through 53 above.

55.   The defendants, who at all material times were employed by and associated with the Corporation, did conduct and participate, directly

and indirectly, in the conduct of affairs of the Corporation, hereinafter the "enterprise," through a pattern of racketeering activity by engaging in acts indictable under 18 U.S.C. §§ 1341 (mail fraud), 1343 (wire fraud), and 201 (bribery), as set forth above during the period from at least early 1980 to the present in violation of 18 U.S.C. § 1962(c).

56.   The defendants who were and/or are officers of the Corporation or XYZ, during the time that they were officers, were directly or indirectly involved in the wrongful acts described above and permitted such criminal activities to take place.

57.   The director defendants, during the time that they were directors of the Corporation, were directly or indirectly involved in the wrongful acts described above and permitted such criminal activities to take place despite an affirmative duty to safeguard the corporation's assets and ensure that the corporation's business was carried on in a lawful manner. All of the director defendants, and in particular those director defendants who were members of the audit and finance committees of the Board of Directors, were directly or indirectly involved in the wrongful acts described above and caused or permitted such criminal activities to take place by allowing the Corporation to maintain books and records that were not in accordance with government rules and regulations and by maintaining an inadequate system of internal controls such that the Corporation's assets could be misused and its affairs could be conducted through a pattern of racketeering activity.

58.   As a direct and proximate result of defendants' conduct of the affairs of the enterprise through a pattern of racketeering activity, the Corporation has been injured in its business and property by reason of said violation of § 1962(c) and, thus, is entitled to recover threefold the damages it has sustained, together with the cost of the suit, including reasonable attorneys' fees.

COUNT II
RICO CONSPIRACY

59.   Plaintiffs repeat and reallege as though fully set forth herein, the allegations contained in paragraphs 1 to 58.

60.   During the period from at least early 1980 to the present, the defendants have conspired to conduct the affairs of the enterprise, the Corporation, through a pattern of racketeering activity in violation of 18 U.S.C. § 1962(d).

61.   In furtherance of the conspiracy, the defendants (in addition to the overt acts previously set forth herein) caused or permitted the following overt acts to be committed:

(a) on or about April 2, 1984, the defendants submitted and caused to be submitted to the Defense Department's Defense Contract Administration Service Plant Representative Office (DCASPRO) and the Defense Department's Defense Contract Audit Agency (DCAA) its 1983 FORS which included overhead billing rates containing cost overruns on design and development contracts, as well as other mischarged development costs, concealed therein;

(b) on or about April 24, 1984, in connection with DCAA's audit of the Corporation's APC charging practices, defendants submitted and caused to be submitted to DCAA and DCASPRO a letter which falsely represented the enclosed "Cost Categorization of Engineering Related Project Costs" as being the Corporation's APC charging policy for the last 25 years;

(c) in or about April 1984, the defendants ordered or permitted and caused to be ordered or permitted the Corporation employees to destroy an internal report and workpapers that suggested that the Corporation's practice of concealing cost overruns on design and development contracts, as well as other mischarged development costs, in APC was not in compliance with certain government regulations;

(d) on or about October 8, 1984, defendants submitted and caused to be submitted to DCASPRO and DCAA its revised 1983 FORS, which included overhead billing rates containing cost overruns on design and development contracts, as well as mischarged development costs, concealed therein;

(e) on or about December 18, 1984, the defendants ordered or permitted and caused to be ordered or permitted a Corporation employee to falsify a report to be given to the DCAA to conceal the fact that a Corporation adjustment to APC charges was being made because the charges resulted from cost overruns on a design and development contract;

(f) on or about June 3, 1985, the defendants submitted and caused to be submitted to DCAA and DCASPRO summary data regarding the Corporation's adjustments to APC charges and the reasons for each adjustment, which summary data falsely represented the reasons for which certain adjustments had been made and omitted the fact that certain adjustments were made because the charges resulted from cost overruns on design and development contracts;

(g) on or about January 30, 1984, the defendants issued or permitted and caused to be issued or permitted a memo to certain Corporation field supervisors advising them of the Corporation's approval of the continued use by field employees in its Washington, D.C. and Dayton, Ohio offices of the term "government employee" in lieu of the individual's name and organization on expense reports when it was considered inappropriate or sensitive to enter the government employee's name, provided the Corporation employee advised his supervisor of the government employee's name, position, and organization by other means prior to the approval of the expense report;

(h) on or about February 20, 1986, the defendants caused or permitted verbal instructions to be given to 20 Corporation field marketing employees throughout the United States that they were authorized to immediately begin using the term "customer" in lieu of a government employee's name on expense reports;

(i) on or about March 6, 1986, the defendants caused or permitted to be added four additional Corporation field marketing employees to those authorized to use the term "customer" in lieu of a government employee's name on expense reports;

(j) on or about March 19, 1986, the defendants instructed and caused to be instructed certain Corporation field service employees to immediately stop using the names of U.S. military personnel, including civilian personnel employed by the military, on expense reports and begin using the term "customer" followed by only a general reason for the expense such as "business discussion";

(k) on or about September 15, 1986, the defendants caused or permitted certain Corporation field supervisors to be advised that despite a recent Corporation directive that additional details be included on expense reports because of new regulations promulgated by Congress and/or the Defense Department, those authorized to use the term "customer" in lieu of a government employee's name on expense reports could continue to do so until further notice;

(l) on or about September 29, 1986, the defendants caused or permitted to be added six additional Corporation field marketing employees to those authorized to use the term "customer" in lieu of a government employee's name on expense reports;

(m) on or about September 29, 1986, the defendants caused or permitted certain Corporation field supervisors to be advised that "customer" should only be used when necessary and should be mixed in with other names when names could be used;

(n) on or about February 24, 1984, the defendants caused or permitted to be executed a new Corporation-SJ contract regarding Aviation parts which did not contain the requirement that the Corporation be present at SJ's disposal of Aviation parts, the language "unless sold to the Corporation" in the provision requiring the removal of Corporation identifiers, and any reference to a buy-back formula, while intending that the Corporation control over Aviation parts shipped to SJ would, in fact, continue in full force;

(o) on or about March 21, 1984, the defendants caused or permitted to be executed a written agreement with SJ containing a buy-back formula that determined the price at which the Corporation reacquired Aviation parts from SJ; and

(p) on or about December 4, 1984, the defendants submitted and caused to be submitted to the IRS the Corporation's response to IDR 170, dated December 22, 1983, asking specific questions regarding the Corporation-SJ relationship, in which response the Corporation concealed and caused to be concealed a material fact, in that in response to questions 1 and 2, the Corporation failed to inform the IRS that SJ's contractually required removal of all Corporation identifiers, including parts numbers, from Aviation parts intended for resale to anyone other than the Corporation rendered those parts unusable on aircraft according to Federal Aviation Administration regulations.

62.   The defendants who were and/or are officers of the Corporation or XYZ during the time that they were officers, were directly or indirectly involved in the wrongful acts described above and permitted such criminal activities to take place.

63.   The director defendants, during the time that they were directors of the Corporation, were directly or indirectly involved in the wrongful acts described above and permitted such criminal activities to take place despite an affirmative duty to safeguard the corporation's assets and ensure that the corporation's business was carried on in a lawful manner. All of the director defendants, and in particular those director defendants who were members of the audit and finance committees of the Board of Directors, were directly or indirectly involved in the wrongful acts described above and caused or permitted such criminal activities to take place by allowing the Corporation to maintain books and records that were not in accordance with government rules and regulations and by maintaining an inadequate system of internal controls such that the Corporation's assets could be misused.

64.   As a direct and proximate result of defendants' conspiracy to conduct the affairs of the enterprise through a pattern of racketeering activity, the Corporation has been injured in its business and property by reason of said violation of § 1962(d) and, thus, is entitled to recover threefold the damages it has sustained, together with the cost of the suit, including reasonable attorneys' fees.

§ 6.6   —Remaining Fraud and Derivative Counts

After the RICO claims, Count Three of the *Shields* complaint alleged an implied private right of action for violations of the Foreign Corrupt

Practices Act.[27] These violations were alleged to have occurred because of the defendants' maintenance of inaccurate financial books, statements, and records by Sundstrand.

Count Four was a derivative claim for violations of the proxy solicitation provisions of § 14(a) of the Securities and Exchange Act of 1934.[28] Here, the complaint alleged that the proxy statements distributed to Sundstrand shareholders were misleading for failing to disclose matters relating to the director defendants' alleged violations of law which would subject Sundstrand to massive fines and penalties. The complaint alleged that these proxy violations occurred for all the years that the directors were allegedly in violation of the law. As a consequence, the plaintiffs alleged that the proxy statements submitted to shareholder votes in 1983 through 1988 were misleading. There were no damages sought in this claim for relief; instead, the plaintiffs alleged that the directors of Sundstrand should be removed and replaced and a new election held.

Count Five was a class claim also for violations of the proxy solicitation provisions of § 14(a) of the Securities and Exchange Act of 1934. Similar in concept to the Fourth Count, this count was brought on behalf of Sundstrand's shareholders of record as of 1988. The Fifth Count sought invalidation of a so-called raincoat provision in the Sundstrand articles of incorporation, an amendment purporting to limit the liability of officers and directors for negligent breaches of their fiduciary duties, adopted that year (during the period of wrongdoing) by Sundstrand's Board of Directors.

Counts Six and Seven of the complaint were common law counts for alleged breaches by the officer and director defendants of fiduciary duties owed to Sundstrand and its shareholders. In these counts, the plaintiffs incorporated the prior allegations of wrongdoing and alleged that the same conduct constituted a breach of such common law duties owed to Sundstrand and shareholders.

The final section of the complaint was the prayer for relief. In summary, the plaintiffs requested a declaration that the director and officer defendants of Sundstrand had committed breaches of trust and breaches of their fiduciary duties owed to both Sundstrand and its shareholders; requested compensatory damages for Sundstrand, such damages to be trebled under

---

[27] 15 U.S.C. §§ 78m, 13(b)(2), and Rules 13b2-1 and 13b2-2 promulgated thereunder. The purpose of § 13(b)(2), when enacted as part of the Foreign Corrupt Practices Act, was to deter bribery of foreign officials by American corporations by requiring proper accounting methods and internal accounting controls. Lewis v. Sporck, 612 F. Supp. 1316, 1332–3 (C.D. Cal. 1983).

[28] 15 U.S.C. § 78n(a) and Rule 14a-9 promulgated thereunder.

RICO; requested restitution to Sundstrand of remuneration and bonuses received by the officer and director defendants during the period of alleged wrongdoing; requested removal of the present directors and requiring a new election of directors; requested a declaration that annulled the raincoat provision added as an amendment to Sundstrand's certificate of incorporation; and requested an award of costs, expenses, and attorneys' fees.[29]

Attached to the *Shields* complaint were five exhibits which provided greater specificity for the allegations of fraud so as to comport with the particularity requirement of Rule 9(b) of the Federal Rules of Civil Procedure. These exhibits were comprised of the plea agreement between Sundstrand and the government, the criminal information brought against Sundstrand based on the fraudulent schemes, the government's offer of a factual basis for Sundstrand's guilty plea, the Board resolution authorizing Sundstrand's guilty plea and payment of $127 million, and a transcript of proceedings relating to the guilty plea.

§ 6.7 Defendants' Motions to Dismiss

Expectedly, the defendants moved to dismiss the *Shields* complaint, including the plaintiffs' civil RICO claims. The defendants' pleading challenge was based on a number of grounds that the practitioner can expect to face after filing a civil RICO complaint.[30]

The defendants' first challenge was the *Shields* complaint's particularity as to the timeframe in which the alleged frauds occurred. The defendants then challenged the complaint's specificity under Rule 9(b) as to the allegations of the defendants' use of wire communications and mails for the predicate acts of wire and mail fraud. The defendants lastly claimed that plaintiffs' civil RICO claims were deficient because there were no specific allegations of wrongdoing by each and every one of the particular defendants.

---

[29] RICO, of course, expressly provides a prevailing plaintiff an award of the cost of the suit, including a reasonable attorneys' fee. 18 U.S.C. § 1964(c).

[30] As with any case, the burden on the private practitioner is to plead and prove the elemental requirements of civil RICO. As a consequence, and especially in a large corporate fraud case, the complaint's allegations must be carefully drafted so as to withstand the substantial pleading and evidentiary challenges which will come from America's largest and most experienced law firms which are happily bankrolled by the management of these corporations.

§ 6.8   —Memorandum Supporting
Motion to Dismiss

Following is a sample memorandum supporting a defendant's motion to dismiss in circumstances like those of the *Shields* case.

IN THE UNITED STATES DISTRICT COURT FOR
THE NORTHERN DISTRICT OF STATE

SHAREHOLDER,
  Derivatively On Behalf Of
THE CORPORATION,
    Plaintiff,
 	
    v.
 	
Defendant A, *et al.*,
    Defendants.
	Civil Action
	No. 88 C 0001
	and related cases
	
	Judge _____

MEMORANDUM IN SUPPORT OF THE
CORPORATION'S MOTION TO DISMISS THE
CONSOLIDATED AMENDED COMPLAINT

Introduction

Between September 23 and November 1, 1990, individual shareholders of THE CORPORATION (the Corporation), without making any prior demand on the Corporation, initiated five separate shareholder derivative actions in this Court.[31] Each action purported to seek, in the Corporation's name, more than $100 million in damages from the Corporation's directors and principal officers, based on alleged violations of various federal statutes (including the Racketeer Influenced and Corrupt Organizations (RICO) Act) and breaches of common law fiduciary duties. All of the actions were inspired by publicity in the national news media concerning the Corporation's agreement to plead guilty to criminal charges, even though those charges did not involve RICO or any RICO predicate act and did not include any allegations of wrongdoing by any of the Corporation's officers and directors.

On November 21, 1990, the Corporation moved to dismiss the first-filed of these actions on the grounds, *inter alia*, (i) that the complaint

---

[31] A sixth derivative action was filed in Delaware Chancery Court on Oct. 19, 1988.

failed to allege with particularity adequate grounds to excuse pre-suit demand on the Corporation, and (ii) that the complaint, which did not contain a single allegation that any individual defendant committed any specific wrongful act, did not allege fraud with the "particularity" required by Federal Rule of Civil Procedure 9(b). Thereafter, the court, with the agreement of all parties, ordered the five cases consolidated and allowed the plaintiffs 14 days in which to file a consolidated amended complaint. The amended complaint was filed on December 16, 1990.

Plaintiffs, therefore, have had ample time to reconsider and to attempt to cure the defects in the initial complaints highlighted by the Corporation's first motion to dismiss. The consolidated amended complaint, however, does not cure these deficiencies in any way. The amended complaint adds no more than a thin veneer to the old allegations, attempting to bolster general references to the criminal proceedings against the Corporation with scattered quotations and massive exhibits. Despite its new veneer, the amended complaint still does not particularize any wrongful act by any individual defendant or state any new or remotely sufficient grounds for excusing demand upon the Corporation. Even with the ample opportunity and time already permitted to amend, plaintiffs' complaint remains fatally defective.

This memorandum will demonstrate that the consolidated amended complaint must be dismissed because it (i) fails to allege adequate reasons for plaintiffs' admitted failure to make pre-suit demand on the Corporation and (ii) fails to allege any specific wrongdoing by any particular defendant, lumping all defendants together in virtually every allegation, and fails to allege the time, place, or circumstances of the purported predicate acts under RICO.

In addition, Counts III, IV and V of the consolidated amended complaint each fail to state a claim upon which relief can be granted under either the Foreign Corrupt Practices Act or the Securities Exchange Act of 1934. These federal securities law claims have been thoroughly briefed in memoranda filed by the individual defendants in support of their respective motions to dismiss. To avoid repetition, the Corporation joins in and adopts the arguments in support of dismissal of the federal securities laws claims set forth in the briefs submitted by the individual defendants. Inasmuch as the federal statutory claims provide the only basis for this court's jurisdiction, the remaining common law claims for breaches of fiduciary duties should also be dismissed for lack of subject matter jurisdiction. Moreover, because the insufficiency of the demand futility allegations is a matter of substantive law, and because plaintiffs already have had an opportunity to cure the fatal defects in their original complaints, the dismissal must be with prejudice.

§ 6.9 —Particularity of Allegations Against Individual Defendants

ARGUMENT

I. The Complaint Fails to Particularize Any Wrongdoing by Any Individual Defendant

Where allegations of a fraudulent scheme involve multiple defendants, Rule 9(b) requires that "the complaint must inform each defendant of the specific fraudulent acts which constitute the basis of the action against that particular defendant." *Rice v. Windsor Industries, Inc.*, No. 85 C 4196, mem. op. at 3 (N.D. Ill. Feb. 26, 1986); *see Adair v. Hunt International Resources Corp.*, 526 F. Supp. 736, 744–46 (N.D. Ill. 1981); *Lincoln National Bank v. Lampe*, 414 F. Supp. 1270, 1278 (N.D. Ill. 1976). A complaint purporting to state fraud claims but "replete with paragraphs beginning with 'The defendants' or 'All defendants'" does not satisfy the Rule 9(b) standard. *Nelson v. National Republic Bank of Chicago*, [1984 Transfer Binder] Fed. Sec. L. Rep. (CCH) ¶ 91,481, at 98,393 (N.D. Ill. 1984). "Plaintiffs may not 'lump' defendants together in general allegations of fraudulent activity, implying that each defendant is responsible for the statements and actions of others." *Coronet Insurance Co. v. Seyfarth*, 665 F. Supp. 661, 666 (N.D. Ill. 1987); *see Lewis v. Sporck*, 612 F. Supp. 1316, 1325 (N.D. Cal. 1985) ("[B]are allegations that each of the defendants 'caused' or 'permitted' certain events to occur are insufficient for Rule 9(b) purposes under any of the RICO provisions.").

These Rule 9(b) standards are applicable to the various alleged frauds asserted as predicate acts for violation of the RICO statute. *Haroco v. American National Bank & Trust*, 747 F.2d 384, 405 (7th Cir. 1984), *aff'd*, 473 U.S. 606 (1985). A RICO complaint "which merely implies, with the conclusory allegation of conspiracy, that a defendant is responsible for someone else's fraudulent acts is insufficient." *Frymire v. Peat, Marwick, Mitchell & Co.*, 657 F. Supp. 889, 895–96 (N.D. Ill. 1987). A civil RICO conspiracy must be pleaded "'with enough specificity to inform multiple defendants of the facts forming the basis of the conspiracy charge. Such allegations must delineate among the defendants as to their participation or responsibilities in making the statements that are the subject of the suit.'" *United States v. Boffa*, 688 F.2d 919, 937 (3d Cir. 1982) (quoting *Van Schaick v. Church of Scientology, Inc.*, 535 F. Supp. 1125, 1141 (D. Mass. 1982)), *cert. denied*, 460 U.S. 1022 (1983).

Rule 9(b) also requires the plaintiff to describe "the time, place, particular contents of the false representations, the identity of the party making the misrepresentation, and the consequences of the misrepresentation." *H.G. Gallimore, Inc. v. Abdula,* 652 F. Supp. 437, 441 (N.D. Ill. 1987); *Tannebaum v. Clark,* No. 88 C 7312, mem. op. at 2 (N.D. Ill. Nov. 29, 1988) (1988 U.S. Dist. LEXIS 13406). A RICO claim asserting mail and wire fraud as predicate acts must "allege how each specific act of mail or wire fraud actually furthered the fraudulent scheme . . . [and] 'must sketch out *who* (i.e., which defendants) caused what to be mailed [or used the telephone] *when,* and *how* the mailing [or phone call] furthered the fraudulent scheme.'" *Landon v. GTE Communications Services Inc.,* No. 88 C 0932, mem. op. at 8 (N.D. Ill. Sept. 28, 1988) (quoting *Balabanos v. North American Investment Group, Ltd.,* 684 F. Supp. 503, 506 (N.D. Ill. 1988)).

The consolidated amended complaint fails to comply with any aspect of these Rule 9(b) requirements. In the 53 paragraphs that purport to allege a "pattern of racketeering activity" (¶¶ 30 through 82), there is not one instance in which the alleged activities of one defendant are distinguished from those of any other defendant. Virtually every paragraph refers to the plural "defendants" or to "the defendants individually and collectively." Moreover, the allegations concerning the use of mail and wire communications (*see* ¶¶ 45, 47, 52, 54, 68, 70, 80 and 82) are cast in the most sweeping terms imaginable; not one communication is identified as to time, place, person, content, or consequences.

Plaintiffs make a feeble attempt in one or two paragraphs of the amended complaint to divide "all defendants" into arbitrarily established groups. Thus, in paragraph 85, plaintiffs allege that the 10 defendants "who were and/or are officers of the Corporation or XYZ . . . were directly or indirectly involved in the wrongful acts." In the next paragraph, the "Director Defendants" (previously identified as a group of 12 defendants) also allegedly "were directly or indirectly involved in the wrongful acts." Amended Complaint ¶ 86. In that same paragraph, plaintiffs further subdivide the "Director Defendants" into a group of six defendants who served on the audit and finance committees, then allege that those six "were directly or indirectly involved in the wrongful acts." Merely typing out the names of various groups of defendants, then alleging that each was involved in the same vague, "direct or indirect" way in the alleged wrongdoing has lengthened the complaint to 65 pages without succeeding in informing any defendant of the charges against him.

The plaintiffs also make a vain attempt to paper over the woeful lack of particulars in the amended complaint by repeatedly referring to, quoting from, and even attaching documents relating to the criminal proceedings concerning the Corporation. Such "catchall general references" to charges in indictments cannot cure a civil RICO claim that is otherwise insufficient, *H.G. Gallimore, Inc. v. Abdula,* 652 F. Supp. at 451, and plagiarizing dates and quotations from the criminal informations adds no more than a veneer of specificity. Plaintiffs still fail to specify which, if any, of the defendants committed any specific act, relying as always on the collective "defendants." Moreover, the informations did not even charge the Corporation with mail fraud, wire fraud, bribery, securities fraud, or any other RICO predicate act. Indeed, because the informations named only the Corporation as a defendant and did not name any of the individual defendants in this action, they cannot properly be considered for purposes of assessing compliance with Rule 9(b). *Lewis v. Sporck,* 612 F. Supp. at 1325.

In short, the consolidated amended complaint, for all its prolixity, does no more than assert that, because the Corporation pled guilty to certain crimes, all directors and officers who were in positions of authority during some or all of the relevant period should be held personally liable in a derivative lawsuit for racketeering activity. These undifferentiated allegations against all possible defendants strongly suggest that plaintiffs' rush to the courthouse is not prompted solely by a sincere effort to vindicate the Corporation's interests. Such hasty and unfounded litigation has been strongly criticized by this court:

> "If plaintiff does not presently possess the relevant indispensable facts to state a fraud claim with particularity, the precepts upon which Rules 9(b) and 11 are founded mandate that he has no business charging a party with fraud on the slim hope that he may use the various and expensive tools of discovery available under the Federal Rules to put meat on the bare bones of his fraud claims. Fraud is too serious a charge, and litigation is too expensive, to allow such tactics; *RICO, even more so.*"
> *Beck v. Cantor, Fitzgerald & Co.,* 621 F. Supp. 1547, 1553 (N.D. Ill. 1985) (emphasis added).[32]

*   *   *

---

[32] Counts I and II of the consolidated amended complaint are also fatally deficient on several grounds in addition to their failure to plead RICO claims with sufficient particularity. Neither Count sufficiently alleges a "pattern" of racketeering activity in that both Counts allege, at most, multiple wrongful acts in furtherance of a single scheme. In the Seventh Circuit, such allegations are insufficient to make out a "pattern" under RICO. *E.g.,* Brandt v. Schal Assocs., Nos. 87-2691, 88-1061, slip op. at 7–11 (7th Cir. Aug. 5, 1988); SK Hand Tool Corp. v. Dresser Indus., Inc., Nos. 87-2294, 87-3067, slip op. at 5–13 (7th Cir. July 18, 1988). Moreover, plaintiffs do not allege any injury that they incurred "by reason of" a RICO violation. *See, e.g.,* Sperber v. Boesky, 849 F.2d 60, 63–66 (2d Cir. 1988) (holding that a plaintiff, who was not the direct target of defendant's alleged racketeering activity and who was injured only by public disclosure of defendant's guilty plea, was not injured "by reason of" racketeering activity); Waste Recovery Corp. v. Mahler, 566 F. Supp. 1466, 1468–69 (S.D.N.Y. 1983) (holding that a plaintiff lacks standing under RICO to sue a defendant whose racketeering activity was not directed toward the plaintiff and which injured the plaintiff only indirectly).

Plaintiffs' failure adequately to specify the alleged RICO violations also makes it impossible to determine which, if any, of plaintiffs' claims are time-barred. The issue

CONCLUSION

The foregoing analysis demonstrates that all derivative claims in the consolidated amended complaint should be dismissed for failure to comply with Rule 23.1 and that plaintiffs' RICO claims (Counts I and II) should be dismissed for failure to comply with Rule 9(b). In addition, briefs submitted by the individual officers and directors in support of their respective motions to dismiss have demonstrated that plaintiffs have failed to state a claim under either the Foreign Corrupt Practices Act or the Securities Exchange Act of 1934. Because plaintiffs' federal statutory claims must be dismissed, their common-law claims for breaches of fiduciary duties (Count VI and "Count IV" [sic]), purportedly pendent to their federal claims, must also be dismissed for lack of subject matter jurisdiction. *United Mine Workers v. Gibbs*, 383 U.S. 715 (1966).

For all of the foregoing reasons, plaintiffs' consolidated amended complaint should be dismissed in its entirety, with prejudice and without leave to amend.

§ 6.10   Plaintiffs' Memorandum Opposing Motion to Dismiss

The following sections contain a sample plaintiffs' memorandum in opposition to the defendants' motion to dismiss found in §§ **6.8** through **6.10**.

IN THE UNITED STATES DISTRICT COURT FOR THE NORTHERN DISTRICT OF STATE

SHAREHOLDER, derivatively on behalf of THE CORPORATION, Plaintiff,	CIVIL ACTION No. 88 C
v.	Judge
Defendant A, *et al.*, Defendants.	

---

of when a civil RICO claim accrues is now pending before this court. *See* Walker v. Aetna Life Ins. Co., No. 87 C 868, mem. op. at 13–14 (N.D. Ill. May 3, 1988) (1988 U.S. Dist. LEXIS 4017).

PLAINTIFFS' MEMORANDUM OF LAW IN OPPOSITION TO DEFENDANTS' MOTIONS TO DISMISS

Plaintiffs submit this memorandum in opposition to defendants' motions to dismiss the Consolidated Amended Complaint (the "Complaint").[33] Defendants' motions are primarily based on the proposition that the Complaint does not plead fraud with sufficient particularity and does not set forth sufficient reasons why demand is excused. That position is totally without merit. The Complaint contains detailed and specific allegations as to fraud and demand and passes muster under the most stringent pleading standards.

Preliminary Statement

This action brings to the forefront the largest and most egregious episode in the burgeoning nationwide defense contractor scandal to date. This action is brought by shareholders of the Corporation on behalf of the Corporation against certain of its present and former officers and/or directors. Plaintiffs allege that the individual defendants caused or permitted the Corporation to fraudulently and criminally overcharge the United States government more than $100 million in connection with certain Defense Department contracts. Those fraudulent and criminal activities have been exposed. The Corporation has pled guilty to five felony counts and agreed to pay almost $200 million to the United States in fines, penalties, and settlement. The individuals who directed and participated in that criminal activity should be held accountable and responsible for the damages incurred by the Corporation.

* * *

As a result of extensive federal law enforcement investigations, two separate grand jury investigations in different parts of the country, and a Defense Department investigation, the criminal conspiracies at the Corporation were uncovered. The individual defendants have caused the Corporation to be damaged in the following ways:

1.   On October 21, 1990, pursuant to a unanimous resolution of the Board of Directors, the Corporation pled guilty to four felony charges in the United States District Court for the Northern District of State (88

---

[33] There are three separate motions to dismiss by: (i) the Sundstrand Corporation; (ii) the individual defendants who were officers (and in some cases also directors) (the Officer Defendants); and (iii) the individual defendants who were directors of the Corporation but were not primarily employed by the Corporation (the Outside Director Defendants). This memorandum will respond to each of the arguments made in the three motions other than the personal jurisdiction arguments. Adjudication of the personal jurisdiction motion has been stayed pending resolution of these motions.

Cr. 0001). As part of the plea agreement, the Corporation paid a criminal fine of $115 million to the United States government—the largest such criminal fine ever imposed on a defense contractor. Complaint ¶ 5.

2. On October 19, 1990, XYZ, a subsidiary of the Corporation, pled guilty to a felony charge in the United States District Court for the Western District of State. As part of that plea agreement, XYZ paid a total of $12,320,000 to the United States. Complaint ¶ 7.

3. The Corporation was suspended and debarred from receiving new government contracts. Complaint ¶ 9.

4. The United States State Department suspended the Corporation's export licenses. Complaint ¶ 9.

5. On or about January 25, 1991, the Corporation settled administrative claims made by the Defense Department by agreeing to pay $71.3 million to the Defense Department and to make substantial and material changes in its accounting systems.

The same individuals who created "a mindset" at the Corporation that it was "all right to cheat and lie and steal" from the government and the same individuals who caused the Corporation to plead guilty to five felony counts and pay almost $200 million to the government, now argue that the Complaint—which tracks and incorporates the relevant criminal informations and plea agreements—is not sufficiently specific to pass muster under Rule 9(b). That position simply strains credulity. It is inconceivable that the individual defendants could on the one hand have sufficient information to justify causing the Corporation to plead guilty to five felonies and pay $200 million and on the other hand claim that they do not have enough information to respond to this Corporation.

Defendants' arguments about demand are similarly misplaced. The Complaint clearly and specifically alleges a continuous course of criminal conduct spanning eight years which directly involved or implicated the entire Board of Directors. Reading the Complaint most favorably to plaintiffs, as required, there is an overwhelming basis for concluding that a majority of the board is not disinterested and that the challenged conduct was not the product of a valid exercise of business judgment. Obviously, the criminal activities alleged here cannot be justified under the business judgment rule. Thus, even under the most stringent standards, demand is excused.[34]

---

[34] Defendants' motions to dismiss plaintiffs' claims under §§ 13(b)(2) and 14(a) of the 1934 Act are without merit. As shown herein there is an implied right of action under § 13(b)(2) on behalf of the Corporation. Viable claims are alleged under § 14(a).

The Complaint and Background Facts

The Complaint and its exhibits provide extensive detail and specificity concerning the different fraudulent schemes engaged in by defendants to cheat and steal from the United States. The relevant facts about the schemes and the individuals who perpetrated them are discussed below.

The Corporation is a leading producer of equipment for the United States Department of Defense. Complaint ¶ 18. The Corporation is based in State and its common stock is listed and traded on the New York Stock Exchange. In 1990 approximately 5,500 shareholders of record owned the Corporation's common stock. Complaint ¶ 18(c). The Corporation is named as a nominal defendant and this action is brought on its behalf.

There are 18 individual defendants named in this action. Complaint ¶ 19. They can be divided into three groups: those defendants who were both officers and directors of the Corporation; those defendants who were directors but not officers of the Corporation; and those defendants who were officers but not directors of the Corporation (or its subsidiaries).

The Complaint sets forth the dates each defendant held positions as an officer or director of the Corporation (Complaint ¶ 19) and alleges that, as executive or operating officers and/or directors of the Corporation, they had positions of authority that allowed them to control the conduct of the Corporation's business. Complaint ¶ 21. They had the power and influence to cause and permit the Corporation to engage in the illegal practices complained of. Complaint ¶¶ 21 and 24. Each defendant, by virtue of his position as an officer and/or director, owed a duty to the Corporation to ensure that its business was being carried on lawfully. Complaint ¶ 22. Each defendant was a direct participant, a coconspirator, or an aider and abettor in the frauds charged in the Complaint, to the extent they took place during his tenure in office. Complaint ¶¶ 25, 85, 86, 91, 92.

Many of the defendants who were officers of the Corporation had direct responsibility over areas where the various frauds were perpetrated. For example, defendant Officer One was the Comptroller of the Corporation and in charge of its books and records. Defendant Officer Two was Group Vice-President for the subsidiary group, from which many of the phony bills were generated. Defendant Officer Three was Vice-President of Finance with direct supervisory responsibility over the Corporation's financial activities. These people as well as the top executive officers (and directors) cannot profess ignorance of the charges alleged in this Complaint.

Those directors who were not primarily employed by the Corporation were also directly involved in the various fraudulent schemes by reason of their membership on the Audit and Finance Committees of the Board of Directors. The members of the audit committee were charged with maintaining the efficacy of the Corporation's internal auditing function and assuring that the books and records were maintained in accordance with all applicable government rules and regulations. Complaint ¶ 20(b). Together with the finance committee, the audit committee had the duty and responsibility to ascertain and assure that the Corporation's financial statements were prepared in accordance with generally accepted accounting principles (GAAP) and that the Corporation's internal accounting and financial controls were adequate and proper. Complaint ¶ 20.

As alleged in the Complaint, the criminal schemes and conspiracies at issue occurred in part because the financial and accounting systems at the Corporation were in shambles. Complaint ¶¶ 3, 10. Internal controls were virtually nonexistent. Costs unrelated to Defense Department contracts were systematically billed to the government. Cost overruns were illegally charged to the government. Executive perks and bribes to government officials were hidden in the books and paid for by the government. An environment existed at the Corporation wherein phony invoices, false bills, and fraudulent claims were submitted, corporate records were falsified, false certificates of compliance were filed, documents were destroyed, and false financial statements were issued. Complaint ¶¶ 3, 10.

The members of the finance and audit committees during the relevant period permitted these schemes and frauds to continue by allowing the Corporation to maintain a grossly inadequate system of internal controls, and thus are liable as direct participants in the wrongdoing. Complaint ¶¶ 86, 92. Moreover, these same defendants knowingly, culpably, recklessly, or in a grossly negligent manner breached their fiduciary duties to the Corporation by failing to establish internal controls sufficient to ensure that the Corporation's business was carried on in a lawful manner and that the reputation and the financial assets of the Corporation were preserved. Complaint ¶ 22.

The Pattern of Racketeering Activity

The Complaint sets forth in detail at least five separate schemes defendants engaged in to defraud the United States and the Defense Department. The Complaint chronicles and details each scheme and the pattern of racketeering activity. Complaint ¶¶ 30–82. Further support and illumination is supplied by exhibits to the Complaint.[35] Because the

---

[35] The exhibits are comprised of (a) the plea agreement between the Corporation and the government, (b) the criminal information brought by the government against the Corporation based on the fraudulent schemes, (c) the government's offer of a factual basis for the Corporation's guilty plea, (d) the Board resolution authorizing the Corporation's plea of guilty and the payment of $127 million in criminal fines, and (e) a

Complaint alleges that defendants were involved in the fraudulent schemes, the exhibits provide even more detailed notice of the charges against them.

The five different schemes to defraud are summarized as follows:

1.   Billing Cost Overruns

The Complaint describes a scheme whereby the individual defendants caused the Corporation to improperly and illegally bill cost overruns on design and development contracts to the Defense Department. Complaint ¶¶ 30–47. Most of the Corporation's design and development contracts were firm, fixed price contracts. Complaint ¶ 31. Under the terms of those contracts, the Corporation was entitled to be reimbursed for certain overhead expenses. Government regulations specifically prohibited including any cost overruns in overhead billing rates. Complaint ¶ 32.

Defendants caused the Corporation to submit low-ball bids to the Defense Department on design and development contracts to assure that the Corporation would obtain the contracts and retain the design rights to the hardware developed pursuant to those contracts. Complaint ¶ 36. In making such low-ball bids, defendants knew that the contract could not be completed at the estimated cost and that there would be cost overruns. Defendants developed an elaborate plan to pass the cost overruns on to the government as overhead. Generally, cost overruns were concealed in the Corporation's overhead billing rates. Complaint ¶¶ 39–40.

At the hearing in which the Corporation's guilty plea was accepted, it was admitted in open court:

> that those participating in this conspiracy took numerous actions to further its objective, including the Corporation's submission to the Defense Department of fraudulent overhead billing rates containing the overruns, and of false statements denying the overruns were included in these rates. As a result of the conspiracy, the Corporation obtained millions of dollars in Defense Department payments to which it was not entitled. Complaint, Exhibit E, p. 21.

2.   Billing Personal Expenses and Misallocating Costs

Defendants also devised a scheme to cause the Corporation to include millions of dollars in personal expenses in its general and administrative overhead billing rate that ultimately was billed to and paid for by

---

transcript of proceedings relating to the Corporation's guilty plea. These exhibits contain even more detailed information about the schemes to defraud, including the dates during which the schemes took place, the dates of some specific activities involved in the schemes, and exhibits reflecting mailings and communications relating to the schemes.

the Defense Department. Complaint ¶¶ 48–54. The personal expenses included, among other things, charges for liquor, gifts, travel by executive spouses, country club memberships, jewelry, and a myriad of other personal costs. Complaint ¶ 50. At the hearing on the guilty plea, it was admitted that "the unallowable general and administrative costs contained in the fraudulent progress payments billing included charges for personal items for employees." Complaint, Exhibit E, p. 47.

3.   Phony Tax Write-Offs

Defendants also caused the Corporation to engage in a scheme to defraud the United States and the IRS by taking millions of dollars in improper tax write-offs. Complaint ¶¶ 55–70. In this regard a series of sham "sales" transactions was set up between the Corporation and SJ Company. (SJ). The Corporation purportedly lost money on the "sales" and took tax write-offs on the "losses." In fact, no bona fide sales took place. Later, the Corporation took steps to conceal the truth from the IRS by making false statements to the IRS about the "sales" and by rewriting the contract with SJ to conceal material facts from the IRS. Complaint ¶ 64.

4.   Bribery of Government Officials

Defendants caused the Corporation to bribe public officials of the Defense Department and other persons, including spouses of public officials, for the purpose of influencing such persons to favor the Corporation. Complaint ¶¶ 71–72. Compounding the crime, defendants also caused the Corporation to hide such bribes on the Corporation's books by recording them as normal business transactions and even billing them to the government as part of the Corporation's overhead.

5.   False Claims by ABC

Defendants caused ABC, a wholly owned subsidiary of the Corporation, to file false, fictitious, and fraudulent claims under a rate agreement with the Department of Defense that wrongfully and illegally included unallowable costs such as patent litigation costs. Complaint ¶¶ 73–82.

The Claims for Relief

Based on the foregoing, plaintiffs assert seven claims for relief against the defendants, alleging violations of RICO, the Securities and Exchange Act of 1934 and state law.

Count I of the Complaint (Complaint ¶¶ 83–87) alleges that the defendants violated RICO in that they directly or indirectly conducted the affairs of the Corporation through a pattern of racketeering activity. Among other things, defendants caused or permitted such criminal and racketeering activities to take place by allowing the Corporation to maintain books and records that were not in accordance with government rules and regulations and by maintaining an inadequate system of internal controls such that the Corporation's assets could be misused and its affairs could be conducted through a pattern of racketeering.

Count II of the Complaint (¶¶ 88–93) alleges that defendants conspired to conduct the affairs of the Corporation through a pattern of racketeering activity in violation of the RICO conspiracy provisions of § 1962(d). The Complaint specifically sets forth 16 overt acts (in addition to the overt acts described above and otherwise set forth in the Complaint) which defendants caused or permitted the Corporation to commit pursuant to the RICO conspiracy. Complaint ¶ 90(a)–(p).

The Complaint also alleges several violations of the Securities and Exchange Act of 1934. Count III (¶¶ 94–99) alleges that the defendants violated § 13(b)(2) of the Act by failing to provide the Corporation with adequate internal financial and accounting controls. Count IV of the Complaint alleges violations of § 14 of the 1934 Act (¶¶ 100–105), on the grounds that various proxy statements issued by the Corporation were materially false and misleading in that they failed to disclose the illegal conduct described above and therefore defendants were improperly re-elected to the Board, and a liability limiting amendment to the Corporation's Certificate of Incorporation was improperly adopted. A class claim for the same violations of § 14 of the Exchange Act is alleged in Count V of the Complaint (Complaint ¶¶ 106–111).

Lastly, the Complaint asserts two claims under state law for intentional breach of fiduciary duties (¶¶ 112–116) and negligent breach of fiduciary duties (¶¶ 117–119).

§ 6.11 —RICO Claims Adequately Stated

ARGUMENT

Point I
Counts I and II State Valid Claims under RICO and the Complaint Fully Complies with Rule 9(b)

Defendants move to dismiss plaintiffs' RICO claims on two grounds. First, they argue that the Complaint does not set forth all of the elements of RICO. Second, they argue that the Complaint is not sufficiently specific under Rule 9(b). Both arguments are totally without merit.[36]

---

[36] In determining the sufficiency of the Complaint, the ultimate issue is whether it states a claim taken as a whole and read most favorably to plaintiffs. Conley v. Gibson, 355

A. Plaintiffs Have Properly Alleged RICO Claims

Nominal defendant the Corporation asserts that Counts I and II of the Complaint are deficient because they do not properly allege a "pattern" of racketeering activity and do not properly allege any injury caused "by reason of" a RICO violation. The outside directors make an additional argument that plaintiffs have not properly alleged a RICO conspiracy under § 1962(d). These arguments should be summarily dismissed.

1. The Complaint Properly Alleges a Pattern of Racketeering Activity

Distinct acts of mail fraud or wire fraud committed over a period of several years in furtherance of at least five distinct and separate schemes to defraud constitute a pattern of the racketeering. As the court held in *Morgan v. Bank of Waukegan,* 804 F.2d 970 (7th Cir. 1986):

In order to be sufficiently continuous to constitute a pattern of racketeering activity, the predicate acts must be ongoing over an identified period of time so that they can fairly be viewed as constituting separate transactions, i.e., "transactions 'somewhat separated in time and place.'"

Id. at 975 (citations omitted). The court went on to find that "the mere fact that the predicate acts relate to the same overall scheme or involve the same victim does not mean that the acts automatically fail to satisfy the pattern requirement." *Id.* at 975–76.[37]

There can be no doubt that plaintiffs have adequately pleaded a pattern of racketeering activity. The Complaint details five or more separate and distinct schemes to defraud the government, all of which continued for a number of years and involved repeated acts of mail and wire fraud in furtherance of the schemes. The Complaint, with its allegations of multiple and distinct schemes with many predicate acts,

---

U.S. 41, 45–46 (1957) ("a complaint should not be dismissed for failure to state a claim unless it appears beyond doubt that plaintiff can prove no set of facts in support of his claim which would entitle him to relief."). When more than one inference can be drawn from the allegations of the Complaint, it must be construed favorably to plaintiffs. Scheuer v. Rhodes, 416 U.S. 232, 236 (1974). City of Milwaukee v. Saxbe, 546 F.2d 693, 704 (7th Cir. 1976). Moreover, in determining the sufficiency of the Complaint, all of the exhibits incorporated in and attached to the Complaint must be considered as a part of the Complaint. Fed. R. Civ. P. 10(c).

[37] *See also* Liquid Air Corp. v. Rogers, 834 F.2d 1297 (7th Cir. 1987), *appeal pending,* "repeated infliction of economic injury upon a single victim of a single scheme is sufficient to establish a pattern of racketeering"); Appley v. West, 832 F.2d 1021 (7th Cir. 1987) (two acts of mail fraud which, although part of the same scheme to defraud, were separate in time and caused a separate injury sufficed for a pattern of racketeering); Deppe v. Tripp, Nos. 86-2893, 86-2894, 87-2514, slip op. (7th Cir. Dec. 21, 1988) (LEXIS 17558) (pattern of racketeering activity was proven with a single injury to two victims based on four predicate acts).

alleges a more concrete "pattern" of racketeering than the complaints upheld in *Morgan, Liquid Air, Appley,* and *Deppe.*[38]

2. The Corporation's Damages Were Caused by Defendants' Criminal Actions

The RICO claims are alleged derivatively on behalf of the Corporation and RICO injuries to the Corporation are clear and direct. Defendants' argument that the Corporation has not suffered injuries "by reason of" RICO violations is meritless on its face. Defendants caused the Corporation to plead guilty to five felony counts and pay almost $200 million in fines and settlements. The Corporation was directly injured, suffering substantial financial loss, as a result of the pattern of racketeering activity engaged in by defendants. *See Carter v. Berger,* 777 F.2d 1173 (7th Cir. 1985).[39]

3. The Complaint Adequately Alleges a RICO Conspiracy

The outside directors argue that plaintiffs have not pleaded a conspiracy under RICO because the Complaint does not allege that each defendant agreed to the operation of the conspiracy. That argument has no substance.

The outside directors are liable under § 1962(d) if they "agree[d] to conduct or participate in the affairs of an enterprise through a pattern of racketeering activity. Under this approach it is only necessary that the defendant agree to the commission of the two predicate acts on behalf of the conspiracy." *United States v. Neapolitan,* 791 F.2d 489, 498 (7th Cir.), *cert. denied,* 479 U.S. 940 (1986). A defendant need not agree personally to violate RICO. Rather "an agreement to conduct or participate in the affairs of an enterprise and an agreement to the commission of at least two predicate acts" constitute a conspiracy to violate RICO. *Id.* at 499. In reality, these two agreements "would be encompassed by the same manifestations of the defendant." *Id.*

---

[38] The cases cited by the Corporation are distinguishable on their facts. In each of them, the court found that there was not a pattern of racketeering activity because the predicate acts were in furtherance of a single episode of fraud against a single victim with only one fraudulent purpose. Brandt v. Schal Assoc., 87-2691, 88-1061, slip op. (7th Cir. Aug. 5, 1988); SK Handtool Corp. v. Dresser Indus., Inc., 87-2294, 87-3067, slip op. (7th Cir. July 18, 1988).

[39] Defendants' authorities are easily distinguishable because the harm to the plaintiffs in those cases clearly did not result from the RICO violation. In Sperber v. Boesky, 849 F.2d 60 (2d Cir. 1988), investors tried to bring a RICO claim against Ivan Boesky, with whom they had absolutely no contact or involvement, on the theory that his illegal insider trading affected the markets generally, thereby affecting the value of their investments. In Waste Recovery Corp. v. Mahler, 566 F. Supp. 1466 (S.D.N.Y. 1983), plaintiffs claimed they would not have purchased a "lemon" company had they known that the seller/defendant had run the business fraudulently. However, the seller's fraud had no bearing on plaintiffs' injury.

Plaintiffs have adequately alleged that defendants agreed to participate in a conspiracy to conduct the Corporation's affairs through a pattern of racketeering activity. Complaint ¶ 89. Plaintiffs further allege numerous acts done in furtherance of the conspiracies. Complaint ¶ 90 (a–p). Combined with the rest of the detailed Complaint, which, as argued *infra*, adequately pleads a pattern of racketeering activity and predicate acts, these allegations suffice for a conspiracy charge under § 1962(d). *See Sutliff, Inc. v. Donovan Companies, Inc.*, 727 F.2d 648, 653–54 (7th Cir. 1984) (allegations that defendants conspired to violate § 1962(a–c) "is a good allegation of a violation of § 1962(d)"); *Bachmeier v. Bank of Ravenswood*, 663 F. Supp. 1207 (N.D. Ill. 1987) (review of entire complaint reflected allegations that defendants had agreed to the fraudulent scheme and participated in it).

As in *Carlstead v. Holiday Inns, Inc.*, No. 86 C 1927, slip op. (N.D. Ill., Oct. 9, 1986), the court can infer from defendants' participation in mail and wire fraud the defendants' agreement to do so. Because the Complaint alleges the defendants' role in the scheme, their participation in mail and wire fraud, and their conspiracy to defraud, its allegations clearly suffice to state a claim for a RICO conspiracy. *Cf. Serpe v. Williams*, No. 85 C 5404, slip op. (N.D. Ill. July 3, 1986) (allegations against defendants collectively were sufficient under both § 1962(a) and (d)).

§ 6.12 —Particularity Requirements of Rule 9(b) Met

B. The Complaint Furnishes Defendants with Detailed Notice of the Charges Against Them and Fully Complies with Rule 9(b)

All three of defendants' memoranda attack plaintiffs' Complaint as failing to comply with Rule 9(b), claiming that the Complaint does not allege enough facts to give them notice of the charges. Defendants' analyses are based on a strained and exaggerated interpretation of Rule 9(b), and their claim that they do not have enough information to answer the charges strains credibility. In fact, the Complaint and its exhibits provide extensive detail and specificity concerning five different schemes engaged in by defendants to defraud the government, causing substantial harm to the Corporation. The complaint alleges in detail the guilty pleas that the Corporation entered and the enormous fines to which the Corporation was subjected, with the direction and approval of the defendants.

1. Rule 9(b) Must Be Read in Conjunction with Rule 8 and Requires only Slightly More Particularity than Notice Pleading

Rule 9(b) provides that the circumstances constituting fraud shall be stated "with particularity." The Rule is designed to ensure that a defendant is sufficiently apprised of the allegations to fashion an answer. As the court stated in *Morgan v. Kobrin Securities, Inc.,* 649 F. Supp. 1023, 1029 (N.D. Ill. 1986):

> The common thread running through these cases is that a complaint can withstand a Rule 9(b) motion if it "sufficiently describes the fraudulent acts and provides the individuals with sufficient information to answer the allegations." Thus, . . . Rule 9(b) is nothing more than Rule 8 raised to a slightly higher level of specificity.

The touchstone is sufficient notice to permit a responsive pleading. The Seventh Circuit has made clear that Rule 9(b) is not an exception to federal notice pleading rules, but must be read together with Rule 8, requiring only that plaintiff give notice of the nature of its claim, simply and concisely, in short and plain statements. *Tomera v. Galt,* 511 F.2d 504, 508 (7th Cir. 1975). Harmonizing Rules 8 and 9, *Tomera* held that the purpose of Rule 9(b) is clear: "Rule 9 lists the actions in which *slightly more* is needed for notice," and allegations describing the "bare bones" of a fraudulent scheme are sufficient to state a cause of action for fraud. *Id.* (emphasis added).

The teachings of *Tomera* have been followed repeatedly. *See I. Rokeach & Sons Inc. v. Eisenbach,* No. 85 C 1106, slip op. (N.D. Ill. Dec. 3, 1985), holding that the "bare bones" of a fraudulent scheme, along with approximate dates and descriptions of the fraudulent acts, sufficed to plead a RICO claim under Rule 9(b); *Frymire v. Peat Marwick Mitchell & Co.,* 657 F. Supp. 889, 895 (N.D. Ill. 1987) (plaintiffs need only allege enough facts to put defendants on notice of the claim and to "sketch out" the elements of the claim).

Contrary to defendants' suggestion, Rule 9(b) is not a static or rigid rule, which requires the same type of detail regardless of the circumstances of the alleged fraud. *Frymire,* 657 F. Supp. at 894. Whether a complaint reasonably notifies each defendant of his or her part in the scheme "will vary with the parties and the nature of the fraudulent scheme alleged." *Morgan,* 649 F. Supp. at 1028. "When the transactions are numerous and take place over an extended period of time, less specificity is required." *Baselski v. Paine, Webber, Jackson & Curtis, Inc.,* 514 F. Supp. 535, 540 (N.D. Ill. 1981).

(a) Rule 9(b) Is Satisfied when a RICO Claim Alleges a Scheme to Defraud, the Identity of Those Involved, and the General Nature of Their Involvement

Time and again, courts have upheld the sufficiency of RICO claims under Rule 9(b) when the scheme to defraud is alleged, the identity of those involved is set forth, and the general nature of their involvement is described.

In *Haroco, Inc. v. American National Bank and Trust Co.,* 747 F.2d 384 (7th Cir. 1984), *aff'd on other grounds,* 473 U.S. 606 (1985), the Seventh Circuit upheld a RICO complaint that simply outlined the allegedly fraudulent transactions, the content of the alleged misrepresentations, the identities of those involved, and the overall scheme to defraud. The court found that the defendants had fair notice of the claims against them under Rule 9(b). 747 F.2d at 405. The court refused to require plaintiffs to identify each instance of fraud with specific dates, places, and circumstances.

Similarly, in *Systems Research, Inc. v. Random, Inc.,* 614 F. Supp. 494 (N.D. Ill. 1985), the court upheld a RICO complaint as sufficient under Rule 9(b), stating:

> First, there must be adequate notice to the defendant of the charges against him to allow him to plead. Second, the pleading must establish enough of a "bare bones" scheme to defraud to exceed conclusory allegations. There is a fine distinction between a faulty, conclusory pleading and one that is consistent with our system of pleading and its emphasis on notice rather than fact or issue pleading.

Id. at 498. The court went on to hold that a pleading sufficiently alleges mail fraud and wire fraud if a "scheme to defraud" is set forth and use of the mails or wires in furtherance of the scheme is alleged. *Id.* at 498–99. Even though the plaintiff in *Systems Research* did not specify the occurrences of mail fraud and wire fraud, the court noted that "plaintiffs do describe, indirectly, the content of the mailings by specifying the business context in which they occurred." *Id.* at 499. The court was able to infer from the allegations made that mailings were part of the scheme to defraud. The court concluded that the defendants would have little difficulty answering the allegations and were given sufficient notice of the charges.

Numerous other cases in this district have held that it is not necessary to plead the distinct occurrences of mail fraud or wire fraud in order to properly plead a RICO claim under Rule 9(b). For example, in *Carlstead v. Holiday Inns, Inc., supra,* this court held that general allegations of mail and wire fraud are sufficient:

> It is not necessary that each conversation or mailing be specifically identified as to date, speaker, contents, etc. It is enough if the complaint identifies a range of time in which the communications occurred, and the general context of those communications, the names of the parties involved, and what defendants obtained by virtue of the communications.

Id. See I. Rokeach, supra (court upheld a RICO claim with general allegations of the means to accomplish a specific fraud); *Olympic Federal v.*

Remp, No. 87 C 8705 (N.D. Ill. June 16, 1988) (LEXIS 5579) (general allegations of wire fraud were sufficient). *See also Pandick, Inc. v. Rooney,* 632 F. Supp. 1430, 1434 (N.D. Ill. 1986) (general allegations of use of the mails sufficient).[40]

(b) The Complaint Fully Apprises Defendants of the Charges Against Them under Accepted Rule 9(b) Standards

There can be no doubt that plaintiffs have adequately alleged RICO claims under the standards enunciated in *Tomera* and applied by this District. Plaintiffs allege in detail the roles and responsibilities of each defendant in relation to the Corporation. Complaint ¶¶ 19–22, 24. The Complaint also sets forth the position and tenure of each defendant (¶ 19) and whether they were members of the Audit and Finance Committees of the Board. Complaint ¶¶ 19–20. The role and responsibilities of those committees is alleged in detail. Complaint ¶ 20. Defendants' power and influence also is alleged. Complaint ¶¶ 21, 22, 24. And it is specifically alleged that each defendant was a direct participant, co-conspirator, or aider and abettor of the criminal frauds set forth in the Complaint, to the extent they took place during his tenure in office. Complaint ¶¶ 25, 85, 86, 91, 92.

As set forth above, the Complaint explicitly details at least five schemes to defraud the government, each of which caused substantial harm to the Corporation. The exhibits to the Complaint provide even more information about the schemes. No more can reasonably be required.

Plaintiffs also have adequately alleged the predicate acts of mail fraud, wire fraud, and bribery. First, plaintiffs allege that defendants used the mails and wires to further their schemes to defraud. Complaint ¶¶ 45, 47, 52, 54, 68, 70, 80, 82. Second, plaintiffs have pleaded numerous acts whereby information was transmitted from defendants to the government in furtherance of the schemes, including, among other things, monthly reports, disclosure statements, responses to IRS requests, and bids for contracts. Complaint ¶¶ 32, 33, 35–40, 50, 58, 60, 64, 65, 74, 77, 90 (a–p). It is reasonable to infer from these allegations that the mails were used to transmit some or all of this material. *See Olympic Federal.* Moreover, Exhibit C of the Complaint contains copies of several letters apparently sent through the mails which were used in furtherance of the fraud. *See* Exhibit C at Government Exhibits 19, 28, 30, 31. Similarly, the use of the telephones and other interstate wire

---

[40] Courts in other jurisdictions have upheld RICO complaints containing allegations against officers and directors similar to those made here. *See* Blake v. Dierdorff, 856 F.2d 1365 (9th Cir. 1988) (allegations made against officers and directors collectively sufficient).

facilities in furtherance of the scheme can be inferred from allegations that defendants made misrepresentations to the government, instructed the Corporation's employees to make misrepresentations to the government, and concealed relevant information in order to defraud the government.

In assessing the sufficiency of these allegations, defendants' protestations of ignorance must be juxtaposed against the fact that these same defendants caused the Corporation to plead guilty to five felony counts that contained charges very similar to the allegations here. Moreover, these same defendants caused the Corporation to pay almost $200 million in fines and settlements in connection with the same charges. ¶¶ 7–8. In causing the Corporation to plead guilty to the criminal information, defendants admitted that those participating in the conspiracy to defraud took numerous actions to further the objectives of the various schemes. Complaint ¶¶ 44, 51, 67, 72.

The detail provided in this Complaint goes far beyond the "bare bones" complaint required in *Tomera* and *I. Rokeach*. It is more than "Rule 8 raised to a slightly higher level of specificity," the standard applied in *Morgan*. For defendants to assert that they do not have notice of the charges against them is ludicrous, particularly in light of the board's approval of the Corporation's plea of guilty to each of the frauds charged in the complaint.[41]

2. Defendants' Arguments about Rule 9(b) Are Totally Without Merit

(a) Rule 9(b) Does Not Require Detailed Pleadings Against Multiple Defendants

Rule 9(b) calls for a flexible standard in pleadings against multiple defendants. It does not require detailed allegations of each defendant's specific involvement in the fraud. "[W]here there are multiple defendants, a pleading is sufficient when it reasonably notifies each defendant of the part he or she plays in the scheme." *Morgan*, 649 F. Supp. at 1028; *Donato v. Merrill Lynch, Pierce, Fenner & Smith, Inc.*, 663 F. Supp. 669, 673 (N.D. Ill. 1987). The Seventh Circuit reached the same result in *Tomera*, 511 F.2d at 508.

---

[41] The director-officers' claim of unfairness in the allegations against defendants D and E, who were not officers or directors of the Corporation at all relevant times, is misplaced. First, parties can be liable for a conspiracy if they were part of it or adopted it at any time. *In re* Cenco Inc. Sec. Litig., 529 F. Supp. 411, 418–19 (N.D. Ill. 1982). Thus, these defendants can be liable for harms which resulted before or after their tenure under a RICO conspiracy theory. Moreover, the complaint alleges the dates of each defendant's tenure as a corporate officer or director, Complaint ¶ 19, and charges defendants with violations of RICO "during the time that they were" officers or directors. Complaint ¶¶ 85, 86, 91, 92. Thus, there is no unfairness.

The nature of the fraudulent scheme and the parties involved has a bearing on the specificity required. *Morgan,* 649 F. Supp. at 1028. For example, in *Donato,* the court inferred the nature of each defendant's involvement in the scheme from the allegations describing his employment and authority. The court in *Olympic Federal* inferred that the defendants willfully participated in the scheme and knew of its fraudulent nature from the overall allegations of the scheme, despite the lack of detailed allegations about each defendant's involvement.[42]

> (b) Rule 9(b) Does Not Require Separate Allegations Against Individual Officers and Directors Who Act Collectively

When a claim is made against officers and directors of a corporation who act collectively, the complaint need not allege each defendant's involvement in the scheme with specificity if sufficient information is provided about the scheme itself to allow defendants to answer. That is the precise holding in *Banowitz v. State Exchange Bank,* 600 F. Supp. 1466, 1469 (N.D. Ill. 1985), a RICO case against, among others, officers and directors of a corporation:

> Defendants argue that where, as here, multiple defendants are involved, the complaint must provide reasonable notice of the part each defendant allegedly played in the scheme. *Lincoln National Bank v. Lampe,* 414 F. Supp. 1270, 1278 (N.D. Ill. 1976); *Adair,* 526 F. Supp. at 744. That rule is modified, however, where the multiple defendants are all corporate insiders. Numerous courts have held that the conduct of such individuals need not be specified and the fraudulent acts complained of need not be attributed to certain persons if the complaint sufficiently describes the fraudulent acts and provides the individuals with sufficient information to answer the allegations. *See, e.g., Pellman v. Cinerama, Inc.,* 503 F. Supp. 107, 111 (S.D.N.Y. 1980) (and cases cited therein).

600 F. Supp. at 1469. *See also, Swanson v. Wabash, Inc.,* 577 F. Supp. 1308 (N.D. Ill. 1983); *Burkhart v. Allson Realty Trust,* 363 F. Supp. 1286 (N.D. Ill. 1973).[43]

---

[42] Courts in other jurisdictions also have followed this rule, allowing pleadings against groups of defendants without requiring specific fraud allegations against each defendant. *See, e.g., In re* Equity Funding Corp. Sec. Litig., 416 F. Supp. 161, 181 (C.D. Cal. 1976) ("Nor is it necessary for the complaint, once it has adequately identified a particular defendant with a category of defendants allegedly responsible for some continuing course of conduct, to plead more than the group conduct of the defendants"); *In re* Consumers Power Co. Sec. Litig., 105 F.R.D. 583, 592–93 (E.D. Mich. 1985); Somerville v. Major Exploration, Inc., 576 F. Supp. 902, 911 (S.D.N.Y. 1983).

[43] Similarly, the Ninth Circuit in *Blake, supra,* 856 F.2d at 1365, held that there is a presumption that corporate actions are the collective actions of the officers and directors, and detailed allegations against individual officers and directors are not required by Rule 9(b) when corporate fraud is specifically alleged. 856 F.2d at 1369. *See also*

(c) Rule 9(b) Does Not Require Plaintiffs to Plead Facts Peculiarly Within Defendants' Knowledge

When, as here, the specific details of the fraudulent acts, including predicate acts under RICO, are peculiarly within defendants' knowledge or control, plaintiffs are not required to plead those facts with specificity to state a claim. In *Hinsdale Women's Clinic, S.C. v. Women's Health Care of Hinsdale,* 690 F. Supp. 658 (N.D. Ill. 1988), the court held that if the complaint sufficiently describes the fraudulent scheme and provides defendants with information to answer the allegations, "it is unnecessary to allege further details that are in the exclusive possession of defendants." *Id.* at 663. *See also Banowitz,* 600 F. Supp. at 1469; *Papai v. Cremosnik,* 635 F. Supp. 1402, 1414 n.11 (N.D. Ill. 1986).

This principle applies with particular force to derivative actions against corporate officers and defendants. In *Schlick v. Penn-Dixie Cement Corp.,* 507 F.2d 374 (2d Cir. 1974), *cert. denied,* 421 U.S. 976 (1975) the court noted that the special pleading requirements of Rule 9(b):

> may be relaxed as to matters peculiarly within the opposing party's knowledge, as where the complaining shareholders in a derivative suit have little information about the manner in which the corporation's internal affairs are conducted and hence are rarely able to provide details as to the alleged fraud.

Id. at 379. *See In re Consumers Power Co.,* 105 F.R.D. at 591–92. It would be an extreme and unfair reading of Rule 9(b) to require shareholders bringing a derivative claim against officers and directors to plead specific facts as to each officer's or director's involvement when that information is exclusively in the defendants' knowledge.

(d) Defendants' Rule 9(b) Authorities Are Inapposite

Defendants' authorities are inapposite or distinguishable on their facts. In finding various complaints insufficient, several cases noted that defendants were not corporate insiders with access to special information or that the complaint lumped corporate insiders together with third parties, such as the company's accountants. *See Rice v. Windsor Industries, Inc.,* 85 C 4196, slip op. (N.D. Ill. Feb. 26, 1986); *Lewis v. Sporck,* 612 F. Supp. 1316 (N.D. Cal. 1985); *Frymire,* 657 F. Supp. at 896 (defendant was an outside auditor, not a corporate insider); *WAIT Radio v. Price Waterhouse,* 691 F. Supp. 102 (N.D. Ill. 1988) (defendant was an outside auditor, not a corporate insider); *McKee v. Pope Ballard Shepard & Fowle Ltd.,* 604 F. Supp. 927 (N.D. Ill. 1985);

DiVittorio v. Equidyne Extractive Indus., Inc., 822 F.2d 1242, 1247 (2d Cir. 1987); Zatkin v. Primuth, 551 F. Supp. 39, 42 (S.D. Cal. 1982); Somerville, 576 F. Supp. at 911.

Nelson v. National Republic Bank, [1984 Transfer Binder] Fed. Sec. L. Rep. (CCH) ¶ 91,481 (N.D. Ill. 1984) (individual defendants were in various positions—both "insiders" and "outsiders"—vis-a-vis plaintiff, with no specification of different roles). *See also Beck v. Cantor, Fitzgerald & Co., Inc.,* 621 F. Supp. 1547 (N.D. Ill. 1985). Clearly that is not the situation here.

Many of the other cases defendants cited involved situations in which the defendants made misrepresentations directly to plaintiffs. In those cases, the courts were naturally reluctant to allow complaints to stand that did not specify the misrepresentations made by particular defendants to particular plaintiffs, especially because that information was within the plaintiffs' knowledge. *See Lincoln National Bank v. Lampe,* 414 F. Supp. 1270 (N.D. Ill. 1976); *Adair v. Hunt International Resources Corp.,* 526 F. Supp. 736 (N.D. Ill. 1981); *Beck,* 621 F. Supp. at 1551. In several other cases cited by defendants the courts simply found there were not enough facts alleged for defendants to frame a responsive answer.[44]

* * *

Conclusion

For the foregoing reasons, defendants' motions to dismiss should be denied in their entirety.[45]

§ 6.13   Court Rulings on Motions to Dismiss

The district court, in a published opinion,[46] did not agree with any of the defendants' arguments in their motion to dismiss. The *Shields* complaint's allegations were sufficient to satisfy plaintiffs' pleading requirements for

---

[44] *See Adair;* Bruss Co. v. Allnet Communications Servs., Inc., 606 F. Supp. 401 (N.D. Ill. 1985) (general allegations that the individual defendants schemed to defraud); Coronet Ins. Co. v. Seyfarth, 665 F. Supp. 661 (N.D. Ill. 1987) (conflicting allegations regarding the roles of the various defendants); Folstad v. Harmon, No. 86 C 4667 (N.D. Ill. Feb. 11, 1987) (vague reference to a kickback scheme in a wrongful termination case with no details alleged); Dileo v. Baumhart, No. 84 C 7305 (N.D. Ill. May 4, 1988) (even after discovery, plaintiffs were unable to plead fraud against outside auditor); Landon v. GTE Communications Servs., Inc., 696 F. Supp. 1213 (N.D. Ill. 1988) (no allegations of defendants' involvement in fraud); Balabanos v. North Am. Inv. Group, Ltd., 684 F. Supp. 503 (N.D. Ill. 1988) (no specific predicate acts alleged).

[45] In an abundance of caution, assuming *arguendo* the court should find that the Complaint is deficient in some respect—which we do not concede—plaintiffs respectfully request leave to replead.

[46] Shields *ex rel.* Sundstrand Corp. v. Erickson, 710 F. Supp. 686 (N.D. Ill. 1989).

their civil RICO claim against the officer and director defendants. Following is that portion of the *Shields* court's opinion relating to defendants' unsuccessful challenges to the complaint's civil RICO allegations:

2. RICO Claims and Rule 9(b): Pleading fraud with particularity.

Defendants allege numerous defects in plaintiffs' RICO count pleadings (Counts I and II) based on the Fed. R. Civ. P. 9(b) requirement, quoted above, that fraud must be plead with particularity. We find no merit to these claims.

First, defendants complain that the pleadings on fraud are insufficiently particular in stating when the alleged activities occurred. Plaintiffs have alleged appropriate time periods, such as "from at least August, 1981 to and including at least June 3, 1985, the defendants . . . devised . . . a scheme . . . to defraud" (Complaint, ¶ 34). Further, they have attached copies of the plea agreements entered by Sundstrand when it plead guilty to the underlying criminal charges. We believe that if the time periods alleged were sufficiently specific to support a corporate plea of guilt to criminal charges, they are also sufficiently specific to apprise the defendants here of plaintiffs' claims. Rule 9(b) must be read in conjunction with Fed. R. Civ. P. 8, which requires only that the complaint provide defendants with notice of plaintiffs' claims. *See Tomera v. Galt,* 511 F.2d 504, 508 (7th Cir. 1975). We think the complaint provides sufficient notice as to the time of the relevant acts. *See Baselski v. Paine, Webber, Jackson & Curtis, Inc.,* 514 F. Supp. 535, 540 (N.D. Ill. 1981) ("when the transactions are numerous and take place over an extended period of time, less specificity is required").

Defendants also allege that the complaint is deficient because it fails to sufficiently allege the use of wire communications and the mails for the predicate acts of wire and mail fraud. We note that plaintiffs' allegations as to these matters tend to be a bit conclusory and do not describe specific phone conversations or mailings. *See, e.g.,* Complaint, ¶ 68 ("for the purpose of executing such scheme and artifice . . . the defendants, placed . . . matter to be sent and delivered by the Postal Service . . ."). However, based on the allegations of the complaint, it is clear that defendants would have had to use interstate mail and wire communications. For example, plaintiffs allege that fraudulent tax returns were filed. This would require the use of interstate mails. Similarly, plaintiffs allege numerous fraudulent transactions with Department of Defense personnel, including bribery, contract negotiations, and over-billing on government contracts, all of which would clearly necessitate the use of interstate mail and wire communications. While the complaint is not particularly well-pleaded with respect to the necessary allegation of the use of the mails and wire communications in furtherance of the scheme, we believe it is sufficient to satisfy the demands of notice pleading in the Federal Rules of Civil Procedure. *See Systems Research, Inc. v. Random, Inc.,* 614 F. Supp. 494 (N.D. Ill. 1985) (no specific allegations of occurrences of mail and wire fraud, but plaintiffs did indirectly describe the contents of the mailings); *Olympic Federal v. Remp,* No. 87 C 8705, 1988 WL 64410, 1988 U.S. Dist. LEXIS 5579 (N.D. Ill. 1988). We believe that we can reasonably infer the existence of the necessary interstate communications from the complaint, particularly in light of plaintiffs' general averments that they occurred.

Defendants further argue that the RICO claims are deficient because they fail to distinguish among the eighteen individual defendants by alleging any specific wrongdoing by any particular defendant or by alleging who in particular among the defendants participated in each of the predicate acts alleged. "[W]here there are multiple defendants, a pleading is sufficient when it reasonably notifies each defendant of the part he or she plays in the scheme." *Morgan v. Kobrin Securities, Inc.,* 649 F. Supp. 1023, 1028 (N.D. Ill. 1986). We think that the complaint suffices to provide defendants with such notice. The complaint extensively describes all the alleged predicate acts of fraud. It further describes the role of each of the defendants as that of having acquiesced in the misconduct and, in essence, negligently and wrongfully failing to properly supervise the corporation and its internal accounting and auditing. We note that:

> Where, as here, multiple defendants are involved, the complaint must provide reasonable notice of the part each defendant allegedly played in the scheme. That rule is modified, however, where the multiple defendants are all corporate insiders. Numerous courts have held that the conduct of such individuals need not be specified and the fraudulent acts complained of need not be attributed to certain persons if the complaint sufficiently describes the fraudulent acts and provides the individuals with sufficient information to answer the allegations.

Banowitz v. State Exchange Bank, 600 F. Supp. 1466, 1469 (N.D. Ill. 1985). *See also Donato v. Merrill Lynch, Pierce, Fenner & Smith,* 663 F. Supp. 669, 673 (N.D. Ill. 1987); *Morgan,* 649 F. Supp. at 1028. In light of the above, we hold that the complaint alleges with sufficient particularity the claims against each of the defendants.

Finally, defendants argue that plaintiffs have failed to properly plead a pattern of racketeering activity and have merely alleged one scheme. We find this claim patently absurd. The Seventh Circuit has noted that a pattern of racketeering activity requires *at least* two acts of racketeering activity, along with continuity plus relationship between the predicate acts. *Morgan v. Bank of Waukegan,* 804 F.2d 970, 974 (7th Cir. 1986). The court held:

> In order to be sufficiently continuous to constitute a pattern of racketeering activity, the predicate acts must be ongoing over an identified period of time so that they can fairly be viewed as constituting separate transactions, *i.e.,* "transactions somewhat separate in time and place." Relevant factors include the number and variety of predicate acts and length of time over which they were committed, the number

of victims, the presence of separate schemes and the occurrence of distinct injuries. However, the mere fact that the predicate acts relate to the same overall scheme or involve the same victim does not mean that the acts automatically fail to satisfy the pattern requirement.

Id. at 975–76 (citations omitted).

We think it clear that plaintiffs have alleged a pattern of racketeering activity. Plaintiffs have alleged that the defendants all participated in at least five schemes to defraud a single victim, the federal government. These schemes included illegally billing cost overruns as part of overhead expenses, billing personal expenses such as gifts, taking improper tax write-offs, bribing government officials, and improperly billing the government for patent litigation costs of a Sundstrand subsidiary. These schemes were ongoing over several years, inflicting distinct injuries, and involved numerous predicate acts. We think it clear that plaintiffs have shown both continuity and relationship. The allegations involve an ongoing pattern of repeated acts and a variety of schemes with a single purpose: to continuously cheat the federal government. The complaint sufficiently states a pattern of racketeering activity.[47]

§ 6.14   Subsequent Litigation and Settlement

After eventually prevailing against defendants' pleading challenges, the plaintiffs sought to conduct merits discovery. Soon thereafter, however, the defendants moved to stay the *Shields* action. The basis for the motion to stay was that the Board of Directors of Sundstrand had empaneled a "special litigation committee" to conduct an investigation into the allegations of the *Shields* action and would thereafter issue a recommendation as to whether the lawsuit should proceed.[48] The district court granted in part and denied in part the defendants' motion to stay the action. In so doing,

---

[47] *Id.* at 686–693 (footnotes omitted).

[48] The appointment of a special litigation committee is a common defensive maneuver by incumbent management challenged in a derivative action. Unfortunately for the shareholder plaintiff, stays sought by such special litigation committees are routinely granted by the courts, during which time the plaintiff is prohibited from conducting merits discovery or otherwise proceeding with the action. In many instances, and with great expense to the corporation, the special litigation committee conducts a lengthy investigation assisted by a large outside law firm. After this investigation, a report is generally issued by the special litigation committee with, more often than not, a recommendation to terminate the litigation. This report is then usually followed by the defendants' motion for summary judgment or motion to dismiss the action based upon the special litigation committee's recommendation. Thereafter, the plaintiff may then be limited to challenging the good faith and reasonableness of the special litigation committee's investigation and recommendation. Only after prevailing on those issues may plaintiff then proceed with the merits of the case.

the district court stayed the derivative portion of the case but allowed plaintiffs to proceed under the class action claim for proxy violations.[49]

Thereafter, the parties began discussing settlement. Before considering any settlement, the plaintiffs' counsel was required to evaluate the nature and extent of Sundstrand's insurance coverage, conduct discovery and interviews relating to the underlying facts, and carefully analyze the actual damages that could probably be recovered on behalf of Sundstrand. Likewise, plaintiffs' counsel had to assess the difficulty of proving that the upper management of Sundstrand engaged in the underlying wrongful conduct as well as taking into consideration the inherent risks attendant with any litigation.

Aside from evaluating the plaintiffs' case, plaintiffs' counsel was also required to consider the defendants' defenses to the plaintiffs' derivative claims under the common law. To the extent the derivative claims implicated the defendants' duty of care to Sundstrand, the defendants could assert the formidable "business judgment rule" as an affirmative defense to those claims.[50]

In assessing the prospects for settlement, plaintiffs' counsel was also required to conduct a damage analysis to ascertain the financial harm that Sundstrand actually suffered by reason of the defendants' alleged wrongdoing. In this regard, to the extent the amounts paid to the government in settlement of the criminal and civil cases were restitution, Sundstrand was not originally entitled to this money and the return of these funds were not damages. Based on this assumption, estimates of direct damages suffered by Sundstrand were limited to actual penalties and fines paid to the government. Sundstrand's settlement of the administrative claims also amounted to restitution and did not involve any fines or penalties.

Under this analysis, it was established that the government considered that of the $115 million paid as a result of the first plea agreement, $15 million represented fines and penalties, and of the $12.32 million paid as a result of the second plea agreement, $1 million represented fines and

---

[49] During the pendency of the stay of the derivative portion of the action, Sundstrand's Board of Directors also impaneled another special committee to focus on the allegations supporting the criminal plea agreements and the remedial actions that had been taken by Sundstrand as a result of those pleas.

[50] Simply stated, the business judgment rule "is a presumption that in making a business decision the directors of a corporation acted on an informed basis in good-faith and in the honest belief that the action taken was in the best interest of the company." Smith v. Van Gorkom, 488 A.2d 858, 872 (Del. 1985). Compounding this obstacle was precedent that, in the corporate governance context as opposed to the tort context, the showing of gross negligence necessary to overcome the presumption of the business judgment rule must approach reckless conduct. See Radkin v. Phillip A. Hunt Chem. Corp., 547 A.2d 962 (Del. Ch. 1986).

penalties, the remainder being restitution.[51] Therefore, Sundstrand paid a total of $16 million in fines or penalties, and the remainder of Sundstrand's payments represented restitution for Sundstrand's wrongful charges under defense contracts with the government.

Finally, as to the class claims in the *Shields* action, extensive remedial measures were effected at Sundstrand to remedy the alleged harm from the proxy violations. These measures included the requirement that Sundstrand's audit committee meet four times a year, instead of the two times a year as it previously had, for at least three years from the date of the settlement.[52] Likewise, a broad range of measures designed to prevent recurrence of the matters that led to Sundstrand's plea agreements were adopted by Sundstrand after the commencement of the action, which provided further consideration in settlement of the *Shields* action.

Upon consideration of all of these factors, and upon recommendation of Sundstrand's special litigation committee, the *Shields* case settled for an insurance-funded amount of $15 million and the adoption of the corporate governance measures outlined above.

---

[51] The quantification of Sundstrand's fine and restitution was based upon, inter alia, a disclosure statement filed with its 1988 federal tax return, statements at the plea hearings, and positions taken by the government in its prosecution of the corporation. Furthermore, although Sundstrand was also suspended for three months from obtaining government contracts, Sundstrand had avoided additional damages by deferring contracts until the end of the suspension period or entering contracts in anticipation of the suspension.

[52] In these meetings, the audit committee also agreed to devote at least one meeting a year substantially to a number of matters, including the following: (a) reviewing all of Sundstrand's proxy materials relating to the compensation of directors and executive officers and charter amendments; (b) monitoring and evaluating the effectiveness of Sundstrand's policies and procedures to ensure compliance with applicable laws concerning the procurement and performance of federal government contracts; (c) monitoring and evaluating the effectiveness of Sundstrand's existing "Government Contract Compliance Educational Program" for managers involved in supervising the procurement or performance of federal government contracts; and (d) requiring all Sundstrand personnel involved in supervising such contracts to certify in writing, on an annual basis, their awareness of and compliance with these policies.

CHAPTER 7

CIVIL RICO AGAINST SUPPLIERS OF FRAUDULENT ENTERPRISES

David H. Schwartz

§ 7.1   The Systematically Fraudulent Enterprise

Systematically fraudulent enterprises injure many victims who cannot recover their losses because the enterprises themselves, and their principals, lack sufficient assets to pay damages. Such fraudulent enterprises frequently have assistance from legitimate businesses that provide the fraudulent enterprise with goods, services, or financing, knowing that they are assisting the fraudulent enterprise in its criminal activities. Such "stand off" third-party suppliers generally felt safe from civil liability because they themselves committed no actionable fraud on the public.

The Racketeer Influence Corrupt Organizations Act,[1] or RICO, offers an opportunity for victims of fraudulent enterprises to impose liability on

---

[1] 18 U.S.C. §§ 1961–68 (1988).

third-party suppliers of goods and services, who are doing business with the fraudulent enterprise knowing of its fraudulent nature; benefitting directly or indirectly from the enterprise's fraudulent activity; and supporting or providing essential goods or services necessary for the fraudulent enterprise to function and carry out its activities.

Enterprises engaging in systematic fraud on consumers and businesses are prevalent in all areas of the United States and in all areas of commercial activity. Mixed among the many legitimate businesses in each field are a certain number of firms which carry out their business by engaging in systematic and repeated fraudulent practices to make their money. Areas where the systematically fraudulent enterprise is especially likely to appear include securities and commodities sales, mortgage brokering, franchising, home improvement services, travel services, nursing and retirement homes, and various types of pyramid selling schemes.

By its very nature, the inherently fraudulent enterprise is unlikely to have the assets to satisfy judgments for persons or businesses who would sue it for compensation. Because such enterprises tend to be centered entirely around their marketing operations, with little or no revenue coming from anything other than the initial sales of their over-hyped products or services, as soon as complaints, either administrative or legal, start to surface, the income of the organization will drop off rapidly.

Even if the purveyor of fraudulent goods or services is still in existence when the victims first seek legal counsel, there is often little opportunity to obtain redress from the assets of the business. It is in the nature of the fraudulent business enterprise to be under-capitalized. Such entities may be highly leveraged.

A significant number of fraudulent enterprises have a "pyramid" type financial structure, such that they can remain in operation only so long as their sales volume continues to increase geometrically or even exponentially. For such enterprises, it often takes only one or two serious lawsuits and the attendant publicity to cause a fall-off in sales followed by financial collapse. Long before a judgment can be obtained, the enterprise is likely to be defunct or have sought protection under the bankruptcy laws.

Suing the individual "entrepreneurs" who found and run such operations is also likely to result in an uncollectible judgment. Often these persons have little personal wealth. Many lead a lavish lifestyle as a "marketing" requirement, the key to convincing their victims that they too can become rich by joining the team and not missing the golden opportunity. Others have truly believed their own misrepresentations. Before a lawsuit can be prosecuted and judgment obtained, the profits which the entrepreneurs who run such enterprises have taken out of them typically have disappeared, having been squandered, hidden, or expended defending criminal and civil prosecutions. While obtaining a judgment against the entrepreneur may be morally gratifying, it will not make the victimized client whole.

Nevertheless, fraudulent and criminal business enterprises do not operate in a commercial vacuum. Like legitimate businesses, the systematically fraudulent enterprise usually needs credit to operate. It consumes goods and requires services just as a legitimate enterprise does. It may have sought public associations with more established and financially sound businesses or individuals as a means of establishing its own legitimacy in the market place. When the fraudulent enterprise goes down, third-party suppliers of goods and services typically "stand off," cry about how they too were taken for a ride, and disclaim any responsibility for the losses suffered by the victims of the fraudulent enterprise.

Such stand off third-party entities are usually insulated from liability for the damage caused by the fraudulent enterprise, and should be so insulated if they acted innocently and without knowledge of the fraudulent nature of the enterprise. But if a stand off third-party supplier of goods or services knows of the fraudulent activity of an enterprise, enters into a business relationship with that enterprise, profits from that relationship, and through the relationship establishes and/or keeps the fraudulent enterprise alive when it would otherwise have failed, the Racketeer Influenced Corrupt Organizations Act often will posit against that third party liability for the injuries occurring to the victims of the fraudulent enterprise.

What is most important and unique about RICO is that if the third-party participant in the fraudulent enterprise is guilty of a RICO violation, then the victims of the fraudulent enterprise may have a private right of action against the third party even though that third party neither participated in the management of the fraudulent enterprise nor had direct contact with the victims.

§ 7.2 Application of RICO

With a good understanding of the reach of the RICO statute, as well as its limitations, the careful practitioner may be able to identify a solvent party with potential liability to the victims of the fraud. The statute's importance is that it may permit the victim to recover from a third-party defendant who profited from the operations of the fraudulent enterprise in the absence of any type of principal/agent relationship, even if the third-party defendant did not directly participate in the actual management of the fraudulent enterprise, and even if there was no traditional privity relationship between the victim of the fraud and the third-party defendant.

Most of the debate over the impact of RICO on the American legal system, and most of the criticism leveled against it, has focused on the treble damage and attorneys' fees provisions and its use in supposedly "garden variety" fraud cases. In the opinion of this author, however, the most striking aspect of RICO is its expansion of legal liability to some morally culpable parties for whom the law previously provided insulation.

What sets RICO apart from other common law and statutory theories of civil liability is that its liability focus is on the criminal behavior of the defendant and whether that behavior furthered the conduct of the enterprise, not on what the defendant did to the victim. If the defendant has engaged in a pattern of conduct amounting to a series of predicate racketeering acts, and has done so in association with a racketeering enterprise, it is not necessary that the defendant have carried out any type of direct fraud on the plaintiff-victim, so long as the pattern of racketeering furthered the existence or operations of the fraudulent enterprise and the victim was injured, "directly or indirectly," by reason of the predicate acts of the defendants. To recover, the plaintiff need not have been the direct intended victim of the racketeering acts,[2] nor does the injury have to be the direct result of the predicate act.[3]

In order to understand the scope of RICO liability for the stand off third-party supplier of goods and services, it is important to examine subsection (c) of 18 U.S.C. § 1962:

> (c) It shall be unlawful for any person employed by or associated with any enterprise engaged in, or the activities of which affect, interstate or foreign commerce, to conduct or participate, directly or indirectly, in the conduct of such enterprise's affairs through a pattern of racketeering activity or collection of unlawful debt.

For our purposes, subsection (c) poses three hurdles for establishing RICO liability: (1) employment or association with the racketeering enterprise; (2) conducting or participating, directly or indirectly, in the conduct of such enterprise's affairs; (3) through a pattern of racketeering activity or collection of unlawful debt.[4]

Employment or association with the racketeering enterprise. The third party must be "employed by or associated with" the racketeering enterprise. "Association" with an enterprise does not require that the defendant be a part of its organizational structure, that the defendant be acting to support the avowed objectives of the enterprise, or even that the defendant deal with the policymakers in the enterprise.[5] Hence, even if the enterprise

---

[2] *See* Terre Du Lac Ass'n, Inc. v. Terre Du Lac, Inc., 772 F.2d 467, 472–73 (8th Cir. 1985).

[3] *See* Bankers Trust Co. v. Rhoades, 859 F.2d 1096 (2d Cir. 1988).

[4] Omitted here is any discussion of the commerce requirement. In most instances this will not be a difficult requirement to meet.

[5] *See, e.g.,* United States v. Yonan, 800 F.2d 164, 166–67 (8th Cir. 1986):

Section 1962(c) literally prohibits persons 'employed by or associated with' an enterprise from illicitly conducting or participating in the conduct of the enterprise's affairs; the statute makes no mention of such persons needing a 'stake or

as a whole is a legitimate business, and the fraudulent business practices are limited to a particular division, segment, or regional or local office of the business, a third-party supplier of goods and services to the offending elements of the business may still be "associated" with the enterprise.

Conducting or participating, directly or indirectly, in the conduct of such enterprise's affairs.   Defendants have repeatedly challenged their civil or criminal prosecutions under subsection (c) on the grounds that this requirement means the defendant must have participated in the management of the racketeering enterprise. Most courts have rejected this, finding that such a requirement would run contrary to the liberal construction to be given to the act. Hence, the requirement that the defendant participate, directly or indirectly, in the conduct of the enterprise's affairs requires showing only some nexus between the pattern of racketeering activity by the defendant and the enterprise's affairs.[6]

A pattern of activity.   The statute requires at least two acts of racketeering within a 10-year period. Whether two acts of racketeering are sufficient to meet the racketeering requirement continues to be a subject of debate. See **Chapter 4**. Another condition imposed on the pattern requirement by some courts is that the racketeering acts occur in separate transactions rather than in the furtherance of only one fraudulent or illegal transaction.

§ 7.3   —Predicate Acts of Racketeering

RICO § 1962 sets forth a large number of statutory violations as predicate acts to meet the racketeering requirement. In the context of the systematically fraudulent business enterprise, the two most likely candidates will be violations of the mail and wire fraud statutes.

Understanding the nature and scope of these statutes is a key to understanding the power of RICO for the defrauded or victimized plaintiff.

---

interest in the goals of the enterprise.' Similarly, there is no statutory requirement that such persons have contact with policymakers or heads of enterprises before they can be said to be associated with it. In the absence of a statutory definition of 'association,' the cases have adopted a common sense reading of the term that focuses on the business of the enterprise and the relationship of the defendant to that business. The cases make clear that the defendant need not have a stake in the enterprise's 'goals,' but can associate with the enterprise by conducting business with it, even if in doing so the defendant is subverting the enterprise's goals.

[6] Virden v. Graphics One, Inc., 623 F. Supp. 1417, 1428–29, (C.D. Cal. 1985).

Proof of a violation of the federal mail or wire fraud statutes does not require proof that a common law fraud occurred.

The elements of mail fraud under 18 U.S.C. § 1341 and wire fraud under 18 U.S.C. § 1343 are (1) the formation of a scheme to defraud, and (2) use of the mails or interstate communications wires in furtherance of the scheme.[7] Thus, the plaintiff must first establish that the defendant specifically intended to participate in the scheme to defraud.[8] "The government proves specific intent if it proves that the scheme was reasonably calculated to deceive persons of ordinary prudence and comprehension."[9] Specific intent can be shown by examining the scheme itself.[10]

Proof of the fraudulent scheme does not necessarily require an affirmative misrepresentation of fact, because it is only necessary to prove that the scheme was calculated to deceive persons of ordinary prudence. Thus, the fraudulent scheme may be demonstrated solely by showing the deceitful concealment of material facts. Most importantly, the mail and wire fraud statutes do not require proof that anyone actually has been defrauded or has suffered damages.[11]

The second element of mail fraud or wire fraud under federal law is the use of the mails or interstate communications wires in furtherance of the scheme to defraud. The court in *Virden v. Graphics One, Inc.* stated that:

> The government may prove that the defendant used the mails or interstate communications wires for the purpose of executing a scheme to defraud by showing that a defendant acted knowing that the use of the mails or wires would follow in the ordinary course of business, or that, even when not intended, such use was reasonably foreseeable. The mailings or wire communications do not have to be an essential part of the contemplated scheme, but they must be made for the purpose of executing the scheme. Direct evidence of the mailing or wire communication is not necessary; circumstantial evidence will suffice.[12]

Hence, the stand-off third-party supplier can be held to have participated in the predicate racketeering acts even if it has not directly

---

[7] United States v. Bohonus, 628 F.2d 1167, 1171 (9th Cir. 1980); United States v. Louderman, 576 F.2d 1383 (9th Cir. 1978).

[8] United States v. Green, 745 F.2d 1205, 1207 (9th Cir. 1984); United States v. Bohonus, 628 F.2d 1167, 1172.

[9] Virden v. Graphics One, Inc., 623 F. Supp. 1417, 1422 (C.D. Cal. 1985).

[10] *Id.* (citing United States v. Green, 745 F.2d 1205, 1207; United States v. Bohonus, 628 F.2d 1167, 1172).

[11] *Id.* (citing United States v. Rasheed, 633 F.2d 843, 850 (9th Cir. 1981), *cert. denied,* 454 U.S. 1157 (1982)).

[12] *Id.* at 1422–23 (citations omitted).

misrepresented information to the plaintiff-victim or sent misleading information through the mails or over wires. If the third-party supplier of goods and services provided or received mailings and wires as a part of the fraudulent enterprise's conduct of a fraudulent scheme, and the third-party supplier can be shown to have the requisite knowledge of the fraud and knowing participation in it, then the third-party stand-off supplier will have RICO liability to those injured by reason of its predicate acts.

§ 7.4   Factual Situation

To illustrate the application of RICO requirements in a third-party supplier situation, consider the following hypothetical case involving a company we shall call Graphics, Inc., which manufactures a line of computerized graphics equipment. A successful sales representative for Graphics, Inc. leaves the company and goes into business for himself. He decides to set up a company, which we shall call GraphixMan, Inc., to sell Graphix-Man franchises or business opportunities.[13] The GraphixMan franchise will be a storefront graphics design and layout business which will get its customers from "quick print" shops that exist all over the country.

Although the salesman has no experience operating a commercial graphics arts business, no meaningful support staff or organization to provide training or support for persons who would purchase and try to operate such a business, no recognized service or trademark, and no successfully proven method for doing business, he feels confident he can sell his franchise to neophyte graphic artists who want to "be their own boss" and have an opportunity to express their "artistic talents."

The salesman begins immediately to market his GraphixMan franchises. He prepares promotional material stating, among other things, that the proven design of the GraphixMan business is a sure winner, that every GraphixMan store has made money within four months of start-up, and that the owner of a GraphixMan franchise does not need to "sell" to make a profit because every GraphixMan shop has a natural market in the quick print shops located nearby.

The salesman knows that to attract such people he must offer a "turnkey" operation, that is, he must provide everything needed to launch his

---

[13] For the purposes of this discussion it is not necessary to distinguish between a mere "business opportunity" and a true franchise, which, because of state and federal statutory schemes, is subject to considerable regulation and often various strict liability requirements with regard to false or misleading promotional information. See **Ch. 2**. The term *franchise* will be used here without an intention to invoke the greater legal implications of that term.

GraphixMan franchisee on a successful career in commercial graphics designing. The salesman sees the centerpiece of the GraphixMan franchise package he would like to sell as a set of computerized graphics equipment and cameras manufactured by his former employer, Graphics, Inc.

The GraphixMan equipment package is comprised of specific items which Graphics, Inc. has traditionally had a difficult time marketing. The former salesman goes to his former bosses at Graphics, Inc. and proposes that he include this package of equipment as his "required equipment" that every GraphixMan franchisee must purchase. Every franchisee will thus be required to purchase a package of the manufacturer's poorly selling equipment. Each franchise sale will also create a market for the supplies, spare parts, and service for the hitherto unpopular Graphics, Inc. equipment. Naturally, the marketing staff at Graphics, Inc. is delighted to accommodate, and it offers the salesman advice on various equipment packages, promotional material and assistance, and, based upon the salesman's optimistic forecasts, prospective volume discounts on equipment packages. Overnight, GraphixMan, Inc. achieves the benefits that are usually given to volume dealers in Graphics, Inc. equipment.

However, the salesman wants something more. His potential franchisees lack the economic resources to obtain credit financing from normal commercial lenders for the $70,000 equipment package. He seeks from the Graphics, Inc.'s captive leasing arm, Graphics Financial, the ability to offer lease financing to his franchisees.

The proposal, including the design of the franchise and some of the franchisor's promotional material, is reviewed by the management of Graphics Financial. A senior credit manager recommends that the proposal for leasing the franchise equipment packages be denied because the representations made in the promotional material can't be true; the credit analysis says there isn't a real market for the services the GraphixMan franchise will provide, hence the GraphixMan franchisee will have to aggressively sell for the business to survive. The analysis also states that in order for the GraphixMan franchisee to meet his or her financial obligations, including the equipment lease payments, the franchisee will have to be highly skilled and experienced in the printing business. In short, the analysis states, each GraphixMan franchise stands a high probability of failure.

Under pressure from Graphics, Inc., the manufacturer parent, the credit manager's recommendation is overruled. The manufacturer agrees to sell the equipment package at discount to GraphixMan, Inc., the franchisor, who will then resell the package to its franchisee, offering lease financing from the Graphics Financial, the manufacturer's captive leasing subsidiary. With this arrangement in place, the salesman is ready to roll.

In fact, the Graphics Financial credit manager was correct. The entrepreneur printed his marketing materials before his organization ever opened or operated a GraphixMan shop. No GraphixMan shop ever does make a profit in the first year, let alone the first four months, and there is no natural market for the graphics services which the business opportunity can provide. To the contrary, the cost of the equipment plus rent and salaries require the GraphixMan shop to price its graphics services higher than the customers of quick-print shops can afford, and the equipment and experience of the GraphixMan franchisees is insufficient to meet the needs of sophisticated commercial printers who otherwise could afford the services.

The salesman is correct, however, that he can sell GraphixMan franchises to a lot of people who wish they had pursued a career in commercial art and are eager to be their own bosses. Learning of the opportunities that await them, they quit their jobs and sign the papers for the GraphixMan franchise. They pay an initial franchise fee of $10,000. They also sign the lease papers for the equipment package purchased through GraphixMan, Inc. Each equipment package is sold to GraphixMan, Inc. for $35,000, with payment due in 30 days. Upon signing the lease papers, GraphixMan receives from Graphics Financial a check for $70,000. GraphixMan thus has immediate income of $35,000 and the use of an additional $35,000 for 30 days. As time goes on this stretches to 90 and 120 days.

GraphixMan, Inc. finds the franchisee a storefront and negotiates the lease. They give the purchaser a few days' instruction on how to use the equipment and a list of suggested prices for services. The GraphixMan franchisee pays lease payments by mailing them directly to Graphics Financial, and buys supplies, spare parts, and service from Graphics, Inc., ordering supplies and service over an 800, toll-free number.

As time goes on, significant numbers of GraphixMan franchisees start to default on their equipment leases, each of which GraphixMan, Inc. has guaranteed. When Graphics Financial begins to put pressure on GraphixMan and the salesman, the salesman goes to the defaulting franchisees and berates them for not getting out and selling and not having their family members helping them with the store. He convinces the franchisees that their failures are due to their own personal inadequacies which can be overcome if they give the GraphixMan stores more time and energy and do not believe that everything will be "handed to them on a platter." To keep the store open (and paying lease payments) for an additional six months or a year, the salesman convinces them they must refinance their homes for the additional cash. Many do, and continue to make lease payments to Graphics Financial until they are economically and emotionally exhausted.

§ 7.5 Analysis of Parties' RICO Liability

On the face of things, Graphics, Inc. has done nothing wrong. It has merely sold equipment packages to GraphixMan and provided supplies, spare parts, and service to GraphixMan franchisees. No franchisee can say that he or she did not get what they paid for from Graphics, Inc. The situation with respect to Graphics Financial is the same. Each franchisee has a lease with Graphics Financial. They have received the equipment they wanted, and the lease terms, by themselves, are not unconscionable or oppressive. Nevertheless, Graphics, Inc. and Graphics Financial can have RICO liability to the victims of GraphixMan, Inc. First, they have associated with the GraphixMan racketeering enterprise; second, they have participated in the conduct of GraphixMan, Inc.'s affairs through a pattern of racketeering activity.

It can be easily established that GraphixMan is operating in violation of the federal mail and wire fraud statutes by utilizing the United States mails and interstate wires to carry out a fraudulent or deceptive scheme. GraphixMan, Inc., is, therefore, a racketeering enterprise.

Graphics, Inc. and Graphics Financial, although they have not directly misrepresented any facts to the franchisees, have provided crucial assistance and support to the GraphixMan racketeering enterprise. Graphics, Inc. has provided the principal equipment for each franchise, the sale of which Graphics, Inc. knows generates the bulk of the revenues for GraphixMan, Inc. Indeed, it is clear that for the salesman, the GraphixMan franchise concept is merely the pretext for selling the Graphics, Inc. equipment to the prospective franchisees. Graphics, Inc. is only too happy to accommodate and sell some of its unpopular equipment.

Graphics Financial has provided the credit crucial for GraphixMan to function. For most of the prospective franchisees, a GraphixMan franchise would be beyond their reach financially without the lease financing available from Graphics Financial. Graphics Financial is extending credit to the new franchisees against its better business judgment and at the request of its manufacturing parent.

By receiving the payment for its equipment through the mail, and receiving orders for supplies and service over interstate telephone lines, Graphics, Inc. has utilized mail and wires to complete the mail fraud and wire fraud initiated by GraphixMan. Similarly, Graphics Financial receives through the mail each month the lease payments from each franchisee. This also completes the act of mail fraud initiated by GraphixMan through its misleading promotions and sale representations.

The remaining element of proof against both Graphics, Inc. and Graphics Financial is *scienter*. If they participated knowing that the equipment purchases, supply purchases, or leases were being entered into by the GraphixMan franchisees as a result of inherently deceptive representations by GraphixMan, Inc., then there is a basis for establishing that Graphics, Inc. and Graphics Financial had the requisite scienter.

A sample complaint based on these hypothetical facts is set out in §§ 7.7 through 7.10.

§ 7.6   A Note on Damages

The persons to whom a RICO violator is liable for damages, and the extent of such damages, remains ill defined. In *Virden v. Graphics One, Inc.,*[14] the court held that the parties in the positions analogous to Graphics, Inc. and Graphics Financial would be liable for damages sustained by GraphixMan franchisees even if those franchisees had not utilized Graphics Financial for their financing, so long as such franchisees could establish a causal nexus between the illegal conduct of the two defendants and the franchisee's damages. Presumably, to the extent the franchisee could establish that GraphixMan would not have been able to make fraudulent sales but for the knowing participation of Graphics, Inc. and Graphics Financial, there would be a causal nexus between the RICO activity and the franchisee's damages.

In order for the plaintiffs in the hypothetical situation of § **5.4** to pursue a RICO claim, they must merely plead and prove that they have been injured in their business or property by reason of a violation of § 1962. To establish a violation of § 1962 the plaintiffs must demonstrate, inter alia, that the defendants engaged in a pattern of racketeering activity composed of predicate acts injuring or affecting someone, not necessarily the plaintiffs. Each RICO plaintiff need not prove that he himself was involved in or injured by one or more of the predicate acts. Obviously, each plaintiff must demonstrate a causal nexus between his own injury and either (1) a predicate act of at least one RICO defendant or (2) the pattern of racketeering activity by which at least one of the RICO defendants participated in the conduct of the enterprise's affairs.[15] The decision in *Virden v. Graphics One, Inc.,* which concerned a fact situation similar to the hypothetical posed in this chapter, is contained in §§ **7.11** through **7.19** in order to illustrate one court's application of the RICO statute to third-party suppliers.

The causal nexus between the RICO activity and damage to the complainants has been accepted in a variety of situations where common law fraud might not reach. For example, a creditor has been found to have standing to pursue RICO claims against individual directors and officers of a debtor corporation for concealing a fraudulent transfer of assets prior to the debtor's bankruptcy,[16] and a homeowner's association was accorded standing to sue for damages it would sustain as a result of having to pay for

---

[14] 623 F. Supp. 1417 (C.D. Cal. 1985).

[15] *Id.* at 1425.

[16] Bankers Trust Co. v. Rhoades, 859 F.2d 1096 (2d Cir. 1988).

improvements which developers fraudulently represented to home purchasers would be installed.[17]

These cases demonstrate that proof of violation of the federal mail and
wire fraud statutes does not require proof of all of the elements of common law fraud. It follows that compensable damages are not limited to
those which flow directly from a fraudulent inducement; just how much
further is an issue which the courts have yet to delineate clearly. For example, defendants who had no contractual relationship with the plaintiff may
nevertheless be liable to the plaintiff for contract damages if they were co-
participants with a defendant who had contracted with the plaintiff and
the non-contracting defendants participated in mail fraud to assist the
contracting defendant's conversion of property rented to that defendant
by the plaintiff.[18]

On the other hand, not every injurious consequence flowing from the
operation of a RICO enterprise will give standing to the injured person to
recover damages by reason of the RICO violation.

> Conducting an enterprise that affects interstate commerce is obviously not
> in itself a violation of § 1962, nor is mere commission of the predicate
> offenses. In addition, the plaintiff only has standing if, and can only re-
> cover to the extent that, he has been injured in his business or property by
> the conduct constituting the violation. As the Seventh Circuit has stated,
> [a] defendant who violates section 1962 is not liable for treble damages to
> everyone he might have injured by other conduct, nor is the defendant
> liable to those who have not been injured. Haroco, Inc. v. American Na-
> tional Bank & Trust Co. of Chicago, 747 F.2d 384, 398 (1984), aff'd, 473
> U.S. 606, 105 S.Ct. 3291, 87 L.Ed.2d 437.[19]

Hence, an employee discharged because he reported to his superiors a
scheme by his employer to violate Canadian customs laws and a subsequent scheme to cover up the violations lacked standing to sue under
RICO, even though the scheme to violate Canadian customs laws would,
itself, constitute a RICO violation.[20] Similarly, when a corporation's stock
was manipulated through predicate acts of securities fraud and mail and

---

[17] Terre Du Lac Ass'n, Inc. v. Terre Du Lac, Inc., 772 F.2d 467 (8th Cir. 1985). *But see*
Sperber v. Boesky, 849 F.2d 60 (2d Cir. 1988), which rejected an argument that an
investor who sought in his own investments to mimic investments being made by a
noted arbitrager because it was public knowledge that the arbitrager had shown himself
to be a very successful investor in the past could claim RICO damages when it was
discovered that the noted arbitrager's successes were due to a pattern of racketeering
activity.

[18] Liquid Air Corp. v. Rogers, 834 F.2d 1297, 1309 (7th Cir. 1987).

[19] Sedima, S.P.R.L. v. Imrex Co., 473 U.S. 479, 496–97 (1985).

[20] Nodine v. Textron, Inc., 819 F.2d 347, 349 (1st Cir. 1987).

wire fraud so that the price was temporarily inflated, the corporation lacked standing to sue under RICO for injuries to its credit worthiness and general business reputation when the scheme was discovered and the stock price plummeted.[21]

The plaintiffs who have been denied standing on the grounds that they were not injured directly or indirectly by the conduct constituting the violation have generally been persons who were outside the class of persons constituting the intended victims of the underlying fraudulent activity. Standing should be afforded to plaintiffs who would fit within the class of intended victims, if they were in fact injured by the conduct constituting the violation, or if it were reasonably foreseeable that a person in the plaintiff's position would suffer injury as a result of the defendant's illegal carrying out of the predicate acts.

§ 7.7   Complaint Against Third-Party Suppliers

UNITED STATES DISTRICT COURT
CENTRAL DISTRICT OF CALIFORNIA

GRAPHIXMAN FRANCHISEES, 　Petitioner/Plaintiffs, vs. GRAPHIXMAN, INC., GRAPHICS, INC., GRAPHICS FINANCIAL, JOE SALESMAN, 　Respondent/Defendants.	CASE NO.: COMPLAINT

1. These claims arise in connection with a "GraphixMan" franchise owned by each plaintiff. Plaintiffs allege that the defendants have: (1) violated the federal RICO statute; (2) committed acts of fraud and misrepresentation; (3) violated the California Franchise Investment Law; (4) violated federal and state antitrust law; (5) violated express contractual obligations and the implied covenants of good faith and fair dealing by failing to perform promissory representations; (6) breached their fiduciary duty; and (7) negligently and intentionally caused them emotional distress. Plaintiffs seek compensatory damages, exemplary damages, injunctive relief, and an award of costs and attorneys' fees.

---

[21] *In re* Crazy Eddie Sec. Litig., 714 F. Supp. 1285, 1290–91 (E.D.N.Y. 1989).

Parties

2. The names and addresses of the plaintiffs are as follows:

    a. GraphixMan Franchisee
        123 Main Street
        Anywhere, USA 12345

Except where the context otherwise indicates, reference to "plaintiffs" refers to all of the named plaintiffs.

3. On information and belief, the names and addresses of the defendant corporations and individuals are as follows:

    a. GraphixMan, Inc. is a California corporation with principal offices at 456 Main Street, Anywhere, USA 67890.

    b. Graphics, Inc. is a Delaware corporation with principal offices at 456 Main Street, Somewhere Else, USA 67890.

    c. Graphics Financial is a Delaware corporation with principal offices at 789 Main Street, Somewhere Else, USA 67890.

    d. Joe Salesman resides in California.

Jurisdiction and Venue

4. This action is instituted pursuant to 28 U.S.C. § 1331 and 18 U.S.C. § 1962, the Racketeer Influenced and Corrupt Organizations Act of 1970, and pursuant to 28 U.S.C. § 1331 and 15 U.S.C. § 15, for violations of the federal antitrust laws; and under the Court's pendent jurisdiction for violation of the California Franchise Investment Law, California Corporations Code § 31000 et seq.; violation of the California antitrust laws, (Cartwright Act, California Business and Professional Code § 16700 et seq.); breach of contract; fraud; promissory estoppel; breach of fiduciary duty; and intentional and negligent infliction of emotional distress.

5. Venue is proper in this district under 28 U.S.C. § 1391(b) because the claims arose in this district, and under 28 U.S.C. § 1391(c) and 15 U.S.C. § 22 because defendants are found in and do business in this district.

6. This Court has personal jurisdiction over the defendants pursuant to California Code of Civil Procedure § 410.10 because: (a) Joe Salesman is a resident of California; (b) GraphixMan, Inc. is incorporated in California and does business in California; (c) Graphics, Inc. does business in California; and (d) Graphics Financial does business in California. The alleged claims relate to the business of each corporate defendant. The California business of each corporate defendant is substantial and continuous.

7. All of the defendants' operations, the system of GraphixMan franchises and the individual franchised businesses owned by the plaintiffs

have involved the use of the U.S. mail and telephone lines, and the transmittal across state lines and in interstate commerce of various equipment, products, chemicals, film, paper, supplies, advertisements, inducements, representations, leases, telephone calls, contracts, communications, and other business matters, transactions, and dealings. Accordingly, plaintiffs, defendants, and the "enterprises" are within the flow of interstate commerce and act as conduits through which printing products, including letterheads, business cards, logos, flyers, brochures, stationery, catalogues, advertising, resumes, and other forms, flow to their ultimate destination. During the relevant period, there has thus been a consistent continuity of movement of said products and services of said defendants in or affecting interstate commerce.

§ 7.8   —Factual Allegations

FACTUAL ALLEGATIONS

8.   Joe Salesman was employed by Graphics, Inc. from approximately 1970 to 1976.

9.   In 1980 Joe Salesman operated as a business consultant specializing in the sale of graphic arts equipment manufactured by Graphics, Inc. He also sold complete "packages" for quick-print centers using such equipment.

10.   Later in 1980 Joe Salesman started GraphixMan, Inc. He was the president and is now the chairman of the board of GraphixMan, Inc. He is also the principal owner of this corporation.

11.   GraphixMan, Inc. has over 40 print centers, primarily on the west coast of the United States, almost all of these centers being owned by franchisees.

12.   GraphixMan, Inc. develops, operates, licenses, and purportedly services the franchise system of GraphixMan centers. These centers operate under franchise agreements with GraphixMan, Inc.

13.   GraphixMan centers were designed to provide at one location all the pre-press needs of printers, advertising companies, and publishers. Pre-press work consists of all the mechanical and creative work that is done prior to printing. This includes typesetting, camera work, layout, and design.

14.   GraphixMan, Inc. advertised in newspapers and magazines to obtain franchisees. GraphixMan, Inc. and Joe Salesman personally also used the mails and telephone lines in the promotion and sale of franchises to the plaintiffs.

15.   By the phone and in person, Joe Salesman and GraphixMan, Inc. representatives made the following false oral representations

to the plaintiffs to induce them to purchase GraphixMan franchises: (a) GraphixMan centers offered unique services at one location; (b) GraphixMan had no competition; (c) GraphixMan, Inc. had a proven formula that guaranteed success; (d) a maximum of $10,000 working capital was needed for three months, to reach the "break-even" point; (e) GraphixMan centers could be run profitably with a small staff; (f) the first GraphixMan center "broke even" within one month; and (g) GraphixMan, Inc. had provided and would continue to provide all the training necessary in order to succeed.

16.   Prior to the purchase of a GraphixMan franchise, Joe Salesman and GraphixMan, Inc. circulated to the plaintiffs through the mail a publication entitled "What's a Graphics Center." The brochure claimed: (a) a GraphixMan franchise "is a multi-service *turnkey* graphic arts business"; (b) GraphixMan franchise owners "are intensively trained by Graphix-Man, Inc. in the operation of state-of-the-art equipment and necessary business management principles and procedures"; (c) GraphixMan "is a unique concept evolved from years of expertise and experience in the printing and graphic industry"; (d) GraphixMan "is a totally unique concept"; (e) that GraphixMan provided "an intensive two-week training course, developed to provide the franchisee with total insight into his business"; (f) that GraphixMan further provided "two weeks of in-store training . . . , plus continuing guidance and assistance"; and (g) "Who is GraphixMan competition? We have none."

17.   By mail, wire, and in person, Joe Salesman and GraphixMan, Inc. directed the plaintiffs in the evaluation, assembly, procuring, and installation of equipment, principally from Graphics, Inc. and Graphics Financial. They offered the plaintiffs the opportunity to lease or to purchase the equipment. Joe Salesman and GraphixMan, Inc. falsely represented that they would secure the lease and financing of equipment through Graphics, Inc. and Graphics Financial at rates lower than the franchisee would otherwise be able to secure. Joe Salesman and GraphixMan, Inc. falsely represented that all of the equipment was new and "state-of-the-art." Joe Salesman and GraphixMan, Inc. provided the franchisees with all the necessary purchase and lease forms and secured financing for them through Graphics Financial.

18.   Defendants Joe Salesman and GraphixMan, Inc. established, promoted, and sold franchises to plaintiffs by making false statements of material fact in documents filed by mail with the California Commissioner of Corporations, as follows:

(a)   Certain individuals affiliated with the franchisor had neither been adjudged bankrupt nor had been an officer or partner in a bankrupt company;

(b)   The franchisor receives no payments from anyone for the placement of financing for such person;

(c) The franchisor provides no average, projected, or forecasted sales, profits, or earnings to its potential franchisees;

(d) The franchisor provides no actual sales figures of its franchised offices to potential franchisees; and,

(e) The franchisor uses or applies the initial franchise payment substantially to specified functions including the training of franchisees, assistance of franchisees in preparing to open and after opening, area survey, and site location.

19. On information and belief as to all matters herein alleged, defendants Graphics, Inc. and/or Graphics Financial:

(a) Directly or indirectly controlled GraphixMan, Inc. and/or Joe Salesman;

(b) Conspired and participated with GraphixMan, Inc. and Joe Salesman; and/or

(c) Were associated with GraphixMan, Inc. and Joe Salesman.

20. On information and belief, Joe Salesman or GraphixMan, Inc., or both of them, were at all times secretly authorized dealers and representatives of Graphics, Inc. and Graphics Financial, but none of them ever disclosed such facts to the plaintiffs and intentionally concealed same from plaintiffs. On information and belief, in all the actions described in the above paragraphs, Joe Salesman acted in his own behalf and as an authorized representative and agent of GraphixMan, Inc. On information and belief, at all times relevant hereto, Joe Salesman was acting as Graphics, Inc.'s and/or Graphics Financial's agent under their actual, apparent, or ostensible authority.

21. Based on these repeated and express assurances, the plaintiffs invested large sums of money in purchasing and establishing GraphixMan franchises.

22. Plaintiffs materially relied on the defendants' aforementioned deceptive and fraudulent promises, representations, conduct, and concealments by purchasing GraphixMan franchises and by continuing to invest time and money in the operation of their GraphixMan franchises.

23. Plaintiffs would not have purchased or continued to invest time and money in the GraphixMan franchises if they had known that any of the promises and representations made by the defendants were false or that the defendants never intended to perform the promises and representations as stated.

24. GraphixMan, Inc.'s franchise agreement requires the purchase or leasing of Graphics, Inc. production supplies.

25. GraphixMan, Inc.'s franchise agreement requires the purchase or leasing of Graphics, Inc. equipment.

26. All of the plaintiffs' leases of equipment were obtained from Graphics Financial. The purchase or lease of Graphics, Inc. equipment is

one of the largest expenses for each plaintiff, in the approximate sum of $70,000 for each franchise.

27.   On information and belief, Graphics, Inc. or Graphics Financial secretly provided Joe Salesman and/or GraphixMan, Inc. with substantial payments, commissions, rebates, and other fees for each lease or purchase of Graphics, Inc. equipment by the plaintiffs.

28.   On information and belief, Graphics, Inc. or Graphics Financial secretly provided Joe Salesman and/or GraphixMan, Inc. with increased payments, commissions, rebates, fees, or other incentives when certain quotas for the lease or purchase of Graphics, Inc. equipment were reached.

29.   On information and belief, Graphics, Inc. and/or Graphics Financial had a secret agreement with GraphixMan, Inc. and/or Joe Salesman that prevented or limited the ability of plaintiffs to receive discounts otherwise available for Graphics, Inc. equipment purchased directly from Graphics Financial.

30.   On information and belief, through Joe Salesman and/or GraphixMan, Inc., Graphics, Inc. and/or Graphics Financial secretly sold or leased Graphics, Inc. equipment repossessed from GraphixMan, Inc. franchisees that had failed to new GraphixMan franchisees.

31.   On information and belief, Graphics, Inc. and/or Graphics Financial had a secret agreement with GraphixMan, Inc. and/or Joe Salesman that specified new or repossessed models of equipment that would be sold or leased to the plaintiffs. These particular models were either outdated at the time they were sold or it was expected that more advanced Graphics, Inc. equipment models would soon be on the market.

32.   On information and belief, Graphics, Inc. and Graphics Financial had knowledge of and actively participated in the fraudulent and other misconduct of GraphixMan, Inc. and Joe Salesman, including but not limited to:

   (a)   Their knowledge of the failures and lack of profitability of the GraphixMan franchises and of the deceptive conduct of GraphixMan, Inc. and Joe Salesman;

   (b)   The setting and/or increase of quotas for the sale or leasing of Graphics, Inc. equipment;

   (c)   The creation of a reserve fund and the requirement of the guarantee of lease payments to Graphics, Inc. to guarantee potential defaults by franchisees; and

   (d)   The continued promotion of sales, leases, and financing by GraphixMan, Inc. and Joe Salesman without the disclosure of this information.

33.   As a further result of the foregoing, each plaintiff has suffered emotional shock, distress, and anguish caused by the defendants' misstatements and misconduct in the promotion, sale, and other acts that

occurred during the continued operation and/or termination of their GM franchises.

§ 7.9 —Claims Based on Franchise Contract

FIRST CLAIM FOR RELIEF
(Breach of Contract)

34.   Plaintiffs reallege paragraphs 1 through 33 above as if fully set forth herein.

35.   Defendants Joe Salesman and GraphixMan, Inc. breached their franchise agreements with the plaintiffs, including the implied covenant of good faith and fair dealing. Such violations caused each plaintiff serious financial damage in an amount not presently ascertainable, but which each plaintiff believes to be in excess of $100,000.

SECOND CLAIM FOR RELIEF
(Promissory Equitable Estoppel)

36.   Plaintiffs reallege paragraphs 1 through 33 above as if fully set forth herein.

37.   Defendants Joe Salesman and GraphixMan, Inc. are estopped from denying that they made the promises and representations described in paragraphs 15 through 18 on which plaintiffs relied reasonably, foreseeably, and to their substantial detriment. The defendants are therefore bound to fulfill such promises and representations. Such violations caused each plaintiff serious financial damage in an amount not presently ascertainable, but which each plaintiff believes to be in excess of $100,000.

THIRD CLAIM FOR RELIEF
(Violation of California Franchise Investment Law)

38.   Plaintiffs reallege paragraphs 1 through 33 above as if fully set forth herein and in particular, paragraphs 15 through 19.

39.   Defendants Joe Salesman and GraphixMan, Inc. established, promoted, and granted franchises in violation of the California Franchise Investment Law § 31000 et seq., including but not limited to:

   (a) Failure to provide the required materials to prospective franchisees within the appropriate time period;

   (b) The making of false statements of material fact or omissions of material facts required to be stated in documents filed with the Commissioner of Corporations, as more specifically set forth in paragraphs 15 through 20, above; and

(c) Offering or selling franchises by written or oral communications that included untrue statements of material fact or omissions of material fact necessary in order to make the statements made, in the light of the circumstances under which they were made, not misleading, including those described in paragraphs 15 through 20.

40.   At the time that the promises and representations were made by defendants, as alleged in paragraphs 15 through 20, plaintiffs had no knowledge that the representations were false or that defendants had no intention of performing on their promises. Within one year last past, and after entering into franchise agreements with defendant Graphix-Man, Inc. and commencing operation of their respective businesses, plaintiffs communicated with one another concerning defendants' failure to perform in a manner consistent with their representations and contractual promises. Plaintiffs learned from one another and others that defendants had almost uniformly failed to honor their promises and representations to all franchisees. After learning this, plaintiffs reasonably concluded that defendants' representations and promises to perform as alleged in paragraphs 15 through 20 must have been false at the time they were made.

41.   Such violations caused each plaintiff serious financial damage in an amount not presently ascertainable, but which each plaintiff believes to be in excess of $100,000.

FOURTH CLAIM FOR RELIEF
(Breach of Trust)

42.   Plaintiffs reallege paragraphs 1 through 33 above as if fully set forth herein.

43.   Defendants Joe Salesman and GraphixMan, Inc. violated the fiduciary duty owed to the plaintiffs. Such violation caused each plaintiff serious financial damage in an amount not presently ascertainable, but which each plaintiff believes to be in excess of $100,000.

FIFTH CLAIM FOR RELIEF
(Fraud and Intentional Misrepresentation)

44.   Plaintiffs reallege paragraphs 1 through 33 above as if fully set forth herein.

45.   With intent to deceive the plaintiffs and to induce them to enter into and operate a GraphixMan franchise and to purchase and/or lease equipment and supplies, defendants knowingly and intentionally made false statements and engaged in the false and fraudulent conduct and concealments described above, particularly in paragraphs 15 through 19.

46. Plaintiffs reasonably relied on such unlawful misrepresentations, concealments, and conduct to their detriment. Such violations caused each plaintiff severe financial damage in an amount not presently ascertainable, but which each plaintiff believes to be in excess of $100,000. Defendants are therefore liable for this fraud.

SIXTH CLAIM FOR RELIEF
(Negligent Misrepresentation)

47. Plaintiffs reallege paragraphs 1 through 33 above as if fully set forth herein.

48. Defendants negligently made false statements to the plaintiffs or concealed the truth from the plaintiffs concerning the franchises and other matters described in paragraphs 15 through 19, with the intent to induce them to enter into franchise agreements, to purchase or lease equipment and supplies, and to operate their GraphixMan franchises. The plaintiffs were thereby induced to enter the franchise agreement and suffered severe damages in an amount which is not presently ascertainable, but which each plaintiff believes to be in excess of $100,000. Defendants are therefore liable for this negligence.

SEVENTH CLAIM FOR RELIEF
(Intentional Infliction of Emotional Distress)

49. Plaintiffs reallege paragraphs 1 through 33 above as if fully set forth herein.

50. The defendants' intentional conduct, misrepresentations, and concealments as described above were outrageous, singly and in the aggregate. Such activities were undertaken by defendants with intent to cause, or reckless disregard of the probability of causing, emotional distress in plaintiffs. It was reasonably foreseeable by the defendants that the plaintiffs would suffer emotional distress as a result of the defendants' activities.

51. Such conduct by the defendants proximately caused each plaintiff severe emotional shock, distress, and anguish, the value of which exceeded $100,000. Defendants are therefore liable for these intentional acts.

EIGHTH CLAIM FOR RELIEF
(Negligent Infliction of Emotional Distress)

52. Plaintiffs reallege paragraphs 1 through 33 and 49 to 50 as if fully set forth herein.

53. The defendants' negligent statements and actions proximately caused reasonably foreseeable emotional shock, distress, and anguish in

each plaintiff, the value of which exceed $100,000. Defendants are therefore liable for this negligence.

§ 7.10   —RICO Counts

NINTH CLAIM FOR RELIEF

(Federal RICO Count Against Joe Salesman, Graphics, Inc., and Graphics Financial)

[This count is directed against Joe Salesman, individually, and the corporate defendants Graphics, Inc. and Graphics Financial for violations of 18 U.S.C. § 1962, the Racketeer Influenced Corrupt Organizations Act of 1970.]

54.   Plaintiffs reallege and incorporate herein the allegations contained in paragraphs 1 through 53 of this complaint.

55.   As to each plaintiff, from at least as early as 1980 and continuing until the date of this complaint, and on two or more occasions, Joe Salesman, Graphics, Inc. and/or Graphics Financial willfully, fraudulently, and intentionally used the United States mails and telephone lines to commit and/or to continue the acts described in paragraphs 7–53 of this complaint.

56.   The acts of Joe Salesman, Graphics, Inc. and/or Graphics Financial described above constitute a pattern of racketeering activity within the meaning of 18 U.S.C. § 1961(1)(B).

57.   Joe Salesman, Graphics, Inc. and/or Graphics Financial received income derived directly or indirectly from the pattern of racketeering activity described above, and invested or used directly or indirectly, part of that income, or the proceeds of such income, to acquire an interest in and/or to establish or operate the legitimate activities of the following "enterprises":

    (a)   GraphixMan, Inc. and/or

    (b)   The system of GraphixMan franchises; and/or

    (c)   The individual franchised businesses owned by plaintiffs. (18 U.S.C. § 1962(a).)

58.   Through the pattern of racketeering activity described above, Joe Salesman, Graphics, Inc., and/or Graphics Financial acquired or maintained, directly or indirectly, an interest in and/or control of the legitimate activities of the above-described "enterprises." (18 U.S.C. § 1962(b).)

59.   Joe Salesman, Graphics, Inc., and/or Graphics Financial, who were associated with any or all of said "enterprises," conducted or

participated, directly or indirectly, in the conduct of each such enterprise's affairs through the pattern of racketeering activity described above. (18 U.S.C. § 1962(c).)

60.   Graphics, Inc. and/or Graphics Financial took the actions described in paragraphs 55 through 59 both as distinct entities and through Joe Salesman.

61.   By reason of defendants' racketeering enterprise conduct as described in paragraphs 57 through 60, each plaintiff has suffered substantial injury in business or property in an amount not yet ascertainable, but believed to exceed $1 million.

TENTH CLAIM FOR RELIEF
(Federal RICO Count Against Graphics, Inc.)

[This count is directed against corporate defendant Graphics, Inc. for violation of 18 U.S.C. § 1962, the Racketeer Influenced Corrupt Organizations Act of 1970.]

62.   Plaintiffs reallege and incorporate herein the allegations contained in paragraphs 1 through 61 of this complaint.

63.   As to each plaintiff, from at least as early as 1980 and continuing until the date of this complaint, and on two or more occasions, GraphixMan, Inc. willfully, fraudulently, and intentionally used the United States mail and telephone lines to commit the acts described in paragraphs 7 through 61 of this complaint.

64.   The acts of GraphixMan, Inc. described above constitute a pattern of racketeering activity within the meaning of U.S.C. § 1961(1)(B).

65.   GraphixMan, Inc. received income derived directly or indirectly from the pattern of racketeering activity described above, and invested or used, directly or indirectly, part of that income, or the proceeds of such income, to acquire an interest in and/or to establish or operate the legitimate activities of the following enterprises:

   (a)   The system of GraphixMan franchises; and/or
   (b)   The individual franchised businesses owned by plaintiffs.
         (18 U.S.C. § 1962(a).)

66.   Through the pattern of racketeering activity described above, GraphixMan, Inc. acquired or maintained, directly or indirectly, an interest in and/or control of the legitimate activities of the above-described "enterprises." (18 U.S.C. § 1962(b).)

67.   GraphixMan, Inc., which was associated with any or all of said "enterprises," conducted or participated, directly or indirectly, in the conduct of each such enterprises' affairs through the pattern of racketeering activity described above. (18 U.S.C. § 1962(c).)

68.   By reason of GraphixMan, Inc.'s racketeering enterprise conduct as described in paragraphs 65 through 67, each plaintiff has suffered

substantial injury in business or property in an amount not yet ascertainable, but believed to exceed $1 million.

ELEVENTH CLAIM FOR RELIEF
(Federal RICO Count Against Graphics, Inc.,
Graphics Financial, and Joe Salesman—Conspiracy)

[This count is directed against corporate defendants Graphics, Inc. and Graphics Financial and Joe Salesman for conspiring to violate 18 U.S.C. § 1962, the Racketeer Influenced Corrupt Organizations Act of 1970.]

69. Plaintiffs reallege and incorporate herein the allegations contained in paragraphs 1 through 53 of this complaint.

70. As to each plaintiff, from at least as early as 1980 and continuing until the date of this complaint, and on two or more occasions the corporate defendants each separately conspired with Joe Salesman and Joe Salesman conspired with each of them to willfully, fraudulently, and intentionally use the United States mail and telephone lines to commit the acts described in paragraphs 7 through 53 of this count.

71. The acts of defendants described above constitute a pattern of racketeering activity within the meaning of 18 U.S.C. § 1961(1)(B).

72. Said defendants conspired to receive income derived directly or indirectly from the pattern of racketeering activity described above, and invested or used, directly or indirectly, part of that income or the proceeds of such income to acquire an interest in and/or to establish or operate the legitimate activities of the following enterprises:

    (a) GraphixMan, Inc.; and/or

    (b) The system of GraphixMan franchises; and/or

    (c) The individual franchised businesses owned by plaintiffs. (18 U.S.C. § 1962(a).)

73. The said defendants conspired to acquire or maintain, directly or indirectly, an interest in and/or control of the legitimate activities of the above-described "enterprises." (18 U.S.C. § 1962(b).)

74. The defendants, who were associated with any or all of said "enterprises," conspired to conduct or participated directly or indirectly, in the conduct of each such enterprise's affairs through the patterns of racketeering activity described above. (18 U.S.C. § 1962(c).)

75. By reason of each defendant's racketeering enterprise conduct as described in paragraphs 72 through 74, each plaintiff has suffered substantial injury in business or property in an amount not yet ascertainable, but believed to exceed $1 million.

WHEREFORE, the plaintiffs pray and demand that the Court:

1. Make a determination of the illegality of the defendants' activities and of the damages thereby proximately caused to the plaintiffs, including:

(a) Treble damages and assessment of attorneys' fees and costs under the federal and state antitrust laws and the federal RICO statute;

(b) Damages for violations of the California Franchise Investment Law, California Business & Professions Code, breach of contract, breach of the implied covenant of good faith and fair dealing, fraud, misrepresentation, breach of fiduciary duty, and infliction of emotional distress;

(c) Restitution of all amounts paid by plaintiffs to GraphixMan, Inc., Graphics Financial, and Graphics, Inc. pursuant to California Business & Professions Code § 17200 et seq., and § 17500 et seq., and payment of attorneys' fees and costs; and

(d) Exemplary damages.

2.   Enter a preliminary injunction ordering the defendants to preserve in their present form and at their present locations any and all documents or records that refer or relate in any way to the facts and matters alleged herein;

3.   Enter a permanent injunction, after making its findings of fact, ordering the defendants to cease from engaging in such violations of statutory and common law as the Court finds to exist;

4.   Alternatively, order that each plaintiff may rescind the GraphixMan franchise agreement and be restored so far as possible to the position occupied by each before entering such agreements; and

5.   Grant the plaintiffs such other relief, in the form of damages, injunction, or otherwise as the Court deems just and proper.

APPENDIX

A. Racketeer Influenced and Corrupt Organizations Statute

APPENDIX A

RACKETEER INFLUENCED AND CORRUPT ORGANIZATIONS STATUTE [U.S.C. §§ 1961–1968]

§ 1961. Definitions

As used in this chapter—

(1) "racketeering activity" means (A) any act or threat involving murder, kidnaping, gambling, arson, robbery, bribery, extortion, dealing in obscene matter, or dealing in narcotic or other dangerous drugs, which is chargeable under State law and punishable by imprisonment for more than one year; (B) any act which is indictable under any of the following provisions of title 18, United States Code: Section 201 (relating to bribery), section 224 (relating to sports bribery), sections 471, 472, and 473 (relating to counterfeiting), section 659 (relating to theft from interstate shipment) if the act indictable under section 659 is felonious, section 664 (relating to embezzlement from pension and welfare funds), sections 891–894 (relating to extortionate credit transactions), section 1029 (relating to fraud and related activity in connection with access devices), section 1084 (relating to the transmission of gambling information), section 1341 (relating to mail fraud), section 1343 (relating to wire fraud), section 1344 (relating to financial institution fraud), sections 1461–1465 (relating to obscene matter), section 1503 (relating to obstruction of justice), section 1510 (relating to obstruction of criminal investigations), section 1511

309

(relating to the obstruction of State or local law enforcement), section 1512 (relating to tampering with a witness, victim, or an informant), section 1513 (relating to retaliating against a witness, victim, or an informant), section 1951 (relating to interference with commerce, robbery, or extortion), section 1952 (relating to racketeering), section 1953 (relating to interstate transportation of wagering paraphernalia), section 1954 (relating to unlawful welfare fund payments), section 1955 (relating to the prohibition of illegal gambling businesses), section 1956 (relating to the laundering of monetary instruments), section 1957 (relating to engaging in monetary transactions in property derived from specified unlawful activity), section 1958 (relating to use of interstate commerce facilities in the commission of murder-for-hire), sections 2312 and 2313 (relating to interstate transportation of stolen motor vehicles), sections 2314 and 2315 (relating to interstate transportation of stolen property), section 2321 (relating to trafficking in certain motor vehicles or motor vehicle parts), sections 2341–2346 (relating to trafficking in contraband cigarettes), sections 2421–24 (relating to white slave traffic), (C) any act which is indictable under title 29, United States Code, section 186 (dealing with restrictions on payments and loans to labor organizations) or section 501(c) (relating to embezzlement from union funds), (D) any offense involving fraud connected with a case under title 11, fraud in the sale of securities, or the felonious manufacture, importation, receiving, concealment, buying, selling, or otherwise dealing in narcotic or other dangerous drugs, punishable under any law of the United States, or (E) any act which is indictable under the Currency and Foreign Transactions Reporting Act;

(2) "State" means any State of the United States, the District of Columbia, the Commonwealth of Puerto Rico, any territory or possession of the United States, any political subdivision, or any department, agency, or instrumentality thereof;

(3) "person" includes any individual or entity capable of holding a legal or beneficial interest in property;

(4) "enterprise" includes any individual, partnership, corporation, association, or other legal entity, and any union or group of individuals associated in fact although not a legal entity;

(5) "pattern of racketeering activity" requires at least two acts of racketeering activity, one of which occurred after the effective date of this chapter and the last of which occurred within ten years (excluding any period of imprisonment) after the commission of a prior act of racketeering activity;

(6) "unlawful debt" means a debt (A) incurred or contracted in gambling activity which was in violation of the law of the United States, a State or political subdivision thereof, or which is unenforceable under State or Federal law in whole or in part as to principal or interest because of the laws relating to usury, and (B) which was incurred in connection

with the business of gambling in violation of the law of the United States, a State or political subdivision thereof, or the business of lending money or a thing of value at a rate usurious under State or Federal law, where the usurious rate is at least twice the enforceable rate;

(7) "racketeering investigator" means any attorney or investigator so designated by the Attorney General and charged with the duty of enforcing or carrying into effect this chapter;

(8) "racketeering investigation" means any inquiry conducted by any racketeering investigator for the purpose of ascertaining whether any person has been involved in any violation of this chapter or of any final order, judgment, or decree of any court of the United States, duly entered in any case or proceeding arising under this chapter;

(9) "documentary material" includes any book, paper, document, record, recording, or other material; and

(10) "Attorney General" includes the Attorney General of the United States, the Deputy Attorney General of the United States, the Associate Attorney General of the United States, any Assistant Attorney General of the United States, or any employee of the Department of Justice or any employee of any department or agency of the United States so designated by the Attorney General to carry out the powers conferred on the Attorney General by this chapter. Any department or agency so designated may use in investigations authorized by this chapter either the investigative provisions of this chapter or the investigative power of such department or agency otherwise conferred by law.

(As amended Pub.L. 98-473, Title II, §§ 901(g), 1020, Oct. 12, 1984, 98 Stat. 2136, 2143; Pub.L. 98-547, Title II, § 205, Oct. 25, 1984, 98 Stat. 2770; Pub.L. 99-570, Title XIII, § 1365(b), Oct. 27, 1986, 100 Stat. 3207-35; Pub.L. 99-646, § 50(a), Nov. 10, 1986, 100 Stat. 3605; Pub.L. 100-690, Title VII, §§ 7013, 7020(c), 7032, 7054, Nov. 18, 1988, 102 Stat. 4395, 4396, 4398, 4402; Pub.L. 101-73, Title IX, § 968, Aug. 9, 1989, 103 Stat. 506; Pub.L. 101-647, Title XXXV, § 3560, Nov. 29, 1990, 104 Stat. 4927.)

§ 1962. Prohibited activities

(a) It shall be unlawful for any person who has received any income derived, directly or indirectly, from a pattern of racketeering activity or through collection of an unlawful debt in which such person has participated as a principal within the meaning of section 2, title 18, United States Code, to use or invest, directly or indirectly, any part of such income, or the proceeds of such income, in acquisition of any interest in, or the establishment or operation of, any enterprise which is engaged in, or the activities of which affect, interstate or foreign commerce. A purchase of securities on the open market for purposes of investment, and without the intention of controlling or participating in the control of the issuer, or of assisting another to do so, shall not be unlawful under this subsection if the securities of the issuer held by the purchaser, the members of his immediate family, and his or their accomplices in any pattern or racketeering activity or the collection of an unlawful debt after such purchase do not amount in the aggregate to one percent of the outstanding securities of any one class, and do not confer, either in law or in fact, the power to elect one or more directors of the issuer.

(b)   It shall be unlawful for any person through a pattern of racketeering activity or through collection of an unlawful debt to acquire or maintain, directly or indirectly, any interest in or control of any enterprise which is engaged in, or the activities of which affect, interstate or foreign commerce.

(c)   It shall be unlawful for any person employed by or associated with any enterprise engaged in, or the activities of which affect, interstate or foreign commerce, to conduct or participate, directly or indirectly, in the conduct of such enterprise's affairs through a pattern of racketeering activity or collection of unlawful debt.

(d)   It shall be unlawful for any person to conspire to violate any of the provisions of subsection (a), (b), or (c) of this section.

(As amended Pub.L. 100-690, Title VII, § 7033, Nov. 18, 1988, 102 Stat. 4398.)

§ 1963. Criminal penalties

(a)   Whoever violates any provision of section 1962 of this chapter shall be fined under this title or imprisoned not more than 20 years (or for life if the violation is based on a racketeering activity for which the maximum penalty includes life imprisonment), or both, and shall forfeit to the United States, irrespective of any provision of State law—

(1) any interest the person has acquired or maintained in violation of section 1962;

(2) any—

(A) interest in;

(B) security of;

(C) claim against; or

(D) property or contractual right of any kind affording a source of influence over;

any enterprise which the person has established, operated, controlled, conducted, or participated in the conduct of in violation of section 1962; and

(3) any property constituting, or derived from, any proceeds which the person obtained, directly or indirectly, from racketeering activity or unlawful debt collection in violation of section 1962.

The court, in imposing sentence on such person shall order, in addition to any other sentence imposed pursuant to this section, that the person forfeit to the United States all property described in this subsection. In lieu of a fine otherwise authorized by this section, a defendant who derives profits or other proceeds from an offense may be fined not more than twice the gross profits or other proceeds.

(b) Property subject to criminal forfeiture under this section includes—

(1) real property, including things growing on, affixed to, and found in land; and

(2) tangible and intangible personal property, including rights, privileges, interests, claims and securities.

(c) All right, title, and interest in property described in subsection (a) vests in the United States upon the commission of the act giving rise to forfeiture under this section. Any such property that is subsequently transferred to a person other than the defendant may be the subject of a special verdict of forfeiture and thereafter shall be ordered forfeited to the United States, unless the transferee establishes in a hearing pursuant to subsection (*l*) that he is a bona fide purchaser for value of such property who at the time of purchase was reasonably without cause to believe that the property was subject to forfeiture under this section.

(d)(1) Upon application of the United States, the court may enter a restraining order or injunction, require the execution of a satisfactory performance bond, or take any other action to preserve the availability of property described in subsection (a) for forfeiture under this section—

(A) upon the filing of an indictment or information charging a violation of section 1962 of this chapter and alleging that the property with respect to which the order is sought would, in the event of conviction, be subject to forfeiture under this section; or

(B) prior to the filing of such an indictment or information, if, after notice to persons appearing to have an interest in the property and opportunity for a hearing, the court determines that—

(i) there is a substantial probability that the United States will prevail on the issue of forfeiture and that failure to enter the order will result in the property being destroyed, removed from the jurisdiction of the court, or otherwise made unavailable for forfeiture; and

(ii) the need to preserve the availability of the property through the entry of the requested order outweighs the hardship on any party against whom the order is to be entered;

Provided, however, That an order entered pursuant to subparagraph (B) shall be effective for not more than ninety days, unless extended by the court for good cause shown or unless an indictment or information described in subparagraph (A) has been filed.

(2) A temporary restraining order under this subsection may be entered upon application of the United States without notice or opportunity for a hearing when an information or indictment has not yet been filed with respect to the property, if the United States demonstrates that there is probable cause to believe that the property with respect to which the order is sought would, in the event of conviction, be subject to forfeiture under this section and that provision of notice will jeopardize the availability of the property for forfeiture. Such a temporary order shall expire not more than ten days after the date on which it is entered, unless extended for good cause shown or unless the party against whom it is entered consents to an extension for a longer period. A hearing requested concerning an order entered under this paragraph shall be held at the earliest possible time, and prior to the expiration of the temporary order.

(3) The court may receive and consider, at a hearing held pursuant to this subsection, evidence and information that would be inadmissible under the Federal Rules of Evidence.

(e) Upon conviction of a person under this section, the court shall enter a judgment of forfeiture of the property to the United States and shall also authorize the Attorney General to seize all property ordered forfeited upon such terms and conditions as the court shall deem proper. Following the entry of an order declaring the property forfeited, the court may, upon application of the United States, enter such appropriate restraining orders or injunctions, require the execution of satisfactory performance bonds, appoint receivers, conservators, appraisers, accountants, or trustees, or take any other action to protect the interest of the United States in the property ordered forfeited. Any income accruing to, or derived from, an enterprise or an interest in an enterprise which has been ordered forfeited under this section may be used to offset ordinary and necessary expenses to the enterprise which are required by law, or which are necessary to protect the interests of the United States or third parties.

(f) Following the seizure of property ordered forfeited under this section, the Attorney General shall direct the disposition of the property by sale or any other commercially feasible means, making due provision for the rights of any innocent persons. Any property right or interest not exercisable by, or transferable for value to, the United States shall expire and shall not revert to the defendant, nor shall the defendant or any person acting in concert with or on behalf of the defendant be eligible to purchase forfeited property at any sale held by the United States. Upon application of a person, other than the defendant or a person acting in concert with or on behalf of the defendant, the court may restrain or stay the sale or disposition of the property pending the conclusion of any appeal of the criminal case giving rise to the forfeiture, if the applicant demonstrates that proceeding with the sale or disposition of the property will result in irreparable injury, harm or loss to him. Notwithstanding 31 U.S.C. 3302(b), the proceeds of any sale or other disposition of property forfeited under this section and any moneys forfeited shall be used to pay all proper expenses for the forfeiture and the sale, including expenses of seizure, maintenance and custody of the property pending its disposition, advertising and court costs. The Attorney General shall deposit in the Treasury any amounts of such proceeds or moneys remaining after the payment of such expenses.

(g)   With respect to property ordered forfeited under this section, the Attorney General is authorized to—

(1) grant petitions for mitigation or remission of forfeiture, restore forfeited property to victims of a violation of this chapter, or take any other action to protect the rights of innocent persons which is in the interest of justice and which is not inconsistent with the provisions of this chapter;

(2) compromise claims arising under this section;

(3) award compensation to persons providing information resulting in a forfeiture under this section;

(4) direct the disposition by the United States of all property ordered forfeited under this section by public sale or any other commercially feasible means, making due provision for the rights of innocent persons; and

(5) take appropriate measures necessary to safeguard and maintain property ordered forfeited under this section pending its disposition.

(h)   The Attorney General may promulgate regulations with respect to—

(1) making reasonable efforts to provide notice to persons who may have an interest in property ordered forfeited under this section;

(2) granting petitions for remission or mitigation of forfeiture;

(3) the restitution of property to victims of an offense petitioning for remission or mitigation of forfeiture under this chapter;

(4) the disposition by the United States of forfeited property by public sale or other commercially feasible means;

(5) the maintenance and safekeeping of any property forfeited under this section pending its disposition; and

(6) the compromise of claims arising under this chapter.

Pending the promulgation of such regulations, all provisions of law relating to the disposition of property, or the proceeds from the sale thereof, or the remission or mitigation of forfeitures for violation of the customs laws, and the compromise of claims and the award of compensation to informers in respect of such forfeitures shall apply to forfeitures incurred, or alleged to have been incurred, under the provisions of this section, insofar as applicable and not inconsistent with the provisions hereof. Such duties as are imposed upon the Customs Service or any person with respect to the disposition of property under the customs law shall be performed under this chapter by the Attorney General.

(i)   Except as provided in subsection (l), no party claiming an interest in property subject to forfeiture under this section may—

(1) intervene in a trial or appeal of a criminal case involving the forfeiture of such property under this section; or

(2) commence an action at law or equity against the United States concerning the validity of his alleged interest in the property subsequent to the filing of an indictment or information alleging that the property is subject to forfeiture under this section.

(j)   The district courts of the United States shall have jurisdiction to enter orders as provided in this section without regard to the location of any property which may be subject to forfeiture under this section or which has been ordered forfeited under this section.

(k)   In order to facilitate the identification or location of property declared forfeited and to facilitate the disposition of petitions for remission or mitigation of forfeiture, after the entry of an order declaring property forfeited to the United States the court may, upon application of the United States, order that the testimony of any witness relating to the property forfeited be taken by deposition and that any designated book, paper, document, record, recording, or other material not privileged be produced at the same time and place, in the same manner as provided for the taking of depositions under Rule 15 of the Federal Rules of Criminal Procedure.

(l)(1) Following the entry of an order of forfeiture under this section, the United States shall publish notice of the order and of its intent to dispose of the property in such manner as the Attorney General may direct. The Government may also, to the extent practicable, provide direct written notice to any person known to have alleged an interest in the property that is the subject of the order of forfeiture as a substitute for published notice as to those persons so notified.

(2) Any person, other than the defendant, asserting a legal interest in property which has been ordered forfeited to the United States pursuant to this section may, within thirty days of the final publication of notice or his receipt of notice under paragraph (1), whichever is earlier, petition the court for a hearing to adjudicate the validity of his alleged

interest in the property. The hearing shall be held before the court alone, without a jury.

(3) The petition shall be signed by the petitioner under penalty of perjury and shall set forth the nature and extent of the petitioner's right, title, or interest in the property, the time and circumstances of the petitioner's acquisition of the right, title, or interest in the property, any additional facts supporting the petitioner's claim, and the relief sought.

(4) The hearing on the petition shall, to the extent practicable and consistent with the interests of justice, be held thirty days of the filing of the petition. The court may consolidate the hearing on the petition with a hearing on any other petition filed by a person other than the defendant under this subsection.

(5) At the hearing, the petitioner may testify and present evidence and witnesses on his own behalf, and cross-examine witnesses who appear at the hearing. The United States may present evidence and witnesses in rebuttal and in defense of its claim to the property and cross-examine witnesses who appear at the hearing. In addition to testimony and evidence presented at the hearing, the court shall consider the relevant portions of the record of the criminal case which resulted in the order of forfeiture.

(6) If, after the hearing, the court determines that the petitioner has established by a preponderance of the evidence that—

(A) the petitioner has a legal right, title, or interest in the property, and such right, title, or interest renders the order of forfeiture invalid in whole or in part because the right, title, or interest was vested in the petitioner rather than the defendant or was superior to any right, title, or interest of the defendant at the time of the commission of the acts which gave rise to the forfeiture of the property under this section; or

(B) the petitioner is a bona fide purchaser for value of the right, title, or interest in the property and was at the time of purchase reasonably without cause to believe that the property was subject to forfeiture under this section;

the court shall amend the order of forfeiture in accordance with its determination.

(7) Following the court's disposition of all petitions filed under this subsection, or if no such petitions are filed following the expiration of the period provided in paragraph (2) for the filing of such petitions, the United States shall have clear title to property that is the subject of the order of forfeiture and may warrant good title to any subsequent purchaser or transferee.

(m) If any of the property described in subsection (a), as a result of any act or omission of the defendant—

(1) cannot be located upon the exercise of due diligence;

(2) has been transferred or sold to, or deposited with, a third party;

(3) has been placed beyond the jurisdiction of the court;

(4) has been substantially diminished in value; or

(5) has been commingled with other property which cannot be divided without difficulty;

the court shall order the forfeiture of any other property of the defendant up to the value of any property described in paragraphs (1) through (5).

(As amended Pub.L. 98-473, Title II, §§ 302, 2301(a)–(c), Oct. 12, 1984, 98 Stat. 2040, 2192; Pub.L. 99-570, Title XI, § 1153(a), Oct. 27, 1986, 100 Stat. 3207-13; Pub.L. 99-646, § 23, Nov. 10, 1986, 100 Stat. 3597; Pub.L. 100-690, Title VII, §§ 7034, 7058(d), Nov. 18, 1988, 102 Stat. 4398, 4403; Pub.L. 101-647, Title XXXV, § 3561, Nov. 29, 1990, 104 Stat. 4927.)

§ 1964. Civil remedies

(a) The district courts of the United States shall have jurisdiction to prevent and restrain violations of section 1962 of this chapter by issuing appropriate orders, including, but not limited to: ordering any person to divest himself of any interest, direct or indirect, in any enterprise; imposing reasonable restrictions on the future activities or investments of any person, including, but not limited to, prohibiting any person from engaging in the same type of endeavor as the enterprise engaged in, the activities of which affect interstate or foreign commerce; or ordering dissolution or reorganization of any enterprise, making due provision for the rights of innocent persons.

(b) The Attorney General may institute proceedings under this section. Pending final determination thereof, the court may at any time enter such restraining orders or prohibitions, or take such other actions, including the acceptance of satisfactory performance bonds, as it shall deem proper.

(c) Any person injured in his business or property by reason of a violation of section 1962 of this chapter may sue therefor in any appropriate United States district court and shall recover threefold the damages he sustains and the cost of the suit, including a reasonable attorney's fee.

(d) A final judgment or decree rendered in favor of the United States in any criminal proceeding brought by the United States under this chapter shall estop the defendant from denying the essential allegations of the criminal offense in any subsequent civil proceeding brought by the United States.

(As amended Pub.L. 98-620, Title IV, § 402(24)(A), Nov. 8, 1984, 98 Stat. 3359.)

§ 1965. Venue and process

(a) Any civil action or proceeding under this chapter against any person may be instituted in the district court of the United States for any district in which such person resides, is found, has an agent, or transacts his affairs.

(b) In any action under section 1964 of this chapter in any district court of the United States in which it is shown that the ends of justice require that other parties residing in any other district be brought before the court, the court may cause such parties to be summoned, and process for that purpose may be served in any judicial district of the United States by the marshal thereof.

(c) In any civil or criminal action or proceeding instituted by the United States under this chapter in the district court of the United States for any judicial district, subpenas issued by such court to compel the attendance of witnesses may be served in any other judicial district, except that in any civil action or proceeding no such subpena shall be issued for service upon any individual who resides in another district at a place more than one hundred miles from the place at which such court is held without approval given by a judge of such court upon a showing of good cause.

(d) All other process in any action or proceeding under this chapter may be served on any person in any judicial district in which such person resides, is found, has an agent, or transacts his affairs.

(Added Pub.L. 91-452, Title IX, § 901(a), Oct. 15, 1970, 84 Stat. 944.)

§ 1966. Expedition of actions

In any civil action instituted under this chapter by the United States in any district court of the United States, the Attorney General may file with the clerk of such court a certificate stating that in his opinion the case is of general public importance. A copy of that certificate shall be furnished immediately by such clerk to the chief judge or in his absence to the presiding district judge of the district in which such action is pending. Upon receipt of such copy, such judge shall designate immediately a judge of that district to hear and determine action.

§ 1967. Evidence

In any proceeding ancillary to or in any civil action instituted by the United States under this chapter the proceedings may be open or closed to the public at the discretion of the court after consideration of the rights of affected persons.

(Added Pub.L. 91-452, Title IX, § 901(a), Oct. 15, 1970, 84 Stat. 944.)

§ 1968. Civil investigative demand

(a) Whenever the Attorney General has reason to believe that any person or enterprise may be in possession, custody, or control of any documentary materials relevant to a racketeering investigation, he may, prior to the institution of a civil or criminal proceeding thereon, issue in writing, and cause to be served upon such person, a civil investigative demand requiring such person to produce such material for examination.

(b) Each such demand shall—

(1) state the nature of the conduct constituting the alleged racketeering violation which is under investigation and the provision of law applicable thereto;

(2) describe the class or classes of documentary material produced thereunder with such definiteness and certainty as to permit such material to be fairly identified;

(3) state that the demand is returnable forthwith or prescribe a return date which will provide a reasonable period of time within which the material so demanded may be assembled and made available for inspection and copying or reproduction; and

(4) identify the custodian to whom such material shall be made available.

(c) No such demand shall—

(1) contain any requirement which would be held to be unreasonable if contained in a subpena duces tecum issued by a court of the United States in aid of a grand jury investigation of such alleged racketeering violation; or

(2) require the production of any documentary evidence which would be privileged from disclosure if demanded by a subpena duces tecum issued by a court of the United States in aid of a grand jury investigation of such alleged racketeering violation.

(d) Service of any such demand or any petition filed under this section may be made upon a person by—

(1) delivering a duly executed copy thereof to any partner, executive officer, managing agent, or general agent thereof, or to any agent thereof authorized by appointment or by law to receive service of process on behalf of such person, or upon any individual person;

(2) delivering a duly executed copy thereof to the principal office or place of business of the person to be served; or

(3) depositing such copy in the United States mail, by registered or certified mail duly addressed to such person at its principal office or place of business.

(e) A verified return by the individual serving any such demand or petition setting forth the manner of such service shall be prima facie proof of such service. In the case of service by registered or certified mail, such return shall be accompanied by the return post office receipt of delivery of such demand.

(f)(1) The Attorney General shall designate a racketeering investigator to serve as racketeer document custodian, and such additional racketeering investigators as he shall determine from time to time to be necessary to serve as deputies to such officer.

(2) Any person upon whom any demand issued under this section has been duly served shall make such material available for inspection and copying or reproduction to the custodian designated therein at the principal place of business of such person, or at such other place as such custodian and such person thereafter may agree and prescribe in writing or as the court may direct, pursuant to this section on the return date specified in such demand, or on such later date as such custodian may prescribe in writing. Such person may upon written agreement between such person and the custodian substitute for copies of all or any part of such material originals thereof.

(3) The custodian to whom any documentary material is so delivered shall take physical possession thereof, and shall be responsible for the use made thereof and for the return thereof pursuant to this chapter. The custodian may cause the preparation of such copies of such documentary material as may be required for official use under regulations which shall be promulgated by the Attorney General. While in the possession of the custodian, no material so produced shall be available for examination, without the consent of the person who produced such material, by any individual other than the Attorney General. Under such reasonable terms and conditions as the Attorney General shall prescribe, documentary material while in the possession of the custodian shall be available for examination by the person who produced such material or any duly authorized representatives of such person.

(4) Whenever any attorney has been designated to appear on behalf of the United States before any court or grand jury in any case or proceeding involving any alleged violation of this chapter, the custodian may deliver to such attorney such documentary material in the possession of the custodian as such attorney determines to be required for use in the presentation of such case or proceeding on behalf of the United States. Upon the conclusion of any such case or proceeding, such attorney shall return to the custodian any documentary material so withdrawn which has not passed into the control of such court or grand jury through the introduction thereof into the record of such case or proceeding.

(5) Upon the completion of—

(i) the racketeering investigation for which any documentary material was produced under this chapter, and

(ii) any case or proceeding arising from such investigation,

the custodian shall return to the person who produced such material all such material other than copies thereof made by the Attorney General pursuant to this subsection which has not passed into the control of any court or grand jury through the introduction thereof into the record of such case or proceeding.

(6) When any documentary material has been produced by any person under this section for use in any racketeering investigation, and no such case or proceeding arising therefrom has been instituted within a reasonable time after completion of the examination and analysis of all evidence assembled in the course of such investigation, such person shall be entitled, upon written demand made upon the Attorney General, to the return of all documentary material other than copies thereof made pursuant to this subsection so produced by such person.

(7) In the event of the death, disability, or separation from service of the custodian of any documentary material produced under any demand issued under this section or the official relief of such custodian from responsibility for the custody and control of such material, the Attorney General shall promptly—

(i) designate another racketeering investigator to serve as custodian thereof, and

(ii) transmit notice in writing to the person who produced such material as to the identity and address of the successor so designated.

Any successor so designated shall have with regard to such materials all duties and responsibilities imposed by this section upon his predecessor in office with regard thereto, except that he shall not be held responsible for any default or dereliction which occurred before his designation as custodian.

(g) Whenever any person fails to comply with any civil investigative demand duly served upon him under this section or whenever satisfactory copying or reproduction of any such material cannot be done and such person refuses to surrender such material, the Attorney General may file, in the district court of the United States for any judicial district in which such person resides, is found, or transacts business, and serve upon such person a petition for an order of such court for the enforcement of this section, except that if such person transacts business in more than one such district such petition shall be filed in the district in which such person maintains his principal place of business, or in such other district in which such person transacts business as may be agreed upon by the parties to such petition.

(h) Within twenty days after the service of any such demand upon any person, or at any time before the return date specified in the demand, whichever period is shorter, such person may file, in the district court of the United States for the judicial district within which such person resides, is found, or transacts business, and serve upon such custodian a petition for an order of such court modifying or setting aside such demand. The time allowed for compliance with the demand in whole or in part as deemed proper and ordered by the court shall not run during the pendency of such petition in the court. Such petition shall specify each ground upon which the petitioner relies in seeking such relief, and may be based upon any failure of such demand to comply with the provisions of this section or upon any constitutional or other legal right or privilege of such person.

(i) At any time during which any custodian is in custody or control of any documentary material delivered by any person in compliance with any such demand, such person may file, in the district court of the United States for the judicial district within which the office of such custodian is situated, and serve upon such custodian a petition for an order of such court requiring the performance by such custodian of any duty imposed upon him by this section.

(j) Whenever any petition is filed in any district court of the United States under this section, such court shall have jurisdiction to hear and determine the matter so presented, and to enter such order or orders as may be required to carry into effect the provisions of this section.

(Added Pub.L. 91-452, Title IX, § 901(a), Oct. 15, 1970, 84 Stat. 944.)

TABLE OF CASES

Case	*Book §*
Landon v. GTE Communications Servs., Inc., 696 F. Supp. 1213 (N.D. Ill. 1988)	§ 6.12
Lever Bros. v. United States, 877 F.2d 101 (D.C. Cir. 1989)	§ 3.2
Lewis v. Sporck, 612 F. Supp. 1316 (C.D. Cal. 1983)	§§ 6.9, 6.12
Lincoln National Bank v. Lampe, 414 F. Supp. 1270 (N.D. Ill. 1976)	§§ 6.9, 6.12
Liquid Air Corp. v. Rogers, 834 F.2d 1297 (7th Cir. 1987)	§§ 6.11, 7.6
Louisiana Power & Light v. United Gas Pipe Line, 642 F. Supp. 781 (E.D. La. 1986)	§ 2.3
Management Computer Servs. Inc. v. Hawkins, Ash, Baptie & Co., 883 F.2d 48 (7th Cir. 1989)	§ 4.3
McKee v. Pope Ballard Shepard & Fowle Ltd., 604 F. Supp. 927 (N.D. Ill. 1985)	§ 6.12
McNally v. United States, 483 U.S. 350 (1987)	§§ 1.6, 2.3, 5.5
Michaels Bldg. Co. v. Ameritrust Co., N.A., 848 F.2d 674 (6th Cir. 1988)	§ 2.11
Miller v. Affiliated Fin. Corp., 600 F. Supp. 987 (N.D. Ill. 1984)	§ 2.5
Miller v. Zable, Civ. No. 88-1195 B(M) (S.D. Cal. 1988)	§ 6.1
Mills v. Electric Auto-Lite Co., 396 U.S. 375 (1970)	§ 6.2
Milwaukee, City of v. Saxbe, 546 F.2d 693 (7th Cir. 1976)	§ 6.11
Mitchell v. Texas Gulf Sulphur Co., 446 F.2d 90 (10th Cir.), *cert. denied,* 404 U.S. 1004 (1971)	§ 3.10
Moll v. U.S. Life Title Ins. Co., 654 F. Supp. 1012 (S.D.N.Y. 1987)	§ 2.6
Morgan v. Bank of Waukegan, 804 F.2d 970 (7th Cir. 1986)	§§ 4.2, 6.11, 6.13
Morgan v. Kobrin Sec., Inc., 649 F. Supp. 1023 (N.D. Ill. 1986)	§§ 6.12, 6.13
NAACP v. Clairborne Hardware, 458 U.S. 886 (1982)	§ 5.6
Nassau-Suffolk Ice Cream v. Integrated Resources, Inc., 662 F. Supp. 1499 (S.D.N.Y. 1987)	§ 2.1
National Org. for Women v. Operation Rescue, 914 F.2d 582 (4th Cir. 1990)	§ 5.6
National Org. for Women v. Operation Rescue, 726 F. Supp. 300 (D.D.C. 1989)	§ 5.2
National Org. for Women v. Operation Rescue, 726 F. Supp. 1483 (E.D. Va. 1989)	§ 5.2
Nelson v. National Republic Bank of Chicago, [1984 Transfer Binder] Fed. Sec. L. Rep. (CCH) ¶ 91,481 (N.D. Ill. 1984)	§§ 6.9, 6.12
New York State Nat'l Org. for Women v. Terry, 704 F. Supp. 1247 (S.D.N.Y.), *aff'd,* 886 F.2d 1339 (2d Cir. 1989)	§ 5.2
New York State Nat'l Org. for Women v. Terry, 697 F. Supp. 1324 (S.D.N.Y. 1988), *aff'd,* 886 F.2d 1339 (2d Cir. 1989)	§§ 5.2, 5.6

334

TABLE

Case	*Book §*
United States v. Weinstein, 762 F.2d 1522 (11th Cir. 1985), *cert. denied,* 475 U.S. 1110 (1986)	§ 3.1
United States v. Yonan, 800 F.2d 164 (8th Cir. 1986)	§ 7.2
Upjohn Co. v. United States, 449 U.S. 383 (1981)	§ 3.8
USACO Coal Co. v. Carbomin Energy, Inc., 689 F.2d 94 (6th Cir. 1982)	§ 1.3
VanDorn Co. v. Howington, 623 F. Supp. 1548 (N.D. Ohio 1985)	§§ 2.3, 2.11, 2.28
Van Schaick v. Church of Scientology, Inc., 535 F. Supp. 1125 (D. Mass. 1982)	§ 6.9
Virden v. Graphics One, Inc., 623 F. Supp. 1417 (C.D. Cal. 1985)	§§ 2.1, 2.3, 7.2, 7.3, 7.6
Vivitar Corp. v. United States, 593 F. Supp. 420 (Ct. Int'l Trade 1984), *aff'd,* 761 F.2d 1552 (Fed. Cir. 1985), *cert. denied,* 474 U.S. 1055 (1986)	§ 3.1
WAIT Radio v. Price Waterhouse, 691 F. Supp. 102 (N.D. Ill. 1988)	§ 6.12
Waste Recovery Corp. v. Mahler, 566 F. Supp. 1466 (S.D.N.Y. 1983)	§ 6.11
Weil Ceramics & Glass, Inc. v. Dash, 878 F.2d 659 (3d Cir.), *cert. denied,* 110 S. Ct. 156 (1989)	§ 3.2
West Hartford, Conn. v. Operation Rescue, 915 F.2d 92 (2d Cir. 1990)	§§ 5.4, 5.5
West Hartford v. Operation Rescue, 726 F. Supp. 371 (D. Conn. 1989)	§§ 5.2, 5.6
W. Goebel Porzellanfabrik v. Action Indus., 589 F. Supp. 763 (S.D.N.Y. 1984)	§ 3.1
Wildflower Partnership v. Hoch, Civ. No. 89-1967 RG(Sx) (C.D. Cal. 1988)	§ 6.1
Williams v. Hall, 683 F. Supp. 639 (E.D. Ky. 1988)	§ 5.1
Wright-Moore Corp. v. RICOH Corp., 908 F.2d 128 (7th Cir. 1990)	§ 2.4
Zatkin v. Primuth, 551 F. Supp. 39 (S.D. Cal. 1982)	§ 6.12
Zola v. Gordon, 685 F. Supp. 354 (S.D.N.Y. 1988)	§ 2.3

INDEX

337